Environmental Evolution

Environmental Evolution

Effects of the Origin and
Evolution of Life on Planet
Earth

edited by
Lynn Margulis
and
Lorraine Olendzenski

The MIT Press
Cambridge, Massachusetts
London, England

Second printing, 1994
© 1992 Massachusetts Institute of Technology

Set in Palatino by DEKR Corporation.
Printed and bound in the United States of America.

Library of Congress Cataloguing-in-Publication Data

Environmental evolution : effects of the origin and evolution of life
  on planet earth / edited by Lynn Margulis and Lorraine Olendzenski.
    p.   cm.
  Includes bibliographical references and index.
  ISBN 0-262-13273-7
  1. Evolution (Biology) 2. Evolution. 3. Biosphere.
I. Margulis, Lynn, 1938–. II. Olendzenski, Lorraine.
QH366.2.E59 1992
575—dc20   91-17981
                                                        CIP

Dedicated to the memory of
our dear colleagues
Elso S. Barghoorn (1914–1984)
and Tony Swain (1922–1987).

Contents

Foreword

Environmental Evolution is an important record of our understanding of holistic biology. Living organisms are an integral part of the universe, not merely an intricate peculiarity of carbon chemistry. A few decades ago biological thought was organized and compartmentalized into a myriad of focused and specialized fields such as genetics, bacteriology, forestry, and embryology. Linkage came with the concept of planetary biology. A few pioneering researchers began to grasp the importance of life's relation to the changing inorganic world. In this newly recognized field of global ecology–biogeochemistry we are shown that life can no longer be considered as a process separate from the rest of the cosmos.

The great Russian scientist Vladimir I. Vernadsky (1863–1945) recognized this idea three quarters of a century ago, and now we are faced with the evidence. Since few people in North America and Europe read Vernadsky's works, we Westerners frequently have to rediscover how geological forces are governed by life. This cosmic vision has been explored by the scientific pioneers represented in this text. These milestones have been carefully and lovingly gathered by a most gifted scientific teacher. Professor Lynn Margulis, with three generations of students and cooperating faculty, has selected the very best scholars in this realm of thought from the dozens of original thinkers of our times. Serving as a key reference, this work will come to be known as a foundation of the new science of planetary evolutionary biogeochemistry.

NASA played a strong role in recognizing the importance of this scientific line of thought. The planetological perspective that emerged from the dramatic successes of the Viking and Voyager missions has been followed by our current fascination and concerns with global change and by the new NASA initiative called Mission to Planet Earth. As project scientist of the Viking mission to Mars (1975–1983), I am acutely aware that biogenesis and planetary biology are intertwined. They fuel the foxfire that drives today's concepts of the origins of life. In this text we see some of the beginnings and the current state of these ideas. The authors, from very different departments in widely spaced universities, are all well-recognized scholars whose work crosses over both time and space in one magnificent leap.

Gerald A. Soffen
Director of University Programs
Goddard Space Flight Center
Greenbelt, Maryland

Preface

This book developed out of Environmental Evolution, a one-semester course in which seniors and graduate students are exposed to audio-taped lectures by eminent researchers exploring the effects of the evolution of life on Planet Earth. The course, developed from 1972 through 1989 at Boston University, is now offered there by the biology and geology departments. Since 1988 it has also been taught, in a dedicated facility, in the botany department at the University of Massachusetts at Amherst.

The book—a study of the history of the environment from prebiotic times to the present—focuses on how the origin and the evolution of life have affected the surface of the Earth and answers the need for an interdisciplinary overview. Aside from serving as the main text for a course in environmental science, it may be used as a secondary text in biology, chemistry, and geology courses.

Scientific "facts" are always changing; the ways in which students create useful models of Earth's past environments change less rapidly. Because the body of material to be covered is potentially unlimited in detail and complexity, we present a series of essential concepts requisite to the reconstruction of the history of life on Earth from clues taken to be representational. The text invites students and professors to join the scientists in discovering the meandering paths of the evolution of life and the environment.

Beginning with the origins of life, the chapters are presented roughly in the chronological order of their subject matter. Each chapter opens with an abstract and is followed by a short list of recommended readings. Wherever possible, the author has revised the transcript to incorporate answers to questions asked by students and faculty members. (Professor Swain died without having revised his chapter in this fashion; the questions are presented in their original form at the end of the chapter and are answered by Robert Buchsbaum. A few of the questions asked of Dr. Lovelock are presented separately because they concern his thoughts about the Gaia Hypothesis ten years after the original lecture was recorded.)

Michael McElroy presents a picture of Earth as a "terrestrial" or inner planet before life emerged. Cyril Ponnamperuma, Clifford Matthews, David Deamer, and Antonio Lazcano introduce us to the problems of reconstructing the origin of life.

Elso Barghoorn recounts his attempts to establish the antiquity of life through the use of fossil evidence. Paul Strother warns us of the temptation to overinterpret the "organized entities" we encounter in the earliest fossil records. Stjepko Golubic explores microbial mats, the ancient benthic communities that bear witness to some of the earliest stable forms of life. Lynn Margulis describes the symbiotic origins of protoctist, animal, fungal, and plant cells and the peculiar sexual-motility systems of the eukaryotic microbial ancestors prior to global expansion. Andrew Knoll examines the sort of evidence we use to derive a picture of the earliest nucleated organisms in planktonic communities: during the Proterozoic eon, floating aquatic microbes settled to the sediment-water interface to be buried in the mud that became shale.

Raymond Siever describes the discoveries that led to the recent revolution in geology, in which the theory of plate tectonics and continental drift replaced a myriad of *ad hoc* geological concepts. Tony Swain and Robert Buchsbaum introduce us to the chemical deterrents, warnings, and punishments that healthy, intact plants communicate to animals that would graze on them. Neil Todd offers a unique explanation of relatively recent mammalian evolution. Looking at the "adaptive radiations" of certain groups of mammals, he attempts to explain the episodes in which many new species of carnivores and artiodactyls appeared—evolutionary changes that are preserved in the mammalian fossil record. Todd correlates the changes in chromosome number that resulted from a process called karyotypic fission with these discontinuous episodes of evolution in representative mammalian groups since the beginning of the Cenozoic era.

In the closing chapter, James Lovelock envisions Earth as a "blue marble" that regulates its surface far differently than would a planet similar in size and in position relative to the sun but devoid of life. In this early lecture, and in his responses to many questions raised by students and colleagues since he first came forth with his new idea about the "environment" as a part of the system itself, we learn from Lovelock about the development of his Gaia Hypothesis.

This book is dedicated to two colleagues who did not live to see it completed. Elso S. Barghoorn, professor of paleobotany at Harvard University, played a crucial role in developing the idea of environmental evolution. A teacher as well as a profound scholar and thinker, he, more than any other biologist of this century, brought about an awareness of the immense amount of biological evolution that preceded the appearance of skeletalized animals. Barghoorn has been called the father of Precambrian paleobiology. As professor, colleague, and friend, he deeply influenced the development of the Environmental Evolution course as well as the careers and the thinking of all of us, especially Stjepko Golubic, Cyril Ponnamperuma, Lynn Margulis, Andrew Knoll, and Paul Strother.

Tony Swain, during his tenure at the Royal Botanical Gardens at Kew and as a professor of biology at Boston University, investigated the evolution of communication between plants and animals. As cofounder (with Lynn Margulis) of the Planetary Biology Internship, which enables advanced students to participate in NASA's research activities in the life sciences, Swain was involved in the Environmental Evolution course as a classroom teacher. He was an inspirational force in the development of the program from 1979 until his death in 1987.

Acknowledgements

We are grateful to Frank Urbanowski and Barry Silverstein, whose generosity permitted the transformation of these materials into a book. We applaud our authors for their unstinting cooperation and participation in this work, some for over 20 years.

The book could not have been completed without the dedicated help of Jon Ashen, Paul Bethge, Christopher Brown, Eileen Crist, David Deamer, Betsey Dyer, Matthew Farmer, William Feder, Stephanie Hiebert, Gregory Hinkle, H. O. Holland, W. Krumbein, Heinz Lowenstam, Kelly McKinney, Laura Nault, Karen Nelson, Dorion Sagan, Joseph Scamardella, R. E. Schultes, John Stolz, S. Tamm, Maud Walsh, and especially Madeline Sunley. We also thank Frank Antonelli, Christopher Baldwin, Daniel Botkin, Gillian Cooper-Driver, Beth Dichter, Michael Enzien, Amanda Ferro, René Fester, Gail Fleischaker, George P. Fulton, Steven Goodwin, David Gorrill, Kate Gyllensvard, Sally Klingener, Thomas Kunz, Thomas Lang, Sheila Manion-Artz, Heather McKhann, Donna Mehos, Bruce Parkhurst, Duncan Phillips, Mitchell Rambler, James G. Schaadt, Jacob Seeler, and James Walker.

We especially acknowledge the inventor of the interactive lecture system, Stewart Wilson, and the Polaroid Corporation, which supported Wilson's work and some of ours by the donation of equipment.

Students at Boston University and at the University of Massachusetts and staff members of the Geddes Language Center at BU provided a continuous flow of aid and criticism; without their enthusiastic cooperation, we would have no book today.

Our greatest debt is to the staff of the NASA Life Sciences Office in Washington. Melvin Averner, Donald DeVincenzi, Arnauld Nicogossian, John Rummel, Gerald Soffen, and Richard Young are among those who have recognized the importance of the emerging science of global ecology in a context of comparative planetology. Since 1970 they have supported the unique research that generated the findings that have made this book possible.

Environmental Evolution

1

Comparison of Planetary Atmospheres: Mars, Venus, and Earth

Michael McElroy

To understand the history of the effects of life as a planetary phenomenon, it is important to recognize Earth as a rocky planet of the inner solar system. Were it not for life, Earth would have an atmosphere much more like those of Mars and Venus. To help us factor out the importance of the planetary background and understand the extent to which Earth is still a typical inner planet, Michael McElroy explores the salient facts about the atmospheres of our neighbors in the solar system. Dr. McElroy, Abbott Lawrence Rotch Professor of Atmospheric Sciences, is the chairman of the Earth and Planetary Sciences Department at Harvard University.

The planets of the inner solar system—Mars, Venus, and Earth (figures 1–3)—appear to share a common origin. All three were formed, in relative close proximity, from the same giant gas cloud. Present differences between these planets, then, seem to be due more to their paths of evolution than to their origin. Radioactive decay, volcanic eruption of gases, and varying levels of sunlight received and retained have shaped the compositions and conditions of these planets' atmospheres since their formation. We must recognize from the start that life makes Earth unique. Living processes exert a major influence on the composition of Earth's atmosphere and may even control its climate. As we try to understand Earth better and to predict its future course, we need an idea of what our planet would be like in the absence of life. Studies of our planetary neighbors provide a broad context for in-depth observations and analysis of the Earth.

Figure 1
Mars as seen through a telescope on Earth. The seasonal polar ice cap in the northern region of the planet is visible.

Figure 2
Venus viewed from the Mariner spacecraft. The entire planet is covered by dense clouds with complex flow patterns, which obscure any surface features.

Figure 3
Earth as seen from the orbiting Apollo spacecraft. It is possible to discern the continents, clouds, and an abundance of liquid water on the surface.

Formation of the Planets

This story begins 4.5 billion years ago. The solar system is an embryonic cloud of hot gas and particulate materials spinning around the protosun. The planets have not yet formed, but their evolution is already underway. Because heat energy radiates into space largely from its outer boundaries, this solar nebula is not uniform in temperature. The material in the center of the cloud retains heat while the nebula becomes cooler toward its edges. As the entire nebula gradually cools, the refractory elements—those that condense at the highest temperatures and generally form heavy compounds—begin to condense. Because of the temperature gradient near the interior of the nebula, these refractory elements tend to solidify. Mercury, the densest planet in the solar system, forms during the earliest stages in nebular condensation, when conditions are ideal for the formation of dense refractory elements. In accordance with that pattern, Earth is less dense than Mercury, and Venus even less dense than Earth.

Refractory material forms the building blocks of the inner planets, condensing initially in the form of very small chunks. These blocks condense together over time. Imagining a motion picture of the solar system forming, we could see planetary formation underway at various points in the nebula. Mercury would form at the inside, perhaps near where it exists today. Venus would form a little more slowly. Further out we would see Earth, and further out still Mars. The formation of the less dense, more gaseous outer planets would just be underway. Only as the nebula cools, toward the final stages, do the most abundant elements—hydrogen, carbon, nitrogen, and oxygen—finally condense. At the temperatures we are accustomed to on the Earth's surface, these elements are not generally present in their solid form. They tend to form gases and liquids, or weakly stable solids which can be readily burned and converted to gases. We consider hydrogen, carbon, nitrogen, and oxygen to be volatiles because they tend to fly away and fill the entire atmosphere. At this stage the planets in the inner solar system are, for the most part, solid. Low-temperature condensing material, rich in hydrogen, carbon, oxygen, and nitrogen, collects around each planet and will eventually form an atmosphere and oceans. As this material rains down, it is bound up in carbon-rich meteorites called *carbonaceous chondrites*, which continue to fall on the planets today.

The second phase of planetary evolution begins as the inner planets begin to acquire more of their own character. The radioactive elements of each of the protoplanets begin to decay and to generate elements that were not present in the initial nebula. The decay of potassium forms argon; uranium and thorium decay and produce helium and other elements. A tremendous amount of heat is released in these radioactive decay processes. This vast source of energy, similar to the internal energy of the sun, profoundly changes these early planets. The planets begin to cook from the inside out and to reorganize themselves: iron and other heavy elements sink to the center to form the core, and lighter elements rise toward the surface. The lighter gases are driven into the atmosphere by volcanoes fueled by this internal energy source. By the end of this second phase, planets such as Earth evolved roughly to their present configurations.

Volatile Inventory of Earth

Having no direct information on these early days of terrestrial history, we rely on inferences based on present-day observations of Earth and other planets. We would like to have a model of evolution that encompasses all the planets. Comparative studies of Mars, Venus, and Earth help us refine our hypotheses. Starting with Earth, we note the composition of the atmosphere, the oceans, and the sediments, trying to reconstruct its volatile inventory. The most abundant volatile on Earth today, and presumably in the beginning, is water— the oceans extend over three-fourths of the Earth's surface to an average depth of almost 4 kilometers.

Perhaps not so obviously, the second most abundant volatile on Earth is carbon. Although there is relatively little carbon dioxide in the atmosphere, and the amount of carbon in living things on the surface is small in comparison with the amount of water in the ocean, we find that the major reservoir of carbon is in the sediments. There, carbon exists in the form of various carbonate minerals, including skeletons of once-living organisms. Most carbonate minerals are tied up with life histories, because they were once part of the mineralized structures of living organisms.

The third most abundant volatile on Earth is nitrogen. Here the atmosphere becomes a primary player: most of the nitrogen that was volatilized by the primitive Earth is still present in the atmosphere. Nitrogen found in living organisms is just a small component of the total nitrogen inventory, and even the sediments do not contain very much. Of the volatiles on Earth, nitrogen tends to be present in the gaseous phase, whereas carbon is present in weakly stable solids (such as carbonates) and water mostly as a liquid.

With this picture of Earth's volatile inventory, we propose the hypothesis that the volatiles on Mars and Venus began with the same relative composition as the volatiles on Earth.

Figure 4
The surface of Mars. The Viking lander sits in the foreground of this view of the
oxidized, iron-rich regolith (loose, rocky covering) on Mars. "Big Ben," a large rock,
is seen in the foreground.

Evolution of the Martian Environment

Let us consider what we would expect Mars to be like. Mars should
have evolved primarily water, with carbon as the second most abundant volatile, followed by nitrogen. NASA's Viking spacecraft, which
landed on Mars in 1976, was sent primarily to search for the presence
of life and to document conditions on the planet. Equipped with
elaborate scientific instrumentation, Viking was capable of making
the first direct measurements of Mars' atmosphere. Photographs of
the Martian surface taken by Viking's automatic cameras revealed a
barren landscape with oxidized, iron-rich rocks and sand. A sky full
of gas and particulate surface material raised by the winds scatters
light brilliantly.

Considering our hypothesis that the distributions of volatiles
should be relatively equal on the inner planets, we would have
expected Mars to have released enormous amounts of water. But on

Mars that water would not form an ocean—at least it certainly would not today. Since Mars is further from the sun than Earth, it is too cold for water to be present in liquid form. The water is present as ice or is bound up in the mineral structures of the planet's upper layers. Even if primitive volcanoes on Mars had released large amounts of liquid water, it would simply have frozen or been incorporated into rock. We infer that Mars does have abundant water— perhaps even more than Earth has—in the upper layers of its lithosphere.

Carbon, the second most abundant volatile element on Mars, follows a similar scenario. Some of it is present in the atmosphere as carbon dioxide. In fact, Mars has much more carbon dioxide in its atmosphere than Earth. All things being equal, this would make photosynthesis an easy process on Mars. As it does with water, Mars' temperature limits the quantity of atmospheric CO_2. The polar cap contains frozen carbon dioxide as well as frozen water. If Mars were to warm up by ten or twenty degrees, it would rapidly acquire an atmosphere containing even more carbon dioxide and would have a surface pressure comparable to Earth's.

We expect nitrogen to be present on Mars mostly in the atmosphere, as on Earth. If we assume not only that the relative abundance of water, carbon, and nitrogen is the same on Mars as on Earth but also that the total masses of these elements are comparable on the two planets, we encounter the first problem with this universal hypothesis: We expect a very dense atmosphere of nitrogen on Mars, but this is not the case. The atmosphere of Mars is composed primarily of carbon dioxide. Nitrogen, though still the second most abundant constituent of the atmosphere, represents only 3 percent of the total atmosphere relative to CO_2. How do we resolve that problem? Since Mars is less massive than Earth, its gravitational field is not quite as strong. It has trouble retaining some of its gaseous elements. Nitrogen, in fact, escapes from Mars by an interesting process recently identified by scientists. Gases tend to ionize in the upper levels of the planetary atmospheres. When they neutralize one another, they break apart and release atoms at fairly high speeds. A speed of 5 km/sec is sufficient for one of nitrogen's primary isotopes, ^{14}N, to escape from the atmosphere. The ^{14}N reaches this critical speed, but the other primary isotope, ^{15}N, generally does not. Nitro-

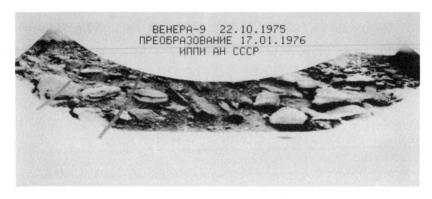

BEHEPA-9 22.10.1975
ПРЕОБРАЗОВАНИЕ 17.01.1976
ИППИ АН СССР

Figure 5
Composite of photographs of the surface of Venus taken by Venera 9.

gen atoms are continually and selectively driven off into space in this manner. We can use this selectivity to test our hypothesis. Since we know the relative abundances of those isotopes on Earth (^{14}N is approximately 100 times as abundant as ^{15}N), and since we presume the ratio to have been the same on early Mars, we can predict the quantity of dispersion. If escape that releases primarily ^{14}N has occurred for 4.5 billion years, we expect to find relatively more ^{15}N on Mars than on Earth. To our satisfaction, one of the first major discoveries of the Viking missions was that atmospheric ^{15}N was almost 60 percent more prevalent than we would expect its initial configuration to be.

In summary, our knowledge of volatiles on Mars is generally consistent with the view that Mars was similar to Earth in its origin but that the two planets have very different histories with respect to nitrogen. In their histories of water and carbon dioxide, Mars and Earth are more similar; temperature is a controlling factor in regulating the composition of the current atmosphere of Mars.

Volatile Inventory of Venus

Now let us consider Venus. A historic photograph of the surface of Venus was taken in the early 1970s from the first Soviet landing vehicle. More recent images of the surface of Venus have been taken from successive Soviet Venera spacecraft (figure 5). Given that the spacecraft had to withstand an atmospheric pressure almost 100 times that on the surface of Earth, these photos represent a remarkable technological achievement. The temperature of the surface of Venus, some 750°K and hot enough to melt metal, compounded the difficulty. These pictures surprised many of us in yet another respect. We did not expect enough light to penetrate beneath the very dense cloud cover of Venus to allow photographs; it seemed comparable to diving into our ocean to a depth of a kilometer to take pictures without artificial lighting. But the Soviet photographs show features of Venus, a rocky landscape, similar to places on Earth and Mars.

What did the probes discover about the volatiles on Venus? The very high pressure on the surface of Venus is exerted largely by carbon dioxide, which constitutes 96.6 percent of Venus' atmosphere. It would be interesting to compare CO_2 levels on Venus and Earth at typical Venus temperatures. If we took all of the carbonate minerals in the sediments on Earth, cooked them, and converted their carbon into carbon dioxide, carbon dioxide would become the most abundant constituent of Earth's atmosphere as well. Though Venus has almost 100 times the surface pressure of Earth, we can account for the higher pressure of Venus and for the abundance of carbon dioxide by changing our initial suggestion: Venus had a richer suite of volatiles from the start. More carbon may have been present at the time of Venus' formation, or more volatiles may have been released during the second phase of planetary evolution than were on Earth. In view of Venus' high temperatures, the presence of large amounts of carbon dioxide in its atmosphere is not a surprise.

What is surprising is the absence of enormous amounts of water on Venus. On Earth and Mars, water is the most abundant volatile. We expected to find a hot, steamy environment on Venus, with a surface pressure (resulting from water vapor) perhaps 1,000 times that of Earth. Yet on Venus water accounts for only about one part in 10,000 (about 100 parts per million) of the atmosphere. Where is the water? If hydrogen escaped from Venus as nitrogen did from Mars, we would expect to find Venus' current hydrogen, or its water, to be a little on the heavy side. Just as nitrogen comes in two isotopes, ^{14}N and ^{15}N, hydrogen comes in two forms: hydrogen, with atomic mass 1 (^1H), and deuterium, with atomic mass 2 (^2H). We know with confidence the abundance of those elements at formation, and we know their relative abundance on Earth by measuring their ratio in the oceans. We were delighted when mass spectroscopy revealed that Venus was in fact enriched in deuterium by about a factor of 100, which was evidence for the early escape of the lighter forms of hydrogen. Venus has the highest relative abundance of deuterium to hydrogen we know of in the solar system. Its water is rapidly switching to favor the heaviest form, rich in deuterium.

We expected Venus to have retained nitrogen; the process that allowed nitrogen to escape from Mars should not work on Venus because of the stronger gravitational field. If Venus was like Earth and Mars at time zero, its atmosphere should have a few percent nitrogen by relative abundance to carbon dioxide. Indeed it does. Nitrogen and carbon dioxide on Venus stand the test. Both support this universal hypothesis for volatiles on the planet, leaving the case of water as the only major unsolved uncertainty. Venus may or may not have formed with a volatile inventory like that of Earth. One scenario suggests that in its earliest stages of evolution Venus may have had a very hot, steamy atmosphere that was lost through evaporation to space. Hydrogen and deuterium, and perhaps oxygen as well, streamed off in an episode of planetary evolution for which we have not discovered any record. After this, another evolutionary phase began with less water, perhaps by a factor of 100, than it had at time zero. A second possibility, which I favor, is that Venus began with less water than either Mars or Earth. Water, more than the other volatiles, is most affected by changing temperatures. The proximity of Venus to the sun may have caused it to lose more of its water initially. The history of Venus is generally similar to that of Earth and Mars, but it is significantly different with regard to water.

Earth's Atmosphere as a Product of Life

As figure 6 shows, the present atmospheres of Mars and Venus are predominantly carbon dioxide whereas that of Earth is predominantly nitrogen. If Earth had not undergone an evolution that involved living organisms, its atmosphere and its surface would look profoundly different. There might be large amounts of nitrogen in the atmosphere, but there probably would be much more carbon dioxide. In contrast with the current level of less than 1 percent, carbon dioxide would be the most abundant constituent of the atmo-

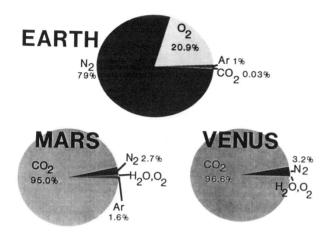

Figure 6
Comparison of major components of the present atmospheres of the terrestrial planets. The percentages represent numbers of molecules, not relative weights. Elements without percentage values are present in trace amounts.

sphere. The oceans might contain most of the hydrogen released in the form of water from the interior of the planet. (The presence of oceans is more a product of the ambient temperature than of life.)

The most dramatic characteristic of Earth's atmosphere, however, is the presence of a large amount of free molecular oxygen. Molecular oxygen is the direct product of life on Earth. Photosynthetic organisms evolved the ability to build biological tissue from carbon dioxide and water using solar energy, liberating oxygen in the process. For every oxygen molecule in Earth's atmosphere, a fossil organic carbon residue lies buried in sediment. Every carbon atom that is present in reduced form in the sediment has an oxygen analog in the atmosphere. The separation took place sometime in the past. When the sediment is uplifted and reoxidized, the carbon reunites with oxygen to form carbon dioxide.

Some episodes of Earth's atmospheric history are easier to make sense of than others. Predicting the future course of the evolution of our planet is difficult because of a number of major paradoxes in its history.

One such paradox is the relative constancy of Earth's temperature. Astronomers believe that at the time of the sun's formation its luminosity was substantially lower. The amount of energy the early Earth received from the sun therefore would have been much lower. Despite this inferred lower amount of solar energy, the geologic record indicates the persistence of a fairly benign global climate. A fluctuation of even 5°C in the average temperature would be capable of inducing catastrophe. The water in the oceans is poised among three phases. If warmed, the water turns to vapor (gas); if cooled, the water turns to solid ice. Water is found in its gaseous phase on Venus, and in its ice phase on Mars. Water absorbs radiation efficiently. If much of Earth's water were to evaporate, the resulting greenhouse would evaporate the remaining water more rapidly, leaving a smoldering, Venus-like surface with a temperature of 750°K— a scenario which obviously did not happen. If the oceans were to freeze, the increased albedo from the icy sheen would reflect much of the sunlight back to space, and the water would quite likely remain frozen. (J. C. G. Walker of the University of Michigan may be correct, however, when he argues that even if the oceans were to freeze over the continuous venting of volcanic gases would produce a greenhouse effect and melt the ice.)

We know a great deal about Earth's past climates because we have the ability to look back in time in a variety of ways. A core of sediment from the floor of an ocean gives us information extending nearly a million years into the past. Sediment cores from continental areas allow us to infer conditions even more ancient. We can also draw climatic conclusions on the basis of the types of life present at various points in time; from data of this type we learn of the planet's temperature constancy despite environmental changes over time.

Mars, it seems, has undergone climatic changes—the presence of deep channels, which probably carried large amounts of liquid water, indicates that temperatures there were once significantly higher. Major climatic variation is less likely to have occurred on Venus; its dense atmosphere acts as a regulator. These observations lead to speculation as to how physical, chemical, and biological processes interact to determine and maintain a relatively constant temperature on Earth.

Comparative planetology is challenged to understand the evolutionary process that brought Earth from its origin to its current state. This challenge involves the biological aspect of the evolutionary history of the planet as well as the physical and chemical aspects. We need to continue to develop this broad perspective to better predict the changes that may occur as we continue to alter the composition of the atmosphere. The increase in carbon dioxide is but one of many global-scale human-induced changes. We mine organic residues of coal and oil, and burn them rapidly. Long-term monitoring shows that atmospheric carbon dioxide amounted to only about 280 parts per million in 1850; by the early 1980s it was 350, and it is increasing steadily. This is attributed (at least in part) to the burning of fossil fuels, and perhaps also to the deforestation of the tropics. Equally dramatic evidence exists for the change in the concentration of atmospheric methane, which is increasing by 1–2 percent per year. Large amounts of methane are produced by bacteria living in cellulose-digesting cattle and other ruminants, the population of which expands along with the human population. And our agricultural practices continue to create environments that favor methanogenic bacteria; for example, the flooding of fields in order to grow rice creates anaerobic conditions favorable to bacterial production of methane. Furthermore, fluorocarbons—for which there are no natural analogs—are appearing in the atmosphere as a result of human activity. Each of these gases can affect the climate by trapping heat radiated by the Earth's surface.

It is believed that Earth's climate has the capacity to change. If, despite the varying levels of atmospheric gases, it does not change, we would like to understand why. Thus the problems of understanding Earth's past and predicting its future merge into one grand scientific challenge of understanding the factors that control the planetary climate. Comparative planetology helps create the broad perspective needed for wise assessment of the future.

Readings

Atreya, S. K., J. B. Pollack, and M. S. Matthews, eds. 1989. *Origin and Evolution of Planetary and Satellite Atmospheres.* University of Arizona Press.

Goldsmith, D., and T. Owen. 1980. *The Search for Life in the Universe.* Benjamin Cummings.

Hunten, D. M., L. Colin, T. M. Donahue, and V. I. Moroz. 1983. *Venus.* University of Arizona Press.

Kasting, J. F., O. B. Toon, and J. B. Pollack. 1988. How climate evolved on the terrestrial planets. *Scientific American* 258, no. 2: 90–97.

McElroy, M. B., Y. L. Yung, and A. O. Nier. 1977. Isotopic composition of nitrogen: Implications for the past history of Mars' atmosphere. *Science* 194: 70.

McElroy, M. B., and M. J. Prather. 1981. Noble gases in the terrestrial planets: Clues to evolution. *Nature* 293: 535–539.

The Planets. Freeman, 1975, 1977–1983.

Weiner, J. 1990. *The Next One Hundred Years: Shaping the Fate of Our Living Earth.* Bantam.

Cosmochemical Evolution
and the Origins of Life

Cyril Ponnamperuma

In this chapter, Cyril Ponnamperuma outlines the successes of experiments in prebiotic chemistry since the famous production of amino acids from gas mixtures by Stanley Miller and Harold Urey in 1953. He views information from meteorites and interstellar matter as indicating that organic materials are common in the cosmos and not unique to Earth. Dr. Ponnamperuma directs the Laboratory for Chemical Evolution at the University of Maryland at College Park and is the science advisor to the President of Sri Lanka.

How life began is a question that has long been on the mind of humankind. Although it is often regarded as too philosophical a problem for scientists, recent scientific advances have transformed the question from a metaphysical one to a physical one.

Astronomy is the domain in which the scientific study of the origin of life begins. The night sky contains billions of stars, each similar in composition and energy to our sun. Since there is life on a planet around our sun, there must be innumerable places for life to arise elsewhere in the universe. Next, we look to the science of biochemistry. Essential to all life, from the tiniest microbe to the most intelligent human being, we find two classes of molecules: the nucleic acids and the proteins. These complex molecules are made up of discrete units. The nucleic acids, RNA and DNA, are composed of five bases: adenine, guanine, cytosine, thymine, and uracil. Two sugars (ribose and deoxyribose) and phosphate residues complete the list of components of these molecules. Proteins contain twenty common amino acids. In all, the proteins and the nucleic acids comprise 28 components—the "letters" that make up the alphabet of life. From this we draw the inescapable conclusion that all life must have

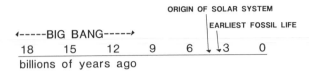

Figure 1
Time line of important events in the history of the universe.

a common chemical origin. Darwinian evolutionary theory is a third basis of inquiry into the origin of life. We now postulate a phase that precedes the biological evolution that Darwin studied: chemical evolution.

Life and Organic Matter in the Universe

A look at the major events in the history of the universe (figure 1) provides a context for the question of chemical evolution. According to the Big Bang theory, the origin of the universe occurred between 10 billion and 20 billion years ago. Astronomers arrive at this rough estimate using an uncertain value that compares the rate of expansion of the galaxies with the distance covered. The dating of the origin of our solar system is much more definite. By measuring the radioactive decay in a wide sampling of meteorites and lunar rocks, geologists conclude that the sun and its planets formed about 4.6 billion years ago. The first evidence of life on Earth is found in microfossils from western Australia and southern Africa, which indicate a relative abundance of life about 3.5 billion years ago. Thus, life on Earth must have begun between 4.6 billion and 3.5 billion years ago.

Whereas biological evolution can account for the changes over the last 3.5 billion years, those of us who study chemical evolution are trying to retrace events from the origins of the universe to the inception of life on Earth. Taking the Earth—the one laboratory in which a successful experiment has been performed—as an example, we postulate that what happened on Earth must have occurred on the billions of other planets around other stars.

Charles Darwin was among the first scientists to speculate on the notion of chemical evolution. In 1861, he wrote to his friend J. D Hooker:

Table 1
Composition of the sun.

Element	Percentage
Hydrogen	87.0
Helium	12.9
Oxygen	0.025
Nitrogen	0.02
Carbon	0.01
Magnesium	0.003
Silicon	0.002
Iron	0.001
Sulfur	0.001
Others	0.038

. . . if we could conceive in some warm little pond with all sorts of ammonia and phosphoric salts, light, heat, electricity, etc., present . . . that a protein compound was chemically formed ready to undergo still more complex changes. . . .

Here Darwin suggests the concept of chemical evolution in a nutshell. According to his theory, life arose from reactions between matter and energy. Our task in the laboratory is to recreate Darwin's warm little pond and see whether reactions necessary for the beginnings of life can be reproduced.

Let us first consider the raw materials available for the origin of life. Spectroscopic studies provide us with data on the abundance of elements in the sun and stars. A glance at the average composition of the sun shows that, apart from helium (which is an inert gas), hydrogen, carbon, nitrogen, and oxygen are the most common elements in our solar system (table 1). This is also true of the universe. These four elements are the major components of living organisms, constituting 99.5 percent of the biosphere. Given the abundance of these elements on the prebiotic Earth, basic chemistry predicts that three important compounds are likely to have formed: methane (CH_4), ammonia (NH_3), and water (H_2O). These gases constituted Earth's primitive atmosphere. As for energy, a wide range of sources were available. Radiation and ultraviolet light from the sun were the major sources. Electrical discharges, cosmic rays, radioactivity, heat from volcanoes, and even the shock waves generated by the impact of meteorites may also have been important.

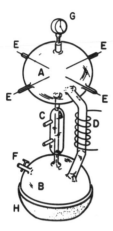

Figure 2
Apparatus used to synthesize amino acids.

Laboratory Approaches to Life's Origins

Our task at this point is to see what happens when these energy sources act upon this sort of atmosphere. Is it possible to synthesize organic matter, or even life itself, from such reactions? This synthetic approach to the origin of life problem has two goals. The first is to see whether the building blocks of life—monomers such as amino acids, purines, pyrimidines, and carbohydrates—can be formed in plausible reactions. The second is to determine whether these monomers can be combined to form polymers, including proteins and nucleic acids.

One type of apparatus used to perform these experiments is illustrated in figure 2. Flask A, containing methane and ammonia, represents the atmosphere; flask B, containing water, represents the primordial seas. The arm D, which is kept hot, enables the heated liquid to reach the upper flask, condense, and fall back through C as "rain" into the "ocean" below. When the electrodes (E) are used to generate sparks, a large amount of dark brown organic matter is synthesized.

To simulate the effect of another energy source, ionizing radiation, we [Ponnamperuma and associates] conducted experiments using a different apparatus. The atmosphere was contained in a long horizontal tube attached to a flask between two heat lamps, representing the ocean. To model the presence of radioactive matter (such as potassium-40) in the primitive oceans, we had a linear accelerator emit a stream of beta particles into the "atmosphere." These beta particles interacted with the atmospheric constituents to form organic molecules. The synthesized organic mixtures were then separated and analyzed by chromatography. A chromatogram from the mixture revealed the presence of a large amount of adenine. What seems to be an almost random experiment yielded the molecule most important for life—adenine is found in DNA, RNA, ATP, and acetyl coenzyme A.

We found it puzzling, at first, that such a complex molecule as adenine could be formed. The presence of a large quantity of hydrogen cyanide provided the key to this. Adenine is simply the pentamer of hydrogen cyanide; five hydrogen cyanides make adenine. Since hydrogen cyanide is generated in this experiment, adenine is easily formed as a by-product; organic chemists have demonstrated this relationship very clearly.

Using methane, nitrogen, and water, we have been able to synthesize all five biological bases. High performance liquid chromatography shows this, and reveals that a nonbiological base (xanthine) was also produced. The production of a nonbiological base is significant because it indicates that the compounds formed are indeed due to chemical reaction rather than possible laboratory contamination. And since we continued to generate hydrogen cyanide in these experiments, we decided to try it as a starting material. Exposing hydrogen cyanide to ultraviolet light produced a large number of organic molecules. A number of amino acids were among the molecules synthesized. Next we tried formaldehyde, another compound commonly formed in these experiments. Exposing formaldehyde to ultraviolet light or ionizing radiation resulted in production of the sugars ribose and deoxyribose.

Having synthesized bases, amino acids, and sugars, we tried next to put them together to form proteins and nucleic acids. During protein polymerization, two amino acids are brought together in a dehydration/condensation reaction. The two components form a dipeptide with the removal of a molecule of water. Two dipeptides joined together make a tetrapeptide, and so on, to build the large protein molecules.

How could such a process have taken place on the prebiotic Earth? J. D. Bernal suggested the possibility that some of the primordial soup may have washed ashore and been evaporated in a lagoon. We simulated a dried-up lagoon in the laboratory. The nucleoside uridine was combined with phosphate and heated to 65°C, a temperature obtainable from direct sunlight on clay. In this experiment, mono- and diphosphates and di-, tri-, and tetranucleotides were formed. In fact, there is now evidence that this process can proceed to combine almost ten nucleotides. These experiments suggest the principle of the formation of complex nucleotides. But of course the entire primordial ocean was not desiccated, so this reaction may also have taken place in aqueous solution. Knowing that living organisms contain enzymes that facilitate these reactions, we tried to catalyze them under prebiotic conditions. The electrical-discharge experiment noted above produced a variety of compounds, as chromatography showed; however, when we first performed this experiment none of the spots on the chromatogram corresponded to simple amino acids. This appeared to contradict the results of Stanley Miller and Harold Urey, who synthesized alanine, glutamic acid, aspartic acid, and glycine by this method in the 1950s. We then looked more carefully at a dark spot at the origin on the chromatogram. This spot indicated heavy material, perhaps macromolecules. After hydrolyzing the mixture we found ten amino acids (figure 3). The amino acids had been formed and then joined together. Apparently a reagent was present that acted as a prebiotic catalyst, a natural condensing agent. Once again hydrogen cyanide played a crucial role. We now understand that hydrogen cyanide can easily produce a tetramer: Four hydrogen cyanides make the compound diaminomaleonitrile (DAMN), a very effective condensing agent that acts as a prebiotic catalyst to bind molecules together. In this case it helped to combine the amino acids into the heavy, dark material.

Thus, we have before us what may be a very simple pathway to the components of life. We expose an atmosphere of methane, ammonia, and water to ultraviolet light, electrical discharges, and ionizing radiation. The simple molecules hydrogen cyanide and formaldehyde are produced. They give rise to the various components of nucleic acids and proteins; hydrogen cyanide yields the bases, formaldehyde yields the sugars, and together they produce amino acids (table 2).

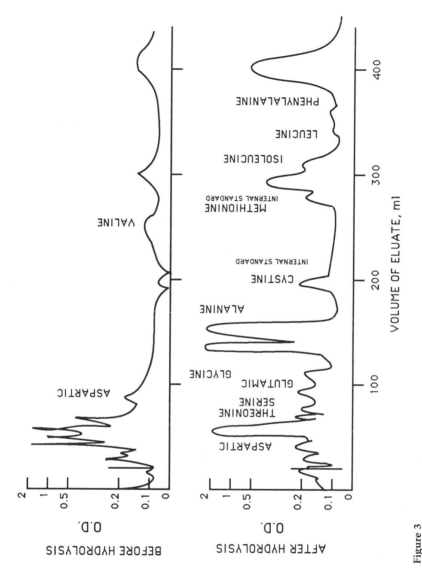

Figure 3
Amino acids from a spark discharge experiment before and after hydrolysis.

Table 2
Examples of precursors and products.

Precursors	Products
Formaldehyde	Sugars (e.g., ribose, deoxyribose)
Cyanide	Bases (e.g., adenine, uracil, thymine)
Formaldehyde and cyanide	Amino acids (e.g., β-alanine)

Through dehydration/condensation reactions the monomers build the large, complex polymers. This scheme, though oversimplified, gives us a sense of the processes that may have taken place on the Archean Earth and which may be taking place elsewhere in the universe. It provides a continuity from atom to human, from atom to Adam.

Over many years of investigation, laboratory chemists have demonstrated that all the requisite components of life can be made under prebiotic conditions. This leads us to the most challenging problem of chemical evolution: How did these components interact? The question of the origin of the genetic code emerges. Can we see how a fragment of a nucleic acid might direct the ordered synthesis of a peptide or a polypeptide in the laboratory?

Organic Molecules in Meteorites

Besides conducting synthesis experiments in the laboratory, scientists approach the question of the origin of life by studying the natural world. In particular, we analyze the rocks of the Earth and fragments of the solar system to find material evidence. Although the oldest rocks on Earth have been crucial to the study of biological evolution, they provide little guidance for the study of chemical evolution. With chemical evolution in mind, we analyzed rock samples from the moon, collected on the United States' Apollo missions. We were looking for amino acids, sugars, nucleic acids, and other organic molecules. We found 200 parts per million of organic, carbon-containing matter in these lunar samples, but no amino acids. Although initially we were disappointed by the test results, we now attribute the absence of organic molecules to the moon's lack of an atmosphere to filter ultraviolet rays, which are capable of breaking apart most carbon-carbon bonds.

Figure 4
Fragment of Murchison meteorite.

Around the time when we were analyzing the lunar samples, an event took place that dramatically affected our research: the carbon-rich Murchison meteorite (figure 4) fell in Australia on September 28, 1969. The first person on the scene reported smelling something like methanol or pyridine, which strongly suggested the presence of organic matter. We were fortunate to be able to study a sample of this meteorite.

Analysis of extracts from the Murchison meteorite showed the presence of a large number of nonbiological amino acids. Living organisms have 20 amino acids, but through abiotic synthesis from 50 to 100 amino acids can be produced. We also noticed a difference in orientation in these amino acids. As the right hand is a mirror image of the left, amino acids occur in dual forms. Amino acids in living organisms are typically left-handed. In this meteorite, however, we found equal amounts of left- and right-handed amino acids. This confirmed their nonbiological origin. Here we had the first unequivocal evidence of nonbiological, extraterrestrial amino acids. The subsequent analysis of another carbonaceous chondrite—the

Murray meteorite, which landed in Kentucky in 1952—substantiated our conclusions. We analyzed a fragment from its center and found the same results: nonbiological amino acids with equal amounts of left- and right-handed orientation. We also analyzed the Murchison meteorite for the presence of bases and found all five biological bases: cytosine, uracil, guanine, thymine, and adenine. The possibility of contamination is slim with respect to bases. Biotic bases are not free to transfer by mere contact, since they are bound inside cells. Moreover, the presence of many nonbiological bases—that is, bases other than cytosine, uracil, guanine, thymine, and adenine—supports the view of indigenous presence of bases. Finally, the presence of a relatively high concentration of bases makes accidental contamination unlikely. Considering these constraints, we feel confident that the Murchison meteorite contained the five bases needed for life. The electric-discharge experiment also generated these five bases. Thus, meteoritic data and evidence from electric-discharge experiments support each other. Synthesis and analysis appear to be congruent.

Organic Molecules in Interstellar Space

Radio astronomers have identified more than 50 different organic molecules in interstellar space. Of these molecules, about 40 are involved in prebiotic processes. Ethyl alcohol, for example, is widespread in the universe. (A colleague at the University of Maryland calculated that the amount of alcohol in the constellation Orion alone is equal to 10^{19} "fifths" of liquor.)

The total picture that we form from laboratory work, meteorite analysis, and radio astronomy is that organic matter is everywhere. Chemical evolution must be cosmic in nature. Since this is the case, life could be commonplace in the universe. A search for intelligent signals might be rewarded with an answer that would prove life exists beyond Earth.

Readings

Honda, Y., R. Navarro-Gonzalez, and C. Ponnamperuma. 1989. A quantitative assay of biologically important compounds in simulated primitive Earth experiments. *Advances in Space Research* 9: 63–66.

Kobayashi, K., L. Hua, P. E. Hare, M. K. Hobish, and C. Ponnamperuma.

1986. Abiotic synthesis of nucleosides by electric discharge in simulated primitive Earth atmosphere. *Origins of Life* 16: 277–278.

Miller, S. L. 1953. A production of amino acids under possible primitive Earth conditions. *Science* 117: 528–529.

Ponnamperuma, C. 1972. *The Origins of Life.* Dutton.

Ponnamperuma, C. 1989. Experimental studies in the origin of life. *Journal of the British Interplanetary Society* 161: 1005.

Ponnamperuma, C., and F. R. Eirich, eds. 1990. *Prebiological Self-Organization of Matter.* Proceedings of the Eighth College Park Colloquium on Chemical Evolution. Deepak.

3   Origin of Life: Polymers before Monomers?

Clifford Matthews

Clifford Matthews' controversial hypothesis on the origin of proteins stands in opposition to the hypothesis presented by Cyril Ponnamperuma in the previous chapter. Matthews believes that protein ancestors—heteropolypeptides—were formed directly from hydrogen cyanide polymers rather than by polymerization of individual amino acid monomers. He describes the implications of this hypothesis for observations of organic matter on comets, meteorites, asteroids, and the outer planets.

Cyril Ponnamperuma's discussion of chemical evolution and the origin of life centers on the widely held belief that the prebiotic formation of primitive proteins on Earth occurred in two steps: First, the synthesis of α-amino acids was brought about by the action of natural energy sources on the components of a reducing atmosphere. Then these monomers somehow linked together through condensation to form polypeptides on the surface of the planet. The pioneering demonstration by Stanley Miller and Harold Urey that α-amino acids are readily obtained from methane, ammonia, and water subjected to electric charges, taken together with the subsequent successful syntheses of peptides from amino acids by various kinds of dehydration reactions, seems to be in accord with this view. When I look more critically at the evidence for condensation, however, I find that the conditions chosen—anhydrous, high-temperature, acidic, for example—are too specific to be characteristic of the surface of the Archean Earth. Troubling questions also arise concerning the concentration, purification, and interaction of the initial products, a host of organic compounds constituting a dilute soup. Even if complex amino acids were present, could they have joined together selectively to form long chains in amounts sufficient for life's beginning? How plausible are these attempted simulations as models of prebiotic chemistry? To me, and to many others, they almost suggest that life could not have started here on Earth!

Misgivings such as these make me question the assumptions underlying Cyril Ponnamperuma's account. In particular, I don't see how the inherent thermodynamic barrier to spontaneous polymerization of α-amino acids could have been overcome. Thus, over the years I have developed an alternative scenario for the origin of proteins which bypasses the amino acid step by postulating the direct synthesis of polypeptides from hydrogen cyanide and water. On this view, the action of sunlight on methane and ammonia in Earth's atmosphere produced clouds of hydrogen cyanide (HCN), which rapidly polymerized to form a complex mixture of long-chain molecules that settled onto Earth's surface, finally interacting with water to form the earliest proteins, potential structural and catalytic macromolecules of life.

Hydrogen Cyanide Polymers Form Polypeptides

How did this come about? A key step was the synthesis of polyaminomalonitrile, a polymer that can be formally derived by addition reactions of aminomalononitrile, $H_2NCH(CN)_2$, a known trimer of hydrogen cyanide. This polyamidine structure made up entirely of HCN molecules can be transformed to the polyamide (or polypeptide) structure of proteins by treatment with cold water (figure 1), since as a rule amidine groups,

—HN—C—
       ‖
      NH,

are readily converted by water to amides,

—HN—C—
       ‖
      O.

Further, the nitrile groups (—C≡N) in each repeating unit are so reactive that cumulative addition of more HCN (as well as acetylene,

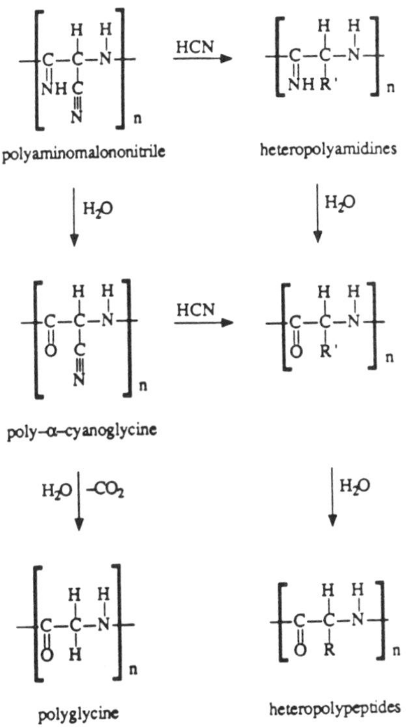

Figure 1
Polypeptides from polyamidines. Polyaminomalononitrile, a polyamidine synthesized directly from HCN, is converted to polyglycine by hydrolysis. Continued addition of HCN molecules to polyaminomalononitrile produces heteropolyamidines, which can be hydrolyzed to heteropolypeptides.

H_2S, etc.) can convert them to side chains (denoted in figure 1 by R')
to give heteropolyamidines. These polyamidines process side chains
that are diverse, not merely repeated. When this modified cyanide
polymer meets water, the amidine groups become amides and R'
becomes R, where R represents the side chains of today's proteins.
What is so intriguing about the parent polymer, polyaminomalononitrile, is that it can be converted by more HCN, and finally by
water, to heteropolypeptides possessing both the backbone and the
side chains of proteins. In principle, then, two of the simplest and
most common molecules in the universe, HCN and H_2O, can give
rise to a variety of these polypeptides, the first informational
macromolecules.

What experiments can we perform to obtain evidence for this hypothesis? First, a variation of Stanley Miller's original demonstration. Bob Moser and I sparked a mixture of methane and ammonia (without water) and obtained a brown-black, sticky solid that covered the inside of the reaction flask. Subsequent treatment with water yielded a yellow-brown powder. Further hydrolysis with boiling water yielded at least six amino acids commonly found in proteins— glycine (mainly), alanine, aspartic acid, glutamic acid, serine, and valine—as well as some nonprotein amino acids. More directly, we found that hydrogen cyanide itself (a colorless liquid that boils at 25°C), with a trace of added ammonia, gradually becomes solid, changing in color from yellow to orange to brown to black. Again, after extraction with cold water we obtained a yellow-brown solid that could be hydrolyzed further to give the same mixture of amino acids. A black insoluble residue was usually formed in substantial amounts at the same time. Comparable results are obtained when liquid cyanide is allowed to polymerize in water or other solvents in the presence of a base such as ammonia or an amine. It seems probable that polypeptides are present in these cyanide products after contact with cold water, since amino acids detected by automatic ion-exchange analyzers or by combined gas chromatography and mass spectrometry are seen only after breakdown induced by drastic hydrolysis.

A more subtle approach, nondestructive analysis of the total solid product obtained from HCN, became possible with the advent of cross-polarization magnetic-angle spinning solid-state nuclear magnetic resonance spectroscopy. With Jake Schaefer and other pioneers of this new technique, Bob Ludicky and I were able to show the unambiguous presence of peptide bonds—the signature of proteins— by studying labeled polymers synthesized from equimolar amounts of $H^{13}CN$ and $HC^{15}N$ and then treated with water. Our continuing investigations of HCN polymerization suggest that the yellow-orange-brown-black products are of two main types: stable ladder structures (black) with conjugated —C≡N— bonds, as proposed by Volker, and polyamidines readily converted by water to polypeptides.

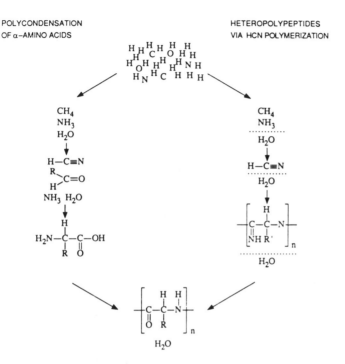

Figure 2
Two opposing models for the origin of proteins. Which came first, amino acids or their polymers? The left pathway shows amino acids somehow condensing in a dilute soup to form polypeptides. The pathway on the right shows HCN polymerizing in the atmosphere to form heteropolyamidines, which subsequently settle in the oceans and become hydrolyzed to heteropolypeptides (primitive proteins).

The Miller-Urey Results Reinterpreted

The two pathways we have considered for the origin of proteins are compared in figure 2. Which came first, amino acids or their polymers? On the left is shown the dilute-soup model whereby amino acids formed by the Miller-Urey route are assumed to have somehow got together to yield primitive proteins. On the right is the cyanide model not requiring water in the atmosphere. Methane and ammonia yield HCN polymers directly, which settle in the oceans to become heteropolypeptides. I have argued against the Miller-Urey view and will now explain what I think really happened in the Miller-Urey experiments.

It seems clear to me from repeated investigations that the primary products were not α-amino acids, as was claimed, but rather HCN polymers, the HCN being formed from methane and ammonia by electric-discharge reactions and perhaps also by elimination from intermediates such as aminoacetonitriles and HCN oligomers (including the tetramer, diaminomaleonitrile, mentioned by Dr. Ponnamperuma). The polymers then became hydrolyzed, first to polypeptides and then to amino acids, either during reflux in the reaction flask or later during the analysis procedure. The same conclusion, I believe, applies to virtually all reported experiments simulating primitive-atmospheric chemistry, as well as to studies of aqueous cyanide reactions by James Ferris and others based on the original work of John Oró. I believe these investigations ostensibly yielding α-amino acids actually supply evidence for the abundant prebiotic existence of protein ancestors—heteropolypeptides synthesized directly from hydrogen cyanide and water.

I believe also that the cyanide model answers the questions I raised earlier with regard to the dramatic results of Miller and Urey. First, why do complex molecules like amino acids appear to be more easily formed than the many simple compounds—hydrocarbons, alcohols, acids, ketones, aldehydes, and amines, for example—expected from reactions of methane, ammonia, and water? Because the major intermediate, by far, is hydrogen cyanide, which then undergoes the rapid polymerization discussed above to eventually yield heteropolypeptides, which can be hydrolyzed to amino acids. What we have here is kinetic control, with a preferred pathway defined by HCN chemistry, rather than thermodynamic control leading to a statistical distribution of products. The next question is how amino acids got together to form primitive proteins. My answer, of course, is that they didn't. Instead, polypeptides appeared first, not via amino acids, but from hydrogen cyanide and water. Finally, would there be enough material deposited on Earth for life to have come about? Indeed, yes, according to the cyanide hypothesis. I am not talking about a dilute soup. Instead I picture an Archean Earth knee-deep in HCN polymers and, eventually, primitive proteins. This model supplies lots of the right stuff, fast.

The ready conversion by water of polyamidines to polypeptides demonstrated by our investigations suggests to me that polyamidines—HCN polymers—might have played yet another essential role in chemical evolution. In the absence of water—on land—they could have been the original condensing agents of prebiotic chemistry. Their reactive amidine groups, eager to become amides, would have brought about the stepwise formation of nucleosides, nucleotides, and polynucleotides from available sugars, phosphates, and nitrogen bases by a series of dehydration reactions. Most significant would have been the parallel synthesis of polypeptides and polynucleotides arising from the dehydrating action of polyamidines on nucleotides:

polyamidines   A–A–A–A–A–A–A   P–P–P–P–P–P–P   polypeptides
    +
nucleotides   N N N N N N N   N–N–N–N–N–N–N   polynucleotides

Optimum conditions might well have existed on the Hadean or early Archean Earth, with photochemical synthesis of organic molecules proceeding in the atmosphere in three overlapping stages defined by the relative volatility of methane, ammonia, and water. Any CO or CO_2 present would not have interfered. With methane as the first major atmospheric component, hydrocarbon chains formed by way of acetylenes. Then, as ammonia became more involved, hydrogen cyanide and cyanoacetylene became major reactants. Polymeric peptide precursors were formed together with nitrogen heterocycles possessing the basic skeletons of purines, pyrimidines, pyridines, and porphyrins. When most of the ammonia had been used up, photolysis of water vapor that had been confined to lower levels became possible; this led to the third stage, in which oxygen-containing molecules such as formaldehyde and sugars were synthesized, as well as phosphates from phosphine. Unlike the prevailing dilute-soup picture of chemical evolution, this atmospheric model supplies the necessary quantity of prebiotic compounds in sequence, in the right place at the right time. As Earth's surface became covered with this organic shower, potential membrane material—carboxylic acids, carbohydrates, polypeptides—accumulated in lakes and oceans, while on land the simultaneous synthesis of polypeptides and polynucleotides was promoted by cyanide polymers, perhaps assisted by clays. Potential metabolic machinery arose separately from the genetic apparatus. Soon this hardware and this software interfaced to produce elementary replicating systems. On our dynamic planet this polypeptide-polynucleotide symbiosis mediated by polyamidines may have set the pattern for the evolution of protein–nucleic acid systems controlled by enzymes, the major characteristic of life today.

Hydrogen Cyanide in the Outer Solar System

The cyanide model has extraterrestrial implications. We know that the four small, warm terrestrial planets of the solar system are oxidizing in character whereas the large, cold outer planets have reducing environments. Thus, the outer planets resemble the early Earth in some important respects. For example, methane, ammonia, and water are present in Jupiter's hydrogen-rich atmosphere, as Urey predicted, together with some hydrogen cyanide. What chemistry, then, is producing those yellow-orange-brown-red streaks seen so clearly by the Pioneer and Voyager missions? I suggest HCN polymerization, since these are the very colors we see in our reaction flasks. We will know more when the Jupiter-orbiting spacecraft Galileo sends back data obtained by instruments parachuted into these colorful layers. Saturn, too, could have layers rich in cyanide polymers. So could Titan, its giant moon, which has an orange haze known to be polymeric.

As Cyril Ponnamperuma notes, amino acids have been found in some meteorites. Again, I believe these are hydrolysis products of cyanide polymers. We have extracted from the Murchison meteorite the same kind of yellow-brown powders that we obtain from HCN; they yield amino acids after drastic hydrolysis. Similar cyanide chemistry would be expected on asteroids (the parent bodies of meteorites), and on comets, with their frozen surfaces rich in methane, ammonia, and water. The black crust covering the nucleus of Halley's Comet very likely consists largely of cyanide polymers, a conclusion supported by the detection in its coma of free hydrogen cyanide, lots of cyanide radicals, and solid particles consisting only of H, C, and N. Most significant is the recent detection by Dale Cruikshank et al. of solid $C\equiv N$-bearing material in several dark bodies of the outer solar system, including comets, asteroids, and Saturn's moon Iapetus. It seems, then, that the primitive Earth may have been covered by HCN polymers through cometary bombardment or terrestrial synthesis as already described.

In sum, laboratory and extraterrestrial studies suggest that hydrogen cyanide polymerization is a truly universal process that accounts not only for the synthesis of the earliest proteins on Earth but also for organic chemistry that proceeds today elsewhere in the solar system, on planetary bodies and satellites around other stars, and in the dusty molecular clouds of spiral galaxies. This preferred pathway suggests to me the existence of widespread life throughout the universe.

I am often asked why my cyanide theory is so controversial. Certainly it touches on, and challenges, much of today's research on chemical evolution. There is technical criticism, of course; it is very welcome, since it leads to further research and additional results, pro and con. But there is also a more profound objection, which I can illustrate by using comments of Cyril Ponnamperuma. In an article from *Science News* reporting our NMR results, Cyril was asked what he thought about the Matthews hypothesis. He found it "an interesting suggestion but probably one that is much too complicated." This surprises me, since I consider simplicity to be its main strength (or weakness). Cyril went on to suggest that the logical approach is to build up more complicated structures (e.g., proteins) from simple building blocks such as amino acids; philosophically it seems more likely that the simple structures came before the complicated ones. Yes, but. . . . The fallacy here lies in the assumption that amino acids were the original building blocks, as they are today. I am arguing that the reverse is true—the blocks came from the buildings. In the beginning—at all beginnings—things have to be different. The first proteins, in all their diversity, arose essentially from HCN polymers.

Readings

Cruikshank, D. P., W. K. Hartmann, D. J. Tholen, L. J. Allamandola, and R. H. Brown. 1990. Solid C≡N bearing material in the outer solar system. *Bulletin of the American Astronomical Society* 22: 1098.

Ferris, J. 1979. HCN did not condense to give heteropolypeptides on the primitive earth. *Science* 203: 1135–1137.

Matthews, C. N. 1984. Chemical evolution: Protons to proteins. *Proceedings of the Royal Institution of Great Britain* 55: 199–207.

Matthews, C. N. 1988. Cosmic metabolism: The origin of macromolecules. In *Bioastronomy: The Next Steps*, ed. G. Marx. Kluwer.

Matthews, C. N., and R. E. Moser. 1967. Peptide synthesis from hydrogen cyanide and water. *Nature* 215: 1230–1234.

Matthews, C. N., R. Ludicky, J. Schaefer, E. O. Stejskal, and R. A. McKay. 1984. Heteropolypeptides from hydrogen cyanide and water? Solid state ^{15}N NMR investigations. *Origins of Life* 14: 243–250.

4   Origins of Membrane Structure

David Deamer

David Deamer uses novel experimental approaches to the question of the origins of life. He recognizes that a critical problem is the first appearance of a material system segregated from its surroundings by a lipid membrane. In his search for the earliest membrane-bounded spheres, the ancestors of all cellular life, Deamer has extracted lipid-like substances from the only available source of concentrated extraterrestrial organic matter: carbonaceous chondrites. This material spontaneously forms membranes that can incorporate photochemically reactive pigment systems. Professor Deamer conducts his experiments at the University of California at Davis, where he is a faculty member.

The structures and functions of contemporary cells are necessarily the starting point for questions related to the origin of life. All cells are bounded by membranes that encapsulate the macromolecular machinery of the life process. How did the first membrane structures on Earth appear?

A focus of research in our laboratory is the chemical and physical nature of lipids, essential components of contemporary cell membranes. Through our research we have gained insight into the lipid-like properties that must have originally permitted certain molecules to self-assemble into the first membranes.

Phospholipids and Contemporary Membranes

Hydrocarbons are organic compounds that contain the elements hydrogen and carbon. The lipids of all contemporary membranes contain hydrocarbon chains, which constitute an oil-like layer that forms the barrier between the internal and external compartments of cells. Proteins, which provide the enzymatic and transport activities that are primary functions of membranes, are embedded in this fluid barrier. Therefore, to understand the origin of membrane structure we need to know how lipids and their hydrocarbon moieties provide the essential barrier properties of membranes. I will use a specific membrane lipid to illustrate this point.

Membrane lipids are typically phospholipid molecules. One of the most common, a constituent of most membranes, is phosphatidyl-choline. The term "phosphatidyl" is derived from phosphate, one of the component groups, and signifies that the phosphate is chemically bound—in this case, to glycerol and choline. The glycerol is linked to two fatty acids, each consisting of an acidic carboxyl group (-COOH) attached to a long hydrocarbon chain. Other common membrane phospholipids include phosphatidylethanolamine and phosphatidylserine.

What kinds of molecules on the early Earth might have had lipid-like properties? Because they are relatively complex, phospholipids probably did not form the earliest membranes. Do molecules simpler than phospholipids assemble into membranes?

Certain molecular structures are polar, with relatively strong electrical charges expressed by their component atoms; others are nonpolar. Polar structures tend to be soluble in water and are usually referred to as *hydrophilic*. Nonpolar structures are *hydrophobic*; that is, they tend to be soluble in oil but not in water. Some compounds (particularly lipids) that have both hydrophilic and hydrophobic residues on the same molecule are referred to as *amphiphilic*.

Hydrocarbons, by themselves, are nonpolar molecules. However, if oxygen is added to a long hydrocarbon chain, the molecule becomes amphiphilic, since the oxygen is typically polar. All lipids have oxygen in their molecular structure, usually as carboxyl and phosphate—oxygen-containing groups chemically linked to nonpolar hydrocarbon chains.

Self-Assembly of Lipids into Bilayers

Amphiphilic molecules have a remarkable property: they self-assemble into stable bilayer structures. When a lipid such as phosphatidylcholine is dried, for example, the lipid molecules form lamellar structures. (*Lamellar* means that the structure has layers of molecules.) If water is then added, water molecules penetrate between the lipid layers along hydrophilic planes, causing the lipid to swell. The swelling produces a variety of fairly stable structures, such as lipid cylinders, each of which contains thousands of concentric lipid bilayers.

Why do the lipid components form a stable bilayer structure in an aqueous environment? For thermodynamic reasons. Hydrocarbon chains can't dissolve in water; water and oil don't mix. When lipid molecules are placed in water, their hydrocarbon chains tend to stay in contact with one another, away from the water phase. This tendency, which is called the *hydrophobic effect,* stabilizes the bilayer structure.

If lipid remains in contact with water, stable spherical structures called *liposomes* form (figure 1). Liposomes represent a good model for the first types of membranes to appear in the origin-of-life saga. However, since no obvious sources for lipid-like molecules seem to exist, where did these compounds come from?

Organic Molecules on the Early Earth

The more general question of how *any* organic molecules appeared on the prebiotic Earth must first be considered. Essentially all present-day organic molecules are products of biological—including human—activity. Before the origin of life, how did organic molecules become available to start up the first biological systems?

One source was chemical reactions within Earth's atmosphere and hydrosphere. This view is supported by experiments described by Cyril Ponnamperuma in chapter 2 of this volume.

Substantial amounts of organic material probably came to the Earth's surface late in the accretion of the planet, about 4 billion years ago, and represent a second source. Organic matter, present throughout the galaxy, forms layers on the surfaces of interstellar dust particles. The dust particles are concentrated in the molecular clouds from which solar systems condense. During condensation, particles bring the organic material along. Most of the dust and gas is incorporated into the sun, some into planets, and the rest into comets and asteroids.

Figure 1
Liposomes. Cylinders of rehydrated phospholipids eventually break to form
rounded liposomes, as seen in the lower half of the photograph.

The process of planet formation is incredibly violent. The temperatures are so high that all organic material is pyrolyzed and gases such as carbon dioxide are produced. However, the last stage of Earth's accretion probably involved a less violent infall of colder materials containing organic compounds: dust, comets, and asteroidal debris. Comets and carbonaceous meteorites contain significant percentages of organic compounds—up to 20 percent by weight. During its late accretion stage, Earth had cooled sufficiently to permit some of the accreting organic material to survive at the surface and in the oceans.

We have estimated the amount of organic material that might have accumulated, assuming such infall occurred. The result is equivalent to a layer approximately 10 centimeters deep over the entire surface of the Earth. Of course, this did not fall all at once, but probably over several hundred million years. The annual accumulation may have been only a few molecules thick. Nonetheless, the total is several hundred times the amount of organic matter now present in the biosphere. From such calculations, it is plausible that a major source of organic matter on the prebiotic Earth was cometary and meteoritic infall.

Organic Structures in Meteorites

Since they represent the only sample we have of the organic compounds present early in Earth's history, we are studying the properties of the organic substances in carbonaceous meteorites. Most of the meteorites that strike Earth today are from the asteroid belt. We assume that asteroids were the parent bodies of the meteorites, and that in the distant past these parent bodies underwent collisions sufficiently energetic to send fragments into Earth-crossing orbits. Actual meteorite falls have been witnessed every 20 years or so, when asteroid fragments captured by Earth's gravitational field produce a spectacular fireworks display as they enter the atmosphere. That meteoritic organic compounds survive atmospheric entry is among the strongest evidence in favor of their contribution to the organic inventory of the prebiotic Earth.

In 1969, the appearance of a fireball in the skies above eastern Australia was followed by a thunderous explosion. Over 100 kilograms of meteoritic material fell near the town of Murchison, just north of Melbourne. The particular specimen of the Murchison meteorite with which we have worked weighs about 90 grams. It was a gift to our laboratory from the Field Museum in Chicago.

Carbonaceous meteorites are stony, rather than metallic, and several percent of their mass is present as organic carbon. The organic material is mostly a polymeric substance which is difficult to extract. Composed of aromatic molecules linked by ether bonds, it resembles refractory soil organics called kerogens. A smaller fraction is composed of molecules that dissolved in water or organic solvents.

To study the material, it was necessary to break open the meteorite. White pebbles several millimeters across, known as chondrules, could be seen. The meteorite was quite friable—it crumbled easily. Even freezing and thawing in water could cause it to break up. From this friability we inferred that the organic components of such meteorites would be readily released to the prebiotic environment.

The freshly fractured meteorite revealed its organic content in the form of microscopic fluorescent particles. The small particles ranged from 1 to 10 micrometers in diameter. Their fluorescence was found to be due to the polycyclic aromatic hydrocarbons present in the organic matter. The simplest (monocyclic) aromatic hydrocarbon is the benzene molecule: six carbons joined in a ring with six hydrogens attached. Two such rings joined together form a compound called napthalene; three form anthracene; and four form pyrene and fluoranthene. Polycyclic aromatic hydrocarbons such as anthracene and pyrene are highly fluorescent. That is, they glow (fluoresce) under ultraviolet light by emitting visible blue-green light. All these compounds were found to be present in the Murchison meteorite, both free and attached to other molecules, and their fluorescence provided useful markers for physical and chemical analyses.

The next step was to partially purify the organic material and examine its chemical and physical properties. We used chromatography to separate the individual components according to the physical differences between the component molecules. (When a mixture is placed in a layer of chromatographic medium and a solvent is drawn into the medium through capillary action, the components usually interact to different degrees with the medium and the solvent. As the solvent moves up through the medium, the most soluble and least interactive components move farthest; the least soluble and most interactive stay nearer the origin, where the mixture was originally spotted.) Organic matter from the meteorite was extracted with lipid solvents such as chloroform, and a sample of the extract was placed at the bottom of a chromatographic plate. The chromatographic separation was carried out first in a solution of hexane and ether; then the plate was turned 90° before separation in chloroform. This technique, called *two-dimensional chromatography*, increases the resolution of the separation process.

Each of the chromatographically separated components was tested for the presence of any amphiphilic molecules that might self-assemble to form membrane structures. Most of the extracted components were fluorescent, and this enabled us to visualize them easily on the chromatographic plate. Some of the separated material contained a complex mixture of amphiphilic compounds. When this material was dried onto a glass microscope slide and an aqueous solution was added, the dried material first broke up into droplets (figure 2). The droplets formed thick-walled fluorescent vesicles (figure 3). At higher magnification, much finer membranous structures were observed at the surface of the droplets (figure 4).

Electron-microscopic examination revealed that even the smallest droplets were surrounded by membranes (figure 5). The inset in the upper right corner of figure 5 is a high-magnification view of part of such a membrane showing a three-layer (dark-light-dark) structure, which is what we expected to see if a bilayer of amphiphilic molecules had self-assembled from the meteoritic components. The presence of a bilayer was confirmed by freeze-fracture electron microscopy (figure 6). (In this technique, a sample of the material is first frozen and then broken open under vacuum. A platinum-carbon replica of the fracture face is then made and viewed in the electron microscope. Because the original fracture plane tends to follow any bilayer structures that are present, the presence of fracture planes is diagnostic of bilayer structure.)

We inferred that membrane structures, formed through self-assembly of relatively simple amphiphilic compounds, were present on the early Earth. Although such materials clearly could have been derived from carbonaceous meteorites, other sources are also possible. Our results simply indicate that self-assembly of membranes is feasible, even under prebiotic conditions.

Membranes and the Origin of Life

If membranes like those we make experimentally were present on the Archean Earth, how could they have contributed to the origin of life? The first cells required some mechanism by which a membrane could encapsulate a system of replicating macromolecules. Although this seems difficult, the drying-wetting procedure offers an easy solution. If membrane-forming lipids are dried in the presence of large molecules, the molecules are "sandwiched" between alternating

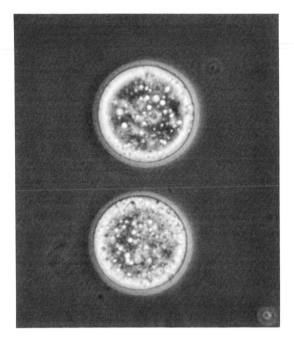

Figure 2
Chromatographically separated amphiphilic compound from the Murchison meteorite. Rehydrated material forms droplets, as seen by phase-contrast microscopy.

lipid bilayers. Upon rehydration, a substantial fraction of the molecules are encapsulated within vesicular membrane structures.

We demonstrated this in a model system containing phosphatidylcholine and a macromolecule (in this case, a protein). The lipid-protein mixture was first dried on a microscope slide, and a clear aqueous buffer solution was added. Within a few minutes there was a vast outpouring of lipid vesicles containing the protein (figure 7). The colorless protein could not be seen inside the vesicles. However, when we used DNA (which can be stained with the fluorescent dye acridine orange) instead of the protein, the membrane-encapsulated macromolecules were clearly visible.

In our view, this simple one-step encapsulation is a plausible mechanism by which the first protocellular structures could have formed, probably in tidal pools subject to periodic drying and wetting. The drying process has the additional advantage of concentrating molecules from dilute solutions.

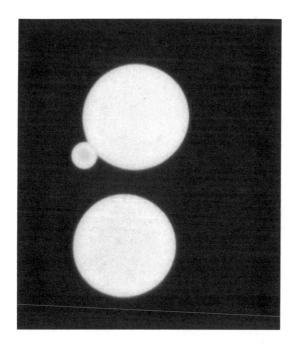

Figure 3
Droplets fluoresce under the microscope when illuminated with ultraviolet light.

We can now return to our original questions concerning the origin of membranes and their role in protocellular structures. We have demonstrated that amphiphilic compounds in meteoritic organic material self-assemble into membranes. The chemistry of the membrane-forming components is still unknown, because even the chromatographically separated material contains hundreds of closely related compounds. However, the compounds are certainly simpler than contemporary membrane phospholipids, and analyses by infrared and mass spectrometry suggest a mixture of organic acids containing cyclic hydrocarbons and carboxyl groups. In earlier work we showed that organic acids as simple as oleic acid (a fatty acid) can form bilayer membranes under conditions like these. The meteoritic amphiphiles probably form membranes by a similar process of self-assembly.

Physical processes predating the origin of life involved the accumulation of organic compounds from a variety of sources, including cometary and meteoritic infall. Chemical evolution of simpler com-

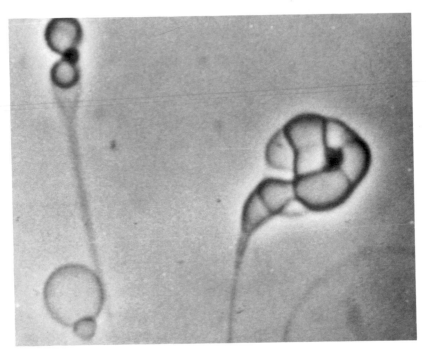

Figure 4
High magnification of material seen forming droplets in figures 2 and 3. Fine membranous structures subdivide and protrude from surface of droplets.

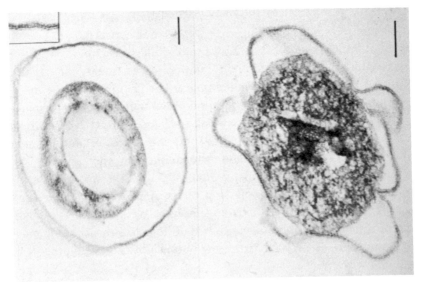

Figure 5
Electron micrographs of membranous boundary formed by lipid-like material from Murchison meteorite. "Membranes" surround amorphous material inside these drops. Scale bars = 0.1 μm. Inset shows bilayer structure of the membranous boundary.

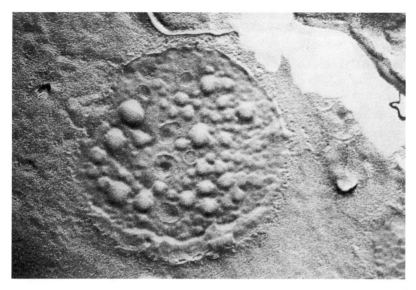

Figure 6
Freeze-fracture electron micrograph of extracted lipid-like material. The circular area
represents a cast of the fracture plane indicating the presence of two layers.

pounds into more complex molecules, and then self-assembly of the
molecules into larger structures, followed. Mechanisms to capture
energy and nutrients from the environment and make them available
to drive the chemical polymerization reactions necessary for the
growth of protocells must have been present as well.

One can imagine a vast number of natural experiments going on
in the rich mixture of organic chemicals and physical environments
available on the Archean Earth. We assume that at some point a
molecular system self-assembled in which catalytic polymers interacted with and aided the assembly of a second class of polymers
having the capacity to store information in a sequence of monomers.
That sequence determined the sequence of monomers in the catalyst,
producing a catalytic-information cycle. In contemporary cells, this
cycle involves enzymatic proteins and nucleic acids.

A primary function of amphiphilic compounds is to provide closed
microenvironments. If a macromolecular catalytic-information system
were encapsulated within a vesicular membrane, the components of
the system would share the same microenvironment. This would be

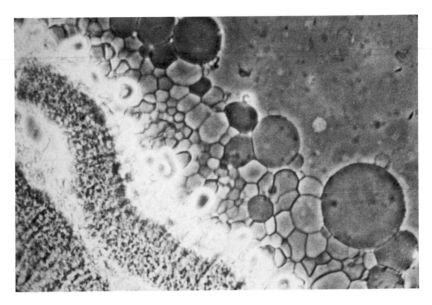

Figure 7
Phase-contrast micrograph of phosphatidylcholine-protein mixture 1 minute after hydration. Protein-containing vesicles can be seen coming from the previously dried mass.

a step toward true cellular function. Encapsulation would also produce individuals; each cell would be different from its neighbors. Only in this way were genetically different individuals selected, a selection based on the ability of a given cell to grow and reproduce.

A second role of early membranes was probably related to energy production, because energy-yielding processes are necessary to provide for growth of the catalytic-information system. In contemporary cells, membranes are central to energy production. Chloroplast membranes capture light energy by means of embedded pigment systems; there must have been some membrane-related process by which light energy was made available to early cells. Light energy may have been used to drive ion transport across membrane barriers. A closed, membrane-bounded structure containing a relatively simple pigment system may have provided energy in the form of ion gradients. These ion gradients could have driven selective transport processes, and then certain synthetic reactions resembling the chemiosmotic synthesis of ATP that takes place on the membranes of bacteria, mitochondria, and chloroplasts today.

The membrane-bounded system described above encompasses a minimal set of basic cellular properties: energy and nutrient capture from the local environment, growth through a catalyzed polymerization mechanism, and replication of an information-storage molecule, all encapsulated within a membranous boundary structure. Such a system, a protocellular stage in the evolutionary process leading to the first life forms, might someday be reproduced under laboratory conditions. However, it should be noted that three essential questions remain to be answered. How did the genetic code originate? Some early mechanism for coding between a nucleotide sequence and a peptide sequence must have evolved. This is still a complete mystery. Second, the synthesis of peptides from activated amino acids must have been catalyzed in some fashion. In contemporary cells the catalysis is carried out by ribosomes, and the origin of such a complex protein synthesis system is difficult to imagine. Last, all life today uses certain forms of amino acids and sugars called *stereoisomers* (L-amino acids and D-sugars). This appears to be a clue to the origin of life, but we still have not penetrated its significance.

We have no answers to these fundamental questions, but the earliest prokaryotes had all the answers over 3.5 billion years ago. The most exciting problems related to the origin of life remain to be worked out through scientific inquiry.

Readings

Anders, E. 1989. Prebiotic organic matter from comets and asteroids. *Nature* 342: 255–258.

Deamer, D. W., and J. Oró. 1980. Role of lipids in prebiotic structures. *BioSystems* 12: 175–176.

Deamer, D. W., and R. M. Pashley. 1989. Amphiphilic components of the Murchison carbonaceous chondrite: Surface properties and membrane formation. *Origins of Life* 19: 21–38.

Ferris, J. P. 1984. The chemistry of life's origins. *Chemical and Engineering News* 62: 22–35.

Ferris, J. P. 1988. Problems and perspectives for the origin of life. *Cold Spring Harbor Symposia on Quantitative Biology* 52: 29.

Fleischaker, G. R. 1990. Origins of life: An operational definition. *Origins of Life and Evolution of the Biosphere* 20: 127–137.

Horgan, J. 1991. In the beginning. . . . *Scientific American* 264, no. 2: 117–125.

Kerridge, J. F., and M. F. Matthews, eds. 1988. *Meteorites and the Early Solar System.* University of Arizona Press.

Miller, S. L., H. C. Urey, and J. Oró. 1976. Origin of organic compounds on the primitive Earth and in meteorites. *Journal of Molecular Evolution* 9: 59–72.

5

Origins of Life: The Historical Development of Recent Theories

Antonio Lazcano

We are almost entirely ignorant of the transition from nonlife to life. Before we knew the chemistry and the cellular structure of all life on Earth, it was easier to believe in frequent and spontaneous generation. In this chapter Antonio Lazcano presents the history of our changing concepts of the origins of life—including experimental approaches—by tracing the development of these concepts in Western Europe, Russia, and North America. He suggests that chemical and biochemical methods will solve the puzzle of the transition from nonlife to life, at least partly, by producing in the laboratory a material system that has the properties of life: information storage, replication, self-maintenance, and boundedness. Professor Lazcano teaches at the Autonomous University of Mexico in Mexico City.

Spontaneous Generation Disproved

In 1859 Charles Darwin published the first edition of *The Origin of Species*, a landmark not only in the field of biology but in Western intellectual history as well. With respect to the question of the origin of life, Darwin seemed to hold the view that the first organisms arose early in the history of the primitive Earth by a process of spontaneous generation (see the passage quoted in chapter 2 of the present volume). Darwin did not use these specific terms, but he seems to have implicitly assumed that the first living beings emerged spontaneously.

In France, also during 1859, Louis Pasteur began the experiments from which he eventually concluded that no spontaneous generation of living organisms ever occurred. In a very simple experiment, Pasteur boiled a concoction of organic materials in a flask and then sealed it. The process of boiling killed all the microbes, leaving the liquid sterile. By breaking the neck of one flask, Pasteur gave airborne bacteria access to the mixture of organic compounds, and they grew; the second flask is still sterile today, whereas the organic matter in the first was quickly decomposed. From these results Pasteur realized that bacteria did not arise spontaneously from decaying organic matter.

Pasteur's experimental demonstration of the nonexistence of spontaneous generation created a problem for biologists studying the origins of life. For example, the famous German evolutionist Ernst Haeckel had theorized that the origins of all living beings could be traced to a common ancestor; after Pasteur's compelling demonstration, Haeckel was unable to conceptualize the root of his "tree of life." Given these circumstances, many people viewed the theme of the origins of life as unscientific and therefore unworthy of study. Others, however, thought that meaningful questions could be asked and answered.

Panspermia

In 1879 Hermann von Helmholtz proposed that life had not emerged on Earth but rather had come to this planet from another part of the universe, perhaps on meteorites or comets. Helmholtz's idea was named *panspermia*, meaning "universality of the germs of life." This idea was quite popular even in the early twentieth century. More recently, the well-respected scientists Fred Hoyle and Francis Crick have tried to revive the theory of panspermia. Despite their efforts, panspermia seems scientifically moribund. The fundamental flaws in the hypothesis of panspermia are that it can never definitively be shown to be right or wrong and that there is as yet no experimental way of showing that life has indeed appeared in other parts of the universe. Panspermia does not solve the problem of the origin of life; it merely transfers the problem to the vastness of space.

Autotrophic Origins

In 1914 a group of scientists, including the physicist Leonard Troland, hypothesized a spontaneous and abiological formation of catalytic molecules in the primitive oceans. These enzymatic molecules were

Figure 1
Herman J. Muller (1890–1967).

thought to be both heterocatalytic (capable of catalyzing reactions in solution) and autocatalytic (capable of self-catalyzation, and possibly self-replication). These ideas were further developed by the American geneticist Herman Muller, who concluded that the first life form on Earth must have been a living gene able to mutate and thus to evolve. Muller's "living genes" gave rise, on his view, to photosynthetic microorganisms ancestral to contemporary plants and, with loss of photosynthesis, to animals themselves. However, most scientists agree that no single molecule or gene can ever be "alive" outside a cell. Muller's viewpoint does not take this into account, and hence many people working in the field of the origin of life feel that it is essential to also explain the emergence of membranes and metabolism.

While Muller and Troland were developing their ideas, the Mexican scientist Alfonso Herrera proposed a theory known as *plasmogenesis*. Herrera devoted more than 50 years to experimenting with different kinds of substances, attempting to produce living photosynthetic cells in the laboratory. At first he used water and oil (or gasoline); later he experimented with hydrogen cyanide and formaldehyde. Though isolated in a conservative society that was incapable of understanding his work or even his motivations, Herrera worked

Figure 2
Alfonso L. Herrera (1868–1942).

tirelessly, publishing the *Bulletin de Laboratoire de Plasmogenie* and maintaining correspondence with scientists all around the world. Many of Herrera's colleagues were absolutely convinced that life could be created in the laboratory, and that the first forms of life had been *autotrophic*—that is, capable of synthesizing organic material for their sustenance.

Formation of Organic Molecules without Life

In November 1923, a book expounding views quite different from Herrera's was published by the young Russian biochemist Alexander Ivanovich Oparin. Oparin's central thesis was that the first organisms to emerge must have been bacteria in an anaerobic environment. Contrary to most of his colleagues at the time, Oparin believed that the first forms of life were heterotrophic—that they could not make their own food but obtained organic material already present on the primitive Earth.

I had the opportunity to ask Oparin how his ideas had originated. As a young student at the Imperial University of Moscow, besides studying biochemistry, botany, and zoology he attended lectures

Figure 3
Alexander Ivanovich Oparin (1894–1980).

given privately by Kliment Arkadievich Timiryazev, a scientist who
had gone to England in order to collect as much material on Darwin
and Darwinism as he could bring back to Russia and who had later
been expelled from the University of Moscow for his political activities. Despite his stern appearance, Timiryazev was a congenial man
who gave lectures on Darwin in his flat in Moscow. Partly because
of his influence, Oparin concluded that on evolutionary grounds it
was impossible to imagine the emergence of a cell that was already
fully autotrophic. Rather, he concluded, the first organisms must
have been heterotrophic.

In order to buttress his intuition, Oparin needed to demonstrate
that organic material could form in the absence of living beings. Two
important pieces of information supported Oparin's claim that the
first organisms were more likely to have been heterotrophic. First,
hydrocarbons and other organic materials were present in meteorites,
and simple organic molecules in comets and in the spectra of stars.
These facts had been known since the middle of the nineteenth
century. Second, as the Russian chemist Mendeleev had demonstrated, long-chain hydrocarbons (oils, fats, and waxes) could be
formed abiologically. On May 3, 1922, Oparin gave a lecture at the

Figure 4
Kliment Arkadievich Timiryazev (1843–1920).

Botanical Society of Moscow in which he made his ideas on the origin of life public. His speculations were not well received.

Most of our current ideas on the origin of life can be traced to Oparin's monograph *The Origins of Life*, published in 1924 in Russian. (As a point of historical interest it is worth noting that the book, though addressed to scientists interested in the origins of life, was published primarily for the ideological purpose of spreading materialistic ideas among workers.) The Soviet revolution had taken place seven years before the book was published; indeed, the first line of the first page reads "workers of all the world unite," the famous closing line of the *Communist Manifesto*. Oparin's book remained largely unknown outside the Soviet Union, though today the seminal nature of Oparin's theses is universally recognized. Oparin proposed that there was no life on Earth when our planet coalesced. The so-called primitive atmosphere of the early Earth was reducing: hydrogen was free in the atmosphere, oxygen was present combined with hydrogen in water vapor, there was no free O_2, carbon existed in the compound methane, and nitrogen was present in the form of ammonia. In this atmosphere, ultraviolet radiation coming from the sun, electrical discharges due to lightning, and heat from volcanos all contributed to the formation of organic compounds, which later collected in the early seas to form the so-called prebiotic soup. According to Oparin these organic materials concentrated into drops, and from these drops the first cells emerged. The first cells were of course prokaryotic (bacterial) and anaerobic, since they had arisen in an environment with no free oxygen. They were probably heterotrophs that used the abiologically produced organic matter that surrounded them as a source of energy and carbon.

Contemporaries of Oparin thought along similar lines. John B. S. Haldane, a versatile British biologist, argued in 1929 that the origin of life could be explained in a context of chemical evolution. The main difference between Oparin's and Haldane's views was that whereas for Oparin the first living beings were cells, for Haldane the first living beings were viruses. Since viruses are not capable of actively maintaining themselves unless they are inside a cell, Haldane's original thoughts ran into a blind alley—the origin of the cell was not explained.

In 1936 Oparin published an enlarged version of his 1924 book. The 1936 edition was far more mature and profound in its philosophical and evolutionary analyses. Oparin not only abandoned his naive and crude materialism, he also provided a thorough presentation and analysis of the literature on the abiotic synthesis of organic material. In addition, Oparin argued that the best model of a system for the concentration of organic material on the primitive Earth, later evolving into the cell, was the coacervate (figure 5). Coacervates are charged, microscopic, organic, colloidal droplets that can concentrate organic materials existing in the medium. Since coacervates form spontaneously when two solutions of macromolecules with opposite charges are mixed, it is quite possible that they were present in the prebiotic milieu. However, they lack the lipid bilayers, present in all known cells, that retain organic matter in high concentrations inside a self-constructed boundary; therefore, they are no longer considered as potentially ancestral to life itself. Coacervates were the favorite model for a considerable time after Oparin's views became widely known, because they were perceived as mimicking the surmised properties of precellular systems. Eventually, however, it was recognized that coacervates tend to fall apart, and that their resemblance to cells is merely superficial. Experimental studies and theoretical

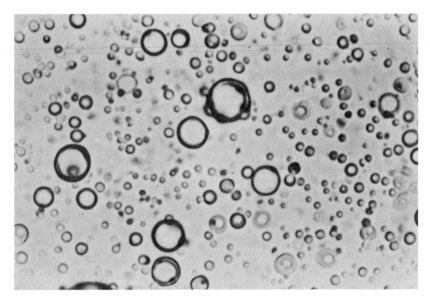

Figure 5
Light micrograph of coacervates.

considerations about colloids and coacervates led to their dismissal
as constituting any steps toward the origins of life.

Laboratory Synthesis

For the next ten years, while World War II raged on, nothing much
happened in the field of the origins of life. After the war, Harold C.
Urey returned to the University of Chicago and, having read Oparin's
book, decided to analyze the primitive atmosphere from a physical-
chemical point of view. Urey published his results in 1952. He suggested that the carbon, nitrogen, oxygen, and sulfur on the primitive
Earth were probably in the most reduced forms: carbon as methane,
nitrogen as ammonium, oxygen as water, and sulfur as hydrogen
sulfide. Urey considered carbon dioxide (CO_2) to have been a minor
constituent of the primitive prebiotic atmosphere. Stanley L. Miller,
one of Urey's brightest students, designed an experiment using a
"simulated primitive atmosphere" based on Urey's conception of the
composition of the early Earth's atmosphere.

Figure 6
Stanley L. Miller.

The question was whether prebiotic synthesis of organic molecules could have taken place in such an environment. The apparatus in which Miller and Urey simulated the primitive atmosphere (see chapter 2) was rather small and did not contain all the chemical compounds that existed in the prebiotic atmosphere. However, the experiment was ingenious—it is considered a classic to this day. The apparatus was composed of two connected flasks. Water was boiled in the lower flask; the water vapor then passed into the upper flask, where it mixed with ammonia, methane, and hydrogen. For about a week Miller and Urey allowed electric charges to go through this mixture of gases. As the water vapor condensed, organic molecules—formed in the gaseous phase—began to accumulate.

Thus Oparin's ideas on the origin of organic molecules, and their possible prebiotic syntheses, were successfully put to the test for the first time. In the years since the Miller-Urey experiment, many of the organic "raw materials" of contemporary cells have been synthesized in the laboratory (table 1). Hydrocarbons and fatty acids form from carbon monoxide (CO) and hydrogen as shown in reaction 1, for example. Small amounts of ribose and deoxyribose, the sugars found in nucleic acids, can be formed from formaldehyde and acetaldehyde. It is now possible to form nonenzymatically the amino acids (reac-

Table 1
Major prebiotic reaction pathways.

1.	$CO + H_2$	FTT (Fischer-Tropsch type) catalysis	Hydrocarbons, fatty acids
2.	CH_2O	Base catalysis	Ribose
3.	CH_3CHO CH_2O	Base catalysis	Deoxyribose
4.	RCHO HCN NH_3	Strecker condensation	Amino acids, hydroxyacids
5.	As above + CH_2S	Strecker condensation	Cysteine, methionine
6.	HCN	Base catalysis	Adenine, guanine
7.	HC_3N + urea	Condensation	Uracil, cytosine
8.	As above + CH_2O	Hydrazine	Thymine
9.	Amino acids	Cyanamide	Oligopeptides
10.	Mononucleotides	Cyanamide	Oligonucleotides
11.	Isoprene	Ultraviolet, ionizing radiation	Polyisoprenoids
12.	Fatty acids, glycerols, phosphates, bases	Cyanamide	Neutral lipids, phospholipids

tions 4 and 5) that make up the proteins in all living beings. As was brilliantly shown by Juan Oró, we can form adenine from hydrogen cyanide, and other simple "prebiotic" reactions lead to the synthesis of guanine, uracil, cytosine, and thymine (reactions 6, 7, and 8). Some of these molecules even condense together to form oligomers or polymers. Under the appropriate conditions, amino acids form oligopeptides and nucleotides form oligonucleotides. Finally (reactions 11 and 12), we can nonenzymatically form the phospholipid components found in all cell membranes. Experiments of this kind suggest that Oparin and Haldane were on the right track. The chemical syntheses of organic compounds on the prebiotic Earth probably

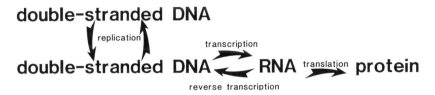

Figure 7
The central dogma of biology: DNA is transcribed to RNA, which is then translated into proteins. Reverse transcription allows RNA to be transcribed back into DNA.

yielded a mixture of many different kinds of molecules, including many of those found in contemporary cells.

Proteins or DNA First?

The problem, of course, is the transition from the mixture of organic compounds we think was present on the primitive Earth to living and reproducing organisms. Two sets of properties distinguish living from nonliving systems: *autopoiesis* and *reproduction*. Autopoiesis, a term derived from Greek, means "self-making." As defined by the Chilean biologists Francisco Varela and Humberto Maturana, it refers to entities that are separated from their environment by an interface or membrane and that *metabolize* (i.e., chemically maintain and perpetuate their identity in fluctuating environments). Autopoiesis is considered a prerequisite for reproduction. All contemporary cells have their genetic information stored in the form of double-stranded DNA. This DNA can replicate itself to produce more DNA; it can also give rise to RNA in a process known as *transcription*. Transcribed RNA contains information derived from the double-stranded DNA. In the process of translation, the information contained in transcribed RNA molecules is used on ribosomes in stringing together amino acids into proteins. Transcription and translation seem to be universal in all contemporary cells. This poses the problem of how such complicated systems arose from the disaggregate mixture of organic molecules on the primitive Earth.

Many people have compared the problem of the origin of life to the chicken-and-egg problem: Which came first, DNA or proteins? On my view neither DNA nor proteins came first. Along with many others, I am convinced that RNA came first. Like DNA, RNA is a molecule that can carry genetic information. Like proteinaceous enzymes, RNA can act as a catalyst. Unlike proteinaceous enzymes or DNA, RNA is autocatalytic. RNA's catalytic activity may be understood as a remnant of times in the prebiotic environment when these molecules were surrounded by lipid membranes.

If RNA came first, this question arises: Why was there a transition in living beings from information stored in RNA to information stored in the form of double-stranded DNA? Several scientists have come to the following conclusions:

• The backbone of single-stranded RNA is much less stable than the equivalent structure in double-stranded DNA. Enhanced stability gives DNA greater fidelity as an information store.

• RNA is much more susceptible to chemical transformations, such as the deamination of cytosine into uracil.

• RNA molecules absorb more ultraviolet radiation than double-stranded DNA, so the chances of the genetic information being damaged by the UV radiation on the primitive Earth were greater for RNA than for DNA.

• RNA polymerase, the enzyme that forms RNA from a DNA template, does not have a proofreading activity. Whereas DNA has many repair mechanisms, RNA has none.

To many, these facts suggest that the evolution of RNA to DNA took place very quickly. Of course these ideas will be developed further, just as the ideas of Herrera, Haldane, Oparin, and Urey have been refined and rewarded. But we can also be absolutely sure that some of these assertions will be abandoned for a more complete idea of the way life appeared on Earth.

Readings

Day, W. 1984. *Genesis on Planet Earth: The Search for Life's Beginning.* Second edition. Yale University Press.

Kamminga, H. 1988. Historical perspective: The problem of the origin of life in the context of developments in biology. *Origins of Life* 18: 1–11.

Lazcano, A., J. Fastag, P. Gariglio, C. Ramírez, and J. Oró. 1988. On the early evolution of RNA polymerase. *Journal of Molecular Evolution* 27: 365–376.

Lazcano, A., R. Guerrero, L. Margulis, and J. Oró. 1988. The evolutionary transition from RNA to DNA in early cells. *Journal of Molecular Evolution* 27: 283–290.

Oparin, A. I. 1953. *The Origin of Life.* Second edition. Dover.

Oró, J., S. L. Miller, and A. Lazcano. 1990. The origin and early evolution of life on Earth. *Annual Review of Earth and Planetary Sciences* 18: 317–356.

Urey, H. 1952. On the early chemical history of the Earth and the origin of life. *Proceedings of the National Academy of Sciences* 38: 351–363.

Varela, F., and H. Maturana. 1974. Autopoiesis: The organization of living systems, its characterization and a model. *BioSystems* 5: 187–196.

6   The Antiquity of Life

Elso S. Barghoorn

Elso S. Barghoorn, professor of paleobotany and geology at Harvard University, was a pioneer in the subject of Precambrian life. His research and wisdom enlightened the Environmental Evolution program.

In the 1950s it became apparent that evidence of the oldest life on Earth could be found in the form of microfossils embedded in glass-like rocks called cherts. Barghoorn was among the first to realize the significance of these spheres and filaments. Here he recounts his discovery of three widely separated ancient-fossil-bearing localities.

Professor Barghoorn died in 1984 without having updated this chapter. Rather than deprive the reader of his inimitable style, we have preserved his writing and added some newer information from the literature that we feel he would have wanted to include.

One could argue that the study of the origin of life as an event is more a philosophical than a scientific pursuit. The fact of the origin of life we can accept, but to actually pinpoint the origin in the history of the Earth is probably not amenable to scientific inquiry in the sense that we cannot actually document it. What I will focus on here, then, is the geological evidence of the antiquity of life on Earth. The sources of information on this subject are widespread and include geologic formations on all the continents (figure 1). Though ancient, these rocks are relatively unmetamorphosed; i.e., they have not been affected to any great degree by high temperatures or extreme pressures. Their surface expression is amenable to direct observation, often of course expedited by mining. In general the source materials are both widespread and within easy access.

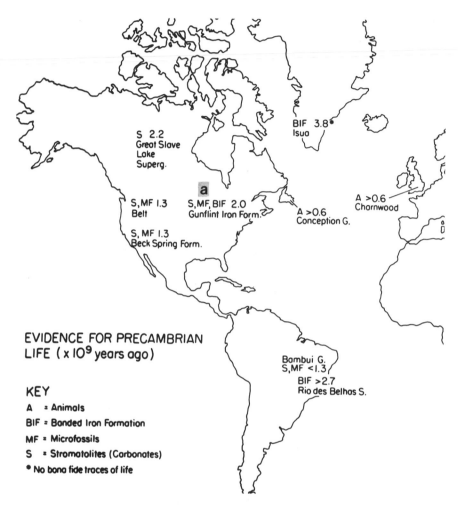

S 2.2
Great Slave
Lake
Superg.

BIF 3.8*
Isua

S, MF 1.3
Belt

S, MF, BIF 2.0
Gunflint Iron Form.

A >0.6
Conception G.

A >0.6
Charnwood

S, MF 1.3
Beck Spring Form.

EVIDENCE FOR PRECAMBRIAN
LIFE (x 10^9 years ago)

KEY
A = Animals
BIF = Banded Iron Formation
MF = Microfossils
S = Stromatolites (Carbonates)
* No bona fide traces of life

Bambui G.
S, MF <1.3
BIF >2.7
Rio des Belhos S.

Figure 1
World map showing evidence of Precambrian life: (a) Gunflint Iron Formation in
Ontario and Minnesota, (b) Fig Tree Formation in Swaziland, (c) Bitter Springs For-
mation in central Australia.

Stromatolites and Microfossils of the Gunflint Iron Formation

My involvement with this problem goes back to the early 1950s. I would like to detail the story in terms of my own chronological experience, so in the exploration of time we will not be following a sequential order from the earliest rocks to the latest, but rather will follow the discoveries as they occurred. My first experience in the search for the antiquity of life was in rocks that fortunately contained abundant evidence of a complex biota approximately 2 billion years old. The formation, aptly named the Gunflint Iron Formation, is found in northern Ontario and adjacent Minnesota and consists of a series of sediments including a thin but persistent unit of rocks called *cherts* or *flints*. Sparks from chert-struck steel ignited gunpowder in the flintlock rifles of yesteryear. These cherts contain large numbers of microorganisms still relatively unaltered in shape, although highly altered in terms of original chemical composition. The Gunflint biota, as we call it, is recognizable at the surface by structures known as *stromatolites* which are preserved in the chert matrix.

Stromatolites are organosedimentary domes formed by the growth of a community of microorganisms often but not always dominated by cyanobacteria. Although most stromatolites consist principally of calcium carbonate, those of the Gunflint Formation are formed of chert—the fineness of silica crystals and the hardness of cherts preserve microfossil structures far better than do carbonates. These stromatolites are clearly visible to the eye and are called *microbial structures*. Typical representatives of both Precambrian stromatolites and their modern counterparts can be seen in figures 2 and 3. The difference between these stromatolites is relatively minor in gross expression but vast in age. The structures shown in figure 2 are on the order of 2 billion years old. Those shown in figure 3 are recent (in fact, living) rock-like masses of cyanobacterial domes found today in western Australia. Precambrian stromatolites are found in great profusion in the Gunflint chert (figure 4). Cut a very thin section of this chert, polish it until light can pass through, and you will find vast numbers of algal pillars with a thimble-like structure.

Here, as in other areas of the world, stromatolites occur in association with abundant silica or carbonate precipitation, which traps the microorganisms in a matrix that upon hardening and crystallization is incompressible. The organisms are in this way preserved and do not undergo any degree of structural alteration sometimes for hundreds of millions of years. A thin section of the Gunflint chert, observed under the microscope, contains a profusion of filaments and small ovoid bodies, very similar in appearance to cyanobacteria that you might typically find in pond scum (figure 5). The Gunflint biota consists of a vast number of types of organisms as well as vast numbers of individuals. These fossil microbes represent some of the more common types of microstructures found in the Gunflint chert and are obviously morphologically diverse. At higher magnification one can observe minute structures that, upon comparison with living microorganisms, demonstrate that these microfossils are indeed bacteria. In the Gunflint chert, then, we have a complicated assemblage of microorganisms, interpreted on the basis of morphology to be cyanobacteria, comprising the productive phase of this biocoenos or stromatolitic assemblage of living and growing bacterial communities.

The Fig Tree Formation

The oldest evidence of life has been pursued in rocks of far greater age in a very different part of the world, southern Africa. The eastern Transvaal of the Republic of South Africa and Swaziland contain a series of rare sediments. (A formation similar in age and composition, the Warrawoona Formation of Australia, is described in chapter 7.) They consist of a series of sedimentary rocks, volcanic rocks, and fluvial deposits with a total thickness of many tens of thousands of feet. Once again, one of the more common rock types in the sequence is black chert. In particular, the middle section of this series, the Fig Tree Formation or Fig Tree Series, contains massive units of dense black cherts containing a relatively high concentration of organic matter. Originally, no stromatolitic organization was evident superficially at the surface, though such organizations have now been described. Closer examination of these rocks by either light or electron microscopy reveals the presence of microstructures comparable to organisms found today—namely bacteria, including cyanobacteria (see chapter 7, figure 3). The bacteria in the Fig Tree biota are in a distinctly bedded arrangement within the rock, indicating growth in

Figure 2
Two-billion-year-old stromatolites at Great Slave Lake, Northwest Territories, Canada.

Figure 3
Present-day, living stromatolites at Carbla Point, Shark Bay, Western Australia.

Figure 4
Stromatolite head in Gunflint chert (Schreiber Outcrop).

shallow, slightly agitated water; they were not preserved in any great profusion. The microstructures are clearly not mineral inclusions, and their organic composition can be readily demonstrated by examination or by simple combustion. The bacterial cells are contained within the matrix of the rock and were present before the rock was silicified. This is determined by the arrangement of the cells in relation to the crystals of silica. The microfossils are extremely minute bacteria, generally less than a micron in size; though infrequent in the rocks, they can be found locally in relative abundance. What makes the microfossils of the Fig Tree rocks interesting to geologists is their great antiquity. The rocks of the Fig Tree system have repeatedly been dated as 3.2 to 3.4 billion years old. Hence, the Fig Tree biota is considerably older than the assemblage from the Gunflint Formation.

In the course of examining other sources of Precambrian organisms, I had the good fortune to be involved in field work in central Australia at about the same time the Fig Tree rocks were being studied in Africa. In the assemblage from Australia we have a rather remarkable complex, but a much younger biota. This Australian biota

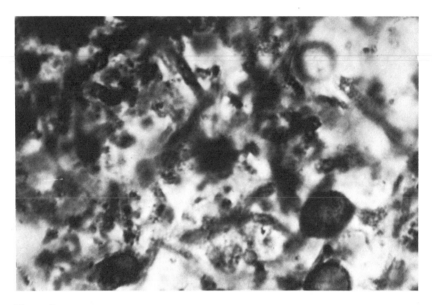

Figure 5
The Gunflint microbiota. Petrographic thin section of chert observed under the microscope reveals 2-billion-year-old filamentous and spherical fossil bacteria.

is called the Bitter Spring assemblage, deriving its name from the rock formation where it was found. This assemblage comprises a larger number of taxa or taxonomic units assignable to a wide range of morphologies of extant or living cyanobacteria. What makes the Bitter Springs assemblage remarkable, though, is the degree of preservation. It is far better preserved, in respect to its original form and probably also in respect to its chemical composition, than the Fig Tree assemblage. The vicissitudes occurring over the enormous length of time since the deposition and formation of the Fig Tree Formation have little changed the biota that made up part of the sediments.

To recapitulate, the early microfossil discoveries were not the earliest in geologic time. The later discoveries are the most elegant in terms of biological sophistication and degree of preservation. In the course of studying the morphologies of the microfossils in various laboratories, it became of interest to focus on the peripheral or ancillary evidence left by the ecological conditions prevalent at the time of deposition. Of course here we enter an area of both demonstrable fact and speculation, but it is of interest to examine some of the paleobiological or paleoecological evidence concerning the organism's physiology and mode of existence.

Chemical Fossils

One obvious and time-honored methodology is to examine the chemicals extractable from the rocks. One substance of the few extractable from these ancient rocks belongs to a class of chemicals identified in the laboratory as porphyrins. Porphyrins are of particular interest because the porphyrin ring complex is central to the photoreceptor system in green plants, in cyanobacteria, and in almost all photosynthetic organisms, regardless of their phylogenetic origin. Porphyrins are also chemically very resistant molecules and can be extracted from ancient rocks in varying amounts and analyzed by infrared absorption techniques. The clearest evidence of ancient porphyrins is from rocks about a billion years old. Porphyrins are found in older rocks to a lesser extent. The potential for the study of ancient biochemical sediments is evidenced by gas chromatography of the extracts from the Gunflint Formation. Such chromatographs show the presence of two probable degradation products of chlorophyll: the hydrocarbons phytane and pristane. Both are side chains on the central tetrapyrrole ring of chlorophyll molecules, whose release during degradation has been demonstrated in the laboratory. The presence of these compounds does not simply prove the chemical resistance of phytane and pristane or establish the presence of porphyrins as a possible prelude to phytane and pristane, but rather implies a biological synthesis. If we have porphyrins and if phytane and pristane are derived from porphyrins, then we are fundamentally demonstrating the all-important physiological process of photosynthesis. [Editor's note: Whether these substituted porphyrin isoprenoid derivatives are direct products of photosynthesis, though, is debatable; porphyrins can come from heme groups, and phytane and pristane can be lipid components of heterotrophic bacteria and have still other origins.] Photosynthesis as a system of life is a milestone in evolution whereby a continually available source of energy, sunlight, is converted to chemical energy and used in a myriad of biochemical and biosynthetic pathways. Hence, the antiquity of photosynthesis is fundamental not only for the origins but also for the energy dynamics of life.

Let us look further at this problem of the origin of photosynthesis. The existence of strongly persuasive, morphological evidence indicating the photosynthetic character of the fossil microorganisms has been demonstrated. Chemical substances extracted from the rocks in minute amounts are reasonably interpreted as degradation products of chlorophyll, a molecule essential to cyanobacteria-type photosynthesis. How else, then, can we drive a wedge into this question of the origin of photosynthesis? It so happens there is a chemical mechanism whereby some putative evidence can be extracted.

Carbon dioxide, one of the two fundamental raw materials (along with water) in the photosynthetic equation, exists in the atmosphere in the form of two stable isotopes: carbon-12 and carbon-13. (Carbon-14, a radiogenic isotope, is an extremely minute constituent of atmospheric carbon dioxide.) The ratio of the two isotopes in the atmosphere is very disproportionate: 99 percent is in the form of the lighter isotope, carbon-12, and about 1 percent in the form of carbon-13. Both isotopes are drawn into the photosynthetic organism during photosynthesis. Because of the kinetics of the molecules, the lighter isotope, being of higher velocity, is selectively concentrated by the plants in the process of photosynthesis. This leads to a fractionation of the two isotopes, so the ratio of carbon isotopes incorporated into the organic material of the body is not in equilibrium with the isotopes of carbon existing in the atmosphere. In other words, the ratio of carbon-13 to carbon-12 in the organism is lower than the ratio of carbon-13 to carbon-12 in the atmosphere. By comparing the ratio of the isotopes against the standard ratio in the atmosphere, one can discriminate between organic carbon and carbon not formed by photosynthetic processes. [Editor's note: Discriminating the history of any material organic carbon simply from the $^{13}C/^{12}C$ ratio is difficult; nonbiological processes (astronomical, diffusion, etc.) fractionate isotopes. However, photo- and lithotrophic carbon fixation so strongly fractionate carbon isotopes, favoring ^{12}C, that it is likely that Barghoorn's intuition is justifiable here.] Nonphotosynthetic carbon such as occurs in the crust of the Earth can be discriminated from carbon incorporated into living organisms via biochemical pathways. Analysis of the organic carbon in Precambrian rocks from various parts of the Earth suggests a photosynthetic origin. This is a big general-ization and obviously must be defended as evidence accumulates, but at the present time we can say it is likely that the oldest organic carbon on the Earth, found dispersed in shales (typical sedimentary rocks derived from muds), was produced by photosynthesis.

Precambrian Micropaleontology and the Origins of Life

What does Precambrian micropaleontology have to tell us about the framework of research on the origin of life? The first organism arose, we can assume, from inorganic sources, but in order to produce life there must previously have been some aggregation of materials into far more sophisticated, organic compounds. Hence, we can postulate major sequences of events between the origin of the Earth and the origin of life as a system of syntheses in which prebiotic or chemical "evolution" was taking place in organism-free molecular systems.

Chemical evolution must have led in the course of time to a fairly high concentration of organic compounds in the seas, with lesser amounts of volatiles in the atmosphere. This mixture of materials presumably then led to the beginnings of life. Now, concomitant with the origin of a self-contained, self-perpetuating (autopoetic) protobiont consumer is the continual depletion of the source mate-rials, namely the organic broth or soup in which these organisms were living. Since we know of course that the organic soup was not completely depleted, some productive innovation among the proto-biota must have arisen. This innovation was, at least in the broad sense, photosynthesis. Photosynthesis, which probably began very early in the history of life on Earth, is connected to sequences we see today in sedimentary rocks. Photosynthesis probably arose well before the time of the earliest recognizable organism, such as those from the Fig Tree rocks. A reasonable date for the origin of oxygenic photosynthesis is, then, somewhere around 3.5 billion years ago. From that point on, there have been major changes in the Earth as a system. These changes are geochemical as well as biological, because organisms influence the geochemical environment in many subtle, often unappreciated ways.

One obvious effect of oxygenic photosynthesis is the oxidation of reduced metals in the oceans and in surface sediments. The transition from a reducing to an oxidative environment may have been gradual and slowly cumulative, but finally, at a date impossible to accurately ascertain, an atmosphere essentially devoid of oxygen was transformed to an atmosphere with oxygen as a significant component. Free oxygen in the atmosphere led to the formation of the gas ozone, the triatomic form of oxygen. A significant influence on the radiochemistry of the Earth, ozone prevents or inhibits the penetration of short-wavelength ultraviolet. Ozone gave rise to a protective layer, freed organisms from the protection afforded by water or thin layers of minerals, and led to the invasion of open surfaces of the land. Just when ozone first appeared we cannot be certain, but it is perfectly obvious and demonstrable that by 2 billion years ago a wide range of microorganisms had evolved. The calibration of this evolutionary diversification is not possible, but we do know that by the end of the Precambrian era—about a billion years ago—cells containing complex structures of the sort associated with eukaryotes had already evolved. This transition from cells without nuclei (prokaryotes) to cells with nuclei (eukaryotes) was arguably the biggest step in cell evolution after the origin of life itself.

After the appearance and diversification of eukaryotic organisms, some 1.8 billion years ago, came one of the most astonishing events in all of evolution: the extraordinary diversification of macroscopic life at the end of the Precambrian era. The vast evolution of morphologically distinct animals at the end of the Precambrian era can only be called explosive. The base of the Phanerozoic eon is delineated by an extreme diversification of the organisms we call invertebrate animals as well as many organisms we assemble under the various groups of the protoctists. (*Phanerozoic* is the name of the present eon, which began at the base of the Cambrian period about 570 million years ago.) The beginning of the Phanerozoic brings us fairly close to the end of the story of our initial efforts to decipher the antiquity of life.

Editor's Note

After the discovery of the microfossils of the Gunflint Iron Formation, Barghoorn continued to study the older Archean rocks of southern Africa. Through his work and that of his students and colleagues

(Stanley M. Awramik, Andrew Knoll, Paul Strother, J. William Schopf, and Maud Walsh, among others) the date for the oldest life on Earth has been pushed back to at least 3.5 billion years ago. Both microfossils and stromatolites have been discovered in two widely separated sequences of lower Archean rocks: the Warrawoona Formation of Western Australia and the Swaziland System of sediments and volcanics described above.

As Maud Walsh of Louisiana State University explains in her videotape *Earliest Life: The Rock Record,* the environments of deposition, the cohesive paleosediment, the filamentous and coccoid microfossils, and the laminated stromatolites and microbial laminates all contribute to a new picture of early life on Earth. The closest relatives of the earliest known organisms exist in the form of microbial-mat communities, which occasionally preserve as stromatolites. All the new information dramatically attests to the validity of studies on the antiquity of life and to what Elso S. Barghoorn began.

Readings

Awramik, S. A., J. W. Schopf, and M. R. Wader. 1983. Filamentous fossil bacteria from the Archean of Western Australia. *Precambrian Research* 20: 357–374.

Barghoorn, E. S. 1971. The oldest fossils. *Scientific American* 244; no. 5: 30–41.

Barghoorn, E. S., and S. A. Tyler. 1965. Microorganisms from the Gunflint chert. *Science* 147: 563–577.

Cloud, P. 1972. A working model of the primitive Earth. *American Journal of Science* 272: 537–548.

Cloud, P. 1987. *Oasis in Space.* Norton.

Engel, M. H., S. A. Macko, and J. A. Silfer. 1990. Carbon isotope composition of individual amino acids in the Murchison meteorite. *Nature* 348: 47–49.

Knoll, A. H., and E. S. Barghoorn. 1977. Archean microfossils showing cell division from the Swaziland System of South Africa. *Science* 198: 396–398.

Knoll, A. H., P. K. Strother, and S. Rossai. 1989. Distribution and diagenesis of microfossils from the Lower Proterozoic Duck Creek Dolomite, Western Australia. *Precambrian Research* 38: 257–279.

Schopf, J. W., ed. 1983. *Earth's Earliest Biosphere: Its Origin and Evolution.* Princeton University Press.

Schopf, J. W., and B. Packer. 1987. Early Archean (3.3 billion to 3.5 billion-year-old) microfossils from Warrawoona Group, Australia. *Science* 237: 70-73.

Tyler, S. A., and E. S. Barghoorn. 1954. Occurrence of structurally preserved plants in pre-Cambrian Rocks of the Canadian Shield. *Science* 119: 606–608.

7

Evidence of Earliest Life

Paul Strother

How can we interpret tiny spheres in ancient rocks? On what basis do we decide that such an object is evidence of the remains of ancient life? Paul Strother confronts us with the paucity of the most ancient fossil record and with the difficulty of interpreting it. Most scientists accept the concept that life originated on Earth at the beginning of the Archean eon, more than 3.5 billion years ago. But upon what is this common belief based? What would the happening of the origin of life on Earth look like if a record of it did persist in the ancient rocks? Dr. Strother develops for us a concept of adequate criteria for biogenicity (origin from living things) that serves us well as we examine putative evidence for life in the remotest past of the Earth's surface.

By what criteria can we determine whether putative microfossils are actually of biological origin? What evidence is there for the existence of life during the Archean eon? What does the geological record say about life on Earth from the time of the first evidence of a solid Earth (about 4 billion years ago) to the beginning of the Proterozoic eon (about 2.5 billion years ago)? After close examination of microstructures in ancient rocks from Greenland, South Africa, and Australia, I attempt here to evaluate their status as inorganic or fossil objects.

Two types of rock sequences or terrains occur in the Archean eon: high-grade metamorphic terrains and greenstone belts. The high-grade metamorphic terrains, by volume, are more significant; they consist of granites and gneiss. The Archean metamorphic rocks represent the primordial fractionation of the upper mantle into crust added to partially melted surface materials. The greenstone belts are volcaniclastic and sedimentary sequences which have been subsequently metamorphosed to produce a suite of minerals, including chlorite, that are characteristically green. These rocks are *metasedi-ments*—sedimentary rocks that are slightly metamorphosed but retain some of the properties, such as texture, that were present when they were unconsolidated sediments. Metamorphism here refers to the processes of increasing heat and temperature that occur with burial during formation of sedimentary sequences over time, rather than the high-grade metamorphic changes that occur when rocks reach a molten state. Because these two general Archean rock types have been metamorphosed, however, the veracity of almost all fossil occurrences from this time period is under question to some extent.

Most of the Precambrian rock samples are studied by making thin sections and observing them microscopically. Objects in these petrographic thin sections are indigenous to the rock sample itself, and any fossil observed must have been incorporated into the rock at the time of its formation. In examining such fossil material, one must know that the samples have not been contaminated. Contamination may occur where there are either microcracks or spaces between individual mineral grains that make up the composite rock. If, in areas of rock sample that were exposed to outside conditions, material is found deposited in these cracks, then the possibility of contamination exists.

Types of Organic Remains in the Archean Eon

Organic remains of the Archean eon are either direct or indirect. *Direct remains* consist of the organic material that originally made up the organism and is still present in the rock. In the Archean eon these consist primarily of individual cells with simple morphologies. *Indirect remains* are trace fossils—sedimentary features or structures indicative of former life activity. A dinosaur footprint or a worm burrow filled by sand is a trace fossil.

Two kinds of Archean indirect remains are most significant (table 1). Mineralized structures of inferred organic origin include organosedimentary structures, called algal laminates or microbial laminates, and stromatolites. Both are sedimentary rocks, or the metamorphosed equivalent of sedimentary rocks, having layering in which the fabric and geometric relationships of the layers, as well as the mineral composition, are mediated by the activity of microorganisms

Table 1
Types of indirect remains of Precambrian organisms.

Mineralized structures of inferred organic origin
    Stromatolites and microbial ("algal") laminates
    Biomineralization products (endo- or extracellular minerals)
Evidence of former biosynthetic activity
    Chemical "fossils" (organic residues)
    $^{12}C/^{13}C$ ratios
    Physical geochemistry
Impressions
Ichnofossils (trace fossils)

(in this case, cyanobacteria). Cyanobacteria are referred to as "algal" in this case, but the term is actually a misnomer since cyanobacteria are prokaryotes and not closely related to the algae (which are eukaryotes). Communities of these organisms trap and bind sediment to form distinctively laminated rocks. These laminated rock types are fairly common. The depositional environments were usually marine, carbonate-rich, shallow water. Surface communities composed primarily of cyanobacteria are inferred. Stromatolites differ from algal laminates in the profile of the laminations. Stromatolite laminations are usually domed, whereas the laminations of algal laminates are flat or wavy-bedded. With the exception of this shape difference, stromatolites and algal laminates are the same.

Since living communities of bacteria form similar structures today, we suspect that Archean structures had the same origin. However, microlaminated structures can occur as part of sedimentary rocks in several ways that are not necessarily related to the trapping and binding of sediment by microbial ecosystems. Furthermore, stromatolites rarely contain fossils. The organisms that produce these porous layered carbonate structures tend to degrade, leaving only layered rock devoid of fossils.

Another source of information about Archean life is organic chemical fossils. Such organic residues retain no morphological structures. Carbon-containing compounds in rocks, comprising complex organic molecules generated only by living systems, have been isolated. For example, porphyrin derivatives found in Archean rocks are strong evidence for the existence of chlorophyll, or at least of living systems, at the time. A major problem with chemical fossils is that all rocks are permeable to some extent; over long periods of time, chemical contamination is likely.

A banded iron formation from an Archean deposit called the Fig Tree Formation, which is located in the Barberton Mountains of South Africa, provides an example of rock remains rich with information about the rise of atmospheric oxygen. This sample (figure 1), which is approximately 3.3 or 3.4 billion years old, is composed of micro-crystalline silica, or chert. The layers are of different colors because of the different oxidation states of the iron oxide mineral compounds, hematite and magnetite, that are indigenous to the rock. A red color, due to oxidized iron, indicates that the rock was formed under oxi-dizing conditions. Gaseous or atmospheric oxygen apparently was present in the sediments at the time the rock formed. What has this to do with the existence of living systems 3.4 billion years ago? Only two sources of atmospheric oxygen are known. One is oxygenic photosynthesis by organisms; the other is the abiological, ultraviolet-light-driven photodissociation of water in the atmosphere. Most the-oretical models indicate that abiological oxygenesis could not have occurred rapidly enough to provide an oxidizing environment in the sediments. Since the Archean atmosphere was probably devoid of free oxygen, oxidized sediments from this age imply very strongly, but do not prove, the existence of at least local pockets of oxygen within the sediments. It is most reasonable to consider this oxygen biogenic.

The origins of these layers in banded iron formations pose a com-plicated problem not yet solved by geologists. The most prominent hypothesis involves the following factors: Iron must have been in solution near the sediment-water interface at the time of sediment formation. This iron must have been in the Fe^{++} state, the valence state of iron in which it is soluble in water. The oxygen tension of the sediment-water interface, or the zone in which the bands were being formed, must have undergone cyclic changes in the amount of oxygen present in the water at that interface. Those relative amounts of oxygen caused the precipitation of iron oxides of different oxidation levels, ultimately causing the bands of color.

Another Archean rock type, found in the Witwatersrand region of South Africa, provides further atmospheric insight. These 2.7-billion-year-old rocks contain rounded clasts of fool's gold, or pyrite. Pyrite

Figure 1
Outcrop of banded iron from the Fig Tree Formation. These laminations correspond
to iron deposited at various oxidation levels and subsequently silicified.

contains iron in a reduced, or unoxidized, form. The rounded shape of these pyrite clasts indicates that they were transported by water. Such pyrite clasts could not be transported and deposited today, because pyrite is very unstable in an oxygen-rich atmosphere. Pyrite clasts transported by water in today's streams and rivers oxidize very rapidly and decompose. Pyrite deposition in Witwatersrand rocks indicates that the oxygen concentration of the Archean atmosphere was low enough to prevent the breakdown of these materials before deposition.

Criteria for Biogenicity of Direct Remains

Direct remains of life in Archean rocks consist of degraded remains of individual cells with simple morphologies. The likelihood that a sample of simple structures is of biological origin can be evaluated using the following criteria: If the fossil consists of a group of cells rather than isolated single cells, the likelihood that the sample has a biological origin increases. Cells found grouped in clusters or in populations that can be described statistically are more likely to be of biological origin.

There are several aspects of morphology that increase this likelihood as well. Putative fossils composed of simple spheres are very difficult to identify. Many different microorganisms appear spherical. However, if the morphology of the microfossil in question is filamentous, colonial, or even more complex, the possibility that the sample is indeed biological is greater.

The preservation, or surface texture, of individual microspheres varies. Direct remains tend to have a highly granular surface texture. Smooth and intact spheres in a rock sample are often suspect. Comparison with degraded organic matter found within a particular deposit may be of value in assessing biogenicity.

Color is also an important criterion, although difficult to assess. Organic materials 3 billion years old are usually entirely carbonized and appear black in thin section through a transmitted-light microscope. Brown or yellow indicates organic materials that have not been fully degraded, implying contamination of some kind. This tendency of organic matter to change color over time is called *organic maturation*. Color changes from yellow to brown to black are accompanied by an increasing relative percentage of carbon. Over time, complex organic matter releases volatile components containing hydrogen, nitrogen, and oxygen from the original organic constituents. The carbon remains, increasing the relative percentage of carbon and the blackness over time as the organic material ages. From the color, we can roughly assess the extent to which the organic matter has been metamorphosed.

Another criterion of biogenicity is the sedimentary context of the microfossils. The sedimentary context of a particular assemblage of direct remains is inferred from the mineralogy of the sample; certain types of minerals are characteristic of particular depositional environments. The Swaziland Supergroup, for example, contains sediments laid down under water, with ripple marks and other evidence of water flow embedded within sandstones. Other examples of sedimentary environments in Archean rock sequences include volcaniclastic deposition, ash flows, ash falls, and subaqueous submarine volcanic deposition as lava flows or pillow lavas.

Analysis of Putative Microfossils

We can now examine some Archean rocks and use this framework to test the biogenicity of potential fossils. A photomicrograph of a sample from the 3.8-billion-year-old Isua group on the west coast of Greenland contains a population of entities once interpreted as fossils (figure 2). However, these structures are not remains of ancient life, for the following reasons: The sample contains actinolite, a mineral characteristic of rock that has been heated to 500°C—too high a temperature for the original structure of organic material to withstand intact. Also, the size range of a measured population of the entities is very large, from less than a micron to over 100 microns. Such a wide range in diameter is not characteristic of living cells. The shapes are also very heterogeneous; one of the specimens is angular, another is ellipsoidal, and another is nearly spherical.

Figure 2 shows a crack running through one of these entities. Under polarized light, the left side appears pink and the right side green, indicating that this crack represents the boundary between two quartz grains. The presence of both brown and clear objects in the same sample is significant, too. The association of brown iron

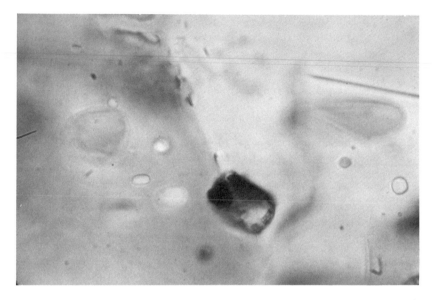

Figure 2
Photomicrograph of a thin section of rock from Isua, Greenland. These spherical inclusions were once thought to be biogenic, but their size, distribution, color, and position relative to the crystals of quartz and the mineral content of the rock suggest that they are abiogenic contaminants.

oxide with the cracks present in the sample suggests that this is not part of the intrinsic organic material but rather that it is associated with a secondary staining or oxidizing phenomenon. The shapes of these entities, reminiscent of minerals, probably represent iron-stained remains of mineral grains that underwent dissolution during metamorphosis. I conclude that this cell-like population does not represent the remains of once-living organisms.

A thin section of a sample from the Barberton Mountainland contains examples of the Swartkoppie microspheres. These were first described by E. S. Barghoorn and J. W. Schopf in 1968 as *Archaeospheroides barbertonensis*, organic spheroids 3.2 to 3.4 billion years old. This microfossil is defined by a roughly spherical shape, a carbon composition, and a coarse granular texture outlining the spherical shape. Populations of these microspheres occur in Archean cherts with organic laminae. Volcaniclastic textures are evident in the sample. Dark organic matter is present. This organic material was deposited in an aqueous environment in which the materials that constitute

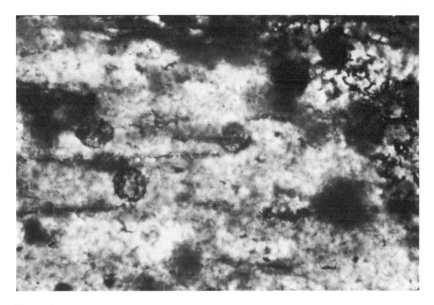

Figure 3
Archaeosphaeroides from the Fig Tree Formation.

the sediment are of volcanic origin. The original organic material has been subsequently enclosed by microcrystalline silica, or chert. *Archaeospheroides barbertonensis*-type microspheres are black in a high-power light micrograph of the layer containing them (figure 3). Part of the original sedimentary context is preserved as slight laminations. The isolated, perfectly spherical small entities have an average diameter of 18 microns and a surface texture that is granular and coarse.

The Barberton spheroids occur as isolated spheres or associated with one or more other cells. They are not particularly well preserved, which is expected of material of this antiquity. The spheres have the same consistent shape, morphology, and continuation of surface texture whether solitary or clustered.

In addition to the populations of *Archaeospheroides barbertonensis*, other populations of cell-like microspheres exist in samples from the Barberton area. Size-frequency diagrams can be used to compare different-size populations, including "ghosts." "Ghosts" are very similar to the *Archaeospheroides barbertonensis*-type spheres, although their texture is slightly different and a bit fainter. They are populations of spheres, very faintly preserved, that occur in clusters within the layered chert of this volcanic sedimentary section. The "ghost" and the *Archaeospheroides* populations are compared in figure 4. Such size-frequency graphs can be compared with similar graphs derived from living populations or from populations from abiogenically produced proteinoid microspheres created in the laboratory, or compared with each other. The mean diameter of the microspheres can be compared, as well as the flatness or the shapes of the histograms. In the upper graph of figure 4 the mean diameter is skewed slightly to the left. In the lower graph the mean diameter is skewed little, if at all, and the histogram is fairly uniform. This suggests that, even within the Barberton material, multiple populations of differing origin are present.

It can be concluded that the environment in which the Archean microstructures of Barberton are contained is a feasible one for microfossils. No inorganic or nonbiological explanations for these microspheres exist—we assume that they are biogenic and that they represent the remains of once-living organisms.

Sidney Fox and his colleagues at the University of Miami have set up an experimental system in which they generate abiogenic microspheres with a uniform morphology. The experiments are basically protometabolic. The microspheres (coacervates—see chapter 5) produced have an inside and an outside, defining a microenvironment inside. With just a simple spheroidal morphology it is difficult to assert evidence of once-living material, protobionts, or proteinoid microspheres. The significance of these experimental proteinoid microspheres in the early evolution of life, however, is debatable. The microspheres we see in the Swaziland and Warrawoona cherts may be evidence of chemical evolution, but I see no geological evidence whatsoever for the existence of proteinoid microspheres.

The Warrawoona Volcanics

Another microfossil-containing environment is represented in rocks about 3.4 or 3.5 billion years old from the Pilbara Block in the Warrawoona Volcanics of Western Australia. Three facies, or general rock types, represent three different depositional environments in the Warrawoona rocks. The first is a laminated chert consisting of black, red, and white layers. Primary sedimentary features are present,

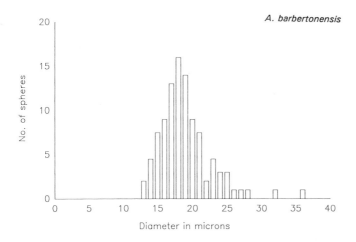

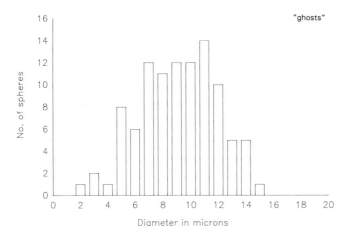

Figure 4
Size-frequency histograms of microsphere populations. The upper graph shows the
distribution of diameters of *Archaeospheroides barbertonensis* microspheres. The lower
graph plots the frequency of sizes of spheroidal "ghost" microfossils.

Figure 5
Pillow lavas in the Warrawoona Volcanics. These lavas were extruded under water.
Their characteristic dome shape has been weathered smooth, leaving ovoid surfaces.

which indicate that the rock has not undergone severe metamorphic change. The second rock type is a fantastic example of pillow lavas, volcanic rocks formed from lava extruded under water, usually in marine conditions. Figure 5 shows an outcrop in which the pillows have been weathered away to give a cross-sectional view of the pillows. The third type of rock is derived from andesite, a silica-rich igneous rock characteristic of continental crust. These rocks occur as thinly layered, light-colored material intruded by a secondary black chert. Silica-rich groundwater percolating through the laminated rock prior to its deposition may have led to cracks or dissolution in particular zones that subsequently became filled with chert. A second possibility is that a warping or bending of the rock during mild tectonic activity allowed silica-rich waters to penetrate.

Within this general sedimentary environment represented by the three rock types, fossils are found. Figure 6 shows a filament from the banded Warrawoona chert. The presence of filaments rather than solitary cells indicates a higher likelihood of biogenicity. An even more complicated fossil from another Warrawoona sample is shown in figure 7. Thin filaments radiate from the dark clustered area near the center. This rosette is so complex that it is difficult to attribute it to an abiogenic source. Such rosette morphology can be seen in modern bacteria. Because the fossiliferous rock was not studied in its immediate sedimentary context, we can only speculate that this Warrawoona sample comes from a setting similar to that in which the Barberton materials were found.

A very typical type of shallow water indicator in the geologic record is mud cracks. Lines that traverse the rock surface represent filled-in desiccation cracks. White, needle-shaped crystals of barium sulfate have replaced the original gypsum, or calcium sulfate, crystals. This replacement mineral, barium sulfate, is called a *mineral pseudomorph*. It retains the same morphology, or crystal habit (form), as gypsum. The source of the barium is unknown. However, the gypsum that has been replaced by barium sulfate is indicative of a highly evaporative environment, one in which a combination of shallow water and oxygen was present. The shallow marine environment of the Warrawoona Formation is feasible for the presence of biogenic remains. The fossils are relatively complex, and stromatolites have also been seen in this rock sequence.

Concluding Remarks

In conclusion, I would like to reiterate some concerns about working with Archean materials. First, the sedimentary context and its metamorphic grade are very important. Only a few unmetamorphosed sedimentary rock types are contained within the greenstone belts. The presence of unmetamorphosed sediments is an absolute prerequisite for finding legitimate organic fossils. Furthermore, not all laminated rocks are stromatolitic, even though they have an undulating texture. The contortions and microlaminations of sinter and siliceous rocks that form by precipitation from high temperatures can resemble an algal laminate or a stromatolite. Sinter is composed of opal (silica) from hot spring water with high mineral concentrations. The genesis of sinter is entirely abiological; it is not related to stromatolites and algal laminates, which form, by definition, by a combination of biological and sedimentary processes.

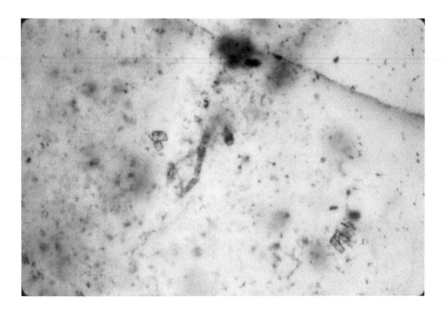

Figure 6
Photomicrograph of thin section from Warrawoona Volcanics, showing septate filaments.

Certain criteria can be used to establish the biogenicity of a particular laminate sample. In the sedimentary context, one must follow the laminae laterally and vertically to determine the strata to the sides of and immediately above and below a presumed stromatolitic horizon. The fabric of the laminate itself must be carefully analyzed; the type, texture, and orientation of the mineral grains making up the laminae must be considered. Extant microbial mats and stromatolites display only certain fabrics. Careful comparison should be made between the microlaminated rocks in question and materials known to be biogenically derived.

The most reliable Archean fossils are direct organic remains. Chemical evidence, and trace fossils such as stromatolitic laminae, are not enough to ascertain biogenicity. The best evidence of biogenic remains comes from samples containing significant populations of fossils. From these, comparisons can be made between Archean and other populations, living and fossil, to help us determine with confidence the nature of the clues to life in the Archean eon.

Figure 7
Rosette-shaped microfossil from Warrawoona.

Readings

Awramik, S. A., J. W. Schopf, and M. R. Walter. 1983. Filamentous fossil bacteria from the Archean of Western Australia. *Precambrian Research* 20: 357–374.

Buick, R. 1990. Microfossil recognition in Archean rocks: An appraisal of spheroids and filaments from a 3,500 m.y. old chert-barite unit at North Pole, Western Australia. *Palaios* 5: 441–459.

Groves, D. I., J. S. R. Dunlop, and R. Buick. 1981. An early habitat of life. *Scientific American* 245, no. 4: 64–73.

Margulis, L. 1984. *Early Life.* Jones and Bartlett.

Roedder, E. 1981. Are the 3,800-myr-old Isua objects microfossils, limmonite-stained fluid inclusion, or neither? *Nature* 239: 459–462.

Walker, J. C. G. 1986. *Earth History: The Several Ages of the Earth.* Jones and Bartlett.

Walsh, M. M., and D. R. Lowe. 1985. Filamentous microfossils from the 3,500-myr-old Onverwacht Group, Barberton Mountainland, South Africa. *Nature* 314: 530–532.

8   Microbial Mats of Abu Dhabi

Stjepko Golubic

Most of the evidence of life during the Archean and Proterozoic eons is in the form of stromatolites—fossilized microbial mats. In this chapter and the next, Stjepko Golubic introduces these microbial landscapes. What is the role of live bacteria in the making of carbonate rocks? Golubic describes the formation of stromatolitic structures at two widely separated locations: Abu Dhabi, on the Arabian/Persian Gulf, and Shark Bay, in Western Australia. After reviewing the main features of the mat communities and their dominant microorganisms, he examines their roles in the dynamic processes that form mats, stromatolites, and salt flats. His discussion addresses ranges of dimension from the microscopic to entire landscapes.

Ancient Microbial Landscapes: Clues to Planetary History

Most of our knowledge of the Earth is limited to the last fifth of its history; we know very little about the first four-fifths, the Precambrian era. The dominant forms of life during these first four-fifths of our planet's history were microorganisms of prokaryotic cellular organization. Prokaryotes, which include all bacteria, are simple cells without inner differentiation into separate functional compartments; eukaryotes have advanced cellular organization with membrane-bounded nuclei and other organelles. In examining the geological record of the Precambrian, one frequently encounters peculiar laminated rocks called *stromatolites*. These were formed by microbial mats dominated by cyanobacteria, which are photosynthetic oxygen-producing prokaryotes. Cyanobacteria were then the dominant primary producers of organic matter on the planet, able to use solar energy and mineral (inorganic) matter as nutrients. Organisms that can turn inorganic nutrients into organic matter are called *autotrophs* (meaning self-feeding). Green plants and algae are the major primary producers today. Cyanobacteria constitute a minor component of modern ecosystems, although these resilient microorganisms often prevail when conditions become extreme. Without autotrophs as the primary producers, life would not be possible for heterotrophs (organisms that feed on organic matter).

Cyanobacteria and other microorganisms associated with them form tightly interwoven microbial mats. The term "microbial mat" refers to entire ecosystems of microorganisms. (In older literature, these structures were called "algal mats." Ultrastructural studies show that they are composed primarily of bacteria. The term "algae" is today restricted to eukaryotic oxygenic photosynthesizers belonging to the kingdom Protoctista.) As in other ecosystems, the energy and nutrients are transferred from primary producers to consumers, including decomposers. While nutrients can be recycled, the energy passes through the system. Because energy transfer in all ecosystems follows the laws of thermodynamics, only a fraction of the energy captured from the sun is transferred to the consumers. The primary producers built most of the biomass and dominated ecosystems in the Precambrian.

Fossil stromatolites are solid, layered rocks composed of alternating organic-rich and mineral-rich laminae. As fossilized remains of microbial mats, these layered rocks are the cumulative record of mat activities. During the vast time spans of the Archean and the Proterozoic, living stromatolitic structures of varying sizes and shapes inhabited the seas and lakes, formed reefs, coated mud flats, and encrusted land.

Along with the study of stromatolites, there is another approach available to learn about microbial ecosystems existing between 3,500 and 600 million years ago: Modern environments can be studied as models of Precambrian conditions. There are a few such environments today, populated and dominated by microbial mats. In these environments we can study the microbial and biogeochemical interactions that occur at the sediment-water interface, and the stromatolitic sequences that develop. By comparing fossils and living organisms we have learned that ancient stromatolites were built by microbes through the trapping and binding of sediment particles, often followed by mineral precipitation which solidified these struc-

Figure 1
Aerial view of sabkha near Abu Dhabi, United Arab Emirates. This lagoonal environment is really a vast microbial landscape. The waters of the Arabian/Persian Gulf are visible at the top of the photograph, and the land at the bottom. The darker areas in the middle constitute the intertidal zone, dominated by the microbial mats that are actually creating the sabkha landscape.

tures. We know that the microorganisms involved in this activity must have been able to stabilize sediment surface by forming mats, and to recolonize the surface, escaping total burial by sediment. The laminated structures we find today originated in the alternation of mat burial by sediment with periods of reestablishment of microbial mats on the surface of the deposited sediment. One of the environments that offers opportunities to study living stromatolites in action is in the Arabian/Persian Gulf area around Abu Dhabi, where the activities of microbial mats have led to the formation of salt flats.

Microbial Mats of Abu Dhabi

Let us focus on a coastal strip in the southernmost part of the Arabian/Persian Gulf, close to Abu Dhabi. The coastline (figure 1) shows a lagoonal environment separated from the land by a wide salt flat (called a *sabkha* in Arabic). Between the lagoon and the sabkha is a broad, darker intertidal zone dominated by microbial mats. This microbial belt is the factory that, over time, creates the large flat landscape of the sabkha.

The intertidal zone, the area between the aquatic and terrestrial environments, is a very harsh environment for life. During high tide the entire zone is flooded; during low tide the seawater retreats and the area is exposed to air and desiccation. Along the coast of Abu Dhabi the air humidity is high, causing dew formation; however, only a few inches of rain fall every three to four years. Evaporation during low tide concentrates the dissolved salts, which pass through saturation stages and then precipitate. This process involves a regular sequence of mineral formation, starting with deposition of calcium carbonate ($CaCO_3$), followed by gypsum ($CaSO_4 \cdot 2H_2O$) and halite (NaCl). The salinity of the lagoons and tidal waters is always above that of the normal seawater. In more humid climates, mats exposed during low tide have their salts diluted by rainwater. Tidal fluctuations expose the organisms to severe shock with respect to both the water supply and the ionic strength of the water. (Some organisms retain some water in their cells and tissues, thereby expanding their physiological activity during low tide; others become dormant.) These coasts are also exposed to high-intensity sunlight, which affects the mats differently during high and low tide. The distinctive zonal distribution of different mat types is the outcome of their competition and adaptation to various degrees of air exposure, desiccation, solar irradiation, and water.

Desiccation and solar irradiation are among the most important factors exerting selective pressures on the organisms. The outcome of these selective pressures is reflected in the distribution of organisms. The upper intertidal zone is drier than the lower intertidal zone. Organisms less sensitive to desiccation can live higher up in the intertidal zone, where they escape competition with those bound to the subtidal and lower intertidal zones. The lower zones are colonized by a larger number of organisms, including those which are more sensitive to desiccation. Here, the dominant form competitively excludes the others; the various degrees of air exposure and desiccation lead to the zonal distribution of mat types.

Very few halophytes (vascular plants which grow in salt-impregnated soils), or eukaryotic organisms in general, can even venture

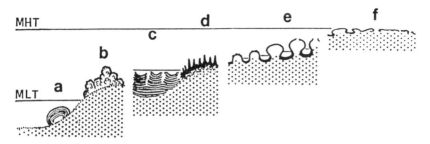

Figure 2
Microbial mat types found in the sabkha. A transition from subtidal (a) to supratidal
(f) mat types occurs over a distance of 2 or 3 km. The various mat types are
described in the text. (a) Laminated biscuits; (b) mamillate mat; (c) low flat mat
(*Microcoleus* mat); (d) high pinnacle mat; (e) convoluted mat; (f) folded mat.

close to this harsh environment. The major primary producers are
photosynthetic prokaryotes, for the most part cyanobacteria (also
called "blue-greens"). Moving from the lagoon across the microbial
belt of the intertidal zone toward land, one crosses a sequence of
zones covered by different types of mats, which are dominated by
different cyanobacteria (figure 2). These mat types, designated here
as types a through f, replace each other over a distance of 2 to 3
kilometers.

a. Gelatinous laminated biscuits are formed by the cyanobacterium
Phormidium hendersonii (figure 3). In cross-section these structures are
finely laminated. The microorganism itself is a small filamentous
cyanobacterium, hardly more than a micron wide, surrounded by a
thin tubular polysaccharide sheath within which it can move by
gliding. Type a represents soft gelatinous colonies scattered in the
subtidal portion of the lagoon. There are no coherent mats in that
zone.

b. Mamillate mat is built by *Entophysalis major*, a coccoid cyanobacterium that occupies the lowest intertidal ranges. It is the first colo-
nizer of mega-ripples in the lower intertidal zone. Mega-ripples are
large sand ripples in lagoons and channels formed by currents that
frequently change direction. They can be up to a meter high and
several meters long. A closer view of the mamillate mat on these
mega-ripples shows it to be a translucent, brownish, gelatinous mass.

Figure 3
Laminated biscuit formed by the cyanobacterium *Phormidium hendersonii*. The small, soft, biscuit-shaped colonies, approximately 2–5 cm across, dot the sandy bottom of the near subtidal zone.

The word *mamillate* is from the Latin *mamilla*, meaning "small wart," and refers to the surface texture of the *Entophysalis* mat, which is characterized by millimeter-size warts.

As we move further landward across the intertidal zone, the somewhat wavy landscape is completely covered by mats. This landscape is differentiated into depressions which retain pools of stagnating water during low tide and are covered by the low flat mat, and slightly elevated, well-drained heights between them that are covered by the high pinnacle mat. Both these mat types are complex microbial communities rather than populations of individual species, and the dynamic processes that take place within them are also more diversified and complex.

c. Low flat mat lines the bottom of pools and tidal channels in the mid-intertidal zone. Low flat mat is a coherent, smooth, leathery microbial mat which appears layered when seen in cross-section.

Figure 4
Photomicrograph of *Lyngbya aestuarii*. This filamentous cyanobacterium is surrounded by a thick, gelatinous sheath and is found with *Microcoleus*, another cyanobacterium, in the low flat mat.

This layering reveals a vertically differentiated microbial community in which each layer constitutes a separate microenvironment that is dominated by the organism best adapted to the prevailing local conditions. The surface layer of the low flat mat is dominated by the filamentous cyanobacterium *Lyngbya aestuarii* (figure 4). This organism is composed of tightly packed discoid cells surrounded by a firm, brown, gelatinous sheath. As in *Entophysalis*, the extracellular gel of these sheaths contains the pigment scytonemine. The layer underlying *Lyngbya* is dominated by *Microcoleus chthonoplastes*, a filamentous cyanobacterium characterized by its habit of forming bundles. Although *Microcoleus* produces sheaths, it does not produce extracellular pigments within them; its solution to the problem of solar radiation is to live beneath a protective layer of *Lyngbya aestuarii*. *Microcoleus* can tolerate low oxygen tension, a property that enables this cyanobacterium to colonize stagnant pools and to spread horizontally along their floors. It therefore constitutes the main structural element of the low flat mat. Below *Microcoleus* is a layer devoid of

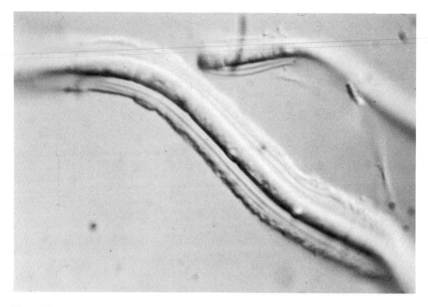

Figure 5
Photomicrograph of *Schizothrix splendida*. This sheathed cyanobacterium is a major component of pinnacled mat.

oxygen where anoxygenic photosynthetic bacteria thrive. Some of these bacteria are filamentous, similar to *Chloroflexus,* known from mats in hot springs. Others are coccoid, motile and nonmotile purple sulfur bacteria. Below the purple zone is a black layer stained by ferrous sulfide (FeS), dominated by sulfate-reducing bacteria. At this level and below a variety of heterotrophic anaerobic bacteria grow, notably fermenters and methanogens. By growing, they enhance decomposition of organic matter produced by the mat photosynthesizers.

d. High pinnacle mat covers the elevated hills between pools, channel levees, and their well-drained slopes. The name comes from its tendency to grow numerous upright pointed cones, or pinnacles, 1 to 2 cm high. As in the low flat mat, the surface layer of this mat is dominated by *Lyngbya aestuarii.* However, the principal organism in the main underlying layer is *Schizothrix splendida* (rather than *Micro-coleus chthonoplastes* as in the low flat mat). *Schizothrix splendida* (figure 5) requires good drainage and a regular oxygen supply. On well-drained sites it receives ample water at high tide and a regular oxygen supply at low tide. Below the blue-green *Schizothrix* layer is a thin, often incompletely developed layer of purple photosynthetic bacteria, and an equally faint black layer, indicating a transient anaerobic zone. The high pinnacle mat is underlain by light-colored, oxidized sediments. This is in contrast to the extensive purple layer (up to a centimeter thick) of the low flat mat, which usually rests on massive, black, organic-rich anaerobic sediments.

e. Convoluted mat is a contiguous leathery mat that is characterized by a folded surface which forms over gas bubbles trapped below the mat. The dominant mat form in the upper intertidal zone, it combines elements of the low flat mat and pinnacle mat, but with different spatial distribution of the microorganisms. Lower portions are dominated by *Microcoleus chthonoplastes,* and the tops by *Schizothrix splendida.* Continuing growth increases the mat surface laterally, forming convolutions that become more and more elaborate. These convolutions increase to about 10 cm in diameter. The lower, upward-concave folds hold water; the convex domes are hollow. The convolutions are thick in the lower portions and thin on top, where they often become perforated. This mat develops at a level where water trapped between tides is long exposed to evaporation. Gypsum precipitates from this highly concentrated brine, both in the mat's surface depressions and within the enclosed bubbles.

f. Folded mat is the final stage in the development of the intertidal microbial mats. With prolonged exposure in the uppermost ranges of the tidal flux, the entire mat periodically dries out. *Microcoleus* is replaced by *Schizothrix* throughout the mat. The consequence of dry conditions is a general slowing of growth at the mat surface. Underneath the mat surface there is a microenvironment with enough protection and moisture available for degradation to continue. The balance between the two processes keeps the mat thin as the degradation rate catches up with the production rate. As the mat gets thinner, the convolutions collapse and flatten, and the mat shrivels and becomes disrupted in places. During low tide the mat dries out completely and becomes mummified. Ultimately, desiccation stops both constructive and destructive processes. The shriveled, mummified mat residues are blown away by the wind.

In addition to the dominant microbial forms mentioned, many more accompanying microorganisms are present within each type of mat. Whereas mat types a and b are largely products of single cyanobacterial species, types c–f are complex, differentiated microbial communities with several dominant members. Recognizable by differences in shape and in the composition and arrangement of microbes, these mats are also characterized by the particular dynamics of the sedimentary and biological processes that occur within each of them.

Now that we have become acquainted with the main participants in the "drama" that unfolds in the Abu Dhabi intertidal landscape, we will turn our attention to the ways these protagonists interact within the system. We will consider some of the dynamic processes that take place across the tidal flat, and then assess the resulting changes in the landscape.

In this improvisational drama of the intertidal zone, the participants follow several rules: (1) Each participant has a set of specific requirements and responses. (2) Each participant will use every opportunity to occupy areas where these conditions are met. In the process, the participant may (3) enhance its own position by optimizing the conditions or (4) change the conditions in a direction that inhibits its own functions (which creates new opportunities for other participants). Relationships between component mat organisms may be complementary, antagonistic, or neutral.

Building on Sand

The subtidal lagoonal environments are dominated by physical forces, and these forces are the major shapers of sedimentary processes. Microbial growth is kept in check by numerous bioturbating animals: grazing cerithid snails and worms which churn through the sandy sediments. Solitary gelatinous biscuits of *Phormidium hendersonii* persist for periods of 30–60 days before they too fall victim to the rapid turnover of organic matter. These biscuits are perfect models of stromatolitic architecture. By day the gliding movement of *Phormidium* is positively phototactic, orienting the filaments upward; by night it changes direction into a horizontal "resting" position. As the microorganism moves, it abandons its sheaths, weaving a laminated structure in which each day is marked by a pair of laminae of horizontally and vertically oriented sheaths. *Phormidium hendersonii* lives by a circadian rhythm and follows a solar clock. Nothing remains from its activity even a few months later, so we cannot refer to ancient stromatolitic records of it; yet from it we can learn the principles that may have operated in constructing countless ancient stromatolites.

With the emergence of sediments in the lower intertidal zone, the microbial mats have a better chance of becoming established. The entire mid-tidal landscape is coated by coherent carpet-like mats. The first mat that colonizes loose sediment in the lower intertidal zone is the mamillate mat of *Entophysalis major*. This coccoid cyanobacterium excretes polysaccharide envelopes at the time of cell division. As a consequence, each cell is embedded in a cushion of gelatinous matter. Within these envelopes the microorganism deposits the extracellular yellow-brown pigment scytonemine. This light-induced pigment stains the surfaces of *Entophysalis* colonies, protecting them from excessive light. Ultraviolet radiation is detrimental to life; visible light, if too strong, can also be detrimental. The sheath pigment scytonemine absorbs in both the ultraviolet and the visible range of the spectrum, although some ultraviolet radiation is also absorbed in the nonpigmented portion of the sheaths. Scytonemine pigment is resistant to degradation and preserves well; the fossil record shows that similar pigments played a protective role in ancient mats and stromatolites.

When cores were taken from the oldest portions of the Abu Dhabi sabkha at a depth of 60–80 cm below the present sabkha surface, they showed distinct lamination. Microbial mats accrete at a rate of several millimeters per year. These 8,000-year-old laminae contained cyanobacterial envelopes and sheaths with their brown pigment still preserved. Since scytonemine pigment develops only under the influence of strong direct sunlight, we can conclude that this portion of sabkha, now well below the surface, was once a surface mat illuminated by the sun. Pigmented sheaths remain preserved in fossils 1 to 2 billion years old, revealing the orientation of the mats with respect to the sun at the time they grew.

Figures 6 and 7 depict the sites of preferred settlement of the

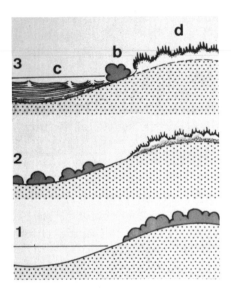

Figure 6
Preferred zones of growth of mamillate mat (*Entophysalis major*). (1) In the lower intertidal zone, mamillate mat (solid) grows on the crests of sand ripples. (2) In the mid-intertidal zone, it prefers to grow in depressions; high pinnacle mat grows on ripple crests. (3) Higher up in the intertidal zone, mamillate mat (b) can grow only along the margins of pools. Low flat mat (c) grows within low pools that contain stagnant water; high pinnacle mat (d) is found on the crests.

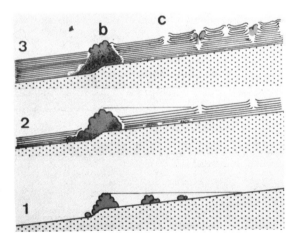

Figure 7
Intertidal succession of mats. *Entophysalis* (b) grows across tidal channels, forming dams (1) and producing stagnant pools where low flat mat (c) thrives.

mamillate mat (*Entophysalis*) at different elevations with respect to the tidal range: lower intertidal (1), mid-intertidal (2), and upper intertidal (3). *Entophysalis* grows best in areas with an optimal combination of water and oxygen supply; in the lowest ranges it covers the crests of mega-ripples [figure 6 (1)], while in the mid-intertidal range it prefers the depressions [figure 6 (2)]. Higher up in the intertidal zone, where the pools retain stagnating water, the crests of mega-ripples have longer exposure to drying during low tide. These conditions are less favorable for the mamillate mat, which is gradually replaced by the low flat mat in the pools [figure 6 (3c)], and by high pinnacle mat on the crests [figure 6 (3d)]. Only along the margins of the intertidal pools is there still sufficient water and air exchange to promote the growth of a narrow rim of mamillate mat [figure 6 (3b)].

Entophysalis settles preferentially in areas with rapid water movement, and tidal channels offer another habitat with ample water supply and turbulence. However, mamillate mat is a fragile structure, vulnerable to erosion, and cannot settle in the larger, swiftly moving channels. (In fact, after each storm large quantities of detached mamillate mat fragments are removed, transported, and deposited elsewhere.) Small tidal channels are the preferred habitat of this mat. *Entophysalis* colonies actually divert the water flow as they grow, causing eddies and more turbulence and further promoting their own growth. Finally, *Entophysalis* growth extends across the channel to form living dams. This creates small waterfalls and areas of enhanced turbulence on top of and below dams, and creates stagnant pools behind them [figure 7 (1)]. The *Entophysalis* colonies behind these dams are flooded, and their further development is hampered by the lowering of oxygen tension. However, these new conditions are favorable for the growth of *Microcoleus chthonoplastes* of the low flat mat, which takes over and paves the bottoms of these pools [figure 7 (2)]. As the low flat mat grows and accumulates, further suppressing the mamillate mat [figure 7 (3b)], it becomes exposed to air for extended periods during low tide. This drying leads to cracking, and the cracks provide new local drainage passages within pools [figure 7 (3c)]. Water turbulence created by this drainage is sufficient to cause localized secondary settlement of *Entophysalis*.

The dynamics of settlement, growth, and replacement of the mamillate mat illustrate a case in which the conditions become increasingly favorable for the organism that creates them. These processes also show negative feedback, in which *Entophysalis* growth is inhibited in the pools behind the dams. The latter case leads to a typical biological succession, in which one organism inhibits its own growth and prepares the conditions that favor its replacement by another one.

The next community of microbes can settle wherever *Entophysalis* has successfully colonized and stabilized loose sand, and this next community can trap and bind sediment particles into their laminated structures.

Trapping, Binding, and Polygonal Cracking

Each layer of a fossilized stromatolite represents an ancient mat, once active at the sediment-water interface, that was involved in trapping and binding sediment particles and/or promoting mineral precipitation. Sediment transport and deposition are essential components of the intertidal environment. Sediments, brought in by tidal currents, are dumped on or trapped in microbial mats. With every change of tide the microorganisms must cope with rapid burial by sediments, and they have found two solutions to this problem: growing and moving. Some species grow through the sediment fast enough to form a new layer on top of it by adding more cells to extend a filament while one end of the filament remains anchored below. Other microorganisms employ a gliding movement to crawl out of their sheaths, which are left buried in the sediment while a new mat is established on the surface of the sediment. As sediment is deposited and the mat grows, the entire landscape becomes slightly higher with each tidal cycle.

There are several ways in which microorganisms trap sediments. Smaller sediment particles adhere to the sticky surfaces of organisms—and since most cyanobacteria produce polysaccharide sheaths that are highly hydrated, they can be very sticky indeed. Mats also act as a filter mesh to trap larger sediment particles, and microbial activity binds sediment together. As microorganisms glide and grow through sediment in order to reestablish themselves on the surface, they intertwine sediment particles and bind them into a coherent fabric.

Low flat mats are among the most efficient sediment traps. The pools they inhabit act as sedimentation basins; the sticky cyanobacterial surfaces retain even the finest particles. In cross-section, the low flat mats show alternating organic-rich and sediment-rich laminae. With every tidal cycle, a mat receives a load of sediment, and the microorganisms struggle to crawl on top of it until the next high tide. Those that do not make it are incorporated in the sediment as part of the organic-rich layer. Extracellular sheaths are invariably left behind. *Microcoleus chthonoplastes*, the principal constituent of such mats, is one of the fastest gliders.

Microcoleus chthonoplastes is well adapted to water-logged conditions because of its tolerance of, or even preference for, low oxygen concentrations. Such organisms are called *oligoaerobic* (from Latin *oligo*, meaning "little," and *aerobic*, meaning "exposed to air") or *microaerophilic* ("loving small amounts of air"). This ability permits *Microcoleus* to survive deeper within the mat, and to function within the transient region between oxygenated and anoxic (oxygen-free) zones within the mat.

The anaerobic layer beneath *Microcoleus* is the realm of bacterial anoxygenic photosynthesis, carried out by green and purple anoxygenic photosynthetic bacteria. These bacteria absorb light in the long-wave portion of the solar spectrum, the portion not absorbed by the overlying cyanobacteria. They are strictly anaerobic when active, taking hydrogen sulfide (H_2S) as a source of electrons and leaving sulfur behind as a by-product. After a good day of activity, the cells of these bacteria are loaded with sulfur granules. Subsequently, this sulfur needs to be further oxidized to a more soluble sulfate (SO_4^{2-}) so that the cells can get rid of their "kidney stones." Sulfate-reducing bacteria (such as *Desulfovibrio desulfuricans*) can use this sulfate by respiring anaerobically and then reduce it back to hydrogen sulfide, thus closing a recycling loop of prokaryotic cooperation. Sulfur compounds are cycled through this portion of the mat between purple sulfur bacteria and chemolithotrophs, on one side, and heterotrophic sulfate reducers, on the other. Some of the sulfide is trapped by iron precipitating out of circulation, and stains the mud black.

There are many different heterotrophic bacteria in the anaerobic zone beneath the mat which help degrade the organic matter produced above them. As long as anoxic conditions are maintained underneath the mat, the microbial processes there will necessarily be anaerobic. These include different types of fermentation, methanogenesis, and anaerobic respiration (mostly sulfate reduction). The gases that develop include hydrogen sulfide, methane, carbon dioxide, ammonia, and hydrogen. Although a complete anaerobic degradation of organic matter is possible, it involves several steps performed by different metabolic types. Since all necessary participants may not be in the right place at the right time, substantial organic residues are left to be buried and preserved. As a consequence, there is a relatively high input of both inorganic and organic matter into the sediment beneath the low flat mat. This accelerates the filling of the pooled depressions, and the mat gets elevated to a position where it will have longer exposure to air and desiccation.

A distinctive characteristic of intertidal microbial mats that are exposed to air is the presence of polygonal desiccation cracks. In smaller tidal channels, the cracking begins transverse to the flow; larger surfaces crack into polygons. The largest polygons form in the relatively moist center of channels, becoming progressively smaller toward the edges, where drying is faster (figure 8). As the points of contraction are evenly distributed over the sediment surface, the cracks develop roughly equidistant from these points; they then join to describe polygon shapes. The size of the polygons is determined by the severity of the dehydration and by the cohesiveness of the shrinking material. Continuing shrinkage causes upright curving of the polygon edges, leaving a central depression.

Water loss and shrinkage are common to the cracking of mud and microbial mats. The main differences in the cracking patterns of barren mud and mat-covered sediment originate in the differences in the cohesiveness of these materials. Mud cracks in straight lines, resulting in geometrically perfect polygons which often subdivide into smaller secondary cracks. In mud cracks, each layer behaves independently in terms of the positioning of the cracks. Cracks may be filled with sediment but cannot heal.

In contrast, microbial mat behaves like a fabric of matted fibers, and the polygons form in ragged, uneven lines. Each polygon shrinks, but rarely does one develop secondary cracks. Microbial mats overgrow the edges of cracks and bridge them. In younger, weaker mats, the healed cracks are prone to cracking again in the

Figure 8
A desiccated tidal channel through the sabkha. Dried mats crack into characteristic desiccation polygons. Larger polygons form in the center of the channel; smaller polygons are found toward the edges.

same place, perpetuating the cracking in subsequent layers. In vertical section, mat polygons can be seen stacked in prisms. Prism cracks have been recognized in the fossil record, and these described features are used to distinguish microbial mats from cracked mud.

The Rise and Fall of Pinnacles

On well-drained elevations in the mid-intertidal range, such as the crests and slopes of mega-ripples, the mamillate mat is gradually replaced by the high pinnacle mat [figure 6 (3d)]. Both mats show a preference for well-drained and aerated conditions. The main determining factor that initiates the succession, apparently, is an extended period of air exposure and drying. At low tide, water drains from the mat and from the pores between sediment grains, and air is sucked in to replace it. This simple suction mechanism supplies the sediment beneath *Schizothrix* with enough oxygen to support bacterial aerobic respiration, which degrades most of the organic matter pro-

Figure 9
Pinnacle mat. The small solid cones characterizing this mat type are made up of
Lyngbya aestuarii and *Schizothrix splendida.*

duced by this mat. Only in a thin zone immediately below *Schizothrix*
is the bacterial respiration intense enough to temporarily remove the
ambient oxygen. This creates a narrow anaerobic niche where purple
sulfur bacteria and sulfate-reducing bacteria can live. With time,
aerobic degradation prevails, leaving only oxidized sediments
beneath the pinnacle mat. Scattered rusty-red spots in a light-colored
sediment mark the locations where dissolved reduced iron was concentrated during a brief anoxic episode.

Some observations may help in better understanding the relationship between organisms and environment in generating the peculiar
morphology of the pinnacle mat, with its countless conical points
(figure 9). First, pinnacles are solid cones. Second, both of the dominant cyanobacterial species, *Lyngbya aestuarii* and *Schizothrix splendida,* participate in pinnacle formation. Third, the layers of purple
sulfur bacteria and degrading bacteria are found below them. Fourth,
on well-drained surfaces the pinnacles are small and numerous; the
largest pinnacles grow adjacent to pooled areas. Fifth, in the upper
distribution ranges of the pinnacle mat, the pinnacles become blunted

at the tips, then rounded, until they disappear altogether. Lastly, the appearance, size, density, and eventual disappearance of pinnacles are not correlated with changes in the composition of the microbial community. Pinnacle formation is but one of the possible phenotypic expressions in microbes genetically equipped for this peculiar growth habit.

Formation of the Fossil Record

The southern coast of the Persian Gulf is a *prograding* coast: the land is expanding, and the sea regressing, because sedimentary processes prevail over erosional ones. The geological terms *transgression* and *regression* refer to changes in the level of the sea in relation to the land. Transgression refers to the relative rise, and regression to the relative fall, of seawater level with respect to land. The 8,000-year geological record at Abu Dhabi is rich in multiple cycles of alternating transgression and regression. Each cycle shows, in stratigraphic sedimentary sequence, a relatively rapid sea-level rise followed by a set of sediments that represent progressively shallower water.

A sedimentary sequence representing one such cycle can be observed in a core taken through the Abu Dhabi sabkha. These sediments have accumulated during the transformation of lagoonal environments to sabkha plains. As the lagoons are gradually filled by sediments, new lagoons form offshore; the entire intertidal zone moves seaward, followed by the ever-expanding sabkha plain. Today's sabkha plain was once a lagoon; today's lagoon will someday become a sabkha plain. A core taken through the sabkha will reveal a sequence of sediments deposited on top of one another at different stages of this coastal progression. Using radiocarbon dating to trace this development, we learn that the process of sea-level decline lasted some 6,000 years here, and that it was preceded by 2,000 years of sea-level rise.

A cross-section through the sediments in the mid-intertidal zone shown in figure 10 clearly shows an uneven distribution of deposits [compare figure 6 (3)]. The low flat mat in the pool (figure 10, left) accumulates sediment significantly faster than the high pinnacle mat covering the heights (right). Moreover, in the pools stained black by hydrogen sulfide there is a high input of reduced organic material

Figure 10
Accumulation of sediment in the low flat mat (left) under conditions tending to anoxia leads to flattening of the landscape and preservation of laminae, seen here in cutaway section.

into the sediment. This is in contrast to the light, oxidized, organic-poor sediment that accumulates much more slowly beneath the pinnacle mat. As a consequence, the resulting profile of the current surface is much milder than at the start of the accumulation process—the landscape is flattening.

The balance of the ongoing processes and their effect on sedimentation rates can be summarized as follows: A relatively high rate of primary production in the flat low mat (figure 11) is combined with a relatively low rate of decomposition under the prevailing anoxic conditions. As soon as the oxygen beneath the mat is depleted, degradation of organic matter by efficient aerobic respiration gives way to much slower anaerobic respiration and fermentation. When the tidal flux of inorganic sediment is added, the accumulation of sediments, as a result of all these factors working together, will be relatively high.

Conditions are somewhat different in the high pinnacle mat (figure 12). Good drainage maintains aerobic conditions in the underlying sediments. Vigorous primary production is counteracted by equally

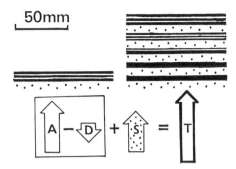

Figure 11
Sedimentation processes in low flat mat. Low flat mats have a relatively high primary production or assimilation rate (A) and a low rate of degradation (D). The tidal influx of inorganic sediment (S) results in a high accumulation rate (T).

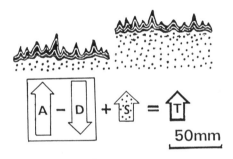

Figure 12
Sedimentation processes in pinnacle mat. In well-aerated pinnacle mat, primary productivity or assimilation rates (A) are matched by a high degradation rate (D). Very little organic matter remains in the sediment (S). Accumulation (T) is much less than in low flat mat environments.

vigorous aerobic decomposition, so practically no organic matter remains in the sediment. When the inorganic sediment is added, the combined sediment accumulation is much less than that in the depressions. As a result, the pools fill up more rapidly, and the landscape flattens.

Twice a day, in combined lunar-solar cyclicity, lagoonal waters rush up the tidal channels and spill over the intertidal flat. During low tide these waters drain into pools and channels, which conduct them back into the lagoon. Throughout the lower- and mid-intertidal zones, the drainage system of pools and channels is fully functional.

However, in the upper tidal ranges the capacity of the drainage system is diminished by the activities of microbial mats and the resulting accelerated sedimentation. As pools and channels become shallower and wider, previously well-drained areas, and ultimately the entire plain, become stagnant. With drainage now impaired, the upper ranges of the intertidal flat retain tidal waters over the entire low-tide period and become soft and marshy. The accompanying lowering of oxygen tension favors the spreading of *Microcoleus chthonoplastes*, and low flat mat becomes established on the territory previously held by the high pinnacle mat. During this phase of development the prevailing degradation of organic matter is anaerobic and relatively slow, so organic compounds are buried and incorporated into the sediment at very high rates.

Ecologically important changes occur when the extended exposure to air and solar heat causes the elevated low flat mat to crack and form polygons. The cracks promote water movement, becoming areas of local drainage and aeration. As the polygons shrink, their concave centers hold water and maintain a flat mat; their edges curl upward into positions of better drainage and air exposure. In response, a secondary growth of the high pinnacle mat around the edges of polygons ensues, and some mamillate mat may settle inside cracks. The environmental and biological factors still favor the three microbial communities described above, but now the differentiation takes place on a scale of centimeters rather than meters and kilometers.

The relative inefficiency of anaerobic decomposition is in sharp contrast to the vigor of bacterial aerobic degradation. In this intertidal environment, oxygen is introduced through the cracks between polygons. From there it spreads laterally, facilitating a complete degradation of the mat. Although the conditions are in some respects similar to those beneath the pinnacle mat, the mat here takes quite a different shape; it is called *convoluted* or *blister* mat [figure 2 (e)].

In spite of conspicuous morphological differences between convoluted mat and the mat types previously described, the microbial composition of the convoluted mat reveals the same familiar elements: *Microcoleus chthonoplastes* dominates the thick, lower, waterlogged folds, and *Schizothrix splendida* occupies the vaults of the upper folds. The same organisms that differentiate in the lows and highs

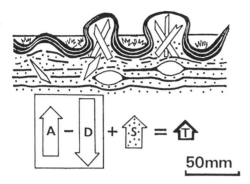

Figure 13
Sedimentation processes in convoluted mat. Growth or assimilation of convoluted mat (A) is low relative to the high rates of aerobic degradation (D) found here. Sediment input (S) is very small, resulting in a very low accumulation rate (T).

of the intertidal zone are here differentiated into contiguous convolutions. Like the secondary settlers on polygonal cracks, these microbial communities microdifferentiate on a centimeter scale in response to local ecological conditions. The observed differences in growth and shape between these mats, therefore, are caused not by specific genetically fixed properties of particular organisms, but rather by their specific responses to microenvironmental conditions and by the interaction between different participants at the community level.

The convoluted mat develops in the upper intertidal ranges, following the "universal flooding" and the consequent prevalence of anaerobic degradation with a high input of organic matter into the sediment. Its development takes place after long exposure to air has caused shrinking, cracking, and aeration of the underlying sediments. At this stage the growth of the convoluted mat (figure 13) is accompanied by an intensive aerobic degradation fueled by the organic input inherited from previous states. Since storms are the only source of substantial amounts of sediment in this zone, the sedimentation is relatively slow and comes mostly from local precipitation of gypsum. This keeps the overall sedimentation input at very low levels. Differences in the thickness of mat folds are consequences of the local balance between growth and degradation.

Water retention in the lower (upward-concave) folds ensures local growth. This growth is followed by temporary oxygen depletion, which slows down the degradation and thinning of the mat. These relationships are inverted in the convexities of the mat where growth is retarded by periodic drying of the mat surface, while aerobic degradation continues within the protected moist "bubble" of the convolution. As a consequence, the convoluted mat is thin in convex and thick in concave curvatures. This also explains the increase of the mat surface by folding. Like an Eskimo igloo that "grows" by freezing outside while melting inside, the hemispherical fold of the mat increases its surface area by growing outside while being degraded inside. When the rate of interior degradation catches up with the rate of mat growth, the bubble perforates. Further desiccation halts both the process of growth and the process of degradation, and the mat surface shrivels to scraps and is blown away by the wind.

This completes the picture of how the biological and sedimentological processes jointly shape the intertidal zone and create the sabkha plain. The intertidal microbial belt holds the key to this transformation process, functioning as the "factory" in which sabkha is produced. Further change beyond the microbial belt is caused by predominantly geochemical processes fostered by further evaporation. Dolomite is formed, gypsum is dehydrated to anhydrite, and the chemistry of the briny ground waters beneath the sabkha is set in motion. Only the highest spring tides and storm tides bring the lagoonal waters up and over the sabkha plain. Although periodic storms recharge the geochemical transformations that operate in the sabkha's interstitial waters, this irregular water supply is insufficient to foster vigorous primary production of microbial mats. Lagoonal waters are hypersaline, with salinities well exceeding 40 parts per thousand (versus approximately 34 ppt in the open ocean). Under arid climatic conditions, it takes much less time to evaporate this water and incorporate the precipitated minerals into the sediment. As the water evaporates on the surface, it is replaced with pore waters from below by capillarity.

The level surface of the sabkha, initially created by the growth and sedimentation of microbial mats, is maintained by wind action and the capillarity of groundwater. When the groundwater level goes down, the surface soon dries out, crumbles, and is blown away by wind. When the groundwater level goes up, the surface is wetted by capillary action, and wind-blown sand grains stick to the sabkha surface. Thus capillarity keeps the sabkha surface at a certain distance from the groundwater level, maintained by alternating aeolian sediment input and erosion, making the surface perfectly parallel to the groundwater level. The sabkha's groundwater is replenished from the land in the background, by groundwater stored beneath the desert dunes, and by lagoonal floods brought by occasional storms. Because the groundwater slowly seeps toward the sea, its level and consequently the level of the sabkha are inclined slightly seaward. Because the fluctuation of the groundwater table is in the range of a few centimeters, so is the range of accretion and destruction of the sabkha surface. Anything buried below that fluctuating zone will not be affected, and the secrets of sabkha formation will be kept in the fossil record. Indeed, because of the alpine orogeny, we now interpret the Lofer Formation high in the Austrian alps to be a fossil counterpart of the Persian Gulf sabkha sediments.

Clocks of the Past

Fossil stromatolites are a record of the rhythmicity of events long past. They were once living microbial communities similar to the ones we have examined here—communities that synthesized organic matter and trapped and bound sediments. Can we examine fossil stromatolites and say, with any degree of certainty, what kind of cyclic events were recorded by the deposition of their laminae?

In order to fossilize, these structures had to harden and turn to rock. We know that today's microbial mats grow best in hypersaline environments flooded by waters which are substantially supersaturated with dissolved minerals. Precipitation of calcium carbonate around sediment particles cements them together, forming hard rock. This process is called *lithification*, a word referring to the hardening and transformation of soft sediment into sedimentary rock. Structures that harden early have a better chance to escape erosion and therefore to be preserved as fossils. Although the process of mineral precipitation depends largely on the physicochemical condition of the solution, it is often promoted by microbes that act as centers for crystal nucleation. Lithification can occur early, contemporaneous with a mat's trapping and binding activities, or late, long after the sediments have been buried and subjected to increased temperature and pressure. Changes in the sediment that lead to rock formation are termed *diagenetic*. Early diagenesis takes place on the biological time scale and often involves microbial activities. Late diagenesis takes place on the geological time scale, after burial of sediments has already occurred.

If the thickness of layers in fossil stromatolites allowed us to accurately interpret ancient deposition rates, we would be able to learn a great deal. When we compare fossil stromatolites with recent ones we find both the organic-rich and the sediment-rich layers in the fossil record to be only small fractions of their original thicknesses. We know from modern examples that the thickness of organic-rich laminae depends primarily on the total biomass of the organisms. However, during mat formation the organic-rich layer is highly hydrated; after death and burial it becomes compacted because of water loss. We also know that the eventual preservation of the biomass depends on two major factors: the cyanobacteria must be efficient in escaping burial by sedimentation, and the degrading bacteria must be relatively inefficient in decomposing and recycling the accumulated biomass. Measuring the sedimentation rate of sediment-rich laminae is somewhat less problematic, yet compaction after burial and recrystallization during diagenesis must be taken into account. For all these reasons, the time span of layer formation is very difficult to determine.

If we assumed that laminae of an ancient stromatolite were caused by diurnal growth and responses of microorganisms to changing light, we could use the modern *Phormidium hendersonii* as our model. Using this model, we could assume that every day when the sun rose the microorganisms grew upward, and that every night they turned to a horizontal position and rested. The accumulation of sediment particles would show a complementary picture. Even with sedimentation at a uniform rate, particles would accumulate while the microbes were resting at night and would be spread and "diluted" by active, upward-growing filaments during the daylight hours. The expected result would be an alternation of sediment-rich and organic-rich layers in a diurnal rhythm. If we could identify an ancient counterpart of our model, we could reconstruct a Proterozoic solar clock and calendar by counting pairs of laminae.

Giorgio Panella, who examined many Proterozoic stromatolites and counted their laminae, inferred that organisms that grew in a protected, undisturbed subtidal environment constituted solar clocks. They lived and lithified under conditions that do not exist today, perhaps because the chemistry of the ocean has changed and perhaps because of interference from the grazing and burrowing animals that have since evolved.

We could use the trapping and binding of sediments by low flat mat in the pools of the lower intertidal zone as a different model, a model in which the sediment-rich laminae would record the tidal cyclicity. A load of sediment brought by every high tide and deposited on the mat would be recorded as a sediment-rich lamina. The microorganisms would respond by moving up through the layer of newly deposited sediment and establishing a new mat on the surface. Those that remained buried would become a fossilized organic-rich lamina. The capacity of microbial mat to cope with heavy loads of tide-distributed sediments has been demonstrated by Conrad Gebelein and Paul Hoffman for the intertidal flats of Cape Sable, Florida. Taking these modern examples as our interpretational models and counting pairs of Proterozoic laminae, we could reconstruct a lunar clock.

The third possible model is offered by sediment deposition in the upper ranges of the intertidal zone, where only storms bring substantial amounts of sediments that become incorporated into mats as laminae. The seasonal distribution of storms could be recorded as clusters of stromatolitic laminae repeated in an annual cycle.

What meanings, then, can we derive from our interpretations of stromatolite lamination? How do we recognize which ancient stromatolites are reliable solar or lunar clocks, which ones recorded storms, and which are a mixed record of various cyclicities? Reading the past from the present is often confusing. Although the basic principles of natural laws operated then as well as now, particular physicochemical conditions may have changed—to a large extent through the very microbial activities that we are trying to reconstruct.

Readings

Cohen, Y., R. W. Castenholtz, and H. O. Halvorson, eds. 1983. *Microbial Mats: Stromatolites*. Alan R. Liss.

Cohen, Y., and E. Rosenberg. 1989. *Microbial Mats: Physiological Ecology of Benthic Microbial Communities.* American Society for Microbiology.

Fisher, A. G. 1964. The Lofer cyclotherm of the Alpine Triassic. *Kansas Geologic Survey Bulletin* 169: 107–149.

Golubic, S. 1973. The relationship between blue-green algae and carbonate deposits. In *The Biology of Blue-Green Algae,* ed. N. Carr and B. Whitton. Blackwell.

Schlegel, H. G., and B. Bowien. 1989. *Autotrophic Bacteria.* Science Tech Publishers.

Schopf, J. W. 1983. *Earth's Earliest Biosphere: Its Origin and Evolution.* Princeton University Press.

9   Stromatolites of Shark Bay

Stjepko Golubic

On the western coast of Australia the Indian Ocean enters a deep embayment called Shark Bay. There, a large hypersaline water body, Hamelin Pool, is separated from the outer bay by a shallow sandbar that restricts water exchange (figure 1). In the late 1950s two Australian geologists—a young professor, Philip Playford, and his graduate student Brian Logan—were exploring the Shark Bay area. As they approached the shores of Hamelin Pool, a landscape of living stromatolites spread before them (see chapter 6, figure 3). Formed by layers of microorganisms, the rocky shore was reminiscent of scientific reconstructions of Proterozoic life. As fossils, the rocky structures were well known to these geologists as the only record of life from the vast Precambrian time span, long before the evolution of any plant or animal.

Plants and animals evolved about 600 million years ago. The more recent fossil record of animals and plants has been intensively studied by geologists and paleontologists for over 200 years. The earlier span of life on Earth, between 3.5 billion and 600 million years ago, was dominated by microorganisms and has only recently been subject to investigation. This chapter focuses on what Playford and Logan saw: contemporary, live, growing stromatolites in the process of lithification.

Stromatolites may be defined as rocks produced by the activities of microbes. How are living structures, composed of layered communities of microorganisms, turned to stone?

The fossil record of stromatolites is rich and diverse. Ancient stromatolites are abundant on the margins of Precambrian shields of all continents. They have been studied intensively in North America, Africa, Asia, and Australia. Modern stromatolites harboring live com-

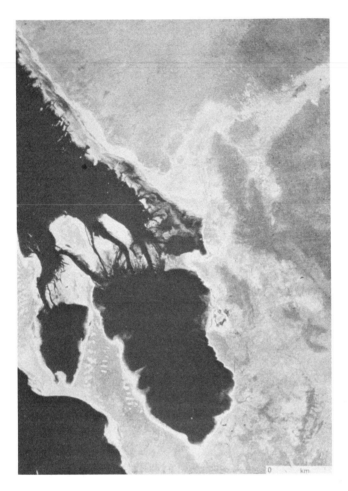

Figure 1
Shark Bay, a deep embayment on the west coast of Australia. This aerial photograph reveals the sandbars that separate Hamelin Pool, the larger body of water in
the photo, from the rest of the bay.

munities of bacteria, discovered on the shore of Hamelin Pool, were quite similar to the ancient stromatolites known to Playford and Logan from the Great Slave Lake area of the Canadian Precambrian shield. In that Arctic region of Canada, denuded by glaciers, the landscape is 1.8 billion years old, and the stromatolites can be observed in their original positions (see chapter 6, figure 2).

A section through a stromatolite reveals alternating layers of organic-rich and mineral-rich material. These layers, or laminae, are the cumulative record of the activities of microbial mats. A microbial mat is a community of microorganisms that occupies the sediment/water interface. These communities of microorganisms form stromatolites by trapping and binding sediment particles; sometimes they promote precipitation of minerals that cement the particles, thereby fortifying the entire structure. These microorganisms cope with rapid sedimentation by growing or crawling upward through each newly deposited sediment layer, thus escaping burial. The intertidal zone, where stromatolites commonly form, provides encouraging conditions of moisture, nutrients, and sunlight for these microbes. It also provides a supply of sediment that is deposited over the mat during tides and storms. With each layer of sediment deposited, the microorganisms of the mat grow from underneath to form a new layer on top. This distinctive layered profile characterizes most stromatolites.

Microbial mats are living communities of bacteria. Those that form stromatolites are found today, mainly in hypersaline basins, all over the world. Such environments include bays in western Australia; enclosed lagoons and ponds near Adelaide, in southern Australia; the coast of Kuwait, Saudi Arabia, and the United Arab Emirates; Solar Lake, on the Sinai Peninsula; bays along the coasts of the Red Sea; and lagoons in Baja California and on Christmas Island. Stromatolites also form in many inland environments, including thermal springs in Yellowstone National Park, the Great Salt Lake of Utah, and the Cuatro Cienegas Basin in northeast Mexico. Saltworks in southern Europe and South America are also good experimental environments in which to study modern stromatolites and microbial mats.

Today's microbial mats are the dominant communities only in extreme environments, such as hypersaline ones. Mat-making microorganisms are able, and may even prefer, to grow in conditions of normal seawater salinity; however, today they rarely form coherent mats or stromatolites there. Peter Garrett observed that on the coasts of the Bahamas subtidal mats are destroyed by grazing and burrowing invertebrate animals as quickly as they form. Stanley Awramik, who studies ancient stromatolites, compiled a record of the diversity of these structures and found that their decline at the end of the Proterozoic coincides with the widespread appearance of invertebrate animals in the fossil record. Garrett and Awramik believe that in Precambrian times stromatolites were abundant in normal marine, freshwater, and other environments, and that they retreated to their present hypersaline refuge after the advent of invertebrates. They conclude that mats persist today only under extreme conditions that preclude the presence of snails, worms, and other animals which feed on them.

Recent discoveries of contemporary stromatolites in freshwater (e.g., the karstic springs of Cuatro Cienegas, Mexico) and normal marine environments (e.g., subtidal stromatolites of Exuma Sound, Bahamas) have raised questions about the universal validity of Garrett and Awramik's conclusions. The absence of invertebrate feeders cannot explain the growth and preservation of those stromatolites that share their habitat with a diverse eukaryotic microbiota, flora and fauna. The distribution of these stromatolites correlates with high rates of sediment cementation and lithification. This observation led to the conclusion that early hardening of the structure by mineral precipitates is the most likely key to success.

Lithification takes place through intergranular precipitation of minerals such as calcium carbonate or silica. Calcification refers to lithification involving calcium carbonate; silicification refers to lithification involving silicon dioxide. Other forms of lithification can involve oxides of metals such as iron and manganese. Microorganisms are preserved better in silica than in far more porous calcium carbonate rock. The main reason for this difference lies in the size of the crystal grains these minerals form. Calcium carbonate grains are generally much larger than those of silica, and larger than the microorganisms they enclose. Their size increases with every recrystallization. In the course of crystal growth, the microorganisms are displaced and crushed in the interfaces of colliding crystal planes. Silica crystallization generally starts with very small grains, which embed the microfossils without destroying them. This is particularly the case with fine fibrous crystals of the mineral chalcedony, which accounts for most of the cherty nodules within which preserved Precambrian microorganisms are commonly found. Thus, microfossils have the best chance for preservation if the material in which they are embedded silicifies early, and if the surrounding rock retains its original mineralogy and does not recrystallize.

Microbial Mats and Stromatolites of Hamelin Pool

The shores of Hamelin Pool provide a living, natural laboratory for the study of processes which may have been operating on Earth for over 3 billion years. An array of different stromatolitic structures form along these shores. Each type is characterized by a unique assemblage of microorganisms, confined to a particular zone with respect to sea level. The degree of lithification in each of these structures varies, indicating that particular microbial communities may influence the process in a specific manner.

When geologists examined these stromatolites, they had difficulty determining which were alive and growing and which were products of past activities, now covered by secondary settlers. Microbes which secondarily encroach on the stromatolites may help protect the structure, may contribute to its destruction, or may have no effect on the rock. Logan, impressed by the degree to which the shapes of intertidal stromatolites reflected the action of environmental forces such as wave scouring, concluded that the intertidal zone is where all stromatolites form. Stromatolites found submersed in the pool were, according to his explanation, relics from times when the sea level was lower. Playford, on the other hand, was convinced that subtidal stromatolites were alive and growing. He placed stainless steel nails in a number of these stromatolites, as measuring sticks, and found that many of them accreted several millimeters per year. When we (S. M. Awramik and S. Golubic) first visited Shark Bay, in 1973, we employed a different method. We analyzed the microbial composition of the mats covering each of the stromatolite types, determined the ambient sedimentation processes, and then tested the continuity of these processes in the formation of stromatolites by studying the structures in cross-section. We concluded that different stromatolite-

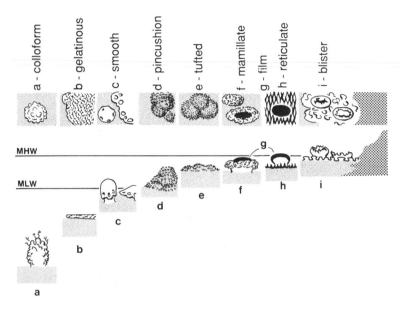

Figure 2
Microbial mat types in Hamelin Pool, arranged along a representative profile from permanently submerged habitats (left) to coastal dunes (right). MLW: mean low water level; MHW: mean high water level.

making communities inhabit the intertidal and subtidal zones, and that both types are actively growing and accreting.

Tidal zonation is one of the most distinctive characteristics of the microbial mats that form stromatolites. A profile perpendicular to the shoreline of Hamelin Pool transects nine coastal zones, characterized by different timing of tidal inundation and air exposure and by different types of microbial mats (figure 2). We will look briefly at the microorganisms in each zone, starting with the permanently submersed subtidal zones and then proceeding landward toward the more hostile intertidal zones, where organisms are exposed to intense solar irradiation and desiccation.

a. Colloform mat and subtidal stromatolites. A diver in the clear waters of Hamelin Pool sees a fascinating landscape, with large stromatolites rising from the sandy bottom like monuments in a sunken graveyard. These subtidal stromatolites, up to 60 cm high, are covered with a translucent beige gelatinous mat, called *colloform mat,* formed principally by a coccoid entophysalidacean cyanobacterium that is new to science. Inside these mats, calcium carbonate precipitates by an unknown mechanism, forming tiny, hollow aragonitic spheres. This kind of precipitate seems to be confined to the colloform mat, since it was not observed in any other mat type. These concretions apparently act as centers which start the lithification process within subtidal stromatolites. In addition to the newly discovered and still undescribed microorganism, the colloform mat contains numerous prokaryotic and eukaryotic organisms, notably the cyanobacterium *Schizothrix* sp., the diatom *Mastogloia*, and the chlorophyte *Acetabularia*. In deeper layers of the colloform mat the encrustation of calcium carbonate gradually increases, so that the interior portions of stromatolites are firmly cemented and hard. This gradual change in the degree of cementation suggests that the process of lithification progresses from the interior outward, and that the same processes were responsible for the buildup and preservation of these subtidal stromatolites.

b. Gelatinous mat is formed by a mixed population of the prokaryotic cyanobacterium *Aphanothece* sp. and certain eukaryotes: stalked diatoms. Calcium carbonate precipitation takes place sporadically within the mat, which rarely forms hard, crust-like horizons.

c. Smooth mat is a leathery beige-pink mat with a smooth surface. It coats dome-shaped stromatolites or covers sand, but it remains largely unlithified. It is composed of a small *Schizothrix* sp. dominating the surface layers and *Microcoleus chthonoplastes* forming a blue-green layer underneath.

d. Pincushion mat is an unlithified mat that traps and binds coarse sediment, often building dome-shaped structures. It is built by *Gardnerula corymbosa*, a large rivulariacean cyanobacterium. In cross-section, this mat shows radiating *Gardnerula* filaments growing in a manner that results in the formation of faint laminations.

e. Tufted mat is formed by a large scytonematacean cyanobacterium. Like the two mat types described above, the tufted mat is not hardened.

f. Mamillate mat is one of the most characteristic and common mats, dominating the middle and upper intertidal ranges. Its name describes its bumpy, warty (in Latin *mamilla* means "wart") texture. This mat is formed by the coccoid cyanobacterium *Entophysalis major.*

g. Film mat settles only on hard, completely lithified surfaces. It is composed of the endolithic cyanobacterium *Hormathonema luteobrunneum* and *H. violaceonigrum,* which penetrate carbonate substrates and contribute to their weakening and destruction.

h. Reticulate mat dominates the water-logged environments of the upper intertidal zone, such as tidal channels and ponds. In this mat the main formative microorganism is the cyanobacterium *Lyngbya aestuarii.* Because of the way it responds to light and to local drainage, its filaments form a fine network of ridges visible to the naked eye. Reticulate mat decomposes anaerobically; the sediment underneath is organic-rich and is stained black by ferrous sulfide. This condition is in sharp contrast to that underneath the mamillate mat, which grows and decomposes in well-aerated environments.

i. Blister mat (also known as convoluted mat) dominates at the upper end of the intertidal zone. The conspicuous blistering is caused by gas release from bacterial decomposition of organic-rich sediments beneath it. The continuing growth of the mat increases its surface and causes it to fold. Many different mats may undergo some blistering, but blistering is most noticeable in mats that have previously been water-logged.

Seasonal Lithification of Intertidal Stromatolites

The waters of Hamelin Pool are hypersaline and supersaturated with calcium carbonate throughout the year. This condition intensifies with continued evaporation at different levels of the intertidal zone. Although some precipitation of calcium carbonate takes place in every type of mat described, the most intensive lithification has been observed in subtidal zones [figure 2 (a)] within the colloform mat and in intertidal zones within the mamillate mat [figure 2 (f)].

When we first studied the mamillate mat and the lithified intertidal stromatolites—during the austral winter, in July 1973—we found healthy mamillate mat overgrowing soft, nonlithified stromatolites in the lower intertidal zone. Nearly identical stromatolite shapes could be observed in the upper intertidal zone, all of which were hardened and covered by the thin dark film mat. In the transitional zone we found hard, lithified stromatolitic structures which had been invaded by a new generation of mamillate mat. Although morphological similarities suggested the same origins of hard and soft structures, we were not able to find transitions between these apparent phases.

The resolution of this puzzle had to await a second field trip, this time during the austral summer in December 1980. We discovered that lithification takes place quickly and suddenly, during a short but critical time interval at the peak of the summer season. We were able to find a few sites where lithification could be caught in the act, so that every phase of the process could be documented. We noted that stromatolites undergoing lithification changed not only in hardness, but also in color (from dark brown to bluish-black).

Calcium carbonate forms minerals in three mineralogically distinct types of crystallographic organization: calcite, aragonite, and (much less frequently) vaterite. Calcite is thermodynamically the most stable form, and is usually the final outcome of diagenetic recrystallization of calcium carbonate. (*Diagenesis* is geochemical alteration of sediments.) In freshwater environments this mineral incorporates very low amounts of magnesium and is referred to as "low-magnesium calcite," or simply "calcite." However, in seawater environments rich in magnesium salts, calcite formation incorporates large proportions of magnesium and is referred to as "high-magnesium calcite," or simply "magnesium calcite." Aragonite is thermodynamically less stable, forming under normal marine conditions, particularly when the process is fast—for example, under conditions of high temperature, or elevated salinity, or in the presence of organic matter. In the formation of aragonite, strontium is incorporated and magnesium is excluded. The crystallographic properties of minerals can be studied using x-ray diffraction; however, when minerals are mixed, or when the samples are too small for standard mineralogical analysis, they can be analyzed for their elemental content. By determining the amount of magnesium and the amount of strontium incorporated

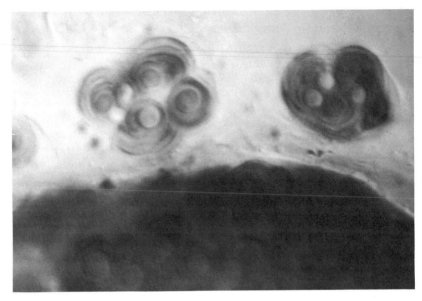

Figure 3
Photomicrograph of *Entophysalis major*, the principal builder of the mamillate mat.
The cells occur in packets surrounded by a thick polysaccharide sheath. Cells of
Entophysalis are approximately 8 microns across.

within the crystals, one can determine whether the mineral in question is calcite or aragonite.

The amorphous carbonate is the least-known form of carbonate. It has been described only a few times in the scientific literature. Chemically it is calcium carbonate, but it is not organized in mineralogical crystal lattices, as are calcite, aragonite, and vaterite. Current thinking is that in the formation of amorphous carbonate the molecular arrangement follows an organic template. With time, carbonate molecules may rearrange, crystallizing as calcite or aragonite.

For most of the year the healthy mamillate mat is bubbly and gelatinous. The cells of its principal builder, *Entophysalis major*, are seen surrounded by gelatinous envelopes (figure 3), which form yellow-brown, wart-like projections. When lithification begins, at the height of summer, it occurs suddenly, starting within the polysaccharide surrounding the cells. Here, the nucleation of calcium carbonate starts simultaneously at several points and spreads rapidly. Petrographic thin sections of a stromatolite in the early stages of the lithification process show that the core of the hardening stromatolite is still stained by the brownish color of *Entophysalis,* the microbe that built the mamillate mat, although the mat is now completely encrusted with calcium carbonate. The exterior part of that same stromatolite has a secondary crust of pure carbonate crystals precipitated on top of this *Entophysalis* layer. The black microorganisms that appear on top of that crust are the first colonizers of the film mat, which constitutes the next stage in the succession.

Examination of the transition between the precipitate inside the *Entophysalis* gel and that outside of it with a scanning electron microscope shows that the carbonate precipitated within the gel appears smoother and more compact in comparison with the more crystalline look of the carbonate in the outer crust. Higher magnification of the precipitate inside the gel reveals a globular morphology without any crystalline orientation. It can be recognized as the amorphous carbonate known to form only in biological systems.

The location of the initial carbonate-crystal nucleation, the rapidity of the process, and the amorphous nature of the precipitate all strongly suggest that the process occurring inside the mat is triggered or mediated by organisms or organismic products. Chemistry alone cannot explain the observed phenomena. The fact that the external crust is composed of aragonite needles is more consistent with the mode of calcium carbonate crystallization, which is normal in the marine chemical environment, yet the uniformity of the crystals suggests that they have formed at roughly the same time and that their formation probably was initiated by biogenic precipitation in the gel below. A similar pattern can be seen in the first mineral lining of cavities, enclosed within the stromatolite. Continuing precipitation in these cavities leads to the formation of large magnesium calcite crystals.

Entophysalis as a Living Fossil

Let us now turn to the destiny of the organisms that were caught in the lithification process. After the encrusting carbonate has been dissolved, the scanning electron microscope clearly reveals shriveled and destroyed cells that fell victim to the disruptive crystal growth, which was accompanied by bacterial degradation. Lithification of the mamillate mat is a recurring catastrophic event that terminates the cycle of mat development, "freezing" it in stone. The hardened surfaces of these lithified stromatolites, initially barren, are exposed to colonization by the film mat. This is an entirely different microbial community, composed of endolith microorganisms that penetrate the carbonate substrates as they grow inside rocks and contribute to their destruction. Within a year, the mamillate mat may recolonize and overgrow those hardened surfaces, thus starting another cycle of stromatolite growth. These dramatic changes explain discontinuities in the process of accretion of stromatolites, as well as the low preservation potential of the microorganisms that build them.

The chances of long-term preservation and fossilization are better if the mat escapes lithification by carbonate precipitation and is silicified instead. Structural degradation in nonlithified mamillate mats is more gradual and less destructive. Characteristic morphological features of cell arrangements and colony construction are sometimes so well preserved as to remain recognizable even after thousands of years of burial in sediment. Silicified Proterozoic microbial fossils were first discovered in the mid-1950s by Taylor and Barghoorn. Since then, many such remains have been described, many of them from stromatolites and microbial mats.

The degradation of modern microbial mats supplies new information about the differential preservability of various structural components of modern microorganisms. The results are applied to interpretation of the preserved structures found in microbial fossils that are billions of years old. We have learned from studying degrading modern mats that cells themselves are more vulnerable to deformation and decay, and thus less preservable, than their gelatinous extracellular envelopes and pigments.

Concluding Remarks

In this section we will review the main morphological characteristics of a healthy, growing mamillate mat, then follow the changes caused by degradation after death by sediment burial. Finally, we will compare these contemporary remnants with those found in a fossil counterpart.

Healthy cells of *Entophysalis major* (figure 3) are spherical and are surrounded by a Gram-negative cell wall (typical of cyanobacteria), which contains peptidoglycan, a cross-linked polymer. The cell wall resists the osmotic pressure and maintains the cell's shape. Externally (outside the cell wall) the *Entophysalis* cells are surrounded by envelopes of the polysaccharide they excrete. Every time a cell divides, it produces a new external envelope around itself and inside the previous external envelope. In the multiple envelopes of polysaccharide gel around each cell, the older envelopes include pairs or tetrads of cells. Small groups of enveloped cells that detach from the mat are carried by tides, contributing to the spreading of the mamillate mat. Scytonemine, the light-induced extracellular pigment embedded in the polysaccharide gel, is most prominent at and near the illuminated surface of the colony.

After the cells die, the osmotic regulation of their plasma membrane ceases. With the loss of turgidity, their cell walls cave in. The molecular cross-linkage of peptidoglycan walls exerts folding forces so strong that the cells collapse into small "star-shaped" bodies. Continuing degradation is accompanied by further size reduction, until the cells become minute granules a small fraction of their original size (figure 4). Surprisingly, the envelopes suffer much less in this process. They shrink proportionally to the water loss from the polysaccharide, but retain their rounded outlines.

A reconstruction of changes in cells and envelopes at different stages of cell division, in the process of *post mortem* degradation, is diagrammed in figure 5. Live cells which are dividing in three perpendicular planes (into packages of two, four, eight, and so on) are shown on the top line. Their altered morphology after death and shrinkage is shown on the bottom line. The multiple envelopes remain recognizable because of the preservation of the pigment scytonemine within them; this aids greatly in our recognition of the cell-division sequence. The cells themselves shrivel down to dots, and sometimes disappear altogether. Cells caught in division at the time of death may shrivel to elongated or dumbbell-shaped specks. Two adjacent specks may indicate cells that died immediately after completing division.

Modern degraded *Entophysalis* (figure 6) is not much different in shape and cellular organization from the mid-Proterozoic microbial fossil *Eoentophysalis* (figure 7), which has been found preserved in

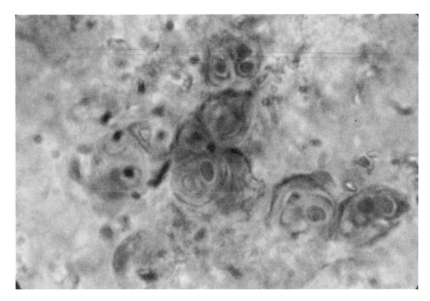

Figure 4
Degrading cells of *Entophysalis*. The cells shrink to a fraction of their original size; the polysaccharide sheaths retain their rounded shape.

silicified stromatolites. The structures are seen in a petrographic thin section as clearly as if they were preserved in glass. The extracellular pigment, the multiple envelopes, and the granular remains of cells are all clearly visible.

Modern *Entophysalis major* and ancient *Eoentophysalis belcherensis* have many morphological features in common, some of which reveal similarities in their life cycles. The cell-division patterns revealed by the arrangements of extracellular envelopes are identical. Both organisms are stained darker outside and lighter inside by a similar light-responsive pigment. Both organisms formed carbonate stromatolites of approximately the same shape and size. Another indication of the similarity of their respective environments is the finding of pseudomorphs of halite (NaCl) within the ancient stromatolites. (*Pseudomorph* means "false form"; it refers to the result of a mineral replacement in which the crystalline form of the original mineral is retained.) Pseudomorphs of halite and gypsum are indicators of a hypersaline and/or evaporitic paleoenvironment. They tell us that during Proterozoic times the Belcher Islands were a part of a coast

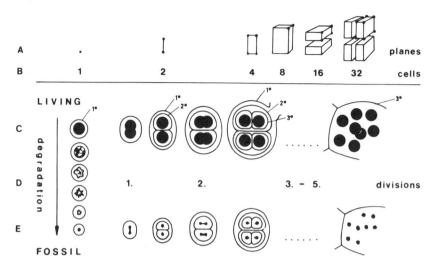

Figure 5
Degradation processes in *Entophysalis*. Cell-division patterns are shown from left to right, and degradation of cells is shown from top to bottom. (A) Spatial arrangements of division planes in the formation of a 32-cell packet. (B) Number of cells at each division. (C) Cell division and envelope formation during five divisions in living *Entophysalis*. (D) Number of cell divisions for stages shown in C. (E) Morphologies of degraded and shrunken cells.

where stromatolites were forming in an intertidal setting similar to the coastal environments of today's Shark Bay.

Eoentophysalis has subsequently been found in younger Proterozoic strata in Amelia Dolomite in Australia (1.6 billion years old), the Gaoyuzhuang Formation in China (1.2 billion years old), the Bitter Springs Formation in Central Australia (800–900 million years old), and in Greenland (700 million years old). Today *Entophysalis* inhabits intertidal zones in the bays of subtropical coasts, such as Shark Bay or the lagoons of the Arabian/Persian Gulf. Its occurrence during the Proterozoic eon encompasses a time span much longer than that which has lapsed between the beginning of the Phanerozoic and the present. *Entophysalis*, the oldest known living fossil, has maintained its form and its function through a geological time span exceeding half the entire history of life on Earth. Living microbial mats and their lithified remains, stromatolites, are among the most valuable clues we have for our reconstruction of planetary conditions during the vast span of history before the evolution of plants and animals.

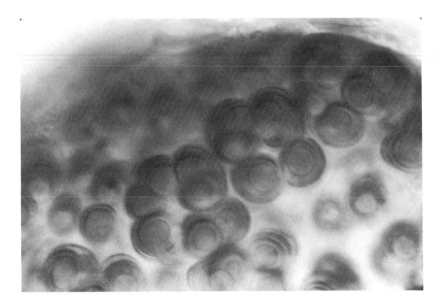

Figure 6
Light micrograph of living *Entophysalis* in vertical section.

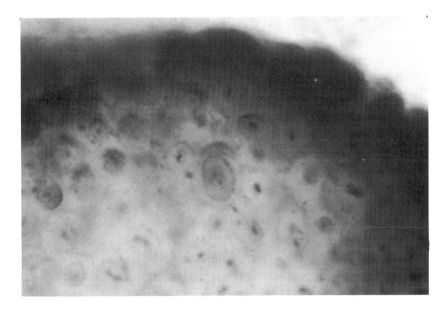

Figure 7
Petrographic thin section of *Eoentophysalis belcherensis* from a 1.8–1.9-billion-year-old silicified stromatolite from Belcher Islands, Hudson Bay, Canada. Paired cells in upper left corner and central region are evidence of cell division.

Readings

Golubic, S. 1976. Organisms that build stromatolites. In *Stromatolites* (Developments in Sedimentology, volume 20), ed. M. R. Walter. Elsevier.

Golubic, S. 1976. Taxonomy of extant stromatolite building cyanophytes. Ibid.

Golubic, S. 1985. Microbial mats and modern stromatolites in Shark Bay, Western Australia. In *Planetary Ecology,* ed. D. E. Caldwell et al. Van Nostrand Reinhold.

Golubic, S., W. E. Krumbein, and J. Schneider. 1979. The carbon cycle. In *Biogeochemical Cycling of Mineral-Forming Elements,* ed. P. A. Trudinger and D. J. Swaine. Elsevier.

Golubic, S., and J. Schneider. 1979. Carbonate dissolution. In ibid.

Golubic, S., and H. J. Hoffmann. 1976. Comparison of modern and mid-Precambrian Entophysalidaceae (Cyanophyta) in stromatolitic algal mats: Cell division and degradation. *Journal of Paleontology* 50: 1074–1082.

Lowenstam, H. A., and S. Weiner. 1989. *On Biomineralization.* Oxford University Press.

Westbroek, P., and E. W. De Jong. 1983. *Biomineralization and Biological Metal Accumulation.* Reidel.

10   Symbiosis Theory: Cells as Microbial Communities

Lynn Margulis

The forerunner of this lecture was recorded in 1972. The molecular-biology revolution and the large amount of new information from experimental and observational biology have necessitated a complete revision. Here Lynn Margulis describes her current view of the origin of the eukaryotic cells of fungi, plants, and animals and of other cells with membrane-bounded nuclei.

I present here the *serial endosymbiosis theory* (SET) of the origin of cells with nuclei. Eukaryotic cells (those constituting animals, plants, fungi, and protoctists) are, I argue, derived from tightly integrated bacterial communities. Eukaryotic cells did evolve from bacteria, but not directly. A single eukaryotic cell is quite different from a single bacterial cell (figure 1). Twenty years ago, when I first recorded these ideas for students, my lecture was called "The Symbiotic Theory of the Origin of Higher Cells." Since then I have realized that to speak in terms of "higher" and "lower" forms of life is meaningless: Charles Darwin was correct when he admonished us not to use the terms "higher" and "lower" for live organisms; all are equally evolved by the very fact of their presence in today's world.

Bacteria may be small, but they are just as "high" as any other life form; they appeared on Earth before any eukaryotes, and in terms of metabolic diversity they are far more capable than animals and plants. Bacteria cycle all of the chemical elements required by life as biogenic gases and solutes. They tolerate extremes of oxygen, temperature, and pressure better than the most resistant eukaryotes. Bacterial, or prokaryotic, cells are *units*: membrane-bounded, protein-synthesizing, self-sufficient little systems. All bacteria have prokaryotic cell structure; they all have DNA, various types of RNA (e.g.,

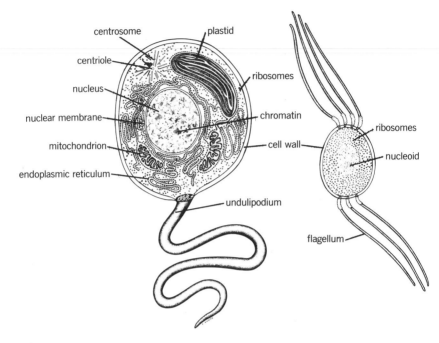

Figure 1
Eukaryotic and prokaryotic cells compared. Eukaryotic cells (left) contain membrane-bounded nuclei and other organelles, including mitochondria, plastids, and unduli-podia (complex motility organelles composed of tubulin and many other proteins). Prokaryotes (right) have DNA that is not surrounded by a membrane, and flagella with shafts composed of a single protein (flagellin).

messenger or mRNA, ribosomal or rRNA, and transfer or tRNA), ribosomes, and a plasma membrane consisting of lipid and protein bounding the whole entity. A minimal cell, with at least 2,000 genes and their products, constitutes the unit bacterial cell. Cell walls, which may or may not be present, are always outside the bacterial plasma membrane. With respect to their limiting structures, bacteria display four possibilities: Gram-negative, Gram-positive, Gram-variable, and no walls at all. All bacteria belong exclusively to one or another of these classes, which refer to staining reactions that indicate the wall's composition.

Organelles From Free-Living Bacteria

The theory of symbiosis states that the three classes of organelles of eukaryotic cells—undulipodia (organelles of motility), mitochondria (organelles of energy transduction), and plastids (organelles of photosynthesis)—originated from bacterial symbionts. If my view is correct, all animal cells have at least three kinds of ancestors, and all plant cells have at least four; all are chimeras.

The phylogeny or "family tree" of eukaryotic cells is depicted in figure 2. The monerans (all the bacteria) are shown at the bottom; as we move chronologically from past to present we ascend the paths of this diagram. Toward the top are the four groups of eukaryotes: plants, animals, fungi, and protoctists. Protoctists, having evolved earlier, are first represented at a lower level.

The major mechanism of evolution put forth by the SET is "serial symbiosis." This term refers to the acquisition of particular symbionts in a certain order. Symbiosis is simply defined as the long-term physical association of organisms that are members of different species. In the serial symbioses described here and envisaged to have established eukaryotic cells, most of the physical association became permanent. Two or more types of symbionts coevolve with time and become integrated into a single organismal unit. This new unit, in turn, is capable of acquiring still other symbionts.

I hypothesize that the first step in the origin of the eukaryotes—the process of eukaryosis—involved the acquisition of motile bacterial symbionts (spirochetes) by a "host." The host—a different prokaryotic cell, much like the *Thermoplasma* of today—fermented sugars via glycolysis (conversion of glucose to pyruvate or lactate). These host bacteria developed symbioses with motile bacteria; they were invaded by surface spirochetes. This first and crucial step in the origins of the nuclear membrane system and of intracellular motility, in which symbiotic spirochetes and their hosts became "undulipodiated mastigotes," is detailed in the next chapter. The spirochete-plus-*Thermoplasma* step, I believe, evolved into a type of protist—a mastigote, but one that lacks mitochondria (see the middle of figure 2). This first symbiotic complex was actively motile; the coevolved microbes became mastigote microbes—protists—representing the first nucleated cells. Most of these acquired mitochondrial symbionts. After this, algae and plants acquired colored, photosynthetic symbionts, whereas fungi and animals evolved directly from mitochondria-rich mastigotes (top of figure 2).

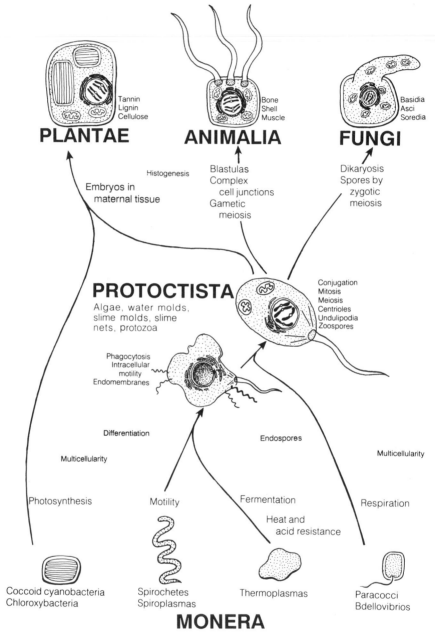

Figure 2
Cells as microbial communities: the serial endosymbiosis theory of the origin of
eukaryotic cells.

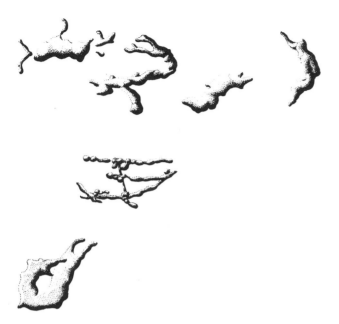

Figure 3
Thermoplasma acidophilum, drawn from electron micrographs.

The Origin of Nucleocytoplasm

The term *nucleocytoplasm* refers to the single, integrated system of the eukaryotes, which is composed of the membrane-bounded nuclear DNA and the ribosome-rich cytoplasm external to the nucleus. Sequences of nucleotide base pairs in nuclear DNA determine complementary sequences in messenger RNA. In short lengths, mRNA travels to the cytoplasm, where the messages are "read" on cytoplasmic ribosomes in such a way that specific proteins are synthesized. No eukaryotic cell lacks this nucleocytoplasmic system. Thus, a central question in eukaryosis is: "What is the evolutionary ancestry of the nucleocytoplasm?"

The leading hypothesis, at least at the University of Massachusetts, is that the nucleocytoplasm originates from bacteria like the *Thermoplasma acidophilum* that Dennis Searcy cultures in his laboratory (figure 3). *Thermoplasma acidophilum,* the best-studied of the thermoplasmas, belongs to the group of bacteria that Carl Woese, of the University of Illinois, calls the kingdom of Archaeobacteria. The possibility that a *Thermoplasma*-like bacterium evolved into nucleocytoplasm is now being tested by Searcy. What characteristics suggest the possibility that *Thermoplasma*-like bacteria are on an ancestral line with nucleocytoplasm? One is that *Thermoplasma* may contain histone-like proteins, as Dennis Searcy has claimed. Nearly absent from bacteria, histone proteins are distinctive features of eukaryotes. The histone-like protein of *Thermoplasma*, called HTA, binds and protects DNA. The DNA-binding behavior of histone proteins directly protects the DNA from heat and radiation. Presence of these proteins is a distinctly eukaryotic feature of these bacteria. Moreover, *Thermoplasma* has an actin-like protein. Actin protein seems to be universal in eukaryotes, where it is a component of the thin fibers involved in generating all movement. Actins are generally absent from bacteria. Whether the actin-like protein of *Thermoplasma* is actually homologous to the actin of eukaryotes is not known with certainty. Nevertheless, Searcy's research suggests the actin of *Thermoplasma* is directly homologous with the actin of eukaryotes. If this is the case, it fortifies his idea that *Thermoplasma* and the nucleocytoplasm have common ancestry.

No bacteria ever divide by mitosis. The appearance of mitosis in the evolution of life occurred in protoctists. Since *Thermoplasma* is a bacterium, we assume that when it divides its DNA is segregated to the two resulting offspring on the cell membrane. Membrane grows between the new cells which emerge with the newly synthesized DNA attached. Because of the difficulty of growing and observing *Thermoplasma*, the details of its division process are still obscure. *Thermoplasma acidophilum* grows best at 60°C and pH 2. At room temperature, which is far too cold for *Thermoplasma*, the tiny cells freeze on a microscope slide. The high temperature and strong acidity in which *Thermoplasma* thrives explain why its DNA is coated with histone-like proteins, almost in eukaryotic nucleosome fashion. *Thermoplasma*'s histone-like proteins may have been preadaptive: the nucleocytoplasmic host may have already contained histone-like proteins that protected its DNA from hydrolysis by acidity and high temperature when such an organism, or its descendants, became ancestral to the nucleocytoplasm as we know it today.

Although irregular in shape, *Thermoplasma*, like all other bacteria, has no nucleus. If we accept Searcy's idea that *Thermoplasma*-like microbes became nucleocytoplasm and established early symbioses with spirochetes and respiring bacteria, the next question involves the origin of the nucleus itself. Minimally, a nucleus must be bounded by a nuclear membrane. I suspect that the nuclear membrane evolved as a consequence of symbiotic associations between *Thermoplasma*-like bacteria and spirochetes that penetrated them. The parrying led to a proliferation of membrane, including endoplasmic reticulum, inside what had been *Thermoplasma*. Newly formed nuclear membrane became involved in the segregation of *Thermoplasma* DNA in the way that membrane originally segregated DNA in *Thermoplasma* before it was beset by would-be symbionts.

The nuclear membrane is just one among many membrane elaborations characteristic of all eukaryotic cells. It is continuous with the other cell membranes: endoplasmic reticular membrane, Golgi-apparatus membrane, the outer membrane of the mitochondria, and the plasma membrane. Membranes are dynamic—they should be thought of as moving belts of fusing and rupturing lipid layers in which proteins are embedded. Membrane is continually produced in the nucleus at DNA attachments and is moved outward; unlike the static drawings typical in textbooks, membranes are fluid, interactive, and asymmetrical. (See chapter 4.) Since membranes often grow vigorously at the site of microbial invasion, I suspect that intracellular membranes in general proliferated in response to once-aggressive microbial associations.

At the beginning of any such symbiotic associations among microbes, the genomes of the unit cells are separate. Host cells and invading bacterial symbiont cells each have their own genomes. Integration of genomes probably occurs only after a great deal of other structural integration. Integration of the genomes of former symbionts is probably a consequence of moving "small replicons." Plasmids, viruses, transposons, and DNA in solution are all examples of small replicons—small lengths of replicating DNA that can be manipulated by enzymes. Such small DNA replicons can move and be incorporated into "large replicons," longer pieces of DNA. Since mechanisms that incorporate plasmids or viruses into larger pieces of DNA are ubiquitous in bacteria, I suspect that integration of small replicons from bacterial symbionts into what became nuclear DNA was an essential aspect of eukaryosis.

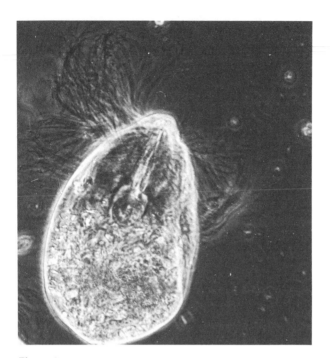

Figure 4
Staurojoenina, a hypermastigote protist symbiotic in termite hindguts, possesses
undulipodia and lacks mitochondria.

With the acquisition of motile spirochete bacteria by a *Thermo-plasma*-like bacterium, the first step toward eukaryosis was taken. Descendants of such a first step toward symbiosis still thrive in anaerobic muds and as gut symbionts in insects. Since many extant mastigotes have microtubule-composed undulipodia but lack mito-chondria, the most tenable view is that the nucleocytoplasm acquired motile spirochetes that eventually became undulipodia before mito-chondria evolved. Hypermastigotes (including *Staurojoenina*, shown in figure 4), devescovinids, and other mastigotes are examples of these; they lack mitochondria yet have undulipodia. The kinetosome-centriole microtubule systems (discussed in chapter 11), nearly uni-versal in eukaryotes, are present in all mastigotes. From the masti-gotes (undulipodiated organisms at the protoctist level of organization) to the origin of fungi, animals, and plants, an uncount-able series of evolutionary steps occurred, leading to many innova-tions—including the origins of mitosis and meiosis.

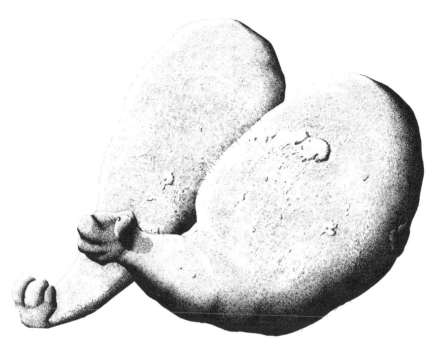

Figure 5
The giant ameba *Pelomyxa palustris.*

The giant ameba *Pelomyxa palustris* (figure 5) is thought to be a relic of an early stage in the origin of nucleated cells. Limited to some pond environments, it cannot be grown in captivity. It can be kept only for about a month before it dies. Each of these giants of the microcosm has many hundreds of nuclei. Since these nuclei are bounded by membranes, *Pelomyxa* is by definition a eukaryote. But here the resemblance to eukaryotes ends. *Pelomyxa* does not divide by mitosis, and it lacks centrioles and all other vestiges of the mitotic apparatus. It has no mitochondria. Stiff, immotile undulipodia-like structures have been reported sticking out of its surface, but they do not show the pattern of the typical [9(2) + 2] microtubule array in cross-section and we do not understand much about them. What *Pelomyxa* does have inside its cell are three kinds of symbiotic bacteria: perinuclear bacteria, found around each little nucleus, and two other types, one larger and one smaller, found in the cytoplasm. *Pelomyxa* is a kind of creeping bacterial community. At least one and maybe even two types of bacteria inside *Pelomyxa* can generate methane. Instead of using the hydrogen atoms from fermenting sugar and attaching the hydrogens to oxygen to form water, as humans and most other eukaryotes do when respiring, *Pelomyxa* passes hydrogen atoms derived from fermentation of sugar to its internal symbiotic bacteria. Inside the intracellular symbiotic bacteria, these hydrogens react with CO_2 (also derived from sugars) to produce methane. Methane gas has been detected in live whole cells of *Pelomyxa palustris* and in cell extracts that contain the intracellular methanogenic bacteria. *Pelomyxa*, as a eukaryotic cell, is clearly on an anaerobic, methanogenic line of evolution quite different from the lines taken by most other eukaryotes. I suspect that *Pelomyxa*, an isolated protist organism with its own set of symbionts, evolved before mitochondria entered the major eukaryote lineages. The very existence of this giant ameba is instructive; the story of its serial symbioses is a spinoff from the main narrative of eukaryotic cell evolution.

Mitochondrial Origins

The next step in this saga is the origin of mitochondria. Whereas the symbiotic acquisition of spirochetes is hypothesized to be central for the origin of mitosis and other forms of cell motility, the acquisition of mitochondria led to the colonization of the aerobic world by descendants of the early mastigotes. Many early mastigotes became aerobes: they either engulfed or were attacked by aerobically respiring, Gram-negative bacteria, such as members of the genera *Paracoccus, Bdellovibrio,* and *Daptobacter.* After the establishment of the membrane-bounded nucleus, with its mitotic motility, there were subsequent symbioses. The acquisition of symbiotic, intracellular, oxygen-respiring bacteria occurred many times. In some cases the bacteria evolved into mitochondria, providing us the next step in my version of the serial endosymbiosis theory.

All plants, algae, fungi, and animals—more than 30 million species—contain mitochondria in each of their cells. This observation suggests that the common ancestor of animals, plants, fungi, and algae—presumably some mastigote protist—possessed mitochondria. Mitochondria, universal in all photosynthetic eukaryotes, were probably already present in cells when plastids appeared in the lineage that eventually gave rise to plants and algae. During the period before plastids were acquired, eukaryotes were heterotrophs (that is, they were unable to make their own food). They all required preformed organic compounds, or other whole organisms, in aqueous solution. Some of the early protists phagocytotically ingested—but did not digest—photosynthetic bacteria. Photosynthetic bacteria—coccoid cyanobacteria, chloroxybacteria such as *Prochloron*, and other phototrophs—began as food for translucent protists; they ended up as plastids. Thus, one of the last steps in the origin of algal and plant eukaryotes was the acquisition by symbiosis of photosynthesis. Bacterial photosynthesizers capable of oxygenic photosynthesis became residents, converting their heterotrophic hosts to algae of various colors, including green.

I believe that the acquisition of photosynthetic symbionts was the most recent step in my version of serial endosymbiosis theory, because the other two classes of organelles—undulipodia and mitochondria—are thoroughly integrated in all cells that contain plastids. This last, most recent, evolutionary step, the acquisition of plastids, is the easiest to document since the plastids have retained most features of free-living cyanobacteria. Eukaryotes did not evolve as bigger and more complex bacteria; rather, according to the SET, all eukaryotes are products of the serial integration of several bacterial symbionts. The coexistence in the same cytoplasm of three originally separate genomes, each with an associated protein-synthesis apparatus, is a crucial aspect of this theory of the origin of eukaryotes. The integration of the symbionts provided not only the source of inherited variation but new individuals at greater levels of complexity.

What is most remarkable about this phylogeny—which by 1988 had reached its current form, with undulipodia preceding mitochondria (figure 2)—is that it was anticipated in its fundamentals by K. S. Mereschkovsky nearly a hundred years ago. Figure 6 depicts a phylogeny of all life forms drawn by this Russian biologist, who was a professor at the University of Kazan at the time. He placed the origin of the bacterial groups at the far left. Following the "tree of life" drawn by the German scientist Ernst Haeckel in 1865, Mereschkovsky named the microorganisms *monerans*. From the set of symbioses depicted as broken lines running from lower left to right, it is appar-

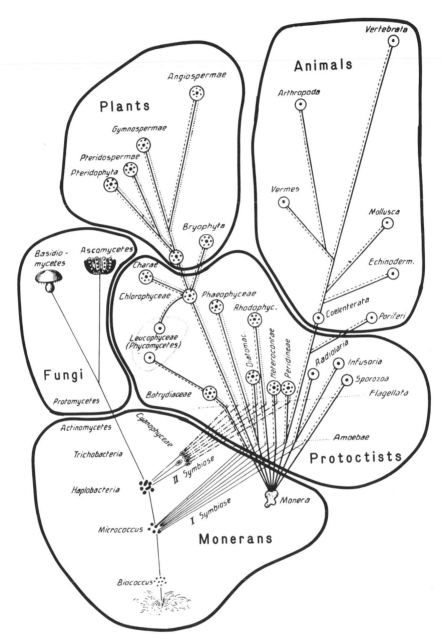

Figure 6
Mereschkovsky's anastomosing phylogeny based on symbiosis. The current five-kingdom classification scheme is superimposed.

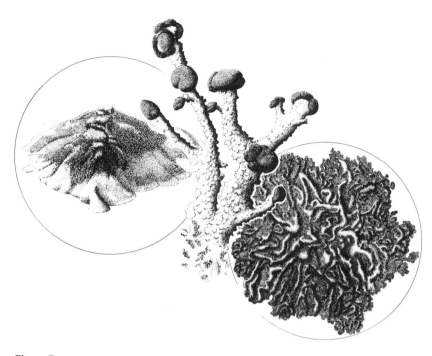

Figure 7
The lichen *Cladonia cristatella,* with the fungus isolated at left and the alga isolated at right. Only when the alga and the fungus grow together does the lichen (center) form.

ent that Mereschkovsky realized that all larger cells had emerged from symbiotic associations. Mereschkovsky derived all "infusoria" and other protists, as well as all animals, from double symbioses. ("Infusoria" is an old name for ciliates.) He showed algae and plants evolving from triple symbioses (nuclei, mitochondria, and plastids, in that order). Of course some of his details are considered incorrect today, but Mereschkovsky anticipated the notion of the origin of eukaryotic cells by symbiosis perfectly well. He called his book "Theory of Two Plasms." Indeed, with the two circles that bring together fungi with algae (phycomycetes) he even depicted the symbiotic origin of a kind of lichen. He was aware that, in the lichen symbiotic partnership, sugars produced by the algae or cyanobacteria are transferred to the fungi, while the fungi extends the ecological niche for the algal partner (figure 7). As far as I know, this fundamental conceptualization of symbiosis, on which I have worked all my professional life, was first developed by Mereschkovsky before 1910. Mereschkovsky's contribution is little known in the West. Similar ideas of symbiogenesis—the origin of evolutionary novelty through symbiotic alliances—were put forward in the United States by Ivan E. Wallin, a professor of anatomy at the University of Colorado who wrote a fascinating small book called *Symbionticism and the Origin of the Species* in 1927. Rejected in its time, Wallin's work is very poorly known today.

Molecular biology and ultrastructure as revealed by electron microscopy, and certain aspects of natural history, have contributed to the revival of early-twentieth-century concepts of the origins of cells by bacterial symbioses. Certain present-day bacteria, such as *Bdellovibrio*, behave just as we might expect some to have acted during the evolution of cell organelles. In the framework of the SET, *Bdellovibrio*'s lifestyle is similar to what might be expected of the ancestors of mitochondria. Tiny *Bdellovibrio* bacteria must attach to their larger bacterial hosts; they cannot survive or grow unless a host such as the Gram-negative bacterium *Spirillum* is available for penetration. In order to feed and reproduce, *Bdellovibrio* must enter the host's outer membrane and come to lie in its periplasm, the space between the outer and inner membranes of the host's Gram-negative cell wall. Penetration and growth by extant *Bdellovibrio* is ultimately lethal to the host. *Bdellovibrio*-like organisms would try to feed on their host from the inside, while the host would resist such a *Bdellovibrio* infection. According to the SET, an initially uneasy truce resulted from such antagonism; with the integration of these two types of genomes in the course of time, the *Bdellovibrio*-like organism and its host coevolved into a new, single, integrated entity. The *Bdellovibrio*-like penetrator respired oxygen and concentrated the fermentation products of its host to CO_2 and water in the new complex organism. In short, a motile, mitochondria-containing eukaryotic organism would have emerged by now. I suspect that as soon as any heterogenomic system (that is, any microbe inside a different sort of microbe) began, the proliferation of membrane of both organisms occurred (as it does now), providing the starting point of the origin of the great diversity of nucleated cells (protoctists) with their complex endomembrane and organellar systems.

Control of Symbionts by Hosts

An objection to these scenarios of symbiosis could be based on the question of the host's survival. Since present-day *Bdellovibrio* kills its host, why don't mitochondria still kill their "nucleocytoplasmic hosts"? Indeed, they may. Cancer may be connected to precisely this kind of intracellular interaction. Some ancestors of mitochondria were lethal to the cells that incorporated them. Philip John argues that an imbalance between mitochondria and the rest of the mammalian cell in which they reside is directly related to carcinogenesis (cancer formation). The number and sometimes the morphology of mitochondria in a cancer cell may vary significantly from those in normal cells of the same tissue. Does the increased number of mitochondria demonstrate mitochondrial overgrowth and induced death of the rest of the cell by which they were originally acquired?

Certain bacterial associations begin as lethal pathogenic infections; they end under control of the host cells. *Amoeba proteus,* grown by Kwang Jeon at the University of Tennessee, is an example of this. The amebas in Jeon's laboratory became infected by bacteria; the consequence was that nearly all the amebas died. Electron-microscope investigation showed that tiny black specks within the infected amebas were bacteria. At first the huge numbers of bacteria inside the amebas' cytoplasm killed nearly all the amebas; however, later the surviving bacteria became symbionts.

How did the pathogenic bacteria kill the amebas at first? This is not known in detail, yet Jeon saw that the amebas fed by taking bacteria into their phagocytotic vacuoles. He showed that digestive enzymes, which kill bacteria, are excreted across the vacuolar membranes. Though very few can, some bacteria debilitate or attack amebas in a way that completely precludes the efficacy of the amebas' digestive enzymes. Such bacteria, since they are not digested, actually penetrate the vacuole membranes and enter the cytoplasm. They find themselves "sitting in the pantry" and start growing. In the early days of Jeon's discovery, great populations of intracellular resistant bacteria were found in ameba cytoplasm—more than 120,000 bacteria per ameba. If the bacteria divide again, before the ameba does, the number of bacteria per ameba goes from 120,000 to 240,000 and the ameba dies. An amazing corollary—which I have only imbibed by hearsay—is that this microbial behavior is extremely similar to that of the bacteria that caused "Legionnaires' disease." Apparently, then-unknown pathogenic bacteria entered the cooling water of the air-conditioning system of a Philadelphia hotel in which an American Legion convention was taking place. Once transmitted to a human, the bacteria were engulfed by white blood cells of the immune system. A number of Legionnaires became fatally ill when their white blood cells were killed by pathogenic bacteria. A young man who had studied Jeon's work recognized the behavior pattern of these bacteria, which were later named *Legionella*. He realized that free-living amebas are similar in morphology to the lymphocytes in human blood. *Legionella* bacteria penetrate the vacuoles of our ameboid lymphocytes, the cells our bodies use to restrain bacteria. Generally, *Legionella* grows in the cytoplasm more rapidly than the lymphocytes can contain it. Lymphocytes, like Jeon's amebas, are under threat of death—they endure enormous selection pressure as they produce inhibitors, shut down DNA and protein synthesis, and behave in other ways to restrain intracellular growth of pathogenic bacteria in themselves. In most cases, the infections continue and the amebas or ameboid lymphocytes are destroyed by bacteria growing inside them.

However, bacterial growth can be restrained by the infected cells. Jeon isolated some amebas in which the quantities of intracellular pathogenic bacteria dropped from 150,000 bacteria per ameba to fewer than 40,000. The infection, in these cases, concomitantly became benign. After 5 years many live amebas contained only 40,000 bacteria per cell; Jeon showed that the descendants of the amebas that had survived the bacterial infection now required those same bacteria for their health and growth. What had once been a pathogenic bacterial infection had—by definition—become a symbiosis; moreover, the formerly invasive bacteria were now organelles! The nucleocytoplasm of the long-infected amebas no longer could survive without the bacteria. This symbiosis was established in only a few years; certainly such events can take place over geological periods of time. Jeon's story is instructively analogous to the origin of mitochondria: pathogenic free-living bacteria infect their hosts and become cytoplasmic resident bacteria under control of their host. A first step in the origin of any obligate endosymbiosis is the host's restraint of the intracellular symbiont's tendency to continue to grow. In the final stages in the development of these relationships, symbiotic assimilation occurs such that the bacteria unequivocally become organelles required for the continued growth of their hosts.

Photosynthetic Animals

As for the symbiotic origin of plastids, many examples exist in natural history where a heterotrophic organism eats but fails to digest a photosynthetic organism and the two continue to evolve as a consortium. One beautiful example is *Hydra viridis*, found in fresh waters all over the world. Such green hydra provide excellent illustrations of heterotrophic organisms that ate and failed to digest algae, developing symbioses over time. The endodermal (inner) layer of the hydra in nature contains the coccoid green algae *Chlorella*. The same animal, *Hydra viridis*, can be treated with chemicals and high-intensity light to induce loss of its *Chlorella* algae. An experimentally derived white hydra, unfed and placed in the dark, will die within days. An unfed green hydra in the dark dies in a few days too. A white hydra, experimentally deprived of its *Chlorella* and placed in the light without any food (*Artemia*—brine shrimp—are their usual food) will also die in a few days. However, green hydra under starvation conditions continue to live in the light for at least 3 or 4 months. If given *Chlorella* as food, a white hydra will "regreen"—the *Chlorella* it eats will not be digested but will become symbionts and will continue to help feed the hydra as long as light is available. Such associations between photosynthetic and heterotrophic entities serve as models for the origin of plastids in algae, some of which eventually evolved into plants.

A recently discovered photosynthetic bacterium called *Prochloron* bears a striking resemblance to the chloroplasts in *Codium*, a free-living green alga. *Prochloron*, an oxygen-producing photosynthetic bacterium with chlorophyll *a* and *b* as pigments, is now the best candidate for what ancestors of the chloroplasts of green plants and algae were like. That chloroplasts derive from free-living photosynthetic organisms such as *Prochloron* is buttressed by the presence of chloroplast DNA, chloroplast messenger and transfer RNA, chloroplast ribosomes, and the observation that all plastids are bounded

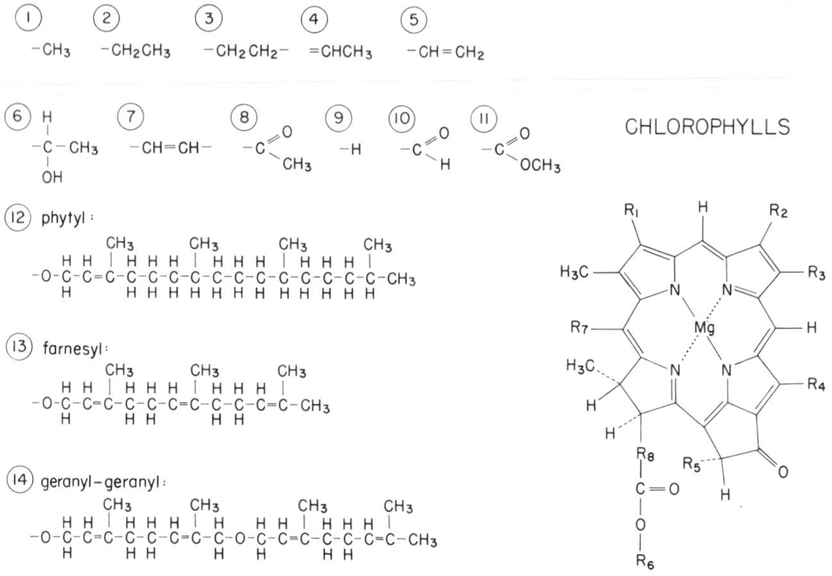

① 　　② 　　　③ 　　　④ 　　⑤
－CH₃　－CH₂CH₃　－CH₂CH₂－　＝CHCH₃　－CH＝CH₂

⑥ H
　｜
－C－CH₃
　｜
　OH

⑦ －CH＝CH－

⑧ －C⟨O / CH₃

⑨ －H

⑩ －C⟨O / H

⑪ －C⟨O / OCH₃

CHLOROPHYLLS

⑫ phytyl :

CH₃　　CH₃　　CH₃　　CH₃
H H ｜ H H H ｜ H H H ｜ H H H ｜
－O－C－C＝C－C－C－C－C－C－C－C－C－C－C－C－CH₃
　H　　H H H H H H H　H H H H H

⑬ farnesyl :

CH₃　　CH₃　　CH₃
H H ｜ H H H ｜ H H H ｜
－O－C－C＝C－C－C－C＝C－C－C－C＝C－CH₃
　H　　H H　　H H

⑭ geranyl–geranyl :

CH₃　　CH₃　　CH₃　　CH₃
H H ｜ H H H ｜ H　H H ｜ H H H ｜
－O－C－C＝C－C－C－C＝C－C－O－C－C＝C－C－C－C＝C－CH₃
　H　　H H　　H　　H　　H H

Figure 8
Distribution and comparison of chlorophyll structure. Structures 1–14 represent the substitutions present in various chlorophylls at sites R_1–R_8. (See also table 1.)

by membranes. Even today, plastids inside plant cells possess macromolecules and structures that are present in all free-living bacteria.

Both *Prochloron* and chloroplasts have DNA, chlorophyll *a* and *b*, and carotenoids. The differences between chlorophyll *a* and chlorophyll *b* and other pigments are shown in figure 8. Both *a* and *b* are chlorophyll molecules: magnesium-chelated tetrapyrroles. They are composed of four pyrrole groups, each chelated to a magnesium atom in the middle, bounded to the nitrogens of the ring. Each chlorophyll has a phytol side chain which is an isoprenoid derivative. These isoprenoid derivatives are up to 19 or 20 carbon atoms in length (see chapter 14, figure 4). The lipophilic phytol group allows the chlorophyll molecule to stick into a membrane. These chlorophyll molecules differ only in their side substitutions. R_1 and R_2 refer to radicals that can be substituted on the chlorophyll rings. The substitution R_1 is exactly the same on chlorophyll *a* and *b*. For R_2, chlorophyll *a* has a methyl group (—CH_3) and chlorophyll *b* has an aldehyde (—$HC=O$). This substitution is the only difference between these

Table 1
Distribution and comparison of chlorophylls.

	R_1	R_2	R_3	R_4	R_5	R_6	R_7	R_8	Organisms
bchl a	8	1	2	1	11	12/13	9	3	⎰Purple photosynthetic
bchl b	8	1	4	1	11	12	9	3	⎱sulphur and non-sulphur bacteria
bchl c	6	1	2	2	9	14	1	3	*Chloroflexus*
bchl d	6	1	2	2	9	14	9	3	⎰Green photosynthetic sulphur bacteria
bchl e	6	10	2	2	9	14	1	3	
bchl g	5	1	4	1	11	13	9	3	*Heliobacterium*
chl a	5	1	2	1	11	12	9	3	⎰Cyanobacteria, all algae, plants
chl b	5	10	2	1	11	12	9	3	⎰Cyanobacteria, green algae, plants
chl c_1	5	1	2	1	11	12	9	7	⎰Diatoms, dinomastigotes, phaeophytes
chl c_2	5	1	5	1	11	12	9	7	⎰Diatoms, dinomastigotes, phaeophytes

two chlorophyll molecules. The small chemical difference probably corresponds to a minor genetic difference. Although just a few mutations were involved in changing the R_2s, these were important from the point of view of the absorption spectra, color, and other properties of the molecule. Cyanobacteria lack chlorophyll b; chlorophyll a and other pigments give them the blue-green color. Chlorophyll a and chlorophyll b together produce the bright green color characteristic of plants, green algae, and certain other protist groups. Today *Prochloron* is found in association with chordate animals called *didemnids;* they are sea squirts, a kind of tunicate. The major difference between the whole *Prochloron* organism and the chloroplast organelles is the presence of a penicillin-sensitive cell wall in *Prochloron*.

The evolution of plastids from photosynthetic, oxygen-producing bacteria is accepted widely as a step in the origin of eukaryotic cells. Plastids undoubtedly evolved from photosynthetic symbionts more than once; they are thus viewed as polyphyletic, acquired several different times in the ancestral lineages. Symbioses of phototrophic bacteria with heterotrophs were established perhaps six, eight, or ten times, as is illustrated by different classes of plastids: grass green (chlorophyll a and b), blue-green plastids of cryptomonad, glaucocystid, and red algae (chlorophyll *a* and phycobiliproteins), and diatoms and brown algae (chlorophyll *a* and *c*). Blue-green and red plastids have many pigments in common; they are nearly identical. Green plastids were symbiotically acquired from organisms of the *Prochloron* group of bacteria, whereas blue-green or red plastids apparently derived from various types of cyanobacteria.

Mitochondria polyphyly also appears very likely. For example, *Pelomyxa*, the karyoblastean giant ameba, has three types of mitochondria-like bodies which, in fact, are not mitochondria at all. As was noted above, each is a different kind of bacterium; two are methanogens. Some typical mitochondria have tubular cristae (tubule-shaped inner membranes); others have flattened cristae. These two types plausibly correspond to acquisitions of two different original types of bacteria. The divergence of morphologies, coupled with 5S and 16S RNA-sequence data, suggests that mitochondria are polyphyletic, and that they originate from a large group of "eubacteria" that contain both respiring and photosynthetic members. Data from molecular biology reinforce the concept that mitochondria were acquired and evolved in more than a single lineage, perhaps three or four times.

Far more controversial, and largely unaccepted at present, is the idea of the origin of undulipodia from spirochetes in the phylogeny of eukaryotic cells (see chapter 11). The question of the polyphyly of undulipodia is difficult. The detailed structural similarity of the kinetosomes and axonemes that comprise undulipodia suggests that the structure is monophyletic—that it emerged only once. But every time I have opted for monophyly I have been wrong. Since the spirochete origin of undulipodia itself is not firmly established, the question of poly- or monophyly becomes a second-order question. We simply do not know.

Symbiosis in the Fossil Record

We probably can infer acquisition of symbionts from the fossil record. The process of symbiont integration is not seen directly, but the products are. Gonzalo Vidal discovered plankton over 100 million years old—these fossil eukaryotes were symbiotic products in my opinion. Andrew Knoll, in chapter 12 of this book, talks about early fossil eukaryotes from the Draken Formation of Spitzbergen. By the time these eukaryotes were present in the fossil record, mitochondria or their equivalents were in the cells and so were nuclei. From 3.5 billion to 2.5 billion years ago, the Archean eon was the age of prokaryotes. Perhaps many symbioses between prokaryotes were established (see figure 9), but none led to the eukaryotic lineage (figure 10). Not until 2.5–1.5 billion years ago do we see evidence of large, elaborate microbes—more than 100 microns in diameter—which we interpret as eukaryotes.

Figure 2 summarizes the concept of the symbiotic origin of eukaryotes. Microbes first appeared in watery, anaerobic environments. A variety of metabolic pathways and abilities evolved in bacteria: motility, fermentation, respiration, sulfate reduction, nitrogen fixation, photosynthesis, and so on. Over time these organisms developed into communities, and from communities into newly integrated individuals. Since the beginning of the Archean eon bacteria have diversified in many different ways. Spirochetes attached and conferred motility on what became the nucleocytoplasm. These associations gave rise to between 200,000 and 500,000 extant protoctista. Other developments include the evolution of mitosis, the incorporation of bacteria which become mitochondria, and the secondary acquisition of photosynthesis in organisms which evolved into algae and eventually plants. Figure 2 reconstructs the phylogenetic development underlying the emergence of plants, animals, and fungi. The latter appear in the fossil record rather suddenly, about 550 million years ago. Plants and animals depended entirely upon the preexistence of consortia of bacteria, from which the "new" kind of eukaryotic cell emerged more than a billion years ago.

Earth was dominated by bacterial communities from the inception of life, around 3.5 billion years ago. From this evolutionary perspective, protoctists and animals are derived from genome integration in fast-moving microbial communities, and plants come from sedentary, photosynthetic, integrated microbial communities. Thus, Earth is still largely dominated by microbial communities!

Symbiogenesis Theory

Why was Mereschkovsky's theory of symbiosis never accepted? Mereschkovsky's diagram shows two direct lineages: one set of microbial

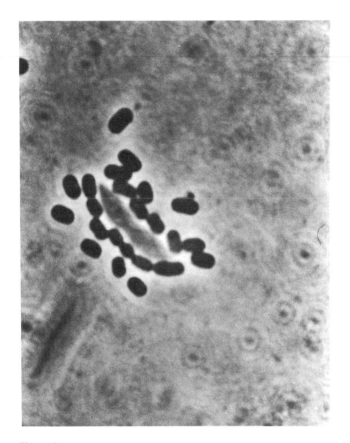

Figure 9
Pelochromatium, a bacterial consortium consisting of a large heterotrophic motile bacterium surrounded by many purple phototrophic bacteria.

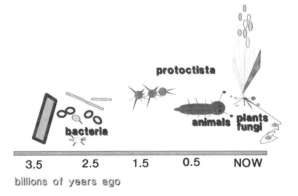

Figure 10
Times of appearance of the five kingdoms in the fossil record.

symbioses leading to protists and animals, and one set leading to algae and plants. The latter clearly represents plastid symbioses; its position at a higher level on the diagram indicates that plastids were the most recent acquisition. The lower set of symbioses has been misinterpreted by many—myself included—as representing mito-chondrial symbioses, though in his text Mereschkovsky explicitly states that these broken lines refer to the microbial symbioses that led to nuclei. Recognizing, of course, that plants, algae, fungi, and animals all have nuclei, Mereschkovsky concluded that symbioses leading to the emergence of nuclei preceded those leading to plastids. Although modern scientists agree that nuclei preceded plastids, few would argue a direct symbiotic origin of the nucleus.

Other scientists also argued for the importance of symbiosis in evolution—among them Mereschkovsky's Russian colleagues A. S. Famintzyn and B. M. Kozo-Polyanski, Paul Portier in France, and Ivan E. Wallin. There was little communication among Russian, French, and American scientists when most of this work was published (between 1900 and 1930). There was disdain for the role of symbiosis in cell evolution even among German scientists such as Paul Buchner, who worked on insect-bacterial symbioses, and until the 1960s no work at all on symbiosis in evolution was done in Great Britain. Within "mainstream evolutionary biology," views on the important role of symbiosis in evolution were uniformly ignored or rejected.

Many complex factors account for this history, but probably the overriding reason that serious biologists rejected the symbiotic origin of cell organelles is that too little was known about the little "dots" inside cells to allow any cohesive scientific judgment. Mereschkovsky, who incorrectly derived fungi directly from bacteria in his spec-ulations about the symbiotic origin of the nucleus, lacked sufficiently detailed information. Early cell biologists (called *cytologists, histolo-gists,* or *cytogeneticists*) had legitimate concerns about generating "artefacts." They were aware that many of the "dots," "lines," and "squiggles" inside the cells they studied were products of the fixation and staining procedures, induced by laboratory treatment. These scientists were extremely suspicious about the nature of any "little bodies." Not until 1963, when glutaraldehyde came into wide use as a fixative for electron microscopy and when biochemistry and genetics were transformed to include molecular genetics, were extensive data on the "dots" inside cells available. From the late 1960s on it became obvious that organelles inside cells (such as plastids in plant cells) were more similar to free-living bacteria outside these cells (e.g., cyanobacteria) than they were to the rest of the cell in which they were embedded. After 80 years, "symbiogenesis"—Mereschkovsky's concept of the importance of symbiosis—is entering "mainstream biology." I expect that in another decade or so the concept that eukaryotic cells are genetically integrated, tightly coevolved communities of bacteria will be fully accepted by all serious biologists.

Readings

Gray, M. W. 1985. The bacterial ancestry of plastids and mitochondria. *BioScience* 33: 693–699.

John, P. 1984. Mitochondrial regulation of cell surface components in relation to carcinogens. *Journal of Theoretical Biology* 110: 377–381.

Lewin, R. A., and L. Cheng. 1989. *Prochloron: A Microbial Enigma*. Chapman and Hall.

Margulis, L. 1981. *Symbiosis in Cell Evolution*. Freeman.

Margulis, L., and D. Sagan. 1986. *Origins of Sex*. Yale University Press.

McMenamin, M. A. S., and D. L. S. Schulte-McMenamin. 1990. *The Emergence of Animals*. Columbia University Press.

Searcy, D. G. 1987. Phylogenetic and phenotypic relationships between the eukaryotic nucleocytoplasm and thermophilic Archaebacteria. *Endocytobiology III* 503: 168–179.

11

Spirochetes and the Origin of Undulipodia

Lynn Margulis

Here Lynn Margulis concentrates on a specific problem, having to do with the origin of eukaryotes, that is currently under investigation in her laboratory: How did centrioles, kinetosomes, and other microtubule-based systems of motility—including the peculiar mitotic-meiotic sexuality that is characteristic of eukaryotes—originate?

The most difficult and controversial aspect of the symbiotic theory of the origin of eukaryotic cells is the hypothesis that undulipodia evolved from spirochetes. However, this proposition is intrinsic to the current version of the serial endosymbiosis theory (SET). In this chapter I survey the relevant research and discuss the origin of undulipodia.

Undulipodia and Flagella Compared

Undulipodium is the generic name for the [9(2) + 2] microtubular structure, the motility organelle that is nearly universal in eukaryotes and is absent from prokaryotes (figure 1). Entirely different from the bacterial flagellum (figure 2), it has had many names: cilium, flagellum, sperm tail, and even pecilokont. Knowledge of undulipodia is crucial to an understanding of the origin of mitosis, the cell-division process unique to eukaryotes.

The origin and evolution of the five major groups of organisms (kingdoms) is depicted in figure 3, where the lower portion represents bacterial evolution and the broken lines trace the symbiotic origins of cell organelles, mitochondria, and plastids. The broken line on the far right represents the origin of undulipodia from spirochetes.

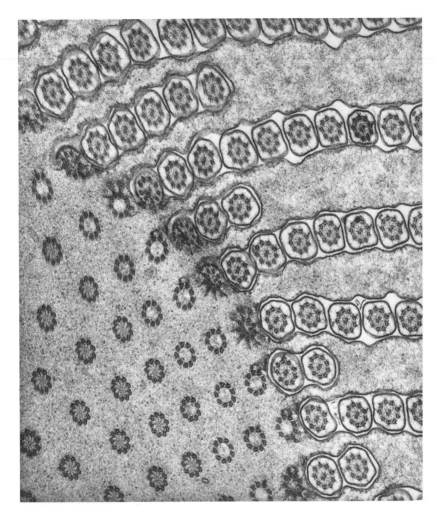

Figure 1
Undulipodia of a termite-hindgut-dwelling protist. The left portion shows clearly the
[9(2) + 2] structure of the axonemes (shaft); toward the right are the [9(3) + 0]
kinetosomes, underlying the axonemes. (Transverse sections in electron
micrograph.)

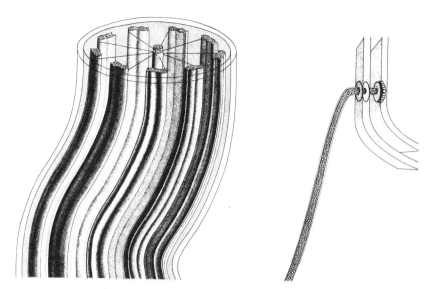

Figure 2
Axoneme (shaft) of undulipodium (left), surrounded by cell membrane, compared with flagellum (right) that penetrates its cell membrane.

This phylogenetic reconstruction views all eukaryotes as symbiotic composites from various bacteria. The central advantage of the hypothesized spirochete symbiosis is precisely that highly motile bacteria conferred rapid motility on a stationary or slow-moving host. From the motile consortium mitosis evolved, and then, in a later series of evolutionary steps, meiosis. Of course, mitosis and meiosis are crucial cell-level prerequisites of the sexuality of animals, plants, and fungi.

The undulipodium—the eukaryotic organelle claimed to have originated symbiotically—is compared with the bacterial flagellum in figures 2 and 4. The only motile portion of the bacterial flagellum is in the basal rotary motor—the flagellum shaft is passive. This wheel-like structure functions as the "rower," while the shaft of the flagellum, analogous to the "oar," transmits but does not generate force.

All undulipodia are composed of nine doublets of microtubules, the walls of which are made of alpha and beta tubulin proteins. In amino acid composition, these tubulins are extraordinarily similar to the alpha and beta tubulins found in the mitotic spindles of animals, plants, and fungi. Each undulipodium is always underlain by its

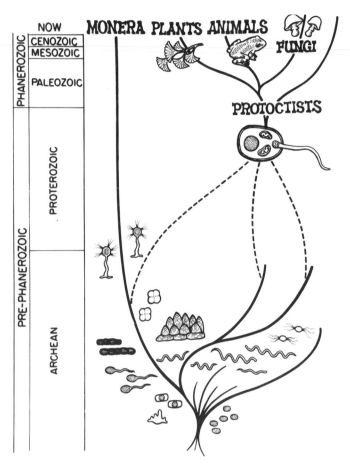

Figure 3
Appearance and evolution of major groups (five kingdoms) in the fossil record. Broken lines represent symbiotic origins of plastids, mitochondria, and undulipodia.

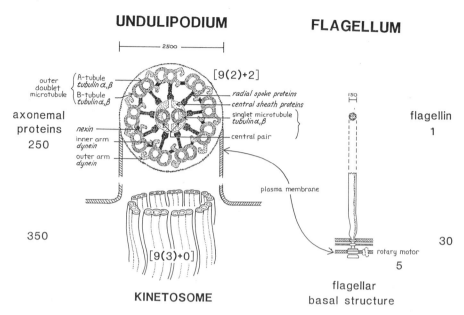

Figure 4

Undulipodium and flagellum compared. The undulipodia of eukaryotic cells are relatively large, complex structures. Approximately 250 nanometers in diameter, they are composed of some 600 proteins: 250 in the axoneme and 350 in the underlying kinetosome. Bacterial flagella, only 15 nm in diameter, contain only one protein (flagellin) in their shafts. The rotary motor is made up of about five proteins involved directly in motility and 25 flagella-assembly proteins; a total of 30 proteins are found in the whole flagellar basal structure.

kinetosome, the [9(3) + 0] microtubular structure. The hypothesis is that the entire undulipodium, including its kinetosome, originated by symbiosis. Before evolving into a cell organelle, the undulating structure was a free-living bacterium. The claim is that the undulipodium originated as a free-living microbe similar to present-day spirochetes that attach to and associate with other bacteria. Eventually parts of the spirochetes, the nucleic acids and certain motility proteins, were deployed inside their host cells. A series of selective steps led to the evolution of at least 100,000 different species of protoctists, as well as to many other cell-organizational developments, all precursors of animal, plant, and fungal meiotic sexuality.

How were motility proteins "deployed" within the first composite microbes— spirochetes and hosts—which became the early eukaryotic cells? "Deployed" in this context essentially means "sent out"—

microtubules and their associated membranes rearranged over evolutionary time. The idea is that helically motile bacteria, largely
resembling extant spirochetes, as they still do today, entered host
cells, eating and growing inside them. These spirochetes brought
with them their constituent motility proteins, including tubulin and
microtubule-associated proteins (MAPs). In the course of evolution,
spirochete constituents were assimilated into the structure of the host
for many other purposes. Membranes fused; some were lost. The
motile proteins moved around to various portions of the host cells,
which began as *Thermoplasma*-like bacteria but became mastigotes.
Eventually microtubules, which had originally entered as part of the
motility apparatus of the spirochetes, were used in the process of
mitosis; they became mitotic microtubules.

Even today tubulins function in the microtubule-based processes
of morphogenetic movement and growth in cells. It is possible that
actin and myosin proteins, which display motility based on their
fibrils, also came in with spirochetes. Importantly, tubulins and tub-
ule-associated proteins of spirochetes were preadapted to evolve into
undulipodia; soon they were used for the intracellular motility so
characteristic of eukaryotes and absent in bacteria. Thus, the integration of spirochetes and the *Thermoplasma*-like host to form a new
entity is, in itself, the first step of eukaryosis.

Spirochete Morphology and Motility

Spirochetes are distinguished from other bacteria by their form. They
are Gram-negative, heterotrophic, helical, and highly motile. None
are photosynthetic. Spirochetes have paired flagella in the periplasm,
inside the outer membrane of the Gram-negative cell wall. By definition, a helically motile bacterium with flagella inside the outer
membrane of the Gram-negative wall is a spirochete. In spirilla and
other bacteria, the flagella actually project from the cell walls. Spirochete flagella are composed of flagellin, a class of proteins comprising bacterial flagella in general. Many different kinds of
spirochetes exist; all are motile and helical. Each spirochete has a
central protoplasmic cylinder, the main body of the cell in which the
ribosomes, DNA, and other structures are found. Microtubules have
been seen in the protoplasmic cylinders of large spirochetes (e.g.,

Pillotina, Hollandina); borrelias and even other large spirochetes (e.g., *Cristispira*) lack cytoplasmic microtubules. Like other motile bacteria, spirochetes possess basal rotary flagellum motors. In some treponema spirochetes tiny cytoplasmic tubules are found on the inner face of these basal rotary motors, suggesting that these microtubules are connected to the motility act of spirochetes.

Helical motility is best described by analogy with the form and movement of a corkscrew, although a helically motile organism is autonomously locomotive. In the shape of a helix, the motile bacterium moves through a viscous medium like a corkscrew moves through cork. This type of movement is characteristic of spirochetes, spirilla, and certain other kinds of bacteria (e.g., *Saprospira*). They can move through dense or viscous media, such as muds and gelatinous materials, far more effectively than rod or coccoid microbes, which are not helically motile.

I suspect that spirochetes, as autonomous heterotrophic organisms, swam in the Archean eon in search of nutrients; today, spirochetes inhabit anaerobic, viscous, organic-rich environments. In such environments, millenia ago, spirochete ancestors associated with other bacteria which inadvertantly disintegrated or photosynthesized and thus spewed all kinds of foodstuffs across their borders. While feeding on exudates of other bacteria, certain spirochetes produced enough sticky substance to cause them to adhere to the surfaces of their potential food sources (figure 5). In some cases, casual adherence to less-motile or nonmotile microorganisms became very strict; in this attached state the spirochetes retained their motility and proceeded to move in various directions. Bundled at one end, spirochetes initiated "motility symbioses." The larger chimeric organism was then able to move with greater facility because of the activities of its adhering spirochetes. Motility was the primary selective advantage in the acquisition of spirochetes.

As I learned about the large number of undulipodiated protists lacking mitochondria and the probability that mitochondria are polyphyletic, I decided that the acquisition of motility preceded that of mitochondria: the integration of a spirochete with a *Thermoplasma*-like archaeobacterium was the first step toward the evolution of the nucleocytoplasmic component of all eukaryotic cells. Present-day spirochetes (figure 6) enter and apparently feed within other cells (fig-

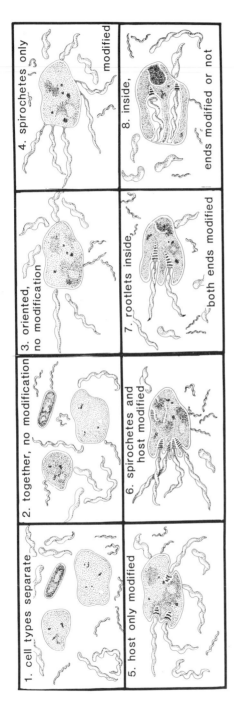

Figure 5
Hypothesized sequence of origin of undulipodia from spirochetes: (1) Spirochetes and archaeobacteria coexist as separate cell types. (2) Unmodified spirochetes feed on metabolic products supplied by archaeobacteria. (3) Spirochetes recognize archaeobacterium, eventually attach, and form close associations. (4) Modified spirochete attachment sites provide the archaeobacterium with enhanced motility. (5) Host is modified at attachment site. (6) and (7) The spirochete-archaeobacterium complex leads to the first lineage of undulipodiated protists. (8) Parts of spirochetes that have been engulfed entirely by their hosts are internally deployed, leading to early protist lineages.

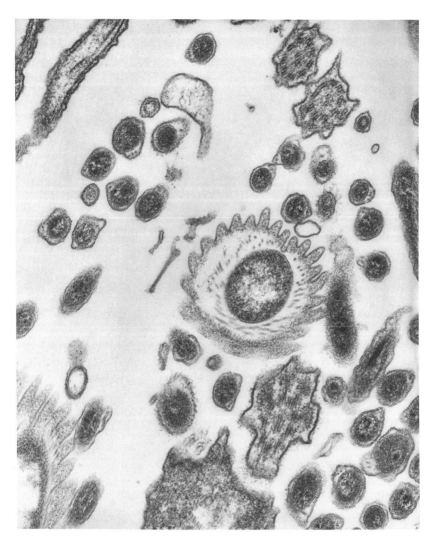

Figure 6
Pillotina and other smaller spirochetes inside the lumen of the hindgut of the termite
Reticulitermes hesperus. Transverse section in electron micrograph.

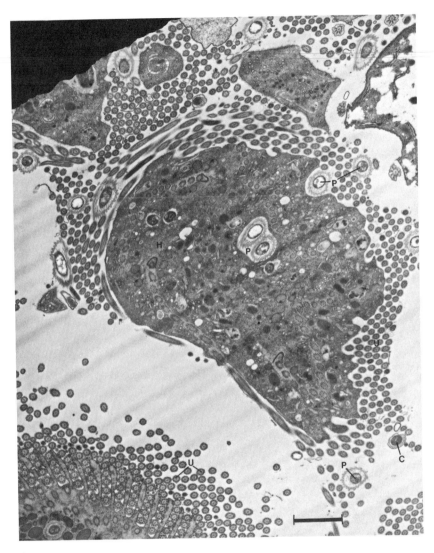

Figure 7

Hypermastigote (H) containing *Pillotina* (P) spirochetes in its cytoplasm with free-swimming *Pillotina* in the hindgut lumen. Bar = 2.0 μm; U = undulipodia; C = *Clevelandina* spirochete.

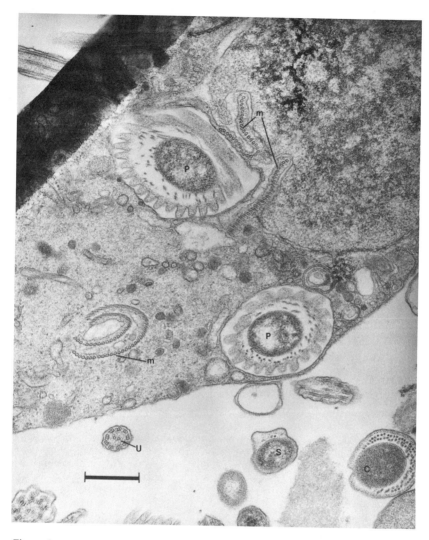

Figure 8
Pillotina inside the cytoplasm of an unidentified pyrsonymphid-like protist. Bar =
0.5 μm; m = microtubules; P = *Pillotina* spirochete; C = *Clevelandina* spirochete; S =
unidentified spirochete; U = undulipodia.

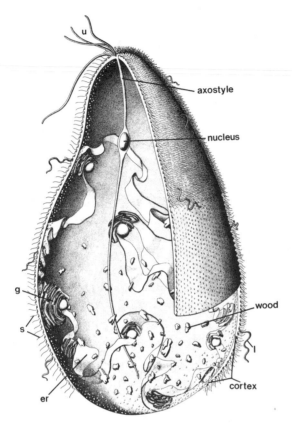

Figure 9
Mixotricha paradoxa hypermastigote protist from termite *Mastotermes darwinensis*. The whole cell is motile by virtue of its symbiotic surface spirochetes. Small spirochetes (s) cover the surface; a few larger spirochetes are also present. *M. paradoxa* also has four undulipodia (u) at the anterior end. g = Golgi apparatus; er = endoplasmic reticulum.

ures 7 and 8). As they do today, spirochetes must have penetrated their hosts. In the symbiotic hypothesis such spirochete penetration eventually led to the assimilation of spirochete replicative mechanisms and the intrinsic motility prerequisite to the emergence of mitosis and meiotic sexuality.

Spirochetes form amazing motility symbioses with other organisms. The organism known as *Mixotricha paradoxa* (figure 9) is exemplary in this respect. Found in the hindgut of an Australian termite,

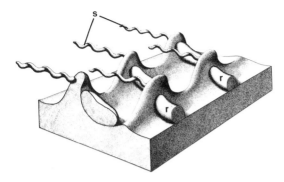

Figure 10
Close-up of *M. paradoxa* cortex. Rod-shaped bacteria (r) lie in grooves on the surface of *M. paradoxa*. Each is associated with a small *Treponema* spirochete (s).

Mixotricha, a large protist, is a eukaryote that lacks mitochondria; it is beset with spirochetes. Bearing approximately half a million spirochetes on its surface, each of these spirochetes reproduces, by transverse cell division, so that just before cell division *Mixotricha* bears about a million spirochetes. After protist cell division there are, once again, about 500,000 spirochetes on each offspring cell. *Mixotricha* moves by virtue of undulating, surface symbiotic spirochetes. The association of the large protist and its spirochetes, coupled with the intrinsic motility of the spirochetes, enables the consortium to swim forward through the termite's gut. *Mixotricha paradoxa* provides a wonderful example of a motility symbiosis, a consortium of a protist not only with surface *Treponema* spirochetes but also with several other kinds of bacteria. Large, arbitrarily associated, unidentified spirochetes decorate *Mixotricha*'s surface. In addition to its spirochetes, *Mixotricha* bears rod-shaped bacteria on its surface and coccoid symbiotic bacteria in its cytoplasm. Cross-sections of the rod-shaped bacteria and attachments of spirochetes are shown in figure 10. These *Mixotricha* spirochetes are certainly not undulipodia. More precisely, they are not cilia, as they superficially appear to be; rather, they are externally attached symbiotic spirochetes. Though *Mixotricha* appears to be a single individual acting as a unified whole, it is in fact an association of at least five originally separate microorganisms.

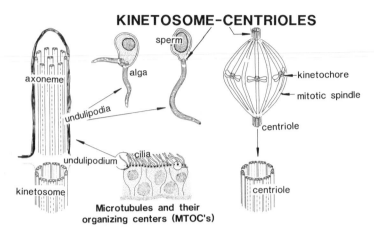

Figure 11
Relation of kinetosomes, centrioles and spindles, [9(2) + 2] microtubules structures in undulipodia, sperm tails, cilia, and ciliated epithelium. Kinetosomes and centrioles are homologous; both have a [9(3) + 0] structure.

Microtubule Structures: Spindles, Kinetosomes, Centrioles, and Undulipodia

This kind of association between spirochetes and other microbes is hypothesized to be a precursor of the origin of mitosis—and then the meiotic sexual process. The directly homologous relationship between undulipodia and the mitotic spindle, long described in the zoological and cytological literature, is diagrammed in figure 11. In some protists (e.g., ciliates), the undulipodia reproduce as a consequence of their kinetosome reproduction (figure 12). In others (e.g., *Lophomonas, Barbulanympha*), the undulipodia reproduce and, as they separate, a proteinaceous spindle apparatus behaves exactly as poles of any mitotic spindle, but the undulipodia are still attached to it. Such well-documented relationships of undulipodia and their kinetosomes with mitotic spindles, as seen today in protists, are interpreted within symbiotic theory as a legacy of undulipodial origin from spirochetes whose components became moving parts of the mitotic spindle. Direct relationships between undulipodia and spindle are readily visible in trypanosomes, retortamonads, dinomastigotes, and other protoctists.

The evolutionary relationship among centrioles, kinetosomes,

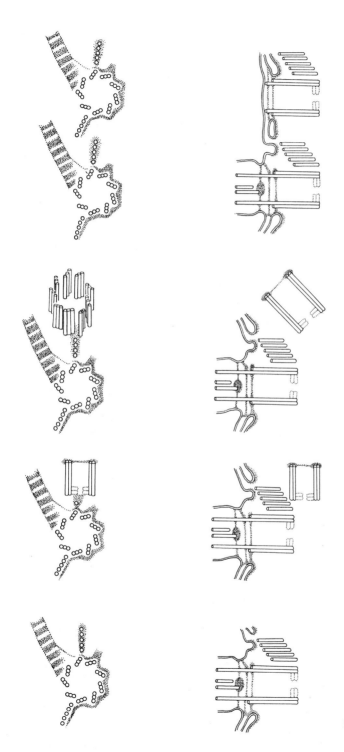

Figure 12
Kinetosome reproduction. This sequence shows the replication of a ciliate kinetosome in transverse (top) and longitudinal (bottom) section. New kinetosomes form at right angles to the old ones and rotate into position adjacent to the parent kinetosome. From the new kinetosome, the axoneme will grow and form the undulipodium.

undulipodia, and the mitotic spindle—the derivation of one from the other over time—can be seen concretely in the dinomastigote *Syndinium*. This organism has two cylinder-shaped organelles, which might be identified as centrioles because a mitotic spindle is formed between them. They are actually kinetosomes from *Syndinium*'s two undulipodia. During mitotic division, *Syndinium*'s undulipodia retract and microtubules form between them; the two former kinetosomes are now centrioles. This microtubule spindle segregates the chromatin. Such mitotic functions may be viewed as the legacy of the use of the motile apparatus of undulipodia in the type of cell motility that segregates chromosomes. The undulipodia plausibly evolved from the earliest acquired symbionts, conferring the immediate selective advantage of rapid motility on the host cell, whereas mitosis arose polyphyletically in a series of evolutionary steps, at least some of which are partially discernible today in protoctists such as *Syndinium*.

A phylogenetic tree of life schematically depicts the possible evolutionary trajectory beginning with bacteria at the roots (see chapter 10, figure 2). Spirochetes, attracted to the nutritious environment of other microbes, eventually attached to these other organisms and, in the course of evolution, formed symbiotic consortia. The attachment of spirochetes to other microbes was selected for primarily because of the advantage of motility—as in the case of *Mixotricha*, which is mobile by virtue of its spirochetes. Moreover, since spirochete feeding proceeded faster inside the microbes, certain spirochetes penetrated their hosts (figure 7). Such attempted penetration probably led to the infection and death of countless hosts. However, the symbiosis hypothesis further suggests that in certain cases the spirochetes must have come under the control of their hosts. Possibly on account of an initially fortuitous congruence between the ratio of spirochete and host-cell divisions, some rate of survival prevailed in spirochete-host associations. At this stage the host bacterium—most likely an archaeobacterium like today's *Thermoplasma*—possessed its own DNA, RNA, ribosomes, and structural proteins. Integration of spirochete and archaeobacteria led to protein deployment in a series of steps resulting in accurate segregation of the two originally separate sets of DNA. Such integrating phenomena led to the emergence of mastigotes, early protists with chromosomes and mitotic spindles.

A very peculiar relationship between the kinetosomes of undulipodia and the "naked kinetosomes" or centrioles in the mitotic spindle division has been observed in many living protists. Biologists generally agree that centrioles [9(3) + 0] are identical in structure to the kinetosomes [9(3) + 0] of undulipodia. The single difference is that a kinetosome bears the shaft (called an axoneme), whereas a centriole, with the same [9(3) + 0] structure, lacks the shaft. This kinetosome-centriole structure is about 0.25 μm × 2.0 μm in nearly all cells studied. It is this "enigmatic" structure that is postulated to have originated from spirochete attachment sites. Centrioles, kinetosomes, and kinetochores and the relationships among them are depicted in figure 12. These structures, when at the poles of mitotic spindles, are called *centrioles*. The centrioles are connected to chromosomes via microtubules, which terminate at points on the chromosomes known as *kinetochores*. Since the development of light microscopy early in the twentieth century, centrioles have been defined as those structures observable at the poles of the spindle during mitosis—especially in large animal cells, such as eggs.

Traditionally, centromeres have been considered equivalents of kinetochores. Until very recently, our understanding of these structures was quite deficient; they had some 27 different names (e.g., spindle fiber attachments, chromosome constrictions, kinetochores, centromeres). Although the kinetochores of animal cells and plant cells differ, they are always found at the junctures where bundles of microtubules (spindle fibers) attach to the chromosomal points (centromeres, kinetochores). The smallest kinetochores are points where a single microtubule attaches to chromatin: the largest ones are complex, with many microtubules and with other structures analogous to a ball-and-socket joint.

The insight that centrioles are [9(3) + 0] microtubules occurred only after the emergence of electron microscopy, which revealed that the ultrastructure of a centriole is identical to that of a kinetosome. A kinetosome is the [9(3) + 0] microtubule structure at the base of an undulipodium. If an axoneme is present the base is called a kinetosome; when no axoneme (and not even a stub of the undulipodium) emerges, the [9(3) + 0] body is defined as a centriole. The [9(3) + 0] microtubular structure that sits at the pole in mitosis is also, by definition, a centriole. Confusion arises in the literature when light-microscopy nomenclature (e.g., "division center," "aster") is applied to structures revealed more precisely through electron microscopy (e.g., the microtubule-organizing center). The fact that these structures are dynamic—centrioles move, disappear, grow, reproduce, and in general become kinetosomes during the life cycle of a cell—leads to further terminological confusion.

The organization of the kinetosome is probably an evolutionary relic of the association between spirochetes and their hosts. A naked centriole does not seem to have a function, as D. N. Wheatley noted in his 1982 book *The Centriole: A Central Enigma of Cell Biology*. At certain times the centriole seems to organize microtubules; it acts as a microtubule organizing center (figure 13). According to symbiosis theory, the centriole is an evolutionary legacy of spirochete motility associations that were prerequisite to eukaryotic cell origins. Centrioles are retained in cells that develop microtubules at later stages of their ontogeny. Thus, centrioles are nearly ubiquitous in protoctists, animals, and motile plant sperm, without always exhibiting an obvious function. They are actually vestiges of evolution.

Spirochete Microtubules?

Is present-day spirochete structure related to the ninefold microtubular array of undulipodia? Can [9(2) + 2] structure be found in spirochetes? The relation between the structure of present-day spirochetes and undulipodia is of central significance. A spirochete with bacterial flagella in its periplasm may also have tubules in its protoplasmic cylinder. There is no evidence whatsoever of flagella or flagellin protein in any undulipodia. If the hypothesis of phylogenetic relatedness is correct, then the immotile, oar-like flagella were lost in the transformation from spirochete to undulipodium. However, motility generation was retained along with internal microtubules in the protoplasmic cylinder. Though [9(2) + 2] tubulin structures are unrelated to bacterial flagella, they may be related to the cytoplasmic tubules found inside spirochete protoplasmic cylinders.

The serial endosymbiosis theory does not require that the [9(2) + 2] symmetry be present in all spirochetes, nor even that it be present in any spirochetes. No known free-living spirochete has the [9(2) + 2] array of microtubules, or even a simple ninefold symmetry of

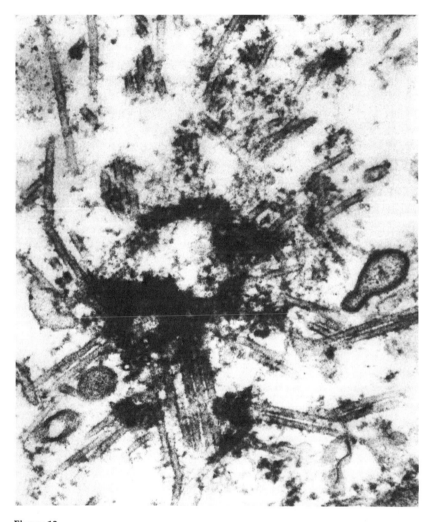

Figure 13
Electron micrograph of microtubule-organizing center (MTOC) in a protist.

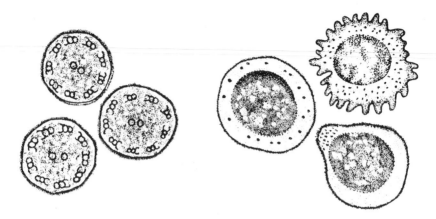

Figure 14
Undulipodia and spirochetes. Axonemes of undulipodia (left) are 0.25 μm in diameter. Large spirochetes vary in diameter from 0.25 μm to 2.0 μm. (Drawing not to scale.)

them; but if one were found, such a spirochete would be the best candidate for the bacterial codescendant of undulipodia. However, the theory does not stand or fall on such a discovery, since microtubules are found in many different arrays in protists and even in the spirochetes in which tubules have been seen. Certain spirochetes may have tubules in a ninefold symmetry, but it is also possible that microtubules formed other patterns which became [9(2) + 2] in the course of undulipodial evolution (figure 14). The ninefold array may be related to the origin of the kinetosome as a spirochete attachment site. In other words, [9(2) + 2] may be an epiphenomenon, a product of the association that was not present in unassociated ancestors. Nevertheless, microtubular tubulins (i.e., proteins associated with motility) are predicted to be present in certain spirochetes: those phylogenetically closest to the ancestors of undulipodia.

The conjecture that spirochete-like bacteria are ancestral to the undulipodium would be strengthened by evidence of features common to undulipodia and present-day spirochetes. Microtubules composed of alpha and beta tubulin protein, major constituents of undulipodia, are characteristically present in eukaryotes but generally absent from prokaryotes. If microtubules originated in spirochetes, then—even though they are, as a rule, absent in other

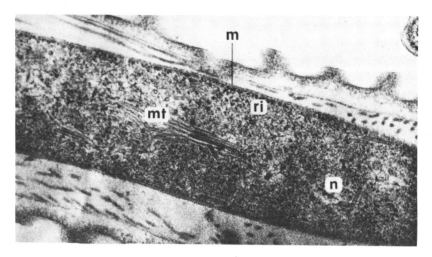

Figure 15
Pillotina spirochete (electron micrograph of longitudinal section, by A. Hollande and
I. Gharazoghou). Cytoplasmic tubules (mt), approximately 24 nm in diameter, are
visible inside the protoplasmic cylinder. ri = ribosomes; n = nucleoid.

arbitrarily chosen bacteria—they may still be present in certain
spirochetes.

Pillotina spirochetes (figure 15) have microtubular structures. With
the exception of this spirochete and a few others, microtubules are
absent from bacteria. My prediction is that if *Pillotina* belongs to that
group of spirochetes which entered consortia and evolved into undulipodia, then the microtubules of *Pillotina* should be composed of
tubulin proteins. It must be stressed that although alpha and beta
tubulins are universal in eukaryotes, they are entirely unknown in
bacteria such as *Escherichia coli* and *Bacillus subtilis*. Tubulin proteins,
microtubules, mitotic spindles, centrioles, and kinetosomes, all distinctive structures of eukaryotes, are conspicuously absent from
E. coli and other prokaryotes. The implication of the hypothesis of
the spirochete origin of undulipodia is that, just as chlorophyll *b* is
present in specific phototrophic bacteria thought to be ancestral to
chloroplasts (e.g., *Prochloron*), microtubules and microtubule proteins
ought to be limited to certain bacteria, such as those spirochetes that
are extant forms of the ancestors to the undulipodia.

Tubulin-Like Proteins in Spirochetes

Are the microtubules observed in spirochetes composed of tubulin? A methodological approach to this question is the labeling of tubulin proteins with specific antibodies. Alpha and beta tubulins, which make up walls of microtubules, are found in all mitotic spindles, centrioles, and kinetosomes, in all undulipodia, and also in the microtubules of the axons and dendrites of nerve cells of the spinal column and brain of all mammals. Found throughout the eukaryotic world but absent from prokaryotes, alpha and beta tubulin are recognized to be homologous proteins. Did these proteins that form tubules originate from spirochetes? Using the technique of immunocytochemistry, an antibody is produced by injecting a rabbit (or some other antibody-producing animal) with tubulin protein from brain, undulipodium, or mitotic spindle. The rabbit makes highly specific antibodies against the brain tubulin. The specific antibody made in the rabbit's blood is purified. Rabbit serum containing the antibody is treated with a solution of immunoglobulin G, a nonspecific antibody made in a goat. The immunoglobulin G "carries a candle"— that is, it is stained, or bound, to fluoroscein, a small fluorescent molecule. These successful treatments allow the identification of a material suspected to be tubulin. The fluorescent antibody reaction can be detected with a fluorescence light microscope. Antibody treatment allows visualization of a specific, fluorescent reaction against authentic tubulin, if tubulin exists. When this specific antitubulin-antibody fluorescence staining reaction is tried with any of the aforementioned tubulins—indeed, with any authentic tubulin—one sees a bright fluorescence indicating the presence of tubulin. Now the crucial question is whether tubulin can be detected by immunofluorescence in spirochetes.

Micrographs of spirochetes illuminated by ultraviolet light reveal the fluorescent material present in spirochetes treated with the antitubulin antibody. The antibody had been made against guinea pig brain microtubules. Various spirochetes glow. In the same preparations, any undulipodia—cilia, sperm tails, etc.—also glow. Antitubulin antibody fluorescence was first detected in spirochetes that cannot be grown in cultures (the large *Pillotina* spirochetes symbiotic in termites); however, *Hollandina*, *Pillotina*, and several other spirochetes (which we cannot, at this point, even identify) exhibited the same fluorescence, and as powerfully as the undulipodia in the same cytological preparations. Working with graduate student Leleng To, I saw strong antitubulin antibody fluorescence in *Spirochaeta bajacaliforniensis*, a spirochete we isolated from the microbial mats of Baja California. David Bermudes extended this work; he showed fluorescence in the purified proteins from *Spirochaeta bajacaliforniensis* and demonstrated the reaction in both *Spirochaeta halophila* and *Spirochaeta littoralis*. He confirmed that treponemes, the spirochetes that cause syphilis, do not exhibit the fluorescence. So far, only the closely related spirochetes of the genus *Spirochaeta*, along with the larger spirochetes of termites, show the antitubulin-antibody fluorescence. *Bacillus subtillis*, *E. coli*, *Arthromitus*, and other bacteria randomly tested do not show this reaction. *Azotobacter*, a bacterium completely different from spirochetes, may also show the antitubulin antibody fluorescence; this claim, which appeared in an unpublished report by Michael Adams of Eastern Connecticut State College, needs to be verified. The presence of proteins with tubulin characteristics in spirochetes and perhaps other bacteria has been demonstrated. Is it coincidental that, among 10,000 or so different kinds of bacteria lacking tubulin, tubulin-like protein is conspicuous in spirochetes? Tubulin-like protein in spirochetes is consistent with—but does not prove—the hypothesis that the undulipodium evolved from free-living spirochetes. The antigenic activity, the existence of a protein that is recognizable by an antitubulin antibody, is consistent with the spirochete hypothesis. But the prediction can be refined further: it should be possible to isolate and characterize tubulin protein in such spirochetes. Since homology is easily demonstrated between the tubulin in sperm tails, in brain tissue, in the mitotic spindle apparatus, and in all other sources of tubulin, such homology—by hypothesis—should be detectable in the tubulin-like proteins of certain spirochetes as well.

Testing the prediction that spirochetes contain proteins homologous to tubulins requires a huge number of spirochetes. Purification steps identical to those used in the standard isolation and purification of brain tubulin were applied to suspensions of spirochetes. When heated, these proteins form fibers; when cooled, they go into solution. The property of transformation from the solid pellet to the liquid

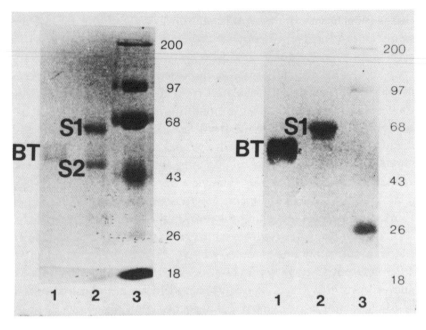

Figure 16
Tubulin-like proteins in spirochetes. Left: Gel-electrophoresis separation of proteins.
Lane 1 contains purified brain tubulin; lane 2 contains tubulin-like proteins S1 and
S2 from spirochetes obtained using tubulin purification techniques; lane 3 is a series
of molecular-weight markers. Right: Western blot of gel-separated proteins. The proteins in the gel at left have been transferred to a special membrane and stained with
an antibody to tubulin. The brain-tubulin band and the S1 band are clearly visible,
indicating a positive result.

phase is quite rare in proteins generally. A photograph derived from
gel electrophoresis of a spirochete preparation is reproduced here as
figure 16. Authentic brain tubulin protein appears in the middle (lane
1, BT). The purified preparations from spirochetes (lane 2) show two
major bands of proteins (S1, S2) resembling the tubulin protein of
brain. The heavier one, S1, is seen toward the top of the gel; it is the
protein closest to authentic brain tubulin, in that it displays the
antibody activity.

Both spirochete protein and brain tubulins are acidic, having a
large number of COOH groups in their structure; accordingly, they
tend to migrate to the positive pole in an electric field. Whereas brain
tubulin has a molecular weight of 50 kilodaltons as calculated from
sequence data, yet shows up as 55 kd on gels, the tubulin-like protein

Table 1
Similarities of brain and undulipodial tubulin with *Spirochaeta bajacaliforniensis* proteins S1 and S2.

	Brain tubulin	*Spirochaeta* tubulin-like protein (S1,S2)
Molecular weight	50 kd	65 kd (S1)
Purification	Temperature cycling (polymerize at 37°C)	Temperature cycling (polymerize at 37°C)
Structure	24-nm tubules	5–7-nm fibers
Antibody to brain tubulin	+,+	+,−
GTP sensitivity	+	−
Isoelectric points	5.1–5.3	5.9, 5.5
Sequence data	Several complete sequences available[a]	Limited[b]
Polymerization: colchicine sensitivity	+,−	−
Stabilization by taxol	+	+

a. M. Little and T. Seehaus, *Comparative Biochemistry and Physiology* 90B (1988): 655–670.
b. G. Tzertzinis, Immunochemical Characterizations and Partial Amino Acid Sequence of Tubulin-like Protein from *Spirochaeta bajacaliforniensis*, Ph.D. dissertation, Boston University, 1989.

S1 of spirochetes on gels has a molecular weight of 65 kd. The protein of spirochetes, although clearly heavier than brain tubulin, shows antigenic activity to an antibody made against brain tubulin. The antibody reaction apparently occurs because tubulin-like protein of spirochetes shares epitopes with brain and undulipodial tubulins. Table 1 lists their similarities.

The antigenic activity alone implies that homology between spirochete tubulin and brain tubulin is highly plausible. The antigenic activity suggests that the percentage of identity in amino acid sequence is 30, 40, or even 80—at least, at the epitope (the part of the protein reacting with the antigen). Even at the level of 10 percent of the sequence in common, a cogent argument for homology can be advanced. For example, a protein in *E. coli* called EFTU (elongation factor–temperature unsensitive) was once thought to be actin on the basis of molecular weight, reaction with calcium, and other physical properties. Later the homology of this protein to muscle actin was firmly rejected on the basis of sequence data. No identity at all in any sequence of more than two amino acids was found. Thus, a common run of four or five amino acids of spirochete tubulin-like protein and brain tubulin would by itself provide a case for homology. George Tzertzinis has acquired amino acid sequence data for the S1 spirochete protein that show some homology to tubulins alpha, beta, and gamma. Although attempts are underway to obtain the entire sequence (approximately 600 amino acid residues), the full extent of homology is still unknown. (R. Obar and G. Tzertzinis have sequenced approximately 80 percent of the gene coding for the S1 protein of *Spirochaeta bajacaliforniensis;* they have unequivocal evidence that the protein belongs to a recently characterized class of proteins, known to be involved in symbiosis, called "chaperonins" or "60-kd heat shock proteins.") A 65-kd protein sharing an antigenic site (an epitope) with brain tubulin is present in at least two spirochetes (*Spirochaeta bajacaliforniensis* and *Spirochaeta halophila*) and absent from other arbitrarily chosen bacteria.

With respect to the question of whether undulipodial (eukaryotic) motility is mono- or polyphyletic, there are many types of spirochetes, and among them many have formed associations with other organisms in today's world. (See figures 5 and 6.) Because of the extremely conservative nature of the [9(2) + 2] structure, I suspect that acquisition of spirochetes gave rise to undulipodial motility monophyletically. However, the origin of mitosis from spirochete-motility-associated ancestors was most likely polyphyletic, appearing in various forms and morphologies in different protists. Clearly there is polyphyly crossing the mitotic border, just as there is polyphyly in flying or swimming among organisms. The distribution of huge quantities of DNA is under severe selection pressure. The problem of moving DNA was solved variously in different organisms. Although most protists have undulipodiated common ancestors, the actual mitotic process itself seems to have evolved independently— perhaps a few dozen times. Independent evolution probably occurred among many different groups, such as the dinomastigotes, the ameba-related groups (slime molds and amebomastigotes, for example), and the hypermastigotes. Nevertheless, all these organisms probably come from common undulipodiated ancestors. Analogously, all animals have common blastula-forming ancestors, yet flying evolved independently in maybe six or seven different insect, reptilian, and mammalian animal groups.

A retrospective overview of the symbiotic theory of the origin of eukaryotes provides a backdrop for the spirochete hypothesis. That mitochondria derive from *Paracoccus*-type respiring bacteria, entering cells in a *Bdellovibrio* fashion, is strongly supported by research comparing the molecular structures of free-living bacteria and mito-chondria. Further, it seems a plausible conjecture that the nucleocy-toplasm may be traced to *Thermoplasma*-like archaeobacteria, but additional research is required. The best-grounded aspect of sym-biotic theory is that all plastids (chloroplasts, chrysoplasts, etc.) evolved by symbiotic acquisition of phototrophic bacteria. The weak-est aspect of symbiotic theory is the hypothesis that spirochetes are the ancestors of undulipodia. A number of predictions that follow from this spirochete hypothesis are currently being tested in the laboratory; whether undulipodia evolved from free-living spirochetes should be definitively established or rejected by the turn of the century. Whether or not the spirochete theory of the origin of undu-lipodia is ultimately correct, the conception of the eukaryotic cell as a consortium, a chimera, a mosaic entity, seems to be as firmly established within biological science as the chromosomal theory of heredity.

Readings

Fracek, S. P., Jr., and J. F. Stoltz. 1985. *Spirochaeta bajacaliforniensis* sp. n. from a microbial mat community at Laguna Figueroa, Baja, California Norte, Mexico. *Archives of Microbiology* 142: 317–325.

Hinkle, G. 1991. Current status of the theory of the symbiotic origin of undulipodia. In *Symbiosis as a Source of Evolutionary Innovation: Speciation and Morphogenesis*, ed. L. Margulis and R. Fester. MIT Press.

Margulis, L. 1992. *Symbiosis in Cell Evolution.* Second edition. Freeman.

Margulis, L., D. Bermudes, and G. Tzertzinis. 1987. Prokaryotic origin of undulipodia: Application of the Panda Principle to the centriole enigma. *Endocytology III* 503: 187–197.

Margulis, L., and M. McMenamin. 1990. Marriage of convenience: The motil-ity of the modern cell may reflect an ancient symbiotic union. *The Sciences,* September-October: 31–37.

Raikov, I. B. 1982. *The Protozoan Nucleus, Morphology and Evolution.* Springer-Verlag.

12

Life in the Late Proterozoic

Andrew Knoll

The late Proterozoic was an age of worldwide expansion of microbial communities, including some in which eukaryotes were common in the open-ocean habitat as plankton. In this chapter Andrew Knoll, Professor of Biology and Geology at Harvard University, describes and interprets sedimentary rocks containing preserved remains of both planktonic and benthic microbial communities from the Draken Formation.

Although the Archean eon and the early Proterozoic encompass nearly 3 billion years, the rock record of these eons provides little direct evidence of the organisms that lived on the young Earth. Sedimentary rocks of this age are limited in volume and are often highly metamorphosed. The few fossils are scattered both in time and in space. Consequently, most of what we know about the earliest history of life must be gleaned from geochemical evidence in the rocks. In contrast, the fossil record of the late Proterozoic eon—particularly of the period from approximately 1 billion years ago to the beginning of the Cambrian period, 570 million years ago—is rich and varied. Late Proterozoic microfossils and stromatolites are found on all continents and in rocks representing a wide diversity of environments. Traditionally, Precambrian microorganisms are discussed in a vertical time sequence; fossil assemblages of varying ages are compared. Here, in order to illustrate the richness and complexity of the record, the focus will be on a single time slice. The ecological and geographical distribution of life at a given moment in late Precambrian history, roughly 800 million years ago, will be examined.

Earth's history begins approximately 4.5 billion years ago with the planet's origin. The oldest known sedimentary rocks, found at Isua in southwestern Greenland, are approximately 3.8 billion years old. Certain features of these rocks—the presence of graphitic carbon and some isotopic fractionation in the carbon—suggest the possibility of life's presence at that time. But because these rocks are highly metamorphosed—that is, altered by heat and pressure—no fossils have been preserved. Slightly younger rocks, about 3.5 billion years old, provide the first firm evidence of life. Rock sequences from southern Africa and western Australia contain evidence of early prokaryotes, including photoautotrophs. Moving along a billion years or so, we come to a major geological transition that separates the Archean eon from the Proterozoic. At this time Earth witnessed a very rapid growth in continental crust. About 2.5 billion years ago, large stable continents emerged for the first time. We recognize this event as the beginning of the Proterozoic eon. Slightly younger, in rocks about 2 billion years old, are the famous biotas of the Gunflint Iron Formation in southern Canada and, equally important, the Belcher microbiota from the Hudson Bay region. Both suggest that the early Proterozoic world contained an essentially modern prokaryotic biota, complete with cyanobacteria and other aerobic and anaerobic prokaryotes. Fossils between 1.6 billion and 1.8 billion years old provide the earliest fairly persuasive evidence of eukaryotic cells. The first record of multicellular tissue, which characterizes the metazoans, is from 670 million years ago. And finally, at 570 million years ago, we have the Precambrian-Cambrian boundary. Here skeletalization becomes widespread, permitting the documentation of an impressive diversity of invertebrate animals and seaweeds.

The Draken Conglomerate Formation: A Fossil Lagoonal Complex

The time slice that I am going to focus on, about 800 million years ago, comes after the origin of the larger, more complex eukaryotes and before the first major diversification of metazoans. Svalbard is an archipelago halfway between Norway and the North Pole. Two islands in this group, Spitzbergen and Nordauslandet, each contain some 6,000 meters of folded but unmetamorphosed late Proterozoic sedimentary rock deposited between 850 million years ago and the base of the Cambrian, 570 million years ago. This succession was deposited in a rapidly subsiding epicontinental basin that eventually opened up to become Iapetus, the forerunner of the Atlantic Ocean. From the compositions, textures, and sedimentary structures of these rocks, it is possible to deduce that they were deposited under a variety of environmental conditions, ranging from supratidal to off-shore marine. Recognize that just as a modern microbial ecologist needs information on physical environments—depth and salinity, for example—the paleoecologist, in trying to deduce environments in which ancient microorganisms lived, is also interested in knowing these factors. This environmental context must be acquired in the field while inspecting the sedimentary rocks in which the microfossils are found. At the outcrop or regional level, one can correlate the physical characteristics of the rock with the types of environments in which sediments are deposited. Features of the rock sequence are compared against modern depositional environments. This analysis is essential because it helps constrain depositional environments and leads to a more accurate picture of life in a particular context.

Hundreds of sample sites in the Svalbard archipelago have yielded fossil remains, but none are more striking than those of the 700–800-million-year-old Draken Conglomerate Formation. The predominantly carbonate rocks in this formation are exposed in U-shaped glacially cut valleys (figure 1). The Draken Formation consists of repeating beds of stromatolites, oolites, and the intraformational carbonate conglomerates from which it takes its name. The most conspicuous indicators of the presence of life in the Draken Formation are stromatolites. Stromatolites are sedimentary rock structures, the remains of the activities of microbial communities. From the diversity and distribution of stromatolites in the Draken and associated formations, it is possible to state that distinctive microbial communities having cyanobacteria as principal mat builders blanketed large expanses of the shallow sea floor 800 million years ago, living wherever such communities were not limited by available light, strong and persistent currents, high rates of sedimentary influx, or the growth of seaweeds. In contrast with the modern situation, then, microbial mats were widely distributed in shallow seas of normal as well as high salinity. Valuable paleobiological information is contained in stromatolites. It is possible to use them as proxies for ancient microbial communities and see something of the environmental heterogeneity and distribution of those ancient communities, even though

Figure 1
The landscape of Spitzbergen. Some 7,000 meters of late Proterozoic carbonate strata are exposed in glacially cut valleys.

the microfossils themselves are not preserved. In fact, very few of the stromatolites from late Proterozoic rocks contain microfossils. The limited record of organically preserved remains of stromatolitic micro-benthos comes mainly from chert nodules, in which stromatolitic carbonate has been replaced by silica.

In the Draken Formation, history is told by the gravel-size bits of carbonate mud that were originally deposited in a quiet lagoon or back reef area and were later ripped up and redeposited locally during periodic floods or storms. The black areas were preferentially silicified after redeposition. The chert itself is colorless; the black color comes from the preservation of organic matter within the silica. For the most part, the silicified shards are ripped fragments of microbial mats. It is here that the best microfossils are found. A look at the properties of carbonate and chert reveals the reasons for this. Carbonates, such as limestone and dolomite, are fairly easy to recrystallize. They are porous, and oxidizing solutions can infiltrate them at any time after formation. Thus, it is difficult for carbonates to preserve organic-walled microfossils in the long term. Chert, which

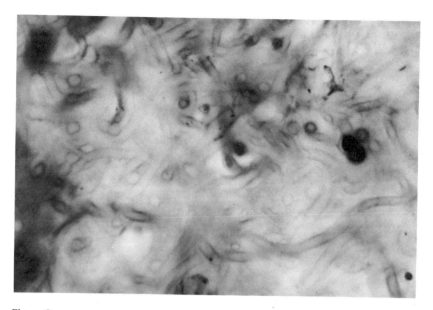

Figure 2

Filaments of *Eomycetopsis*, a cyanobacterial mat builder from the Draken Formation, are visible in this petrographic thin section of microbial-mat fragment. The filaments are 5–8 μm in diameter.

does not recrystallize readily and is much less permeable, in essence acts like bioplastic; it encases the organic microbial remains in a protective silica medium. One can simply take a sample of the chert and make a paper-thin section, a fairly standard geological procedure. The thin section is viewed under the optical microscope in much the same way live preparations of modern microbes are viewed.

Mat-Dwelling Prokaryotes and Lagoonal Plankton

Some 40 species of microfossils have been identified from the Draken Formation to date. Figure 2 is a highly magnified photomicrograph of one of those ripped-up microbial-mat clasts. Those individual squiggles can be resolved into filamentous cyanobacteria 5–8 μm in diameter. Based on the high density and the interwoven pattern of individuals in this population, I interpret them to be principal mat builders within a portion of the Draken lagoon. In fact, five morpho-

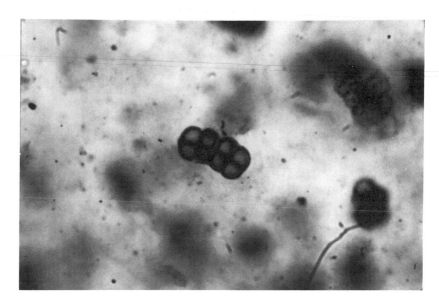

Figure 3
The spherical mat-dwelling organism *Sphaerophycus wilsonii*. In this group of individuals, arranged in a double tetrad, each individual cell is about 4 μm in diameter.

logically distinct types of mat builders have been identified within these deposits, representing differentiated microbial-mat communities that lived along the supratidal-to-subtidal gradient. Mat-dwelling microorganisms are also preserved in this chert. We find that, in general, mat dwellers are specific to a given type of mat-builder association, and that the dweller density is highest in the lower intertidal zone, where subaerial exposure was limited. These recurrent associations of species represent the preserved remnants of microbial-mat communities.

The Draken Formation contains a wide variety of mat dwellers. A well-preserved group of individuals from a very large population of microorganisms is shown in figure 3. The individual cells within this fossil are approximately 4 μm in diameter. Within this population, one sees individuals, dyads, tetrads, and (as pictured here) double tetrads. Other essentially spheroidal groups of cells resemble a blastula at the 32-cell and 64-cell phases. It is possible to reconstruct the entire life history of these organisms on the basis of the various forms observed within a given population. It is important to note that this kind of paleoecological analysis is based not on isolated morphologies but on the distribution of populations and morphologies within many rock samples.

In addition to what are very clearly microbenthic associations, we find free-floating, or planktonic, individuals that are not restricted to any one mat community. These microfossils occur in all three mat types as well as in nonstromatolitic muds of the same formation. One example is a cluster of spheroidal cells about 15 μm in diameter that were probably planktonic microorganisms living in the lagoonal water column above the microbial mats. Besides their size (10–20 μm in diameter) and their scattered distribution, they provide little morphologic information that suggests their ecological affinities. We don't know whether these are even prokaryotic or eukaryotic. A limited diversity of these organisms exists in the Draken Formation. Most have uncertain identities, but other lagoonal populations include assuredly eukaryotic spine-bearing cells up to 2.5 mm in diameter.

This glimpse of the biota found in the Draken Formation illustrates significant ecological heterogeneity within a single area. This is not merely a monolithic accumulation of cyanobacteria and other microfossils. Preserved in this 800-million-year-old formation are recurrent associations within microbial communities that very closely approximate the types and levels of ecological heterogeneity in comparable microbenthos today.

Late Proterozoic Plankton

The fossil evidence of the Draken Formation raises an important question: This 800-million-year-old group of rocks is older than the earliest large animals, yet in all of the Draken samples there are fewer than a dozen taxa that are unequivocally the remains of the eukaryotes—complex, nucleated cells. Where is the fuller record of Proterozoic eukaryotic diversity? To answer this question, let us turn to the Hunnberg Formation. This is also 800 million years old and part of the Svalbard archipelago. Important sedimentological information is conveyed in the Hunnberg outcrop. A succession occurs here from fine-grained detrital carbonates, becoming increasingly coarse, up to stromatolitic structures. This is interpreted as the remnants of a

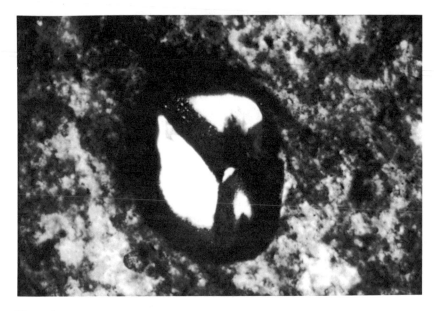

Figure 4
A eukaryotic microfossil of the open coastal plankton *Chuaria circularis.*

coastal marine environment. The gradient includes unrestricted marine conditions up to what acted as a barrier reef shielding a back reef lagoon. We see interesting assemblages of fossils preserved in all three of these environments. In the lagoon, the most environmentally restricted portion of this formation, the biota is similar to that of the Draken Formation. This is particularly true for the planktonic component. Here again are large numbers of individuals with very low diversity, dominated by one or two species of fossils. The plankton represented in the open coastal rocks, however, constitute an assemblage completely different from both the lagoonal portion of Hunnberg and the Draken Formation.

This open coastal environment contains evidence of a highly diverse eukaryotic biota. Large wrinkle-walled forms, 60 μm in diameter, seem to represent the reproductive cyst of a eukaryotic planktonic alga. *Chuaria circularis* (figure 4), a large planktonic organism (some specimens are almost 2 mm in diameter) with a robust wall, is clearly a eukaryote. Planktonic organisms with increasingly complex cell structures were also present in this region. The spheroidal organism shown in figure 5 is about 450–500 μm in diameter. Inspect-

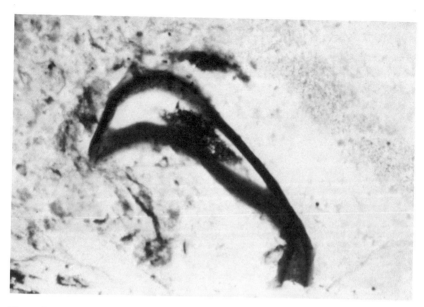

Figure 5
Trachyhystrichosphaera vidalii.

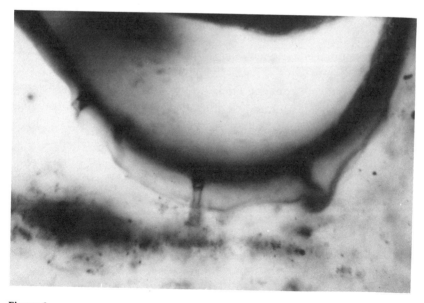

Figure 6
Close-up of *Trachyhystrichosphaera vidalii* showing processes that emerge from inner wall.

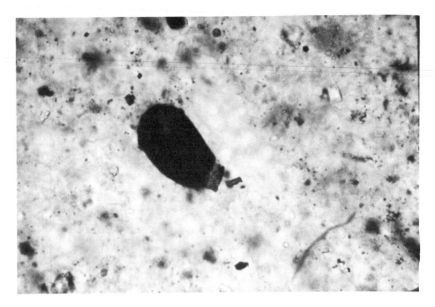

Figure 7
The vase-shaped microfossil of an unidentified heterotrophic protist.

ing its edges, one sees structures that look very much like spines. A close-up of this individual (figure 6) reveals a thick inner wall that gives rise to pillar-like projections which support an outer membrane. These projections are 6–10 μm in diameter—the same diameter as the average unicell from the Draken Formation. Though it does not provide definitive taxonomic identification, this complex morphological form is characteristically eukaryotic. Finally, the coastal beds contain fossils that are not spheroidal at all. The vase-shaped form shown in figure 7 is rounded at one end, with a distinct collar region and apical opening at the other. This individual is 90 μm long; others of its kind reach lengths upwards of 200 μm. Not only is it eukaryotic, but it may be the fossil of a heterotrophic protist. Protists of this type are limited to rocks 800 million years old and younger, although that represents evolution of this degradationally resistant vase-shaped form and not of heterotrophic protists *per se*. Heterotrophic protists are most assuredly more than twice that old.

Within the Hunnberg Formation we have seen a high level of species and ecosystem diversity. Lagoonal portions of this formation have only limited diversity of planktonic biota, but the open coastal waters supported over 25 species of complex eukaryotic plankton, including both photoautotrophs and heterotrophs. Here we see differences in species diversity that are directly related to differences in original ecological settings.

The classic 800–850-million-year-old biota of the Bitter Springs Formation in central Australia shows similar distributions. This formation was discovered by Elso Barghoorn in 1965, and was described in part by J. William Schopf. The best-known portion of the Bitter Springs consists of well-preserved mat-building associations that lived in a hypersaline coastal lake. Originally this biota was thought to be a homogeneous, diverse association of cyanobacteria. Recent paleoecological studies, however, have shown recurring associations of microfossils that are the remains of at least five distinct microbial communities.

Elsewhere, in black shales of the lower Bitter Springs Formation, a very different biota has been discovered by Zang Wenlong of the Australian National University. These rocks contain planktonic eukaryotes similar to those found in the open coastal region of the Hunnberg Formation. In the Bitter Springs Formation, we again see the effects of ecological distribution on fossil diversity. It is intriguing that the planktonic biota of the more open parts of the Bitter Springs Formation is similar, but not identical, to biota of similar ecological settings in the Northern Hemisphere. This suggests that there is still a great deal to be learned about biogeographical distribution of biotas, and about ecological and stratigraphic distributions of individual taxa.

What can be concluded from these highlights of just a few of the more than 100 localities known from this 800-million-year time slice? Certainly the number and variety of life forms found demonstrate the rich diversity of the fossil record at this time in history. But more interesting is the suggestion of an alternative way of looking at the fossil record generally. Most evolutionary interpretations of the Precambrian fossil record have assumed that differences between two microbiotas of differing age reflect evolutionary change. However, it is clear from this overview that a wide variety of fossil assemblages are found in rocks of a single age. Therefore, evolutionary change can be inferred only if ecological differences and degradational histories can be ruled out as sources of the variation observed. A review of the rock record will help underscore this point. First, let us look at the stromatolitic microbenthos in the Bitter Springs and Draken-type biotas. Early Proterozoic biotas are scarce and come from a limited variety of environments. Either these early Proterozoic environments have no late Proterozoic equivalents, or else the younger examples contain essentially the same types of fossils. One might be led to a tentative conclusion that the prokaryotic microbenthos diversified and achieved its modern dimensions early on, in the early Proterozoic era. This does not mean that no evolution among prokaryotic microbenthos occurred in the rest of the Proterozoic, but that the major outlines were set near the beginning of the era. The evolutionary history regarding eukaryotic plankton is not as uniform. In rocks older than 1.7 billion years there are very few remains of planktonic organisms of any type, yet rocks 900 million to 1.4 billion years old contain abundant eukaryotic microfossils.

Beginning about 900 million years ago, we see a mushrooming of morphological diversity in the plankton. Equally interesting, many of these fairly complex planktonic species disappeared about 600 million years ago. Finally, near the beginning of the Cambrian period, about 550 million years ago, a rediversification of plankton gave rise to entirely new forms not closely related to the complex organisms that had evolved in the late Precambrian. Here we are definitely seeing evolutionary change through time in the planktonic realm. In terms of emerging ideas on evolution, it is important to note that the hand of extinction is evident in the regulation of the evolution of the early plankton.

In light of this remarkable diversity of fossil remains, one cannot view differences among biotas as necessarily reflecting evolutionary change. Consideration of the environmental conditions is essential. The late Proterozoic era saw both the fine tuning of a stromatolitic, prokaryotic microbenthos that had originated more than a billion years earlier and the rapid and dramatic diversification of eukaryotes. Of course, by the end of this period the diversification of eukaryotes had reached a new level in the evolution of metazoans. The theory for just why all these evolutionary changes occurred must be sought in the regulatory genetics of living organisms, but the evidence documenting its occurrence—including timing and possible environmental influences—can be found in these diverse biotas of late Precambrian rocks.

Readings

Butterfield, N. J., A. H. Knoll, and K. Swett. 1988. Exceptional preservation of fossils in an Upper Proterozoic shale. *Nature* 334: 424–427.

Green, J., A. H. Knoll, S. Golubic, and K. Swett. 1987. Paleobiology of distinctive benthic microfossils from the Upper Proterozoic Limestone-Dolomite "Series," central East Greenland. *American Journal of Botany* 62: 835–852.

Knoll, A. H. 1981. Paleoecology of late Precambrian microbial assemblages. In *Paleobotany, Paleoecology, and Evolution*, volume 1, ed. K. J. Niklas. Praeger.

Knoll, A. H. 1985. Exceptional preservation of photosynthetic organisms in silicified carbonates and silicified peats. *Philosophical Transactions of the Royal Society of London* 311: 111–122.

Knoll, A. H. 1989. The paleomicrobiological information in Proterozoic rocks. In *Microbial Mats: Physiological Ecology of Microbial Communities*, ed. Y. Cohen and E. Rosenberg. American Society for Microbiology.

Knoll, A. H., K. Swett, and J. Mark. 1991. Paleobiology of a Neoproterozoic tidal flat/lagoonal complex: The Draken Conglomerate Formation, Spitsbergen. *Journal of Paleontology* 65: 531–570.

Schopf, J. W. 1968. Microflora of the Bitter Springs Formation, Late Precambrian, Central Australia. *Journal of Paleontology* 42: 651–688.

Vidal, G. 1984. The oldest eukaryotic cells. *Scientific American* 250, no. 2: 48–55.

13

Continental Drift and Plate Tectonics

Raymond Siever

In this chapter, Raymond Siever traces the development of the discoveries and ideas that led to the synthetic theory of the workings of the Earth's surface, the grand unifying concept of geology: plate tectonics. Echo soundings and magnetometer tracings of the deep ocean, distribution of volcanoes and earthquakes, paleontological studies of fossil reptiles, and other disparate sources of information reveal a new view of our dynamic Earth. Siever is currently Professor of Geology at Harvard University.

The old ideas that oceans and continents were permanently in their present positions were rooted in our emotional need for something firm in our lives: the Earth beneath us, always still and always stable. People living in earthquake zones always knew that the Earth shook, yet it didn't seem to move around between earthquakes. The concept of stabilism, taken for granted at least since the early 1800s, was assumed in geology as a consequence of a very important doctrine: uniformitarianism. Uniformitarianism, enunciated early in the nineteenth century, states that processes at the Earth's surface operated in the past as they operate today. Rivers excavate valleys as rivers always excavated valleys in the past. Although not specifically written, it seemed obvious that if past geological processes always worked the way they do now the continents must also have always been in the same positions.

All this has changed now. The comprehensive theory of plate tectonics has kept geologists busy since its synthesis in the late 1960s. It is odd for me, having been involved in plate tectonics from the beginning as an onlooker, to consider plate tectonics now as an old theory, as old as some ideas about Earth that held sway before. Earlier "theories" were not really scientific theories. They were fanciful notions, like "the cooling Earth contracted like an orange, and mountains were created when the orange peel was crenulated and ridged." Until about 1965 no one had good ideas of why or how the Earth's surface behaves. Mountains, volcanoes, and the distribution of earthquakes were known—we had explanations of how these features acted, but no concepts to tie them together. The discovery of coal beds in the far north at Spitzbergen and in Antarctica disturbed the standard geological world view. Nothing like subtropical forests can grow in these climates now, yet such coal beds must have come from swamp vegetation that grew under hot and humid conditions.

Evidence for Drifting of the Continents

"Continental drift" was one of the earliest ideas people had after looking at decent maps. This idea may have already occurred to Francis Bacon; in 1620 he commented on the fit of Africa and South America. In 1858, Antonio Schneider, a mapmaker, constructed a map of the Atlantic Ocean showing how South America and Africa may have drifted apart. But the true father of continental drift was Alfred Wegener, a German who studied world climatology. Wegener helped discover the tropical *Glossopteris* flora of the southern hemisphere. He questioned why glaciations had occurred at times in the past on continents which are now tropical. The ideas of Wegener (and, later, of others who believed in continental drift) were not accepted by most geologists. Wegener was an outcast because he wasn't a "true geologist"; his ideas were also rejected because he simply had no decent mechanism for "continental drift."

Wegener presented the first serious challenge to stabilism when he noted not only that the contours of South America and South Africa fit but that the fossils of the west coast of Africa matched those of the east coast of South America. There was, for example, fossil evidence that a small late-Paleozoic reptile known as *Mesosaurus* lived a little over 250 million years ago in what is now South America and Africa. Wegener thought it exceedingly unlikely that *Mesosaurus*, a freshwater swimmer, would be limited to those two continental locations without having spread to many other environments. If it could swim across the Atlantic Ocean, why did one find *Mesosaurus* only

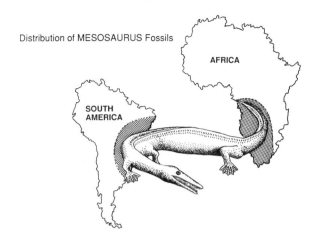

Distribution of MESOSAURUS Fossils

AFRICA

SOUTH
AMERICA

Figure 1
The distribution of fossils of the dinosaur *Mesosaurus* on the west coast of Africa and the east coast of South America.

at a few specific locations (figure 1)? Indeed *Mesosaurus* was not much of a swimmer; it probably could not have crossed the ocean. Wegener reasoned that *Mesosaurus* fossils were found in rocks of the same age at these disparate places because, in the late Paleozoic, these two continents were together. Wegener generated many other biological arguments based on his proposal that the continents, known from geophysical evidence to be approximately 25–30 kilometers thick and overlying a much denser substratum of the Earth, drifted in the oceanic crust like floating pieces of ice in the sea.

The defenders of stabilism responded almost immediately. Biologists and paleontologists invented ingenious alternative explanations for the distribution of fossils. The example of *Mesosaurus*, for example, was explained by the supposed existence of a sunken and eroded land bridge across the South Atlantic Ocean. Wegener argued that continental material is so different from oceanic crustal material in density and composition that a sunken land bridge would be detectable. Geophysicists, for their part, rejected any process of continental movement; they could not conceive of any dynamic mechanism by which continents 25–30 km thick could plow through oceanic crust. Without a mechanism, Wegener's concept of continental drift remained at the periphery of mainstream science.

A general theory of the formation of mountains was lacking as recently as 1960. Geologists believed in continental accretion—that continents grew steadily during geologic history but always stayed in the same place with respect to the ocean basins. The first scientist who proposed a reasonable mechanism was Arthur Holmes, a famous geologist from Scotland. In the 1920s Holmes proposed that the mantle, the interior of the Earth, convected heat, like hot coffee rising unevenly to the top in a just-poured cup. The mantle, beginning approximately 30 km down in the interior of the Earth, was known to be very hot relative to the cooler outer part of the Earth, the crust. Large convective forces transmitting heat from below to above would set up "convection cells" responsible for mountain production.

The Earth's convection, as any convective current, is the result of a temperature difference in the gravity field. The hotter the material is, the lower its density. The material that heats up in some portion of the hotter mantle will become less dense as a result of increased temperature and will tend to move upward, seeking and finding its own level of density. The cooler material tends to sink. This is the behavior of any convection cell.

Holmes held that where the crust and the mantle meet, down-bows in the Earth's crust would be responsible for the first building of geosynclines believed to cause continental accretion. (Geosynclines were defined as linear belts of thick accumulations of sediment that were later deformed into mountain belts.) Sediments would accumulate at continental edges: as motion continued, crumpling, so said Holmes, would erect large mountain belts, introducing great bodies of molten rock appearing on the surface as volcanoes. Lava extrusion, deformations resulting in mountains, Holmes suggested, could be accounted for by convective cells. Holmes' good idea was not easily tested; it rested for 30 years until the period of ocean exploration that started just before World War II.

Mapping the Sea Floor

The major development leading to the measurement of ocean topography, echo sounding, started in the 1920s. Ships on the ocean's surface sent down pulses of sound, which were reflected back up to them. From the travel time of these sound waves and an accurate knowledge of the velocity of sound in water, the distance to the bottom was deduced. Every ship with an echo sounder detected subsea hills. A topography of an ocean floor, typified by the Atlantic Ocean, was revealed (figure 2). From sea level down to about 200 meters is a broad, shallow apron bordering the continents, the so-called *continental shelf*, followed by a steeper slope of about 5°, the *continental slope*. Below the slope is the *continental rise*, a great pile of sediment derived from continental erosion settling out into deeper ocean waters. Further out, at depths greater than about 4,000 meters, are smoother expanses called the *abyssal plains*. These plains give way farther out to a hilly topography that culminates in a high ridge of mountains, the mid-Atlantic ridge, running down the middle of the Atlantic Ocean. In the Pacific Ocean the same general pattern was found, plus another kind of topography: some abyssal plains or hills are bounded by very deep trenches, some 10,000 meters below sea level.

The discoveries that led up to the theory of plate tectonics occurred around 1965—mostly as results of the work of Maurice Ewing and his associates at Columbia University's Lamont-Doherty Geological Observatory, who mapped the ocean floors extensively in collaboration with scientists from other oceanographic institutions. A relatively recent map (figure 3) reveals mountains, valleys, plains, and the peculiar topography of the sea floor surrounding the continents. The sea floor has mountain ranges similar to those of the Alps and Himalayas but arranged somewhat differently. The work corroborated the suspicion of the Challenger Expedition of the late nineteenth century: the mid-Atlantic ridge is a series of high mountains running down the center of the Atlantic Ocean. The center of this high ridge of mountains is a deep valley: a symmetrical cleft or crack running along the middle. We now know that these mid-ocean ridges (MORs) are distributed around the globe. The mid-Atlantic ridge, for example, can be traced into the Indian Ocean. Ridges cross the other oceans as well. The East Pacific rise is like the mid-Atlantic ridge but lower and broader.

The explanation of these ridges was at first a mystery. What did these cracks signify? The ridges were receiving very little sediment: they were floored with only a thin layer. Beneath the thin layers of sediment was a rough surface, opaque to any further transmission

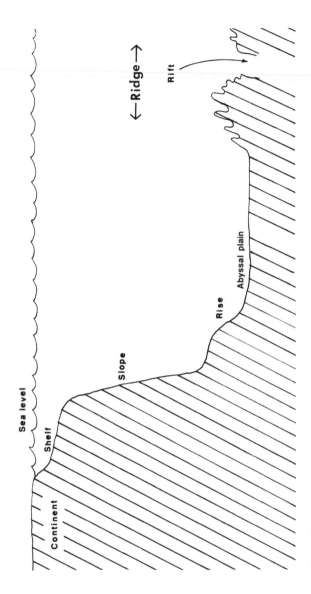

Figure 2
Topography of the Atlantic Basin. The continental shelf runs from sea level to a depth of 200 meters. At the bottom of the steeper continental slope is the continental rise, formed from accumulated continental sediment. At depths greater than 4,000 meters are the very flat abyssal plains that border the underwater mountain range of the mid-Atlantic Ridge.

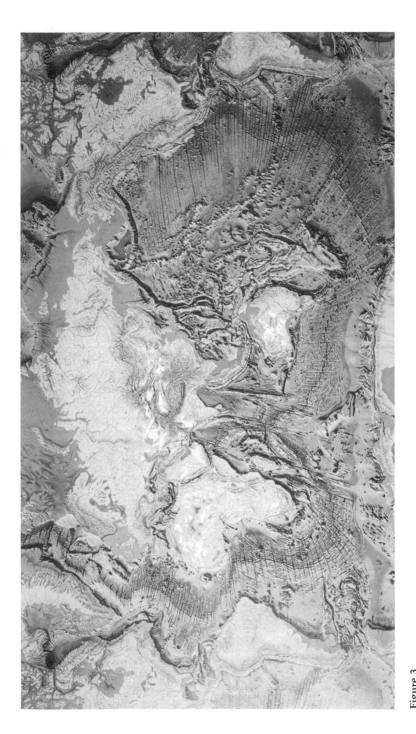

Figure 3
A map showing some of the underwater mountain ranges that traverse the globe.

of sound. Some rock down there seemed to be much denser; it was opaque and would not transmit anything. Signals coming back from this "layer B" were later identified as a worldwide substratum of basalt. Layer B could be dredged, and pieces were broken off from the top; it outcropped in part of the abyssal hills and then in the mid-ocean ridges.

Putting together the detailed discovery of mid-ocean ridges with the discovery of basalts in the 1960s, Harry Hess of Princeton University enunciated the idea of sea-floor spreading. Hess, a mineralogist who had been a submarine commander during World War II, became involved in the history of the oceans. He had worked on the history of the Caribbean, still an inexplicable geological problem. Hess came up with the idea that the mid-ocean ridges had been created as the deep interior of the Earth welled up, producing molten basalt. Basalt, a dark igneous rock, is the product of lava flows. One of the most abundant rock types on Earth, it constitutes much of the lower part of the crust everywhere beneath the continents. It erupts at the surface in a great variety of volcanoes, typified by Kilauea and Mauna Loa on the Hawaiian Islands. Basalt contains many small pieces of a glassy material and very fine fragmented crystalline materials, which suggest that it is formed by the rapid quenching of a very hot igneous rock melt or magma. The temperatures of volcanoes underlain by basaltic lava have been measured as 1,000–1,100°C. When basaltic material is spewed high into the air as volcanic eruptions of the explosive type, or when it pours out onto the surface as lava streams, as observed on Kilauea, it quickly cools, forming glass; thus, it offers little opportunity for systematic and orderly growth of crystals. Basalt outflows have been known all over the continents from regions of vast upwellings, typified by the Snake River and the Columbia Plateau of the state of Washington, in which thousands and thousands of square miles are covered by dark basalt lavas that flowed out in the last 50 or 60 million years. The central fissure eruptions of Iceland are basaltic. This rock type, which is present in so many different areas of the Earth and is known to be one of the lower layers of the crust, assumes special significance when it wells up in the mid-Atlantic and other mid-ocean rises to form the new parts of the crust. Basalt is the material that comes out of the Earth's interior to make the new parts of the plates.

As basalt wells up, the ocean floor splits, rifts, and then continues to spread apart. Hess' problem was urgent: "Where did the floor of the ocean go?" Many of us accepted Hess' mechanism of sea-floor spreading at the rift almost as soon as he presented it. But what happened to the old rock? We could not believe that the Earth was expanding. The expanding-Earth hypothesis, periodically proposed, was always demolished—with good reason. The search was on.

Hess combined Arthur Holmes' ideas of convection currents with the new ocean data: a convective upwelling of basalt was formed by the rise of deep mantle material. The central valley was a rift; material moved apart and out at this point. Hess envisaged a giant "conveyer belt" bringing up material from deep inside the mantle that gradually spread out farther from mid-ocean centers. I went out in 1965 to the mid-Atlantic ridge, at about 20° north latitude, to study sediment basins on and alongside the ridge. Very thin layers of sediment were near the ridge; the sediment became thicker the farther out one went. We also discovered manganese oxide being deposited at a slow rate in the form of crusts that became thicker as one moved away from the ridge. These discoveries were consistent with the idea that the hills farther away from the rift were older. As the ocean floor was made by basalt coming up at the rift, the conveyer belt operated and materials moved away.

Magnetic Anomalies: Clues to Sea-Floor Spreading

Then came the crucial explanation of sea-floor spreading, which was based on the discovery of magnetic anomalies. Fred Vine and Drummond Matthews, of Princeton University, set this picture in order. Magnetometer readings from several different traverses taken at different places in the ocean could be lined up. In its simplest form, a magnetometer is a magnetic compass needle, suspended by a fiber in the Earth's magnetic field. A bar magnet of known strength is brought within a known distance of the compass needle. Knowing the strength of this magnet, we calculate the attractive force. This attractive force will be countered by the force of the Earth's magnetic field attracting the compass to the north. The needle will be deflected toward the magnet, but not as far as it would be if the Earth's magnetic field were not there. The fundamental principle of how a magnetometer works is that it simply compares the Earth's magnetic field with a known magnet of some kind to deduce the strength, at that site, of the Earth's magnetic field. The most sensitive magnetometers available now are ones that depend on the atomic magnetic properties of the proton.

Vine and Matthews discovered that the curves of the strength of the magnetic field along different traverses could be lined up. These anomalies formed striped patterns, which covered the ocean floor. Although they didn't know what caused these anomalies, Vine and Matthews established that the patterns were produced by magnetic reversals. Every so often in the Earth's history the magnetic field suddenly flipped: where there had been a north-seeking pole, the magnetic field became south, and vice versa. Vine and Matthews discovered that layers of rocks of different polarity alternated.

These patterns can be explained by the dynamics of the sea floor (figure 4). Imagine magma coming up from the hot part of the mantle. The dark basaltic lava flows from the partial melting zone out onto the sea floor. As it cools into rock, the temperature of the material descends from roughly 1,000°C to about 500°C. Tiny amounts of iron in the rock act as little magnets. As the lava crystallizes below 500°C (which is called the Curie point, in honor of Marie Curie), the magnetism is locked into the rock in such a way as to record the direction of the Earth's magnetic poles at the time the rock congealed. As long as the polarity of the Earth's magnetic field remains the same, the magma retains the same signature. Operating much as a tape recorder does, the ocean floor preserves a record of the Earth's magnetic field, recording the magnetic orientation in the basalts or lavas as they flow out on the surface. The lavas are carried out by sea-floor spreading. The lavas that are magnetized thus carry a record of the direction of the magnetic field. In addition, they are a taped record of the time when they were deposited, and thus of how fast the sea floor was spreading. Before Vine and Matthews, most magnetic stratigraphy measurements were made on land.

The time scale of magnetic reversal (figure 5) shows that the present polarity has existed less than a million years. Then there was a short period at the beginning of the Matuyama reverse period when north was south and south was north. Flip-flops occur on an irregular time scale of over 3 million years, beginning well over 100 million

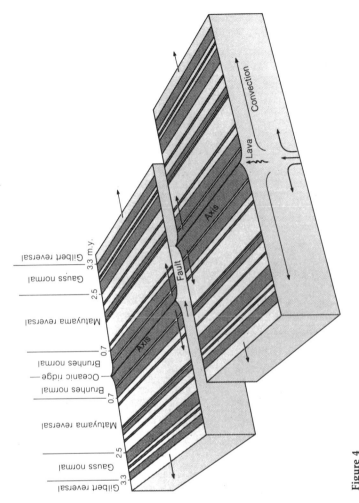

Figure 4
Symmetrical patterns of magnetism on either side of a mid-ocean ridge.

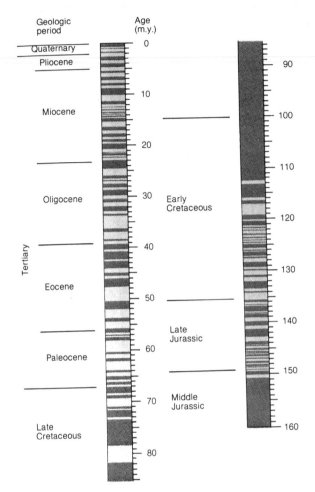

Figure 5

A time scale, stretching back from the present to the Jurassic, based on magnetic reversals. The darker bands represent periods of so-called normal polarity, when the North and South magnetic poles corresponded to their present positions; the lighter bands represent periods of reversed polarity.

years ago. We have only recently begun to find out why reversals occur.

We know from steady and consistent measurements made at magnetic observatories that the Earth's magnetic field has been decreasing in the last 140 years. We are probably on the way to another magnetic reversal, which will occur as the present magnetic field decays down to zero and then builds back up again with a reverse polarity. Reversals take place every 10,000 to 100,000 years or so; thus, we can confidently expect one to happen again sooner or later, particularly since we have been in a normal era for many thousands of years. During the reversal, as the magnetic field declines to zero, magnetic compasses will be confused, for there will be no North or South Pole to attract the compass needle. Since the magnetic field acts to deflect some of the radiation impinging on the Earth from outer space, we may temporarily get more radiation. Yet the history of life suggests that during the many reversals no conspicuous effects on the nature of life occurred.

By early 1965 another clue to the tectonic puzzle had been found: paleomagnetism. The poles "wandered" (figure 6). Nearly all rocks retain a small amount of the magnetism that is induced at the time of their formation. If we look carefully at the magnetic signature of a lava that is approximately 10 million years old, we discover that the north magnetic pole was then in a different place than it is now. If the rock contains a record of the ancient magnetic pole positions, then we can take a great many rocks formed at a great many different times and note how the poles' position seems to have changed over time. Now fathom this: If all the continents were in exactly the same positions relative to one another then as now, all polar wandering paths should be identical, there being at one time only a single magnetic field with one north and one south pole of the Earth. No theory suggests any magnetic field that involves more than just the north and south poles. The fact that the data yield different "polar wandering paths" means that the continents have moved with respect to one another. In the 1960s, in the midst of all of the ferment about an extremely active sea floor, these precise "polar-wandering curves" really upset the applecart. Geophysicists started considering ideas of moving continents, even though geologists were still a little bit reluctant.

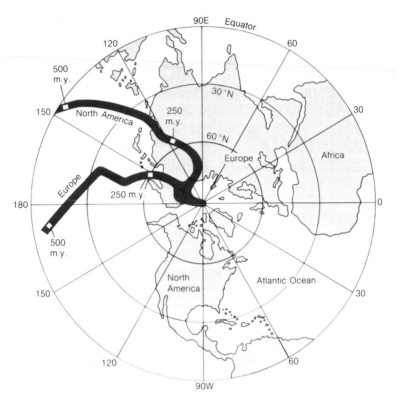

Figure 6
Polar wandering curves of North America and Europe.

Disappearance of Crust at Subduction Zones

In 1965, Hess' original question still needed answering: If new basalt crust is appearing at the mid-ocean ridges, and the earth is not expanding, where does the crust disappear? The oceanwide, world-wide earthquake-sensing network, set up mainly to monitor seismic results of underground atomic explosions, made it possible for the first time to understand the distribution of earthquakes. When the map reproduced here as figure 7 first appeared, it was considered remarkable that all of the rift-ridge and trench zones under the oceans were outlined. An enormous volcanic ring of fire consisting of all the volcanoes around the Pacific Basin was revealed. Earthquakes outline the mid-Atlantic ridge between the Americas and Europe and between South America and Africa; they also delineate the area

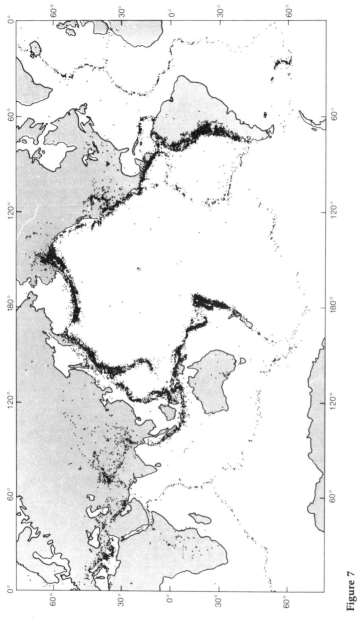

Figure 7
Distribution of earthquakes recorded during the years 1961–1967.

between Africa and Antarctica. Why are earthquakes patterned like this?

The tearing that gives rise to earthquake waves takes place at varying depths, some as deep as 700 km. Shallow-focus earthquakes characterize the mid-Atlantic ridge and the East Pacific rise running from North America southward to the coast of South America. The deep-focus earthquakes are typically in the trenches on the western side of the Pacific Ocean. Deep-sea trenches are great deep folds in the oceanic crust. Lynn Sykes established that in the trenches the earthquakes are distributed in a descending zone, going deeper and deeper as one moves from the trench toward volcanic islands associated with the trench. The trenches are areas of abnormally low heat flow, whereas over the ridges (such as the mid-Atlantic ridge and the East Pacific rise) heat flow is much higher. The high heat flow results from upwardly moving convection currents transmitting heat from deeper in the mantle to the surface. This implies that in the trenches there is a downward movement of cool material, since this is an area of low heat flow relative to the heat flow of the ridges.

The fact that trenches are areas of downward movement of cool crust and the descending distribution of earthquakes indicate that oceanic lithosphere is sliding down the trench, moving deeper into the mantle. The places where this happens are *subduction zones*. That subduction zones are where the plates go was realized by Dan Mac-kenzie and too many other people to name in late 1966 and early 1967. The final picture of plate tectonics fell into place: the ocean ridges are where basalt comes up, creating the lithospheric plates, which move out as rigid bodies until a subduction zone is met. At the subduction zone, the crustal plates start to dive down, completing the cycle.

Movement of Lithospheric Plates: The Essence of Plate Tectonics

A final clue that made everything fit into place was the concept of lithospheric plates, varying in thickness from 70 to 100 km. Below the plates lies the asthenosphere, defined as the partially plastic upper part of the mantle. The asthenosphere can flow and deform by plastic flow, whereas lithospheric plates behave as rigid bodies. This view of the Earth came primarily from a detailed study of the transmission of seismic waves. The Earth's surface consists of rigid plates riding on a relatively plastic and movable asthenosphere. By matching the North American, South American, and African continents and the western part of the Eurasian continent plus Greenland, one can obtain the best possible fit using the continental-shelf lines— rather than the shoreline—where properly speaking, the continents end. Wegener did this—but now we understand the mechanics. The great cry of the geophysicists in the 1920s was that continental drift couldn't work because a continental crust couldn't plow through the oceanic crust in even a shallow ocean. Now we realize that constituents of the lithospheric plates, about 100 km thick, do not plow through oceanic crust; they simply ride over a plastic asthenosphere. The continents are simply the uppermost portions of the moving lithospheric plates, and the oceanic crust is produced at the trailing end of the plate and consumed by subduction at the leading end. The paleomagnetism and the magnetic time scale tell us when and how rapidly the plates move. The rate of sea-floor spreading may be as small as 2–4 centimeters per year. For example, the rift in the center of Iceland is moving apart at an annual rate of about 2 cm.

Between 1965 and the spring of 1967, new ideas floated around the geological, geochemical, geophysical, and oceanographic communities. The new geological ideas led to an explosion of papers in 1967 and 1968 by half a dozen geophysicists, all of them very young and active in oceanography and geophysics: Xavier LePichon, a French geophysicist working at Lamont-Doherty Geological Observatory; Lynn Sykes, a seismologist at Lamont-Doherty; Dan MacKenzie, a geophysicist from Cambridge, England; Jason Morgan from Princeton; and many others. Each was working furiously on a piece of these developments. They visited one another's laboratories, jumped on and off ship, and flew to other ships. The whole picture then emerged. Tested and confirmed in so many different areas, "plate tectonics" is now completely accepted as the major driving force of the dynamics of the Earth.

To understand plate tectonics we must consider the structure of the outer zones of the Earth. The thin outer crust of the Earth is cool relative to the hot interior beneath both the oceanic crust and the continental crust. Continental crust is somewhat thicker than oceanic crust; each is part of the lithosphere. The lithosphere comprises the outer layer of rock, which is more or less rigid, solid, and brittle. Below the lithosphere is the darker zone of partial melting, the top of the asthenosphere. Pressures and temperatures, particularly in the zone of partial melting, are so high in the asthenosphere that its material deforms as a plastic solid. As any other fluid, the asthenosphere's material is characterized by a viscosity, but the asthenosphere is 22–23 orders of magnitude more viscous than the fluids with which we are accustomed. The materials of the asthenosphere move very slowly. The asthenosphere is heated by sources inside the Earth—primarily by the incorporation of radioactive uranium and thorium minerals, and a little-known but very important radioactive isotope, potassium 40. These materials all contribute to the heat of the Earth, which is slowly being transmitted to and through the surface. The interior of the Earth is not all molten, although the core is. For years geophysicists worried about the heat flow because so much heat from the Earth could not be transmitted to the surface by heat conduction. (Heat conduction is a familiar phenomenon; if you sit on a radiator, you get hot because of direct conduction of heat from the heat source to you.) Thermally, the Earth is a lot like a brick: it takes a long time to heat up, and it takes a similarly long time to cool off; thermal conductivity is extremely slow. Almost 100 years ago it was shown that the Earth produced internal heat by radioactive decay at such a rate that it could not possibly lose it all only by heat conduction. Another major way of losing heat is by convection, the way a radiator heats a room: The hot air rises because it is less dense; in some other part of the room, the dense, colder air sinks to the bottom. The easiest way to see convection currents is in a cup of coffee with the proper angle of illumination of light coming in at the borders. These convection "cells" constantly form and break up as the coffee cools from the top layer and then heats up from the hot interior.

The mantle turns over constantly, losing heat in the same way that a room loses its heat in winter even though the radiator continually pumps heat into the room. The cool upper surface of the mantle is at the boundary where the oceanic crust meets the lithospheric crust. As the mantle convects, it brings material to the top, where it cools off more directly than it would by heat conduction throughout the great thickness of the mantle. Hot material from the zone of partial melting in the mantle is brought from the interior to the surface and extruded on the surface at mid-ocean ridges, where it quickly quenches under seawater or cools if it comes up on land (as in Iceland, where the mid-Atlantic ridge passes through the large island).

Plate tectonics even explains how Earth keeps the same radius even though new ocean floor is constantly being formed. The idea that Earth has a constant mass is old; it has not been changed by plate tectonic theory—rather, it supports the concept that plate tectonics is not the result of an expanding Earth. The analysis of Earth's constant radius derives from its constant mass. Not much of Earth's material is lost to space. Hydrogen gas does have sufficient escape velocity to leave the atmosphere. Small amounts of helium may leave by gaseous escape from the outer atmosphere, but Earth's gravitational pull is so strong that few other materials leave. The planet has a constant mass, for practical purposes, and the value of gravity always has been about what it is today. The gravitational compression pulling the planet together accounts for the high density and temperature of its interior. Earth long ago reached equilibrium with respect to gravity, which holds it together. The sun, since it has nuclear fusion in its interior, could conceivably expand; however, no such nuclear mechanism exists for the much cooler Earth. Therefore, if material is produced on the sea floor, we must find a place to which it returns. Plate tectonic theory solved the problem of where the lithosphere, coming up and created at mid-ocean ridges, disappears. The answer is at the subduction zones.

The basalt, cooled from the ascending magma, comes up, and the sea floor, the lithosphere, moves out from each side of the rift (figures 8 and 9). At the subduction zone, crust dives down into the mantle where it is resorbed. The cool lithospheric plates go down into the trench. The material cools down as it travels along. The cool, waterlogged sediments enter a deeper zone of the mantle (figure 10; left and right in figure 9). They enter a zone where materials start melting from the top layers, work their way up, and ultimately form volcanoes.

Several kinds of subduction zones exist. One is the *Marianas* type, which formed the island arcs of the Pacific; another is the *Andean* type, which created the Andes Mountains of South America. As a

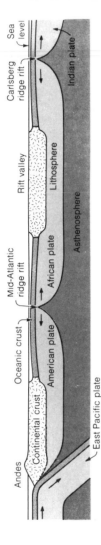

Figure 8
The American plate and the African plate are moving apart at the mid-Atlantic ridge. The East Pacific plate is being subducted under the western edge of the South American plate, creating the Andes.

Figure 9
The East Pacific Plate, moving away from the East Pacific ridge, is subducted under thin oceanic crust, creating the island arc of Japan.

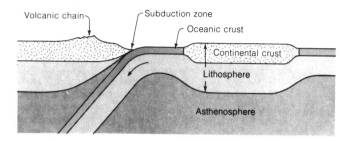

Figure 10
Subduction zones occur when oceanic and continental plates converge.

subducting plate dives below continental crust, the melting rock comes up underneath, creating huge volcanic mountain chains like the Andes. Where plates are subducted underneath thin oceanic crust, island arcs such as the Marianas, the Tongas, and the Japanese islands form.

Transform faults are the accommodations the Earth makes when plates slide past each other (figure 11). In mid-ocean ridges a transform fault appears as a crack and a lateral movement. Although they were understood before the advent of the theory of plate tectonics, transform faults were quickly included in the overarching concept. When mid-ocean ridges curve around and change direction, they tend to tear along such transform faults. The infamous San Andreas fault in California, responsible most recently for the 1989 San Francisco earthquake, is a large transform fault. The mid-East Pacific rise, running south from Baja California under the continent, shifts so

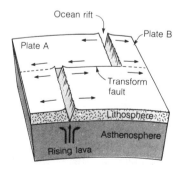

Figure 11
Transform faults occur when plates that are separating slip past one another.

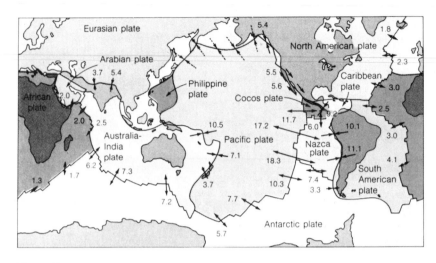

Figure 12
Modern plate boundaries. Opposed arrows indicate converging plates. Diverging arrows represent spreading at ocean ridges. Relative velocities of plate movements are given in centimeters per year.

that the Pacific plate moves laterally northwest relative to the North American plate; California is moving about a centimeter or two per year. As the Pacific plate moves to the northwest it slides past the North American plate, yielding many earthquakes that are an order of magnitude greater than the earthquake of 1989. These movements will continue as the plates move. "Baja" California will move up opposite to the interior of "Alta" California. Eventually Los Angeles will be pushed opposite Berkeley, with results we cannot predict.

How permanent is the current configuration of continents and oceans? We can construct a map of how the plates of the world are divided and in what directions they are moving (figure 12). The African continent seems firmly anchored, but the Atlantic Ocean grows wider by about 2 cm per year. The East Pacific rise moves apart much more rapidly.

Volcanic lava continues to come up at "hot spots," such as the Hawaiian Islands and Iceland. Hot spots may be controlled by the same forces that move plates, but we are still not sure. Hot spots are plumes of magma coming from perhaps as deep as the boundary between the mantle and the molten core, near the center of the Earth—much deeper in the mantle than the partial melting zone.

Hot spots are fixed locations: as a plate moves across a hot spot, it leaves a trail of volcanoes. The Hawaiian Islands, at the end of a trail of a series of extinct volcanoes, were created as the Pacific plate moved northwestward across a hot spot.

Jason Morgan of Princeton University realized that hot spots had to somehow connect to plate tectonics. For the first time in the history of geology, it was felt that everything about the Earth's surface should be included in plate tectonic theory: the sea floor, mountains, volcanoes, volcanic island arcs, the Hawaiian Islands, and so on. And we now can explain continental drift: Continents happen to ride on the plates. The plates, not the continents, are drifting. The continents, as elevated portions of the plates, are passengers.

Glaciers, too, fit in beautifully with plate tectonics. Active glaciers now are limited to extremely high mountains or to polar regions. But certain rocks containing coal beds must have moved; formed in tropical, humid climates, they are now in glaciated regions. Past glaciations inferred from glacial features now in the tropics must have originated when these continents were closer to the poles.

Reconstructing Past Movements

Plate tectonics has inspired research into how mountains were created, into paleo-plate tectonics, and into a topic important for evolutionary biology: extinctions and the disappearance of hordes of phyla at the end of the Paleozoic era. These extinctions can be attributed to the restriction of coastal and continental shelf areas when the continents were together.

The example of paleo-plate tectonics and Earth history helps spell out how we now use plate tectonics to reconstruct mountain-building events. During the development of a passive plate margin, upwarping occurs where molten rock comes up from below, bows up continental crust, and splits it apart into a rift valley. The rift valley widens and deepens; then the sea may invade. The Red Sea and the Gulf of Aden are examples of such valleys. The Dead Sea is a candidate for future marine invasion. The rift widens, seawater penetrates, and the continental margin cools. As it cools down, the plate contracts, and the margin gradually receives eroded sediment from the continents and thus subsides. The full development of a passive

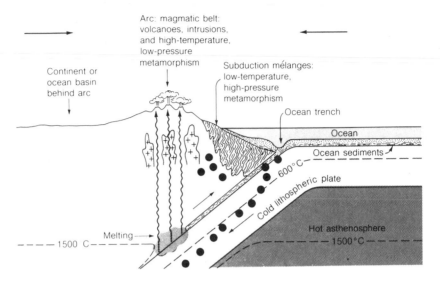

Figure 13
Andean-type subduction zone, an example of active plate margins. Collision of an oceanic plate with continental crust results in formation of trenches, accompanied by metamorphism, volcanism and earthquakes (represented by black dots).

ocean margin is typical of the Atlantic Ocean, where extensive continental shelves delimit former plate boundaries. At active margins, Andean-type subduction zones, oceanic crust dives beneath the continental crust (figure 13). When a plate carrying a continent dives below another plate carrying another continent, the continents collide and are not subducted. The Himalayan Mountains were created in this way when the Indian subcontinent collided with the Eurasian plate. The processes occurring at active plate boundaries account for the development of most of the mountain belts of the world.

How do we reconstruct continental drift through geologic time (figure 14)? Turning the clock back, we see the Atlantic Ocean narrowing. Moving back 120 million years, we see South America and Africa joined. At 180 million years ago, North America also joins. By 240 million years ago, the configuration of the giant supercontinent, Pangaea, is formed.

The names Pangaea, Laurasia, and Gondwanaland were invented by the advocates of continental drift. In 1915 Alfred Wegener, the promulgator of continental drift, named Pangaea. The modern continents put back together give us the enormous ancient central con-

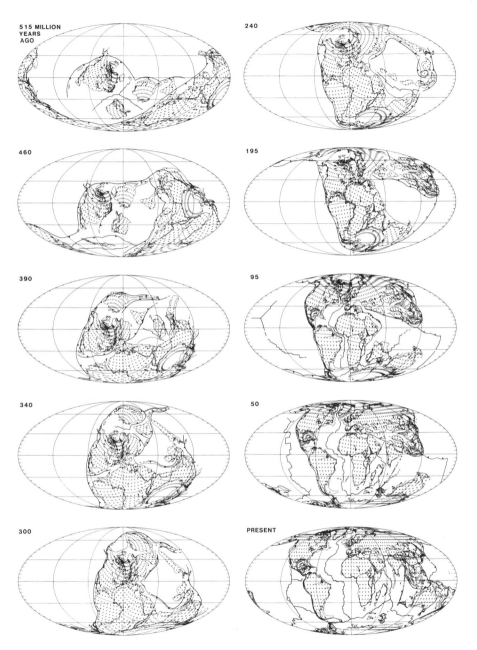

Figure 14
Reconstruction of drifting continents from 540 million years ago to the present.

tinent combining South America, Africa, North America, Asia, Europe, Australia, and the Antarctic. Pangaea was Wegener's creation. He also used the term Gondwanaland, invented around 1885 by Edward Seuss, a Swiss geologist. Seuss had noticed, as had others, that fossils of certain distinctive land plants, the *Glossopteris* flora, occurred in the Gondwana Formation of India. This flora was also characteristic of fossils of the same age in South America and Africa. Seuss assumed that peninsular India was once somehow connected to the other southern continents. No one at that time knew about Antarctica. Wegener added the northern supercontinent (called Laurasia after Asia and the Laurentian Mountains of the Precambrian shield of Canada) to Gondwanaland to make Pangaea. The earlier Atlantic Ocean, present from 540 million to 300 million years ago, was called the Iapetus Sea. At 540 million years ago, just after metazoan life evolved, there was a strange, unrecognizable configuration of continents. Most every type of extant plant and animal organism on Earth—except perhaps some kinds of vascular plants and small, insignificant phyla—evolved between 540 and 300 million years ago, before the gradual assembly of the supercontinent. Pangaea was complete by 240 million years ago. Between 240 and 180 million years ago, nothing much happens tectonically except in the outer Pacific continents. The central and northern Atlantic Ocean begins to open by 120 million years ago, the south Atlantic by 60 million years ago. During the Cenozoic era, beginning 65 million years ago, Greenland opens up, and so does the north Atlantic off the coast of Scotland. We arrive at the current configuration when the Indian subcontinent drifts northward from Antarctica and rams up against the Asian continent to form the Himalayan Mountains.

In the last few years it has become possible to put together a geological map of the world (figure 15). The banded parts show relatively simple ocean basins dominated by the magnetic anomalies. An orderly pattern, symmetrical around the ridge, shows basalt covered by various layers of sediment. The continents, which preserve a record to almost 4 billion years ago, are more disorderly. The North American Cordillera from the Rocky Mountains to the Pacific Coast is an example of an exceedingly complex terrain: various slivers of continent were moved around by plate motions, docked at the main continental mass, and accreted to it.

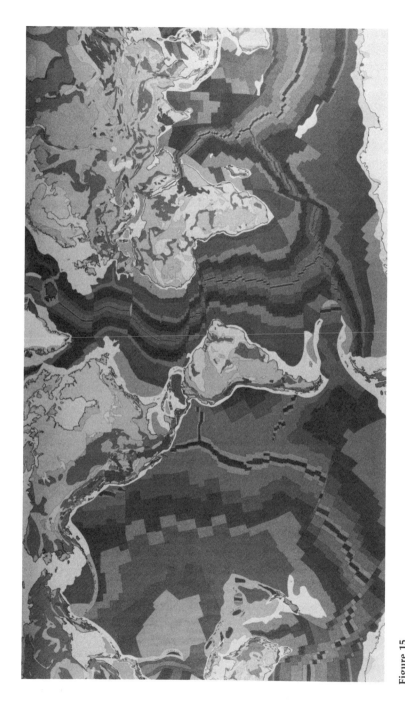

Figure 15
The bedrock geology of the world. Ocean basins are easily recognized by the parallel patterns of magnetic reversals.

When did plate tectonics begin? A few believe that these patterns characterize only the last 100 or 200 million years of geologic history, but most place the inception much earlier. A great many geologists now agree that there is evidence of plate tectonics in the Vendian (late Precambrian). Whether plate tectonics was established as far back as the Archean eon, the period before 2.5 billion years ago, is subject to some debate among specialists. We grope for mechanisms responsible for the cooling of the early Earth. Did magnetic reversals operate in the same way in the ancient past as they have in the recent past? How big were the early continents? We suspect they were much smaller than the continents today, but that's another story.)

Similar geophysical processes, such as convection currents, probably have been at work on the moon, on Mars, and maybe on other planets. However, the thickness of a lithosphere is very much a function of the temperature and thus of the heat flow from the interior of the planet. The moon has lost most of its interior heat. Although the moon's lithosphere may be as much as 400 km thick— too thick to allow any breakage and movement—there is probably little or no convection in its interior. Mars appears to be an intermediate stage. Mars, like the moon, was more active earlier in its history. It may still be intermittently active, or maybe it will become active if enough heat builds up. No evidence exists now for plate motions on Mars, and we don't know whether any convective motion occurs in the Martian mantle. Plate motions can only be inferred from surface manifestations of convection currents. Venus, we believe, has enough interior heat to maintain a sufficiently thin lithosphere so that plate movements and mountains may occur. Venus is blanketed by a dense atmosphere through which we can see only by means of sensitive instruments. There is evidence of volcanoes on Venus, but we still do not know enough about the surface of Venus to infer plate tectonics there. We expect the results of the Magellan mission to be illuminating.

Plate tectonics is an enormous milestone in our understanding of the history of the Earth. We now have an all-encompassing theory that explains the major features of our planet's surface, both the continents and the ocean basins. Further, the theory, based on fundamentally sound geophysical ideas of how the Earth loses heat, links the history of the atmosphere to that of the oceans, providing a mechanism for chemical exchange from the interior to the exterior of the Earth. Together, plate tectonics and continental drift theory are to twentieth-century geology what Newtonian mechanics was to pre-relativistic physics. The theory still lacks details of the mechanics. What dynamical forces pull the plates apart? Many think that lateral plate movement is driven less by "push" from mid-ocean ridges than by "pull" as plates descend into the mantle. Many questions need answering—but plate tectonic theory, constantly in revision, is very much alive. For those of us working on the mechanisms of the Earth's surface, and particularly on the interaction of those mechanisms with life, plate tectonics is the foundation on which future theories of all surface interactions on the Earth will be based.

Readings

Cox, A., ed. 1973. *Plate Tectonics and Geometric Reversals*. Freeman.

Menard, H. W. 1986. *The Ocean of Truth: A Personal History of Global Tectonics*. Princeton University Press.

Press, F., and R. Siever. 1986. *Earth*. Freeman.

Uyeda, S. 1978. *The New View of the Earth: Moving Continents and Moving Oceans*. Freeman.

Van Andel, T. H. 1985. *New View of an Old Planet: Continental Drift and the History of the Earth*. Cambridge University Press.

14 Chemical Signals from Plants and Phanerozoic Evolution

Tony Swain

Secondary compounds are not just waste products of no further use to the organisms that produce them; many are, in fact, "ecological hormones." These compounds have ecological roles as semiochemicals (chemicals that mediate interactions between organisms in the environment)—that is, they are chemical signals. Two types of semiochemicals are recognized: *pheromones* (compounds produced by and targeted toward members of the same species) and *allelochemicals* (compounds produced by members of one species and evoking responses in members of different species).

It has long been recognized that plants and animals profoundly affect the characteristics of one another during the course of their evolution. We have only to consider the case of pollination of flowering plants to see the truth of this statement. Both flowers and their pollinators, whether they are insects, birds, or bats, have developed specialized adaptations to promote success of the operation. Flowers attracting animals with bright colors ensure that pollinators enter their tissue by rewarding the animals with pollen and nectar. This form of signaling between plants and animals is really the essence of biochemical coevolution.

Chemical signals between organisms are largely due to compounds that are not part of primary metabolism. Primary metabolites are absolute requirements for existence and reproduction, such as carbohydrates, nucleic acids and their components (nucleotides, nucleosides, etc.), proteins, amino acids, and lipids. Chemical signals emitted by organisms have been described in the literature as "secondary compounds" or "secondary metabolites," presumably to indicate that they are not as important as primary metabolites. Organic chemists have traditionally referred to these compounds as "natural products" to distinguish them from synthetic compounds made in laboratories. From the ecological and evolutionary point of view, the term *semiochemicals* (from the Greek word *semio,* meaning "signal" or "sign") is more appropriate than these other terms, since it emphasizes their role as chemical signals between organisms. Semiochemicals can serve many ecological roles, such as prey or mate attractants, feeding deterrents, or warnings and deterrents to potential predators or competitors. Semiochemicals are produced by an organism; then either they are emitted into the environment or they remain within the tissues of the producer and eventually evoke a response in another organism.

In animals, neuroreceptors receive chemical signals, and these neuroreceptors send signals to the brain. In most mammals the nose and the mouth are the only organs that receive both smells and tastes, but in insects we find receptors very similar to taste receptors on the feet and other parts of the body. Many insects have feathery protrusions from the tops of their heads which, like our noses, are able to receive and amplify chemical signals of volatile compounds. The emission and reception of these compounds from one insect to another helps regulate their mating, aggregation, defense, and other behaviors.

In this chapter we examine only those semiochemicals produced by plants. We ask how some may have changed during the course of evolution in response to the insects that coevolved with the plants. Among extant organisms, we find that land plants, by and large, produce the largest number of semiochemicals. Plant semiochemicals can be assigned to several different classes on the basis of their chemical structures. We consider here one or two examples from the three major classes: phenols, terpenes, and alkaloids (table 1). The nearly 11,000 known structures are only the tip of the iceberg; the number of compounds present in nature is probably 10 or even 20 times greater.

Phenols as Semiochemicals

A typical phenolic compound, a flavonoid compound called an anthocyanin, is shown in figure 1A. One common anthocyanin, cyan-

Table 1
Major classes of semiochemicals.

	Approximate number of structures known
Phenols	
flavonoids[a]	
tannins	} 1,000
lignins	not well characterized (structurally complex)
Terpenes[b]	
monoterpenes	1,000
sesquiterpenes	600
diterpenes	1,000
triterpenes	800
tetraterpenes	350
polyterpenes	?
Alkaloids	6,000

a. See figure 1A.
b. See figure 1C.

idin, is responsible for the red color in roses and in the skins of winesap apples and other red fruits, such as cherries. The bright red of this anthocyanin is important for flower pollinators that see the color, and, in the case of seed dispersal, for animals that see the red color of fruits such as apples, plums, and cherries. Related anthocyanins are responsible for scarlet, pink, violet, blue, and even black pigments in flowers.

The flavonoids are phenols because they have aromatic or benzene rings, to which hydroxyl (—OH) groups are attached. Flavonoids are probably present in all of the flowering plants, the angiosperms, but they are mostly absent from seedless vascular plants. Some are present in the green algal group, the Characeae, believed to be the closest relatives to plants. They are certainly not present in either bacteria or fungi.

Tannins and lignins are two other groups of phenolic compounds that are essential in many interactions between vascular plants, herbivores, and plant pathogens. The condensed tannins are polymeric molecules, usually containing five to ten flavonoid units joined together (figure 2). Their molecular weights range from 1,500 to 3,000 daltons. A second group of tannins, the hydrolyzable tannins, have

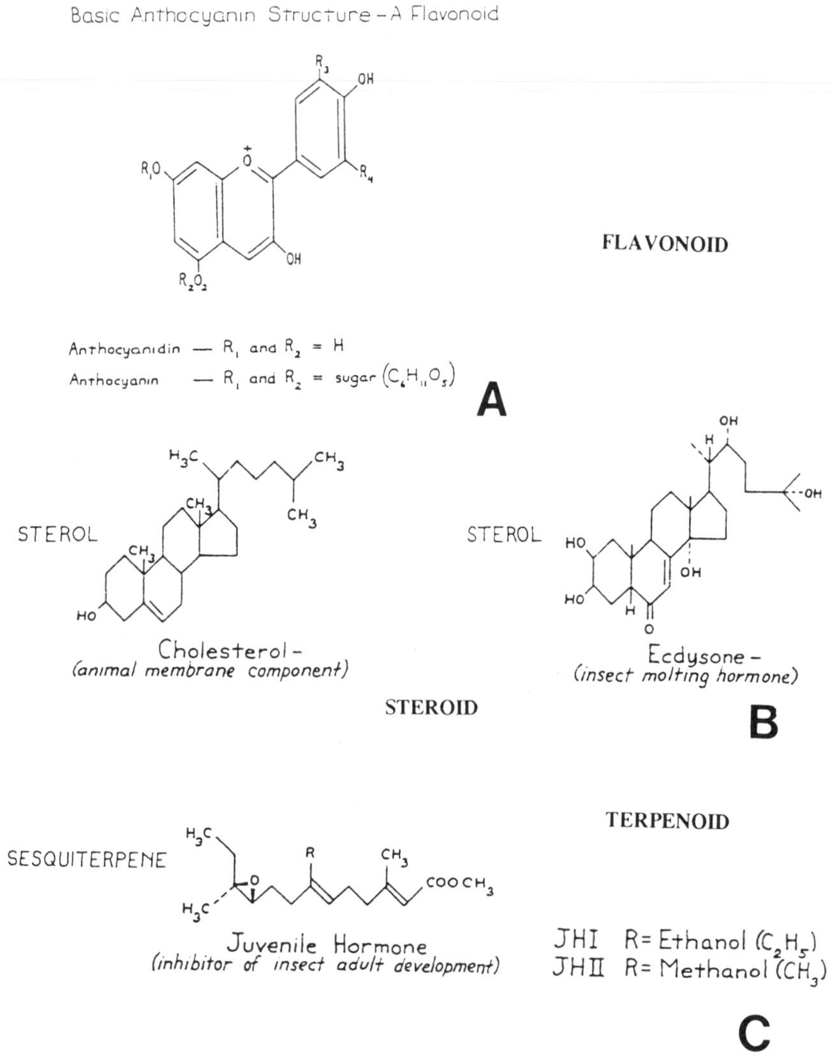

Basic Anthocyanin Structure – A Flavonoid

FLAVONOID

Anthocyanidin — R_1 and R_2 = H

Anthocyanin — R_1 and R_2 = sugar $(C_6H_{11}O_5)$

A

STEROL

Cholesterol –
(animal membrane component)

STEROL

Ecdysone –
(insect molting hormone)

STEROID

B

TERPENOID

SESQUITERPENE

Juvenile Hormone
(inhibitor of insect adult development)

JHI   R = Ethanol (C_2H_5)
JHII R = Methanol (CH_3)

C

Figure 1
A: An anthocyanin, a type of flavonoid that is an important flower color constituent. An anthocyanidin possesses hydrogen at R_1 and R_2; an anthocyanin has sugars substituted at these points. B: The triterpenoid sterols, cholesterol and ecdysone. Ecdysone, chemically very similar to cholesterol, is an insect hormone involved in molting. C: The sesquiterpenoid insect juvenile hormone.

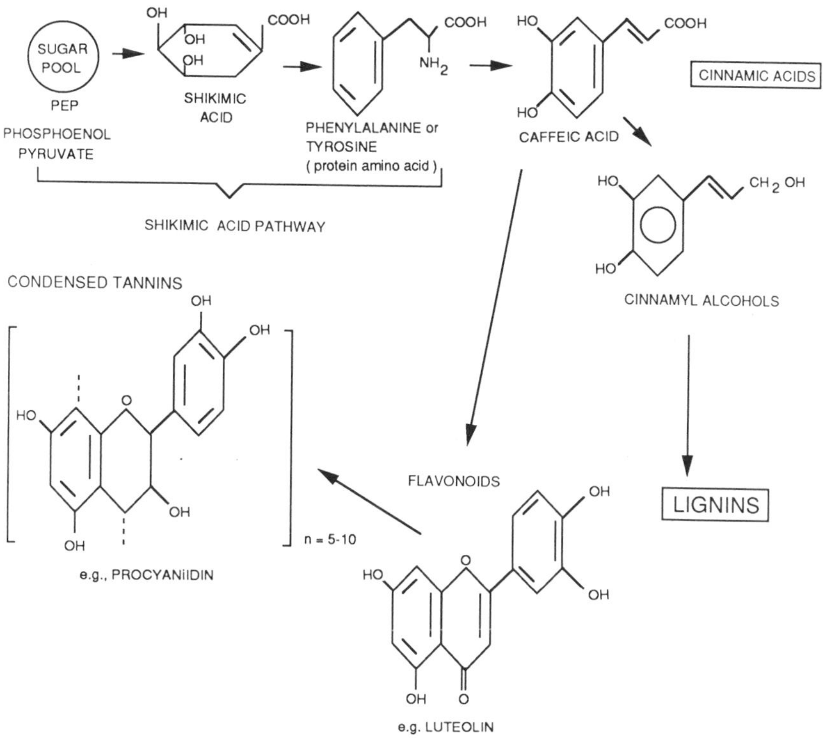

Figure 2
Biosynthetic relationships among flavonoids, tannins, and lignins. Phenylalanine and tyrosine, protein amino acids derived from phosphophenyl pyruvate via the shikimic acid pathway, are the precursors of cinnamic acids. Cinnamic acids are used to make flavonoids and lignins. Condensed tannins are derived from flavonoids.

a "core" sugar molecule to which various simple phenol molecules are attached. Tannins act as deterrents in nature by forming hydrogen bonds between their phenolic hydroxyl groups and the peptide links and other reactive groups of proteins or the hydroxyl groups of polysaccharides. All phenols bind with proteins to some extent; however, the particular effectiveness of tannins as defense compounds in plants relates to their ability to form large insoluble complexes with digestive enzymes of animals, plant proteins, and carbohydrates. This interferes with the digestion and assimilation of nutrients by animals.

Humans, like many animals, avoid plants high in tannins if given a choice. Most of the plants eaten by humans have been selected over many centuries by agriculturists and food producers to be low in distasteful substances such as tannins and other deterrents. If you want to experience for yourself what tannins taste like, bite through an unripe persimmon, grape seeds, or a banana peel. The dry, puckery taste quality of tannins is known as *astringency*.

Tannins are particularly characteristic of woody plants. Although they may occur in all parts of the plant, they are typically most abundant in woody tissues, where they not only deter herbivores but also deter diseases and delay decomposition by fungi. Plants that evolved early in geologic time, such as mosses, liverworts, and lycopods, lack tannins. The first group of land plants to contain tannins, the ferns, evolved in the early Carboniferous or perhaps the late Devonian period, around 360 million years ago. Modifications in the biosynthetic pathways of flavonoids in this group allowed the evolution of tannins in ferns, gymnosperms, and angiosperms. Hydrolyzable tannins are of even more recent origin, since they occur only in dicots.

Lignins are well-known phenols because they are part and parcel of the cell wall of woody plants. Lignins are what we might call the essence of woodiness. They act as plastic glues, locking in the long-chain cellulose molecules that act as reinforcing bars of the cell walls. This makes cell walls tough and woody, and therefore not desirable as food.

The lignins evolved somewhat earlier than the tannins. We find lignin in all plants that contain transporting vessels, including the modern representatives of the very earliest plants visible in the fossil record. We find no lignins in protists or in bacteria, as we might expect. They do occur, however, in *Psilotum*, a present-day remnant of the Rhyniophyta (figure 3). They also occur in lycopods, in horsetails, in ferns, and, of course, in the gymnosperms and angiosperms.

At the end of the Devonian period, around 360 million years ago, there were among the lycopods some trees 100–120 feet tall. It seems likely that lignins were necessary not only to ensure upward growth, but also to ensure the strength of the vessels that transported water up from the roots.

The evolution of these phenolic compounds and their biosynthesis is probably very ancient. They all arise from the aromatic protein amino acids phenylalanine and tyrosine. These universal metabolites

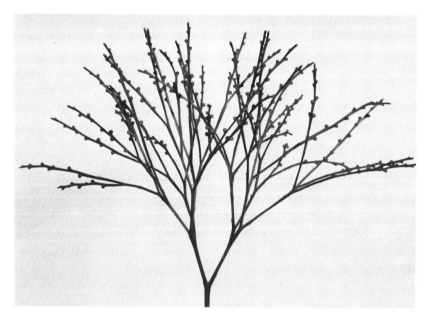

Figure 3
Psilotum, a member of the Rhyniophyta, is a living relative of the earliest vascular plants.

are found in bacteria; we assume they appeared in the early Archean eon or before. The aromatic amino acids are formed from the sugar pool by a relatively straightforward route which includes the simple alicyclic (not aromatic) compound shikimic acid.

The biosynthetic and evolutionary relationships among flavonoids, lignins, and tannins are depicted in figure 2. Flavonoids are present in primitive land plants (*Psilotum,* lycopods, etc.) and, as mentioned above, in one group of green algae: the Characeae of lakes and slow-moving streams. These compounds may initially have developed as light screens to protect early land plants against photodestruction by ultraviolet light of nucleic acids and some coenzymes. The complexity of these compounds increases with evolution; the most recently appearing plants have the most complex flavonoids. Lignins first appear in early land plants, imparting structural rigidity in air. Tannins first appear as flavonoid derivatives in ferns.

The evolution of phenols as defense compounds is related to the movement of plants to land. Plants first coming onto land were probably accompanied by some herbivorous insects. The amphibians did not evolve until much later, followed even later by reptiles and mammals, many of which are voracious plant eaters. Nevertheless, the early insects were probably important herbivores of land plants, eating spores or sucking plant juices. Certainly, a large number of early insects were detritivores, chewing up plant remains along with the bacteria and fungi that accompanied plants onto land.

These herbivore-deterrent compounds, especially tannins and lignins, are obviously important in relation to the development of insects. As lignin enabled plants to evolve into taller forms, insects evolved wings; therefore, height did not provide plants with complete protection from insects. Although insect wings may have evolved at first to regulate body temperature, they allowed insects to fly higher and to exert selection pressure on plants such that even taller plants evolved. Similarly, the development of tannins in leaves and stems, but not in spores, prevented herbivores from chewing on those tissues in plants. We may suppose that lignins and tannins had a marked effect in that a large number of plant remains were not eaten during the Carboniferous period, leading to the extensive coal measures that we find from that period.

Isoprene Units and Terpenoid Formation

The terpenoids are another class of compounds that certainly had enormous effects on the coevolution of plants and animals. Turpentine, produced from pine trees, is an oily liquid formed from a number of terpenoid compounds present in many gymnosperms. The terpenoids are formed from a spiky C-5 unit called isoprene (figure 4). The basic unit that condenses to form the polymers is not isoprene itself but a pyrophosphate derivative called isopentenyl pyrophosphate (IPP) and its isomer dimethylallyl pyrophosphate (DMAPP). The synthesis of isopentenyl pyrophosphate, which comes from the universal 2-carbon metabolite acetate, is shown in figure 4. IPP condenses in a head-to-tail fashion (figure 5) to give dimers, trimers, and so on containing 5, 10, 15, 20, or more carbons. The biosynthetic pathways of the isoprenoids are obviously very ancient, because such compounds occur in many of the quinones that we find even in anaerobic bacteria, used in the transport of electrons from one side of a membrane to another. Bacteria also use isoprenoid compounds, usually containing 50–80 carbon atoms (10–16 isoprene units) to transport sugars from where they are manufactured within the cell to the cell wall for incorporation into the various units there. Another group of terpenoids—the carotenoids (figure 6), required in all photosynthetic systems—are present in photosynthetic bacteria and all photosynthetic eukaryotes. Bacteria chlorophylls also contain a side chain onto which three or four isoprene units are attached. These examples indicate that the pathway to produce three or four isoprene units is a very ancient one.

Terpenoids as Semiochemicals

I have mentioned terpenoid quinones, and terpenoids that transfer sugars in bacteria, and the carotenoids. Making an enormous jump in time, let us now shift to the flowering plants (which evolved only 120 million years ago) and to the gymnosperms (which are a little older, having evolved about 220 million years ago). Both groups of plants contain a vast number of semiochemical terpenoid compounds which act as signals.

Semiochemical terpenoids tend to be simple, containing only two or three isoprene units (that is, 10 or 15 carbon atoms condensed head to tail). They are called monoterpenes if they have 10 carbon atoms, sesquiterpenes if they have 15 carbon atoms (figure 7). Four isoprene units can condense to form diterpenes. Mono-, sesqui-, and diterpenes can be semiochemicals in seed plants, but they are rare or virtually absent in plants that lack seeds. They are absent or uncommon in fungi, animals, and protists. They are completely absent from the bacteria. So, we have a paradox here. The early method of biosynthesis, which could produce large numbers of isoprene units joined together, has been superseded by one which gives simpler types. We can think of this in relation to the biosynthesis of fatty acids. The majority of fatty acids we find in membranes or in storage cells, in plants and animals, contain 16 or 18 carbon atoms, and they are made by the continued addition of two-carbon acetate units to produce the final 16 and 18 carbon atoms. Fatty acids containing fewer carbons are much rarer, pointing to the same paradox: low-carbon-number terpenoids are nearly absent in the predecessors

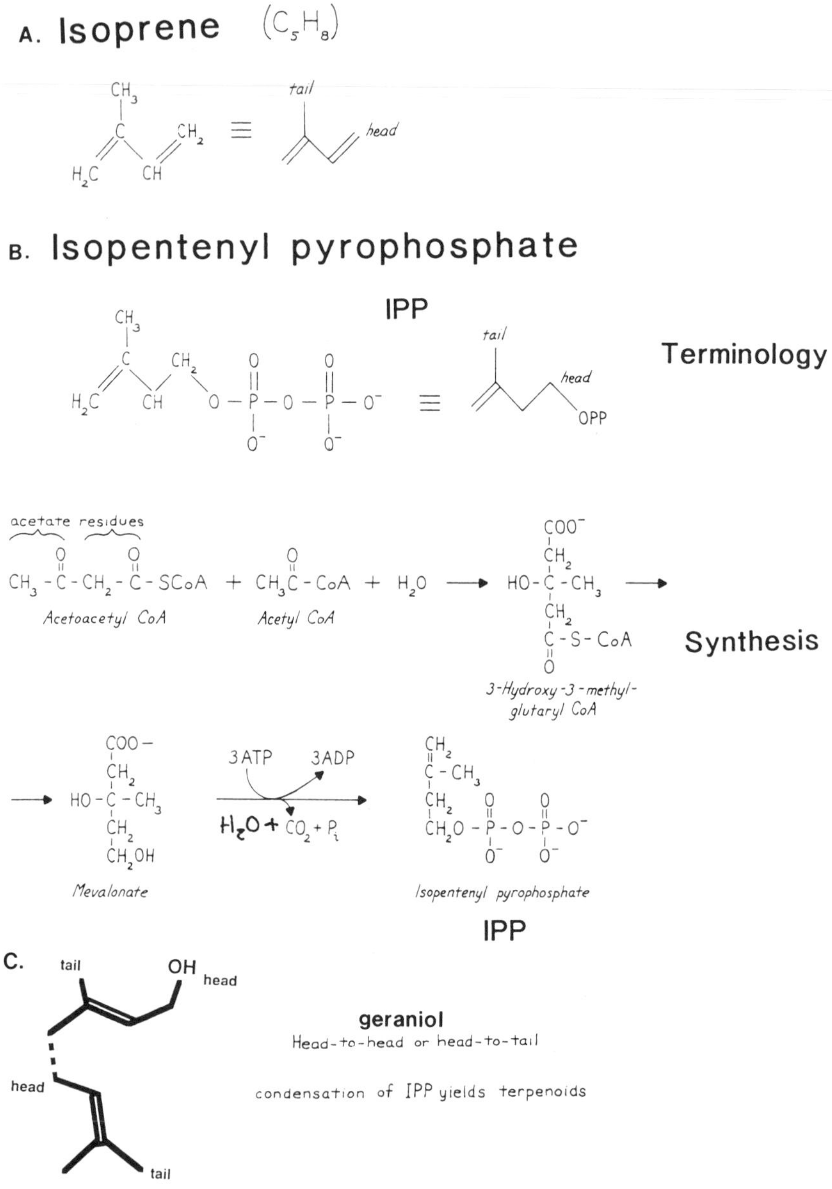

A. Isoprene (C_5H_8)

B. Isopentenyl pyrophosphate

IPP

Terminology

Synthesis

IPP

C.

geraniol
Head-to-head or head-to-tail

condensation of IPP yields terpenoids

Figure 4
A: Isoprene and isopentenyl pyrophosphate. Terpenoids are composed of units of
the five-carbon compound isoprene. The pyrophosphate derivative of isoprene, isopentenyl pyrophosphate, condenses to form the terpenoids. B: Isopentenyl pyrophosphate is synthesized from acetate in the form of acetoacetyl CoA and acetyl
CoA. C: Geraniol is a typical monoterpene, formed by the head-to-tail condensation
(broken line) of two isoprene units.

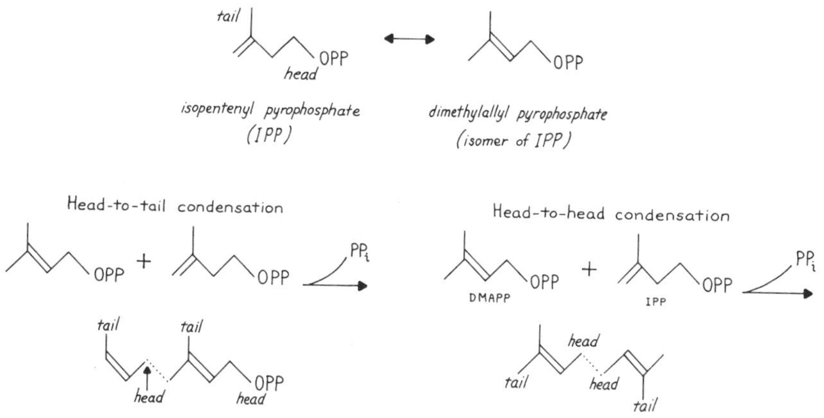

Figure 5
Head-to-tail or head-to-head condensation of isopentenyl pyrophosphate (IPP) and its isomer, dimethylallyl pyrophosphate (DMAPP), yields terpenoids.

to plants. Their evolution was presumably due to some challenge from animals that led plants to vary the control of their terpenoid biosynthetic pathway so that they produce these low-molecular-weight compounds that act as semiochemicals.

How do mono-, sesqui-, and diterpenes act as semiochemicals? The low-molecular-weight monoterpenes are mainly volatile. They account for the piney smell in conifer forests, and for most of the scents of angiosperm flowers. They provide a background of scents that can be attractive to pollinators, but also can act as a kind of hazing mechanism, which prevents insect volatile scents from being properly evaluated by the receivers.

The sesquiterpenes are far less volatile. Their importance, like that of many of the alkaloids, lies in deterring feeding by their bitter taste. This applies especially to those sesquiterpenoids that have one or more hydroxyl or other oxygen residues substituted in the molecule, giving rise to internal lactones. The very bitter sesquiterpenoid lactones deter feeding by insects and mammals. Some also affect the growth and development of insects, and perhaps the development of other animals as well. Diterpenoids, which also affect animal growth, act as feeding deterrents; many of them, especially those that contain oxygen, are bitter.

Sesquiterpenoids very similar in structure to a hormone of insects occur in some gymnosperms. "Juvenile hormone," when released by an insect during molting, retains the insect in an immature phase, preventing it from maturing to an adult. In butterflies and moths, the caterpillar grows in size, going through its various molts, but juvenile hormone keeps the insect as a caterpillar until the very last molt, where it develops not into a larger caterpillar but into a pupa. In this last molt the insect juvenile hormone is not released. Some plant analogues of insect juvenile hormone have an enormous effect on some insects: they ensure that these insects become very giant juveniles and never mature into adults.

One more class of terpenoids, extremely important to us all, is the triterpenoids. Like the carotenoids, triterpenoids are formed by a final head-to-head joining, but in this case isoprenes (two C-15 units) join to give a final 30-carbon compound that then forms rings. The importance of the triterpenoids is that they also yield sterols. Sterols are important in membranes of all eukaryotes. In animals they also act inside the body as internal messengers which we call hormones. (The structure of cholesterol is shown in figure 1B.)

A large number of triterpenes also are feeding deterrents because of their bitter taste. These compounds are present in many plants that we would find bitter. Cucumbers, for example, would be extremely distasteful were it not for selective breeding for low concentration of triterpenes. Ecdysones are among the most important of the triterpenoids. These are again insect hormones affecting the overall molting procedure; they are produced from sterols by small chemical changes in the side chain (figures 1B and 1C). Unlike juvenile hormone, which merely keeps the insect juvenile, ecdysones act as hormones that ensure molting will take place. Ecdysones are very similar to the common sterol cholesterol, which is present in our bodies and those of all mammals. Many ferns, and some gymnosperms, produce very large amounts of terpenoids that mimic insect hormones. It is suspected that until insects evolved ways to properly detoxify and cope with them, these sterols were extremely troublesome. They certainly do not entirely inhibit the development of modern insects, but we assume that during the course of evolution such sterols affected some kinds of insects drastically. Some may still do so.

The carotenoids are a ubiquitous class of terpenoids that contain eight isoprene units, consisting of two groups of four head-to-tail isoprene units joined together head to head (figure 6). The carotenoids are present not only in photosynthetic organisms but also in heterotrophic bacteria, as well as in protists, fungi, and animals. A large number of animals sequester carotenoids from plants and use them for their own coloring. The color of lobsters, for example, is due to a carotenoid-protein complex. The use of different terpenoids must have varied during the course of evolution. Carotenoids provide a good example of how this may have happened. Carotenoids are present in all photosynthetic bacteria; they are essential to the light-harvesting system. However, in flowering plants, carotenoids have taken their part, as with the flavonoids, in petal pigments of flowers and in the skin color of fruits. The bright yellow of daffodils and the red of tomatoes are good examples. Evolutionary processes seem to use ancient chemical pathways to produce signals which lead to plant and animal coevolution.

Alkaloids from Amino Acids

Most of us are aware of the last group of semiochemicals to be discussed here, the alkaloids, since we drink coffee which contains caffeine. Many of us are familiar too with poisonous alkaloids like strychnine, which are still used to rid houses of mice, rats, and other rodents. And, of course, many of us are acquainted with the dangers of the alkaloids morphine, heroin, and cocaine.

Most alkaloids are plant products, although a few are produced by animals. For example, the skins of certain frogs and toads in South America contain alkaloids. The main characteristic of alkaloids is that they all contain nitrogen and, in solution, they all act to take up protons (i.e., as "bases" in the sense of raising pH to create alkaline solutions). Usually the nitrogen is present within a six-member ring. These heterocyclic rings, as they are called, often contain five carbon atoms and a nitrogen atom. Another defining characteristic of alkaloids is that they are highly physiologically active on animals. Some, like strychnine, are poisonous; others, like heroin, have deleterious or psychological effects. Although people may at first consider the effects of morphine and heroin euphoric and pleasant, heavy use of these substances leads to dependence and degradation and even

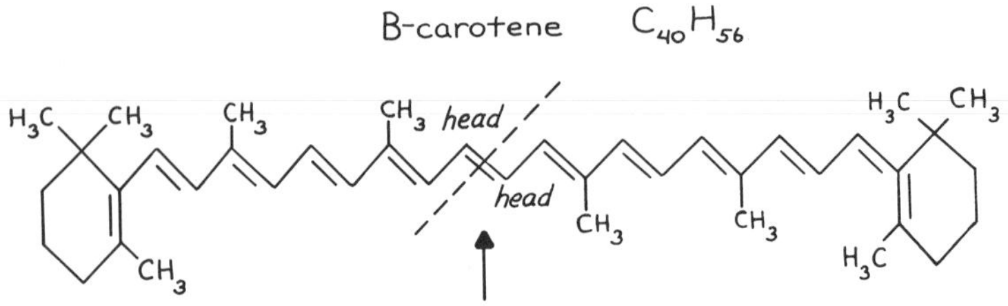

Figure 6
Carotenoids, C_{40} compounds, contain a total of eight isoprene units. They are composed of two groups of four isoprene units condensed head to tail, which are then joined (at the arrow) by head-to-head condensation.

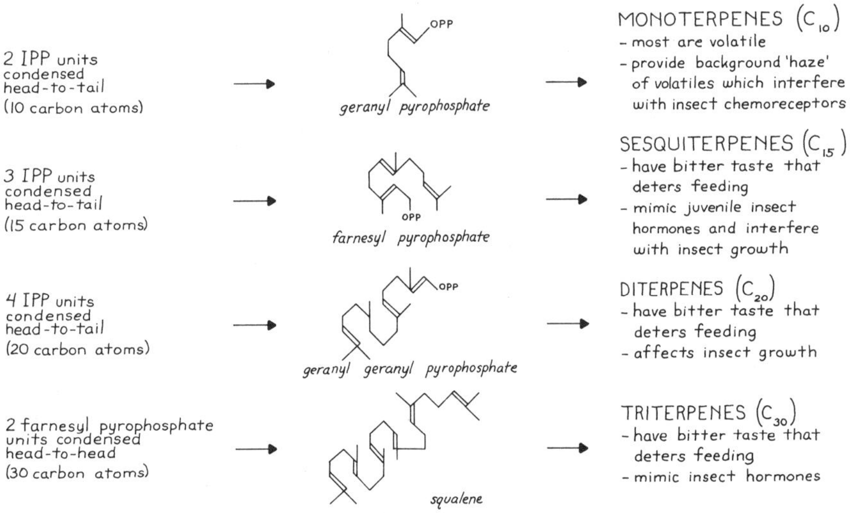

Figure 7
Terpenoid compounds: components, representative structures, and properties of monoterpenes, sesquiterpenes, diterpenes, and triterpenes.

death. Alkaloids have the same kind of effects on many animals, acting as deterrents or attractants as the case may be.

Unlike the other two classes of compounds, terpenoids and phenolics, almost 99 percent of all known alkaloids occur only in the flowering plants; therefore, they have evolved only during the last 120 million years or so. Some alkaloids are found in fungi, some in lycopods, and one or two in gymnosperms. The alkaloids contained in lycopods are based on lysine. The pathway from lysine to some alkaloids is relatively early; even the general route to the protein amino acid lysine may include some cyclic compounds. But, by and large, we are surprised that not until the mammals evolved did plants scramble to produce the large number of new biosynthetic pathways that enabled them to synthesize the extraordinary variety of alkaloids that deter insects and mammals today. Certainly no alkaloids have been reported to be synthesized by protoctists or prokaryotes. Let us consider exactly how alkaloids are formed in the flowering plants.

I am limiting my discussion here to alkaloids formed from amino acids. They fall into two classes: those formed from the aromatic amino acids phenylalanine, tyrosine, and tryptophan, and those formed from the diaminoaliphatic amino acids lysine and ornithine.

Not until the evolution of the flowering plants were these alkaloids produced in sufficient quantities to act as feeding deterrents, yet their mode of biosynthesis from primary metabolites is relatively simple (figure 8). Phenylalanine is decarboxylated, and the resulting amine, phenylethylamine, is condensed with an aldehyde to close the ring and create the various alkaloids (figures 8 and 9). The same is generally true of the nonaromatic amino acids, such as lysine, except here the amino acid is not only decarboxylated; it also loses the alpha-amino group, and its terminal amino group forms a ring which closes to produce alkaloids such as cocaine and nicotine (figures 8 and 10).

The most physiologically active of the alkaloids are those derived from aromatic amino acids. These include benzoisoquinoline alkaloids (figure 9), which lead to the formation of compounds such as morphine and which are known not only in flowering plants but also in certain fungi.

The alkaloids, almost without exception, have a bitter taste. They may be extremely bitter or only slightly so. Their taste gives us and

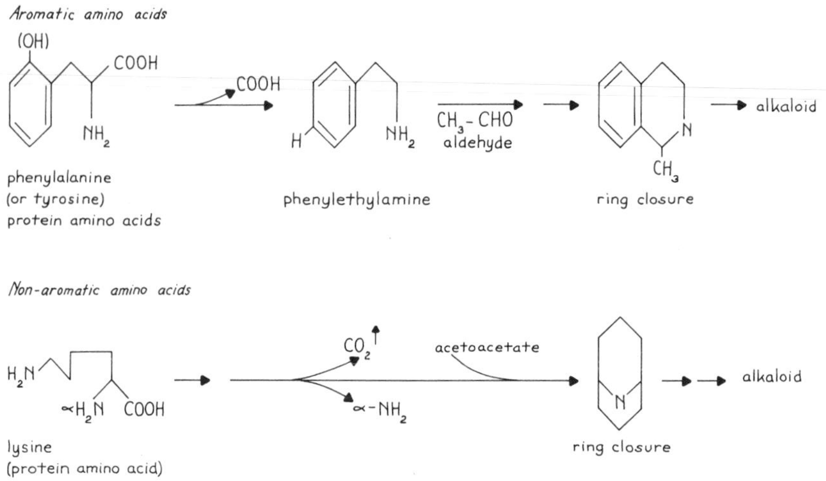

Figure 8
Aromatic amino acids are decarboxylated and condensed with an aldehyde to form
the closed nitrogen-containing ring structure of various alkaloids. In nonaromatic
amino acids, the α-amino group is lost during decarboxylation and condensation
with acetoacetate. The terminal amino group becomes incorporated into the closed
ring of the resulting alkaloid.

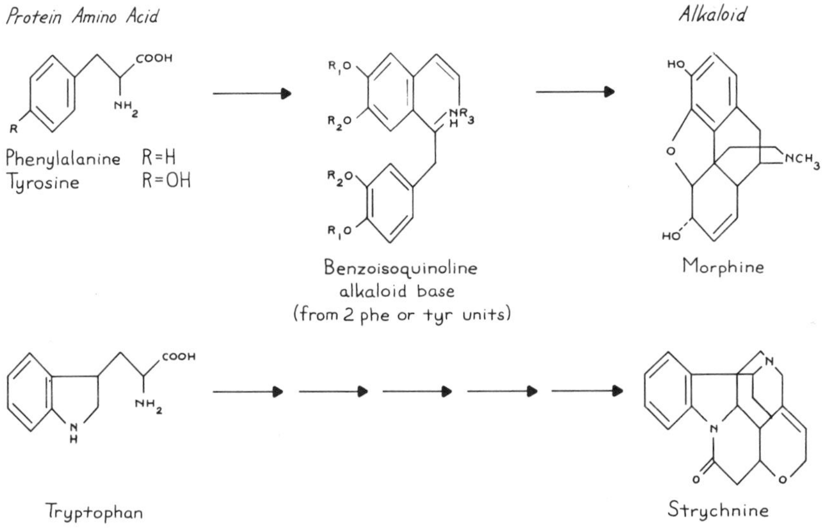

Figure 9
Alkaloids derived from aromatic amino acids. The synthesis of morphine from
phenylalanine and tyrosine involves the formation of benzoisoquinoline alkaloid
intermediates. Strychnine is made from tryptophan in a many-step metabolic
pathway.

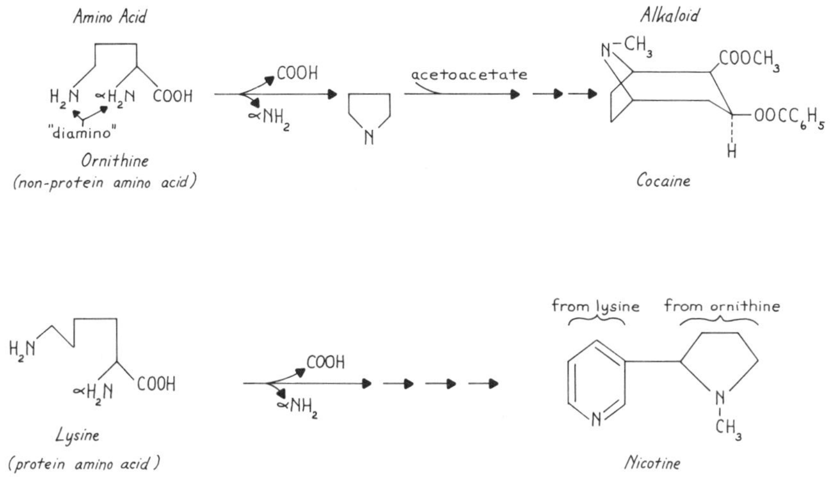

Figure 10
Cocaine and nicotine are formed from the diaminoaliphatic amino acids ornithine and lysine, respectively.

other mammals a clue to their occurrence. Excessive bitterness in food tends to repulse most organisms. I believe "bitterness" is the most primitive of all the taste sensations. Alkaloids synthesized from the aromatic amino acids are often the most bitter and usually the most toxic.

Returning to the biochemical coevolution of plants and animals, we can start looking at land plants and land animals from the early Devonian period to the present. Plants, early in their evolutionary history, had to cope not only with insects and other animals but also with fungal, bacterial, and viral pathogens.

The Role of Semiochemicals in the Evolution of Land Plants

We do not know if the first land plants had to cope with attack by nematodes, earthworms, or the land snails present as soil fauna today, because the fossil record on this issue is sparse. The first accounts of land snails do not occur until about 330 million years ago. Nevertheless, plants have thrived on land since the Devonian period. They must have had bacterial, fungal, and animal helpers that insured production of soil. Detritus was enzymatically chewed up, and particles of sediment were attracted and collected. Such coevolution suggests not only fierce battles between plants and animals but also strong cooperative interactions. The evolution of lignins and then tannins during the late Devonian/early Carboniferous period provided a way for plants to avoid the fiercer insect herbivores that had evolved by then. Perhaps at this time plants developed insect hormones, such as juvenile hormone and the ecdysones responsible for molting. During the Carboniferous period, when a great diversity of large land plants thrived and prospered, detritus was not readily decomposed. Perhaps some plant defenses were far too strong for the animals, mainly insects, living at that time.

The first of the land vertebrates, the amphibians, probably did not have much of an effect on plants. Most modern amphibians are carnivores, eating insects; perhaps the early ones were also. Not until the reptiles evolved, toward the end of the Paleozoic Era (about 290 million years ago), moved away from the river and lakeside habitats of the amphibians, and became the dominant animals were plants forced to cope with more voracious herbivores. Probably during that time the gymnosperms, the ferns, and a number of other plant orders that have since died out developed new types of deterrents. The various terpenoids we find in present-day gymnosperms (monoterpenoids, sesquiterpenoids, diterpenoids, and triterpenoids) apparently evolved in response to these challenges.

When the angiosperms finally evolved, about 120 million years ago, they radiated extensively, becoming dominant plants very quickly—within 60 million years. Concurrently, a large number of new types of compounds evolved, including chemical signals produced using old biosynthetic pathways. Colored compounds and a host of alkaloids and terpenoids developed and were used in different ways. Plants had long been using lignin and tannins as deterrents; animals and other organisms still have not devised suitable ways to overcome them. (Of course, humans, beavers, and packrats have exploited the elastic lignin for various uses, including firewood, homes, and buildings.)

We can look forward to knowing more and more about the biochemical coevolution of plants and animals as more work is devoted not just to the structures of natural products so beloved by the organic chemists but also to the way in which these compounds act as semiochemicals and the way in which animals have devised detoxification and other mechanisms to overcome them.

Questions and Answers
Robert Buchsbaum

In 1986, Robert Buchsbaum, a former student of the late Tony Swain, addressed questions raised by Swain's lecture. Dr. Buchsbaum, now the Massachusetts Audubon Society's Coastal Ecologist, is researching semiochemical interactions between marine plants, animals, and microorganisms. His laboratory is located on a nature preserve on the Atlantic coast of northeastern Massachusetts.

What classes of volatile chemicals can our noses detect?

Our noses can detect monoterpenes, simple phenols, amines, and sulfur-based compounds. Monoterpenes include many familiar odors of flowers and flavorings: e.g., lemon, lime, and menthol. Simple phenols include compounds such as cinnamon and vanilla. The amines are responsible for the odors of cooking and rotting meat. For example, the amines putrescine and cadaverine are named for their smell. The smells of garlic and onions, as well as the skunky odors that are found throughout nature, are due to sulfur compounds. We do detect other classes of compounds, but these are the major ones.

Are animal receptors sensitive to specific plant chemicals, or is the sensitivity generalized?

In some cases, particularly with invertebrates, there seem to be specific receptors; for example, lobsters have a specific receptor for glutamine. In vertebrates, it seems that the receptor is fairly generalized. The reference by Visser provides more information (see "Readings" below).

Plants seem to show more evolutionary change in their chemistry than animals; furthermore, plants apparently evolved chemical defenses against animals. Are these generalizations accurate?

Plants display more chemical evolution because they don't "behave"; they can't run away the way animals do. The major response by plants to attack by animal herbivory is the evolution of defensive chemicals. Plants, of course, respond or evolve to many different factors (not just to herbivores), including light, nitrates, phosphates, and other nutrients, and to the attraction of pollinators.

How do animals generally adapt to evolutionary changes in plants?

Animals tend to change their behavior and, with time, evolve different behavioral mechanisms. They may simply avoid eating toxic plants, or they may avoid toxic parts of plants, as aphids do by feeding on phloem sap.

In addition (and this is fairly well studied), a variety of enzymes in animal guts, such as mixed-function oxidases, act to detoxify secondary compounds; they are very general in their activity. Animals also have an enzyme called rotenase, which detoxifies cyanide, a very toxic semiochemical in a number of plants. The addition of a thiosulfate group to cyanide, by this enzyme, yields thiocyanate, a compound much less toxic than cyanide.

How does hydrogen bonding of tannins to plant proteins and polysaccharides disrupt the ability of herbivores to digest the plant? Does the hydrogen bonding itself make them indigestible or bitter tasting? Can any animals or bacteria metabolize tannins?

According to current views, and there is still a lot of controversy on this issue, hydrogen bonding of tannins to proteins and polysaccharides occurs because the tannins are able to cross-link several protein molecules, creating large insoluble complexes. Chemical cross-linking occurs readily, but we don't know if it is the actual mechanism of their deterrence. Hydrogen bonding of tannins to proteins may make them indigestible, but they may also be repellent because of the astringent taste.

We assume that bacteria can metabolize tannins, and that is the way tannins are eventually broken down in the ecosystem. However, some insects deal with tannins by binding them within the gut to a membrane or lining, which is eventually egested.

What is the definition of an astringent? Are most astringents condensed tannins?

An astringent, in medicine, is something that constricts tissue, such as a substance that causes a wound to close. In the pharmacological sense, astringents such as alum are not necessarily condensed tannins. In ecological chemistry, astringency refers to the cross-linking of proteins, which gives a dry, puckery feeling in the mouth.

Are there animals that do not taste tannins as "bitter"?

We assume that other animals taste the tannins as what we call "astringent," just as humans do, but it's impossible to say with any assurance that these compounds cause other mammals or insects to experience the same taste we do.

In discussing terpenoids, [Professor Swain] refer[s] to head-to-tail and head-to-head condensation. Please explain these condensations and their significance.

Terpenoids consist of "spiky" five-carbon building blocks called isoprene units. The "head" and the "tail" are the two ends of the isoprene unit. The tail is at the spiky end of the molecule.

In the monoterpene geraniol (figure 4 above), a head-to-tail condensation of two isoprene units yields the ten-carbon compound. A generalized head-to-tail condensation is also illustrated on the left side of figure 5.

Smaller terpenoids (monoterpenes, sesquiterpenes, and diterpenes) are composed entirely of isoprene units (two, three, and four units, respectively) joined head to tail.

A head-to-head condensation is shown on the right in figure 5. For steroids and other triterpenes, two sesquiterpenes are joined together head to head to form a compound composed of six isoprene units. In the synthesis of carotenoids, two diterpenes are joined together head to head to form a forty-carbon compound (figure 6). The basic units of the carotenoids and other C_{40} terpenoids are isoprene units put together head to tail, but the final step in their synthesis involves one head-to-head condensation of C_{20} units.

Is there any evidence that monoterpenes prevent insect reproductive success?

Geraniol is a typical monoterpene, a terpene with ten carbon atoms (figure 4). Notice the "spiky" structure. Geraniol is an alcohol with a hydroxyl group. Monoterpenes are often feeding deterrents, or occasionally feeding attractants, so their effect on insect reproduction is indirect. Because the gymnosperms contain vast mixtures of monoterpenes, it is hard to determine the effects of a single monoterpene on insect reproductive success. The article by McClure and Hare in the "Readings" list below examines the effects of monoterpenes on the fecundity of scale insects.

How do sesqui- and diterpenes affect insect growth and development?

A monoterpene is made of ten carbon atoms, or two C-5 units, the basic isoprenoid building blocks of terpenoids. A sesquiterpene is composed of fifteen carbon atoms, and a diterpene contains twenty. Insect juvenile hormones are sesquiterpenes, and a number of plants (particularly the gymnosperms) produce mimics of juvenile hormones.

Sesquiterpene lactones comprise a well-known group of very bitter toxic compounds which occur primarily in sunflowers and other composites. Diterpenes are toxic or defense compounds in rhododendrons, *Kalmia* (mountain laurel), *Solidago* (goldenrod), and some chenopods (members of the spinach family). Gillian Cooper-Driver has worked on diterpenes and their effects on beetles feeding on *Solidago*. More examples are in the Mabry and Gill article listed below.

What functions do the carotenoids have in plants? What is their function in bacteria? Are carotenoids limited to photosynthetic organisms?

Carotenoids are accessory pigments in all oxygenic photosynthesis, absorbing light in the parts of the spectrum where chlorophyll *a* does not. For example, the peaks of absorbance of carotenoids are 460 nm and 500 nm, whereas those for chlorophyll *a* are around 440 nm and 670 nm. Their conjugated structure, which includes a combination of single and double bonds, also protects plants from photo-oxidation. These double bonds can absorb ultraviolet light, and presumably work as UV screens. Present in all photosynthetic organisms (even bacteria), carotenoids are responsible for the red, orange, and yellow colors in some flowers and fruits (for example, tomatoes, *Calendula*, and lilies). Most of the yellows in flowers like *Rudbeckia*, the Black-Eyed Susan, are hydroxylated or oxygenated carotenoids called xanthophylls. Brown algae, diatoms, and other algae also possess oxygenated carotenoids.

The pink color of flamingos is due to carotenoids, which the birds obtain indirectly from the algae they eat. Vitamin A is a product of beta carotene cleavage, or carotenoid cleavage; retinine is an oxidation product of vitamin A. In summary, carotenoids are conspicuous in all photosynthetic organisms, including bacteria, but they are also present, in lower concentrations, in other organisms.

Please discuss the effects of terpenoids on growth in animals.

Most of the studies of terpenoids have considered their effects as feeding deterrents of animals, primarily insects. I would like to point out that this is a very large question, because of the great diversity of terpenoid structures. If we want to remember that steroids are terpenoids, we can mention molting hormones and note the important metabolic effects of steroids. For a general reference, see the paper by Mabry and Gill listed below.

Are alkaloids present in most flowering plants? How do you explain the recent development and the distribution of these chemicals?

While nearly all known alkaloids are produced by flowering plants, they occur in only about 20 percent of them, primarily dicots.

Alkaloids are a large group of compounds characterized by heterocyclic rings of nitrogen and carbon atoms. They are basic compounds in the sense that they are soluble in acid and take up protons (H^+ ions); hence the name "alkaloid." They are also characterized by being physiologically active. Alkaloids are synthesized via a variety of metabolic routes. Although most are derived from amino acids, some alkaloids are derived from steroids. Alkaloids are not homologous to each other, nor do they have a single origin; rather, this vast group of compounds is defined by their chemical characteristics.

Please discuss the extent of the ability among animals to detoxify phenols, terpenes, and alkaloids.

Animals vary greatly in their ability to detoxify phenols, terpenes, and alkaloids. Briefly, it seems that many animals have, among other mechanisms for dealing with toxicity, mixed-function oxidases (MFOs). The speed with which these enzymes are produced often varies among insects. In generalist-feeding insects, MFOs are induced very rapidly. More specialized feeders, insects that have only one or few food sources, must deal in other ways with toxins from their particular food plants. These mechanisms vary greatly, and depend on the evolutionary history of the animal.

Please discuss the range of alkaloid toxicity in various groups of animals. Are the same alkaloids toxic to some animals and not to others?

Toxicity of alkaloids varies greatly among animals. Nicotine, for example, is used as an insecticide, yet the tobacco horn worm, the cabbage looper, and the tobacco bud worm are all resistant to it. Another group of alkaloids, the pyrrolizidene alkaloids found in ragworts (*Senecio*), are hepatotoxins. They are toxic to the liver of mammals, but not to certain moths, and they are used as sex attractants by danaid butterflies.

How did flowering plants develop terpenes less complex than those of the earlier vascular plants? Does the biosynthesis of the longer polymers require more energy? How is it that longer-chain terpenes are found in the plants and bacteria that appear earlier in the fossil record?

In answering why flowering plants developed terpenes simpler than those of earlier vascular plants, there is the assumption that the longer polymers would be harder to synthesize and therefore would take longer to evolve. In fact, it is appropriate to realize that carotenoids and other long-chain terpenoids are absolute requirements for photosynthesis. Later, certain plants developed the ability to modify simpler mono- and sesquiterpenes into ecologically useful compounds. We see this particularly in gymnosperms and angiosperms, which make a great variety of the simpler terpenoids. The pathway to the production of terpenoids has been a part of metabolism since the Archean eon. The ability to modify terpenoids into useful, ecologically relevant compounds, as in many gymnosperms and angiosperms, apparently evolved more recently, during the Phanerozoic eon.

What allowed some insects to continue to feed on early plants even when these plants produced compounds toxic to the insects?

We can only infer that the same diverse mechanisms that were present in the past are also present today; these include simple behavioral mechanisms such as taste avoidance and more complex detoxification mechanisms. Some insects evolved specializations in which they adapted to particular plants and became able to detoxify the specific compounds present in those plants. As long as the insect food is limited to those plants, no harm comes to them from these secondary metabolites. Animal physiological mechanisms for dealing with toxic plants include rapid excretion of toxins, sequestering of toxins, detoxification mechanisms (including gut microbiota that can deal with secondary metabolites), surfactants which break down lipid compounds or solubilize water-insoluble compounds so they can be excreted, and various degrees of tolerance to toxins.

Insects seem to evolve faster than flowering plants, perhaps because they have more rapid generation times. They apparently have the ability to produce a great amount of genetic variation from which mechanisms for dealing with plant toxins could evolve.

With what frequency does color vision occur in major plant-eating groups of animals (i.e., insects, birds, and mammals)?

There is color vision in insects and birds. This is obvious from the way flowers attract insect and bird pollinators; it is also suggested by the simple observation that these groups of organisms are often very colorful themselves. Most mammals, except the primates, seem to lack color vision.

Over what span of time did the evolution of semiochemicals (e.g., alkaloids or terpenoids) take place?

How long it takes a metabolic pathway to evolve is a very speculative question. Alkaloids evolved relatively recently within flowering plants—in the Cretaceous period of the Mesozoic era, about 100 million years ago. Some of what are considered the more primitive groups of angiosperms, such as the Magnoliales and Ranunculales, are alkaloid-containing groups, so we assume that certain alkaloids evolved early in the history of the group. Alkaloids are also present in some lycopods and horsetails (but not in ferns), in a few conifers, and in the gnetophytes (e.g., *Ephedra* and *Welwitschia*), yet the vast majority are found in the dicotyledonous flowering plants.

The terpenoid pathway, on the other hand, is extremely old; terpenoids are involved in the electron-transport chain and in photosynthesis. All chlorophyll molecules, for example, contain an isoprene derivative. The ability to make terpenoids must therefore be very old, perhaps as old as life itself.

Please discuss plant-to-plant semiochemical interactions (e.g., chemical communication between alders and willows when attacked by insects). Over what sort of distances can plants communicate via semiochemicals?

The idea of plant-to-plant semiochemical communication (i.e., that trees "talk" to each other) is really an open question now; whether it really occurs is still under consideration. I think the data for it is not terribly strong. Some plants may do it, other plants definitely do not. The best study is that of Rhoades, listed below.

Also, keep in mind that no one has looked at interspecific communication, such as willows communicating with alders, as the question asks. Rhoades found that only the near neighbors of the same species of an attacked tree gave any indication of having received any kind of signal. It is an interesting area of research. There is still a fair amount of controversy over whether plants can chemically communicate with each other.

Readings

Brattsten, L. B. 1979. Biochemical defense mechanisms in herbivores against plant allelochemics. In *Herbivores: Their Interaction with Secondary Plant Metabolites*, ed. G. Rosenthal and D. Janzen. Academic Press.

Cooper-Driver, G. A., and P. W. LeQuesne. 1987. Diterpenoids as insect antifeedants and growth inhibitors: Role in *Solidago* species. In *Allelochemicals: Role in Agriculture and Forestry*, ed. G. R. Walker. American Chemical Society.

Fenecal, T. 1982. Natural products chemistry in the marine environment. *Science* 215: 923–937.

Harborne, J. G. 1982. *Introduction to Ecological Biochemistry.* Second edition. Academic Press.

Mabry, T. J., and J. E. Gill. 1979. Sesquiterpenoid lactones and other terpenoids. In *Herbivores: Their Interaction with Secondary Plant Metabolites*, ed. G. Rosenthal and D. Janzen. Academic Press.

McClure, M. S., and J. D. Hare. 1984. Foliar terpenoids in *Tsuga* species and the fecundity of scale insects. *Oecologia* 63: 185–193.

Rhoades, D. F. 1983. Responses of alder and willow to attack by tent caterpillars: Evidence for pheromonal sensitivity of willows. In *Plant Resistance to Insects*, ed. P. A. Heden. American Chemical Society.

Robinson, T. 1979. The evolutionary ecology of alkaloids. In *Herbivores: Their Interaction with Secondary Plant Metabolites*, ed. G. Rosenthal and D. Janzen. Academic Press.

Swain, T. 1977. Secondary compounds as protective agents. *Annual Review of Plant Physiology* 28: 479–501.

Visser, J. H. 1983. Differential sensory perception of plant compounds by insects. In *Plant Resistance to Insects*, ed. P. A. Heden. American Chemical Society.

15

Mammalian Evolution:
Karyotypic Fission Theory

Neil Todd

Neil Todd has noted correlations between chromosome numbers in living organisms and sudden and impressive episodes of adaptive radiation in mammals in the fossil record. Karyotypic fission is a mechanism of "macromutation"—rapid rather than gradual evolutionary change.

Todd has worked on his concept of karyotypic fission in the context of carnivores, especially dogs and artiodactyls (pigs, camels, horses, and their relatives). His ideas have not been understood or criticized seriously in the mainstream literature of neo-Darwinism. In this chapter he describes the essentials of his theory.

Karyotypic fission is a theory of chromosomal evolution I developed to explain certain phenomena of mammalian evolution. I believe that karyotypic fissioning is a major mechanism of speciation that applies to all tetrapods (amphibians, reptiles, birds, and mammals) and to other species of animals whose sex is determined by a pair of sex chromosomes.

A karyotype is a representation of the mitotic metaphase chromosomes arranged in accordance with a specific convention by homologous pairs. Take, for example, the karyotype of a long-nosed bandicoot, an Australian marsupial (figure 1). The diploid number of chromosomes of the bandicoot is 14. The autosomal chromosomes are depicted in two rows in order of decreasing length, followed by the two sex chromosomes, X and Y. The arms of each chromosome join in a region called the *centromere*. The *kinetochore*, a microtubule-chromatin junction visible by electron microscopy, forms at the centromere region before chromosome segregation during mitosis. Karyotypic fissioning corresponds to the duplication and dissociation of the centromeres such that both arms of any two-armed chromosome

Order: MARSUPIALIA   Family: PERAMELIDAE

Perameles nasuta (Long-nosed bandicoot)

2N=14
male
2N=12M+XY

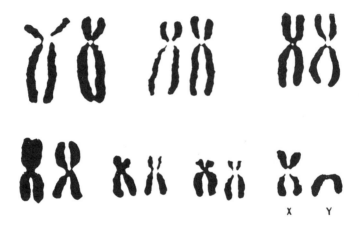

X   Y

N= haploid number of chromosomes
M= mediocentric chromosome

Figure 1
Karyotype of *Perameles nasuta* (long-nosed bandicoot).

become two independent chromosomes or genetic linkage groups
(figure 2). A linkage group consists of all the genes or genetic loci on
a single chromosome. Karyotypic fission usually involves the entire
chromosomal complement of the cell in which it occurs, although
the eventual karyotype may be modulated by many other factors.
Thus, it is not the karyotypes that actually fission, but rather the
chromosomes or linkage groups from which karyotypes are constructed. Since recognition involves the comparison of karyotypes,
the phenomenon is called *karyotypic fission* rather than chromosomal
fission. Chromosome fission may yield various products, as figure 2

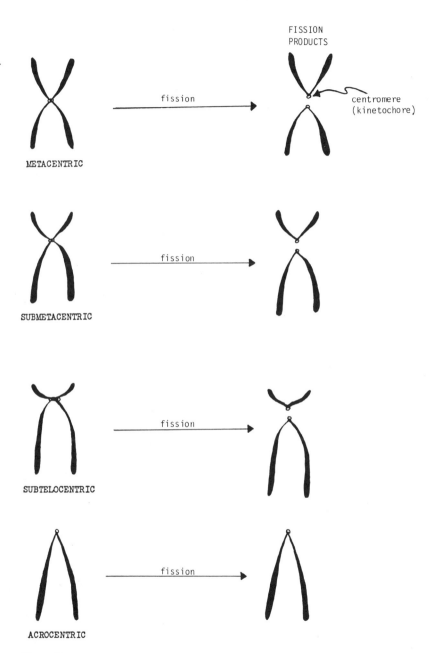

Figure 2
Products of chromosomal fission.

shows. If the centromere of a particular chromosome is central, after fission two chromosomes exist where there was originally one. If the centromere is terminal, the chromosome and the linkage relation of the genes on that chromosome remain essentially unchanged.

Hypothetical Phylogenies of Fissioned Karyotypes

Karyotypic fission can be correlated to the phylogeny of mammals as reconstructed from the fossil record. Phylogenies are hypothesized genealogical sequences, often diagrammed as a branching tree, of ancestor-descendant relationships. Mammals first appear at the Triassic-Jurassic boundary, about 180 million years ago. Since then between 20,000 and 40,000 species have evolved, though today there may be only 4,000 or more extant species. The reasonably good fossil record and the various kinds of comparative studies allow the overall relationships and pedigrees of many of the surviving lines to be established. Exactly how many species have been karyotyped is not known, but estimates are in the vicinity of 2,000 in a good cross-section of mammals. As might be expected, the karyotypes of some groups are much better known than those of others. The diploid number of chromosomes in mammals ranges from 6 to 92. A deer, *Muntiacus muntjak*, is at the low extreme, with a diploid number of 6 in the female and 7 in the male (figure 3); a South American dog, *Atelocynus microtis*, has a diploid number of 74 (figure 4).

Despite this somewhat bewildering range, there are also fundamental similarities among mammalian genomes. These similarities are critical to the understanding and interpretation of the relation of karyotypic fission to mammalian evolution. The total DNA content of the mammalian genome is remarkably constant. DNA content varies from about 85 percent to 105 percent of that of the *Homo sapiens* genome. The sex of any animal is determined by a pair of sex chromosomes. The presence of two X chromosomes determines the sex as female, whereas all males are XY. The X chromosome, although sometimes involved in peculiar translocations, represents approximately 5 percent of the haploid genome in all mammalian species. In most mammals the X chromosome is of medium size and is mediocentric (that is, the centromere is near the middle). From these facts certain inferences can be drawn: First, all differences in mammalian karyotypes result primarily from the repackaging of a seminal genome, not from the addition or the subtraction of material. Second, the sex-determining mechanism is largely refractory to rearrangement—in other words, the X chromosome usually survives and is present in very disparate lineages, no matter what the diploid number. The Muntjac deer has essentially the same X chromosome (although it is attached to an autosome) as the South American dog; the total amount of DNA in these two karyotypes is not grossly different.

In the construction of a phylogeny of a particular group, it is possible to proceed to an analysis of the distribution of the karyotypes in all the extant derivatives within this group. In a hypothetical phylogenetic tree, a common ancestor is the starting point from which lineages (including extinct ones) can be traced (figure 5). The aim is to reveal the sequence of events (especially adaptive radiations or cladistic episodes) in each lineage—in short, the emergence of diverse species from an ancestral form. One descendant (the one on the left in figure 5) has more or less extended into the present, and is not a derivative of any large adaptive radiation. Although this species may be quite different from the ancestral species in terms of particular specializations, it has had no tendency to diversify. An episode of adaptive radiation appearing in this line is termed the *first cladistic episode* or the *primary radiation;* a second cladistic episode, if recognizable, is called the *secondary radiation,* and so on. If the diploid number of the species descending directly to the present is, for example, 14 ($2n = 14$), then we assume this is the ancestral diploid number. As we look at derivatives of a single cladistic episode, we find the diploid number elevated to the mid 20s. If a derivative line descends through two adaptive radiations, the diploid number will be higher still, roughly in the high 30s or the 40s. If a third episode of adaptive radiation in this line of descent emerges, diploid numbers in the 60s or the 70s, or higher, may be found. Today such patterns of diploid numbers are known to exist in numerous lineages of mammals, although never as ideally as in this hypothetical construction.

The ploidy of $2n = 14$ postulated in the last example was not a random choice. Marsupials are found in Australia and South America, and the few North American representatives are descendants of

Order: ARTIODACTYLA   Family: CERVIDAE
         (even-toed ungulates)   (deer, antelope)

Muntiacus muntjak (Indian or red muntjac)

2n=♂7, ♀6

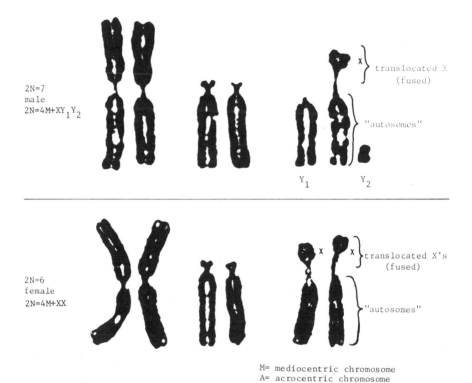

2N=7
male
2N=4M+XY$_1$Y$_2$

X } translocated X
      (fused)

"autosomes"

Y$_1$ Y$_2$

2N=6
female
2N=4M+XX

X   X } translocated X's
        (fused)

"autosomes"

M= mediocentric chromosome
A= acrocentric chromosome

Figure 3
A deer karyotype: *Muntiacus muntjak* (Indian or red muntjac).

Order: CARNIVORA

Family: CANIDAE
(dogs)

Atelocynus microtis (round-eared dog or small-eared dog)

2N=74
female
2N=72A+XX

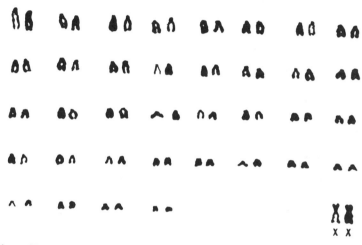

M= mediocentric chromosome
A= acrocentric chromosome

Figure 4

A dog karyotype: *Atelocynus microtis* (round-eared or small-eared dog).

South American Pleiocene migrants. The extant South American marsupials are considered vestiges of the once-diverse marsupial fauna,
which has been reduced to a dozen or so species by competition with
placentals. Australia and South America were once joined with Antarctica in a large continental mass known as Gondwanaland. Since
the breakup of Gondwanaland, South America and Australia have
been drifting apart for at least 100 million years. The long-term separation of the continents explains the major features of the present
distribution of the marsupials, including their karyotypes. Even

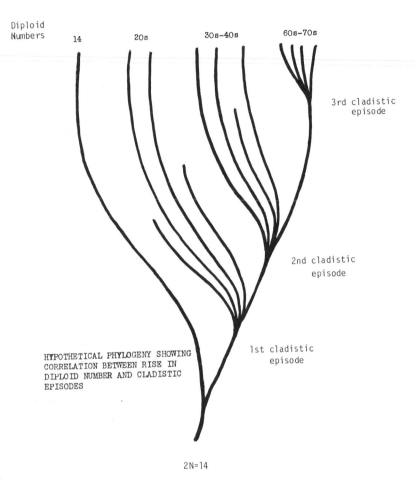

Figure 5
Hypothetical phylogeny (based on chromosome numbers), showing correlation
between diploid values and cladistic episodes.

though the marsupials in South America and Australia are morphologically very different, they have virtually identical karyotypes, with
a diploid number of 14. Diploid numbers up to 30 do occur, but these
karyotypes do not much resemble one another either within or
between the two continental faunas. The similarity of ploidy is con-
vincing evidence that the primitive diploid number for marsupials
was 14. In placentals a diploid number of 14 has been reported for a
peculiar little group: the Macroscelididae (better known as elephant
shrews, though they are neither elephants nor shrews). This report
needs confirmation but would be a very important finding for phylogenetic placement, for the Macroscelididae lie somewhere between
marsupials and placentals, albeit much nearer the latter. A diploid
number of 14 occurs in the South American rodent *Akodon,* although
several other species in the same genus have diploid numbers in the
50s. Finally, in a modified form, the karyotype of *Muntiacus muntjak*
(figure 3) can be "dissected" to give the 14 elements found in the
basic marsupial karyotype. Hence, though $2n = 14$ is not common
in placental mammals, it is found in diverse representatives. That
the earliest marsupials had a diploid chromosome number of 14 is
certainly an appropriate hypothesis, and the similar diploid number
of diverse placental mammals indicates to me that 14 is fundamental
to all mammals as the ancestral mammalian karyotype.

Chromosome Polymorphisms May Lead to Speciation

A more detailed examination of chromosome terminology may clarify
the issues. Chromosomes are designated and distinguished according to the ratio of their arm length, and are placed in four classes
(figure 6). If the centromere lies at the center, the chromosome is
called *metacentric.* If the centromere lies nearer the center than the
end, the chromosome is *submetacentric.* When the centromere is
nearer the end than the middle, the chromosome is *subtelocentric.* If
the centromere is terminal, the chromosome is *acrocentric.* Acrocentric
(derived from the Greek *acros,* meaning "edge") is preferred to telo-
centric (derived from *telos,* meaning "end"), as it is difficult in practice
to determine that there are absolutely no functional genetic loci
beyond the centromere.

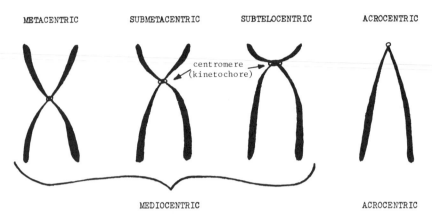

METACENTRIC   SUBMETACENTRIC   SUBTELOCENTRIC   ACROCENTRIC

centromere
(kinetochore)

MEDIOCENTRIC   ACROCENTRIC

Figure 6
Chromosome nomenclature.

Karyotypic-fission theory is concerned only with two broad groups of chromosomes: mediocentric (the three types with nonterminal centromeres) and acrocentric. After fission, a mediocentric chromosome yields two independent linkage groups; an acrocentric chromosome is still acrocentric and does not create new linkage groups. In other words, fission only elevates the diploid number in proportion to the mediocentric chromosomes present in the karyotype. In any population one may find polymorphisms for these various classes of chromosomes. One individual may have a large mediocentric chromosomal pair, whereas another may have two smaller matching acrocentric pairs. This in itself does not provide evidence of chromosome fission or fusion, although a careful analysis of banding patterns might reveal differences. Breeding these animals, however, provides a definitive test. Domestic pigs generally have a diploid number of 38, but some have 37 or 36. Karyotype comparison shows the presence of a mediocentric-acrocentric linkage polymorphism group (figure 7). Pigs with a diploid number of 36 have a pair of medium-size mediocentric chromosomes. Those with 37 have one such chromosome and two smaller acrocentrics that represent the same linkage group. Those with 38 do not have the medium-size mediocentric linkage at all but are called *homomorphic* because they have two pairs of small acrocentrics. Remarkably, the differences are transmitted in a simple Mendelian fashion, with no evidence of reduced viability or fertility between any of the morphs. Two pigs

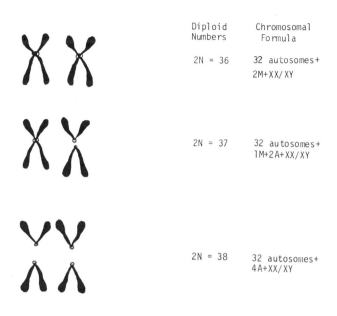

M= mediocentric chromosome
A= acrocentric chromosome

Figure 7
Chromosomal polymorphisms: fission polymorphs in pigs.

with diploid numbers of 37 (heteromorphic) can interbreed and will produce offspring with 36, 37, and 38 chromosomes in a 1:2:1 ratio. The inescapable conclusion is that the two smaller acrocentrics function as one linkage group in the heteromorphic individual.

A second kind of polymorphism commonly found in some groups involves a transformation of a mediocentric chromosome to an acrocentric one (figure 8). This polymorphism is a particular linkage group in the form of either an acrocentric or a mediocentric chromosome. The transformation is caused by *pericentric inversion;* that is, the centromere changes position. Pericentric inversions are widespread—for example, in the deer mouse *Peromyscus* 20 or more chromosomal pairs are involved. Evidence suggests no physiological impairment or infertility when mating individuals have such different karyotype morphologies. Indeed, many of these morphs are distributed in clines (that is, in gradients from high to low frequencies along a geographic transect through the population). Pericentric inversions

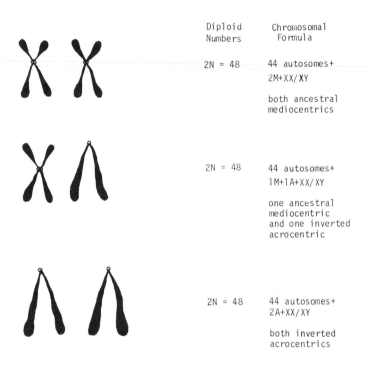

	Diploid Numbers	Chromosomal Formula
	2N = 48	44 autosomes+ 2M+XX/XY both ancestral mediocentrics
	2N = 48	44 autosomes+ 1M+1A+XX/XY one ancestral mediocentric and one inverted acrocentric
	2N = 48	44 autosomes+ 2A+XX/XY both inverted acrocentrics

M= mediocentric chromosome
A= acrocentric chromosome

Figure 8
Chromosomal polymorphisms: pericentric-inversion polymorphs in the genus *Peromyscus* (deer mouse).

do not change the diploid number. Because of fission, populations of *Peromyscus* also have differences in diploid number. Neither fission polymorphisms nor pericentric inversions appear to create any problems on their own; however, the simultaneous occurrence of a fission event and a pericentric inversion seems to severely limit interbreeding. One can imagine the consequences of breeding individuals with two different polymorphisms (figure 9). On the left side of the illustration is an individual with the polymorphism for the pericentric inversion (as seen, for instance, in *Peromyscus*). On the right side is an individual with a polymorphism for the fission product (as seen in the case of the domestic pig). Individuals with either of these two types have no overt physiological problems; however, if they mate

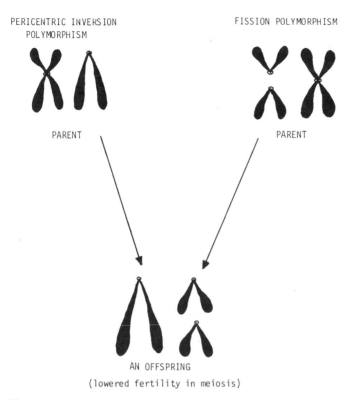

PERICENTRIC INVERSION
POLYMORPHISM

FISSION POLYMORPHISM

PARENT

PARENT

AN OFFSPRING
(lowered fertility in meiosis)

Figure 9
Chromosomal polymorphisms: result of mating individuals with fission polymorphism and pericentric-inversion polymorphism.

with each other, among the offspring types will be the one portrayed at the bottom. This individual will tend to be infertile because it will have great difficulty producing gametes; the two centromeres of the fission product will not align properly during meiotic synapsis. Individuals with this karyotype will produce a high percentage of inviable gametes. Thus, this karyotype will tend to be lost in the population.

Central to our inquiry are the questions of where karyotypic fission occurs and how it becomes established in a population. There are various scenarios. One involves an individual who carries in his or her germ line a fully fissioned karyotype. This individual might introduce a fissioned complement of chromosomes into the population again and again. Such a case has been documented in a popu-

Table 1
Extant genera of dogs and their karyotypes.

Canis	2N = 78 = 76A + XX/XY
Chrysocyon	2N = 76 = 74A + XX/XY
Atelocynus	2N = 74 = 72A + XX/XY
Dusicyon	2N = 74 = 72A + XX/XY
Urocyon	2N = 66 = 2M + 62A + XX/XY

lation of lizards. In my view there tends to be a selective advantage in breeding between animals with the same karyotypes—although breeding between morphs with chromosome alterations occurs, it may lead to reproductive impediments. Many mammals exhibit some kind of mating preference. Mole rats (*Spalax*) seem to somehow differentiate between potential mates with 56 or 58 or 60 chromosomes. Having this faculty for distinction, they tend to mate with their own kind. With a mechanism for generating new karyotypes and the ability to somehow distinguish karyotypes, single (i.e., interbreeding) populations can suddenly be fractured by these chromosomal changes. In a population in which a pericentric inversion polymorphism is distributed as a cline, fission may occur in one portion of the population in which the inversion is absent and spread until individuals encounter others with the pericentric inversion. At this point interbreeding breaks down and the animals, if they have the faculty for making a distinction, rapidly avoid mating with individuals with a karyotype distinct from their own. In this manner two distinct, reproductively isolated populations—in other words, two diverse species—arise. Other selective pressures, such as pre-mating isolation or mating behavior, can reinforce this isolation.

Evolution of Dog Genera: Application of Karyotypic-Fission Theory

The karyotypes of modern dogs provide a useful example of the explanatory power of karyotypic fission in the resolution of phylogenies. Table 1 details the karyotypes of the extant genera of dogs: *Canis* (the domestic dog, the wolf, the coyote, and the jackal), *Chrysocyon* (the maned wolf), *Atelocynus* (the small-eared dog), *Dusicyon* (several closely related subspecies, including the Andean wild dog

Table 2
Hypothetical ancestral karyotypes.

2N = 42 = 36M + 4A + XX/XY	Incipient *Canis*
2N = 42 = 34M + 6A + XX/XY	Incipient *Chrysocyon*
2N = 42 = 32M + 8A + XX/XY	Incipient *Atelocynus, Dusicyon*
2N = 42 = 26M + 14A + XX/XY	Incipient *Urocyon*

known as the "lobo"), and *Urocyon* (the grey fox). Today *Canis* is distributed over much of the world; *Chrysocyon, Atelocynus,* and *Dusicyon* are confined to South America, and *Urocyon* to North America. The fossil record indicates that North America was the ancestral home of the stocks that gave rise to all these modern genera. A hypothetical array of karyotypes, all having a diploid number of 42 but differing in the proportions of mediocentric and acrocentric chromosomes, can be constructed (table 2). Fission of one of these putative karyotypes could have led to the present karyotype of *Urocyon* as follows:

$$2M + 24M + 14A + XX/XY \xrightarrow[\substack{\text{retention} \\ \text{of two} \\ \text{ancestral} \\ \text{mediocentrics}}]{\substack{\text{fission} \\ +}} 2M + 48A + 14A + XX/XY$$

In table 1, the high number of chromosomes and the complete absence of mediocentric chromosomes (except for one pair in *Urocyon*) suggest a recent fission event. My assumption is that acrocentric chromosomes are gradually converted to mediocentrics, since a mediocentric linkage is presumably more stable during mitosis than an acrocentric. This stability is a function of the length of the chromosomes; the location of the centromere will have little to do with the likelihood of breakage along a small chromosome during mitosis. Here the aim is to deduce the karyotype and the diploid number of the last common ancestor of this derivative group. My estimate is that the ancestral diploid number was not lower than 40; this is based on the fact that it requires 38 mediocentrics plus the XX/XY sex chromosomes to yield 76 acrocentrics plus the XX/XY chromosomes in a single fission event. However, for reasons that will become clear,

I am going to designate a diploid number of 42 as the ancestral diploid number.

All of what I believe were the four karyotypes of the five incipient genera have the same diploid number (42), but there are differences in the morphology of the chromosomes—in other words, in the karyotypes (table 2). The group is an interbreeding population with a polymorphism for several mediocentric-acrocentric pairs, not unlike polymorphisms reported for several extant species. If the migration of the populations coincided with this polymorphism, then we have constructed a cline found in extant populations of dogs. A fission event occurring in the incipient *Canis* population, if introduced into each of the other incipient groups, yields exactly the karyotypes of the five modern genera. The only wrinkle in this example is in *Urocyon*, where in addition to the fission a single pair of ancestral mediocentric chromosomes must have been conserved.

I hypothesize that the steps that led to the *Urocyon* karyotype involved the nonfission of two mediocentric chromosomes of the original 26; these chromosomes remained in the ancestral state, as was diagrammed above. This hypothesis could be dismissed as simply the juggling of chromosome numbers to achieve the desired outcome were it not for the existence of *Nyctereutes vivarinus*, the raccoon dog. The karyotype of *N. vivarinus* includes 40 mediocentrics and the two sex chromosomes. Of these mediocentrics, one assumes that 14 of the original autosomes were acrocentric but have subsequently been converted by pericentric inversion to mediocentrics. Evidence from the fossil record shows that the ancestral stock of modern dogs crossed the Bering Strait into Asia. The Asian population of dogs subsequently became geographically isolated when the Bering land bridge was submerged. Thus, *Nyctereutes*, according to the facts of zoogeography, is the ancestral form. I admit that this example of the evolution of dog genera is exceptional in terms of the completeness of the fossil record, the knowledge of migration, and the survival of an ancestral representative; nonetheless, it establishes confidence in the relevance of paleokaryology.

Karyotypic fission also offers an explanation for the observation that evolution, contrary to expectations based on the theory of population genetics, appears to occur in spurts. In other words, morphological change and diversification occur suddenly, not gradually, and are followed by a period of relative stasis (Gould and Eldridge 1977). The proposition of punctuated evolution was long held to be an artifact of incomplete sampling; however, the theory of punctuated equilibria has been sufficiently documented to at least call into question the uncritical acceptance of gradualism. Recent findings and interpretations of the hominid fossil record indicate that spurts are real. No adequate or satisfying genetic explanation for the sudden emergence of new traits has been offered, but I submit that—at least for mammals—karyotypic fission is a good candidate, for it explains two fundamental aspects of evolutionary events. First, by providing a plausible mechanism for the generation of reproductively isolated populations, karyotypic fission explains the rapidity of speciation. Second, any event of karyotypic fission imposes a period in which derivatives have no potential for repeating the process. In other words, fission dictates a pause. During this pause, surviving lineages must accumulate mediocentric linkages before they can enter another phase of fission. The time required for such repotentiation can reasonably be expected to be millions of generations.

Karyotypic fission addresses some rather controversial evolutionary topics. It provides a mechanism for sympatric speciation. It addresses the topic of punctuated equilibria in evolution. It provides a potential explanation of adaptive radiations. In general, karyotypic fission seems a very promising approach to the analysis of tetrapod evolution. To date, karyotypic-fission theory has been applied only in limited cases: Canidae (Todd 1970), primates (Stanyon 1983; Giusto and Margulis 1983), artiodactyls (Todd 1975), and, to a limited extent, perissadactyls and their relatives (Todd 1975). A brief overview of other groups suggests that they are amenable to this experimental approach. I am sufficiently confident in the power of karyotypic-fission theory to explain the interrelations of extant species that I believe it is possible to reconstruct the evolutionary history of these species even in the absence of a fossil record. This may be particularly useful for those groups for which fossil records are poor, such as bats and whales. Karyotypic fission theory has been applied to a limited number of animals by a limited number of workers. Fewer than 100 of the 4,000 species of mammals have been analyzed. Ample opportunity exists for work relating to the remaining thousands of species. Numerous projects await our attention.

Readings

Gould, S. J., and N. Eldridge. 1977. Punctuated equilibria: The tempo and mode of evolution reconsidered. *Paleobiology* 3: 115–151.

Giusto, J. P., and L. Margulis. 1981. Karyotypic fission theory and the evolution of old world monkeys and apes. *Biosystems* 13: 267–302.

Giusto, J. P., and L. Margulis. 1983. Karyotypic fissioning (letter to the editor). *Biosystems* 16: 169–172.

Stanyon, R. 1983. A test of the karyotypic fissioning theory of primate evolution. *Biosystems* 16: 57–63.

Todd, N. B. 1970. Karyotypic fissioning and canid phylogeny. *Journal of Theoretical Biology* 26: 445–480.

Todd, N. B. 1975. Chromosomal mechanisms in the evolution of artiodactyls. *Paleobiology* 1: 175–188.

16

The Gaia Hypothesis

James E. Lovelock

When James Lovelock was first working out his Gaia concept of the physicochemical regulation of the Earth's surface, he visited the Environmental Evolution class several times. The disparate data and observations that led him to suggest a new view of life and the environment are revealed in this early lecture (from 1973) and in his responses to questions posed more than 10 years later. We have presented them here both for historical interest and to illustrate the process of the development of scientific thought.

What has come to be called the Gaian view considers the atmosphere to be an integral part of the biosphere; the atmosphere here is not just a separate physicochemical system which interacts passively with life on Earth. Many will regard this as mere speculation, but I will try to prove that it is not. Even if I fail in this attempt, I think you will find that the Gaian view elicits new questions which otherwise might never have been asked.

Where are we? The small thatched building depicted in the foreground of figure 1 is my former laboratory at Bowerchalke in South Wiltshire. Built over 400 years ago, it is, as far as I know, the only thatched space laboratory in the world. I am not introducing this territory as a bit of cozy folk science; the environment, as always, entails the organism.

The ground on which this laboratory was built is a well-known inorganic chemical substance calcium carbonate, or limestone: $CaCO_3$. The air—which, as you can see, is quite clear—is made up of oxygen (O_2), nitrogen (N_2), carbon dioxide (CO_2), water vapor (H_2O), and other inorganic chemicals. The plant segment of the biosphere colors the biosphere green. The animals are not so con-

Figure 1
The author's laboratory in southwest England.

spicuous, but they exist. Life amid inanimate surroundings, life in its inert environment: this is the ordinary, traditional view of the biosphere. By contrast, the picture I'm developing is that the air and the ground are not independent inorganic chemicals, but that the sediments and atmosphere are part of a living system. On the other hand, despite its seeming position as part of pristine, unspoilt nature, even the green that surrounds my laboratory is not "natural": it is nearly all man-made, biology wittingly or unwittingly ordered by man over the course of time. Without people, this part of southern England would probably be primeval scrub forest.

From this point of view, air pollution on a global scale might perturb not just the atmosphere but the biosphere. The possibility of air pollution on a global scale began to attract professional interest in the early 1970s. My interest was sparked by the reports *Man's Impact on the Global Environment* and *Inadvertent Climate Modification*, published by the MIT Press in 1970 and 1971. When I read them, it occurred to me that a special view of the Earth was denied to the distinguished groups that produced the reports, a view that was more consonant with those of my colleagues working in the planetary sciences. This special view came from a need to look at the planet in its entirety, and in an interdisciplinary manner. By contrast, the view of these otherwise wholly excellent books is limited by the division of science into arbitrary disciplines. For example, the meteorologists state explicitly that they do not at all consider the chemistry or the biology of the Earth. The atmospheric chemists, for their part, say that meteorology lies beyond their territory; they make no reference to biology. This recognition of territorial rights is instinctive to most male animals, and this includes scientific experts and university professors especially. Such a comment may seem glib, yet it accurately accounts not only for the limitations of the MIT reports but also for those of current science in spite of the growing interest in and sympathy toward more interdisciplinary approaches.

Earth's Atmosphere: Evidence for Life

The problem of detecting the presence (or, much more likely, the absence) of life on other planets demands a less divided view. The search for life elsewhere brings biologists and engineers, for example, together in constructive conversations. For some years I have, with colleagues such as these, been interested in the possibility of detecting the presence of life on other planets merely from the knowledge of the chemical composition of the planet's atmosphere. I hypothesized that Mars would be without nitrogen, since it was probably without life; at least, this is what we surmised after seeing the cratered, moon-like surface revealed by the first Mariner mission. To understand the reasons for this educated guess, let us consider the relationship of nitrogen in the atmosphere to the presence or absence of life on Earth.

The cosmic abundance of elements is fairly constant, and (apart from an absence of hydrogen, which may have escaped to space) Earth is fairly representative of the general distribution of elements. These elements tend to combine to the state at which the lowest potential energy is reached; this is a law of chemistry. Comparison of the major constituents of Earth's atmosphere with those of Mars

Table 1
Major features of the planetary atmospheres compared: percent by weight of the reactive gases carbon dioxide, nitrogen, and oxygen; water in precipitable meters over the planet if all vapor precipitated out of the atmosphere; pressure; and mean annual surface temperature.

	Venus	Earth	Mars
CO_2	98%	0.03%	95%
N_2	1.7%	79%	2.7%
O_2	trace	21%	0.13%
H_2O	0.003 m	3,000 m	0.00001 m
Pressure	90 bars	1 bar	0.0064 bar
Temperature	477°C	17°C	−47°C

and Venus (table 1), however, reveals that Earth's atmosphere is anomalous with respect to these gases. With the chemical mixture present in the Earth's atmosphere, the element nitrogen is expected to form its most stable compound, which is not N_2 but the nitrate ion (NO_3^-). One would expect NO_3^- to be present either on the surface or in the seas as a potassium or sodium salt. Conversion of the nitrate ion to nitrogen gas is an "uphill" process which requires the presence of life. The expected chemical conversion of nitrate makes the presence of nearly 80 percent molecular nitrogen in Earth's atmosphere an indication of the presence of life.

The next Mariner mission found only 2.7 percent nitrogen in the Martian atmosphere. The large amount of nitrogen on Earth relative to Mars supported my view that life on Earth shows itself as a global chemical phenomenon.

When I was a young man, the atmosphere of Earth was said to have originated in the primeval outgassings from the Earth's interior; outgassing is a process, particularly important in the early history of the Earth, whereby gaseous and volatile compounds escape from the interior of the planet and help produce the early oceans and atmosphere.

Oxygen, for example, was explained to have come from the photodissociation of water vapor by sunlight followed by hydrogen escape. Nitrogen was said to have been a stable, inert constituent throughout Earth's history. Until a few years ago, this view was largely unchallenged. Indeed, it is widely held, and you will still find it in many textbooks on the Earth's atmosphere. In spite of the

distinguished science done by such workers as L. V. Berkner and
L. C. Marshall, who proposed a wholly biological origin for atmospheric oxygen, most aeronomists still believe that life, responsible
for no net increment of oxygen, merely recycles oxygen gas. Oxygen,
that is, just happens to be in the air at exactly the right concentration
for most life because of blind inorganic processes. Or, if it is your
preference, oxygen was arranged by some beneficent providence. To
me this view of the air as a product of wholly inorganic processes is
the most magnificent nonsense; indeed, one of the most intriguing
puzzles in the history of science is how it has managed to persist for
so long. G. N. Lewis and M. Randall in the 1920s, G. E. Hutchinson
in the 1950s and, most recently, L. G. Sillen all showed that at the
pH and the redox potential of the Earth molecular nitrogen is thermodynamically unstable. The element nitrogen, given these conditions, should be present on Earth not as the gas but as nitrate ion in
seas. From an inorganic viewpoint, the presence of oxygen is, in fact,
equally anomalous when Earth is compared with its neighboring
planets, Mars and Venus, which lack atmospheric oxygen. That Mars
and Venus have no free oxygen is not unexpected. It is, rather, the
presence of free, extremely reactive atmospheric oxygen on Earth
that is a complete anomaly. The once-reducing atmosphere of the
Earth is today an oxidizing one.

The opposed terms *reducing* and *oxidizing*, roughly equivalent to
"hydrogen-rich" and "hydrogen-poor," come from old-fashioned
chemistry. A reducing substance, such as hydrogen, will combine
with the oxygen of a metal oxide, such as iron oxide (rust), to give
the oxide of the reducer (in this case water) and also free iron as the
metal. In a reducing atmosphere, iron would remain as metal. In an
oxidizing atmosphere, it rusts—that is, iron recombines with oxygen
to give its oxide again.

Another shibboleth which has held up progress in this branch of
science is that the climate and the chemical composition of the Earth
are uniquely favorable for life. This is the one you will find in most
science fiction stories, sad to say. I say it is sad because, on the
whole, science fiction tends to be a little less blind that science itself.
Indeed, it is not commonly appreciated that seemingly quite small
changes would render Earth unsuited to contemporary life.

Life Regulates the Environment

What would happen, for example, if oxygen were to increase in concentration? If it were just over 25 percent, the probability of a fire starting by a lightning flash would be so high that even tropical rain forests would be at risk. For each 1 percent increase in oxygen concentration over the current level, the probability of initiating combustion doubles. Interestingly, if the oxygen concentration were to fall to 13 percent one could not start any sort of fire at all. Nearly no difference exists in flammability between O_2 concentrations of 40 percent and 100 percent. Indeed, the current 21 percent O_2 concentration is just about ideal for the existence of trees, which participate in making oxygen: at higher levels trees would be burnt up; at lower ones there might well be too few animals and other oxygen consumers to maintain an ecological balance.

For another example of a quite small change that would have drastic consequences for present life forms, consider that a change in atmospheric pressure of merely 10 percent, assuming that the composition of air was unaltered, would result in a 4°C change in the world's mean surface temperature! Such a change would set Earth on a highly unfavorable climatic course. These examples, which show just how well suited the present atmosphere is to the present form of life on Earth, could be multiplied. I think the biota, the sum of all living organisms, interacts actively with its environment so as to maintain the environment at values of its own "choosing." The notion that blind chance led to such a perfectly adjusted atmosphere, by contrast, seems untenable.

Early in its evolution, life acquired the capacity, I believe, to control the global environment to suit its needs. The capacity for environmental maintenance has persisted; it is still active. The sum total of all the species that go to fill up the biosphere is far more than just a catalog; like other associations in biology, this global biota is an entity with properties greater than the sum of its parts. Such a large creature, with the powerful capacity to air-condition the whole planet, may be only hypothetical at the moment; nonetheless, it needs a name. I am grateful to Mr. William Golding, who lives in my village, for the suggestion of the word *Gaia*: the Greek personification of Mother Earth. It has various advantages, not least of which is its status as a four-letter word with the capacity to focus the attention of my scientific colleagues; certainly "Gaia" is a lot easier to say than "a biological cybernetic system with homeostatic tendencies."

Any theory stating that the Earth's surface is wholly a product of biological processes must be considered wrong. Comprehensive biological explanations of atmospheric composition are difficult to formulate. At the root of this problem is the fact that there exists no formal scientific statement of life as a process. I know of no single and exclusive test that could prove or disprove the existence of Gaia as a living entity. Biologists, fortunately, usually are not deterred by such a lack of rigor. Even if eventually prepared, such a formal physical statement of life is liable to be statistical, mechanical, very mathematical, and quite unsuited to the design of simple experiments to test for the presence of Gaia.

Most biologists, indeed most people, upon seeing a giraffe even for the first time, and especially if it moved, would be able to pronounce it alive without any conscious use of chemistry or physics. Life is still much in the realm of phenomenology. One scientific approach attractive to interdisciplinary biologists would attempt to prove the presence of life by seeing if the entity tested were able to maintain a constant temperature and compatible chemical composition in the face of environmental change or perturbation. From such a phenomenological basis, what evidence points to the existence of Gaia, a creature made up of the biosphere but more than just the sum of its parts?

We believe that during the period in which life has existed on Earth, from at least 300 million years ago to the present, the reduction-oxidation (redox) potential of the atmosphere has shifted from a pE of −5 (reducing) to a pE of +13 (oxidizing). (A useful way of indicating the oxidizing or reducing tendencies of a system, pE, the logarithm of the reciprocal of the electron concentration, is expressed in gram-molecules per liter.) During the time in which the pE changed from −5 to +13, the atmospheric composition changed concomitantly. The change from a reducing to an oxidizing atmosphere led to many correlated changes in atmospheric composition and total pressure. The early atmosphere was probably rich in hydrogen and ammonia. At the same time, as it moves along the standard course for average stars, the energy output of the sun has increased at least 30 percent. This increase in solar luminosity is one of the few relatively certain facts of astronomy. In spite of extensive atmospheric chemical changes and changes in output of radiant solar energy, the geological record, with its demonstrable persistence of life, indicates that at no time in the last 3 billion years did the Earth's mean temperature change more than a few degrees from what it is now. What sort of remarkable coincidence might account for such physical constancy, which is exactly what is required for the continued existence of life? Indeed, I am doubtful that this is coincidence; I think it very much more likely that a biological regulatory system has been and is working, ensuring planetary homeostasis at physical and chemical states appropriate to the global biota at a given time.

Life Regulates Global Mean Temperature

The most important evidence for Gaia is found in the constancy of the Earth's mean temperature through time. Since liquid water has always been present, the average temperature is unlikely ever to have exceeded 50°C or to have decreased much below the mean temperatures during the Pleistocene ice ages. Our sun, like all mainsequence stars, has been increasing in luminosity since its origin. Near the origin of the Earth and life, some 400 million years ago, the sun is thought to have been 30 percent fainter than at present. Quite clearly, even a comparatively short time ago, the Earth's temperature, if it responded passively to solar luminosity in the same atmosphere, would have been much lower than it is now. This paradox—the fact that the solar output was much weaker in the past, and yet Earth's mean temperature seems to have remained within certain boundaries—has been called "the Faint Young Sun Paradox."

To maintain a constant surface temperature, assuming current atmospheric composition, a decrease in atmospheric pressure would have to have occurred over time. On a mountain at a point where the pressure has dropped by 10 percent, you will find that the temperature has fallen by 4°C. Similarly, if you descend 1,000 feet below sea level (as in a deep depression at the Dead Sea), you will find an equivalent rise in temperature. A 10 percent increase in atmospheric pressure corresponds to a rise in temperature of about 4°C. Meteorologists refer to this as the *adiabatic lapse rate*. Atmospheric pressure would have had to decrease to compensate for the increasing output of the sun with time.

What atmospheric composition provided higher atmospheric pressure in the past, leading to maintenance of constant temperature over geologic time? A greater amount of oxygen in the past is precluded. Even small changes in oxygen levels would render disastrous effects. Drastic CO_2 rise is precluded by inorganic equilibria in water which hold this gas fairly near present level. The only gas that changes easily is nitrogen. About 1.5 billion years ago, about 20 percent more nitrogen may have been in the atmosphere than now. We can check this by seeing if younger rocks contain more nitrogen than older ones, since some of this extra nitrogen would have to have been buried to reduce the amount of nitrogen in the younger atmosphere. In fact, younger rocks do, I believe, by and large, contain more nitrogen than older ones. I view this as one possibility of "gaian" pressure and hence temperature regulation of the atmosphere, via manipulation of the quantity of atmospheric nitrogen.

But affairs are more critically balanced. If the mean surface temperature of Earth falls by more than 2 or 3°C, then positive feedback mechanisms associated with the increase of snow cover hasten the falling temperature, as is well established in meteorology. The Earth cools to a point where even the oceans may freeze. Earth's temperature is poised between hot and cold extremes. A 2 or 3°C rise would increase greenhouse gases in the atmosphere and, by a similar positive-feedback mechanism, cause further increased heating. With a sufficient rise in temperature, a thermal "runaway effect" would occur. Yet the temperature has remained relatively constant in the face of perturbation. To me this is the best evidence of the existence of Gaia: a system that controls the conditions at the surface of the planet.

If all of the life on Earth were deleted at one stroke, many inorganic atmospheric reactions—from electrical discharges and ionizing radiation to solar ultraviolet rays—would permit oxygen and nitrogen to react with one another. A predominant end product of these reactions of O_2 with N_2 would be the nitrate ion, which would wash into the sea. Nitrogen so removed would not return to the air: biological processes alone perform nitrate reduction to molecular nitrogen. Whereas the burying of nitrogen from the sea in plate-tectonic processes involves relatively slow recycling, we are concerned here with relatively short periods of about a million years. Small quantities of oxygen might be supplied by water or CO_2 photolysis (the breakup of carbon dioxide via lightning), ensuring the removal of the remaining nitrogen after the last of the oxygen has reacted. The end result of the steady-state inorganic equilibrium, in the absence of life, would be an atmosphere of CO_2, water vapor, carbon monoxide, and rare gases; only trace amounts of oxygen and nitrogen would persist. This scenario for the chemical composition of the atmosphere of a lifeless Earth is a very reasonable interpolation between the atmospheres of present-day Mars and Venus. The redox Earth, compared with its imaginary sterile twin, as well as oxidizing Venus and Mars on the one hand, and reducing Jupiter on the other, is portrayed in the bar graphs in figure 2.

Biotic Emissions Have Global Effects

Now let us consider: Do the activities of man have atmospheric effects, adverse or otherwise, on a global scale? The various gases of the atmosphere, their concentrations, their emission rates from the biosphere, their atmospheric residence times in years, and their emission rates from man-made sources are shown in table 2.

   The first thing you will notice when you look at this table is the overwhelming dominance of the biota. The gases turn over quickly; most of them have short residence times. Oxygen, for example, although fully 21 percent of the total atmosphere, turns over once every thousand years. The residence time for N_2 is measured on the order of a million years—longer than other elements but still short compared to the time that life has been present on Earth. Carbon monoxide and oxides of nitrogen are produced not solely from the exhaust of cars but by the biota as well. Many creatures in the sea find carbon monoxide an essential part of their everyday business. Siphonophores float using little bladders filled with 80 percent carbon monoxide. Even *Fucus*, a common brown seaweed, has 0.1 percent carbon monoxide in its bladders. Carbon monoxide is not a noxious toxic emission, but part of the vital existence of these marine organisms. At least 1.2 billion tons of ammonia are annually produced by the biota. I say "at least" because the figures are probably underes-

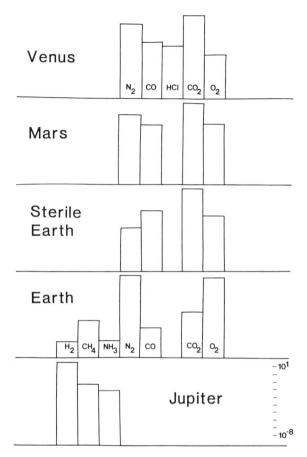

Figure 2
Concentrations of reactive gases in the atmospheres of the inner planets of the solar system on a log scale (from 10^{-9} to 100%). From most reducing (left) to most oxidizing (right): hydrogen, methane, ammonia, nitrogen, carbon monoxide, hydrogen chloride, carbon dioxide, oxygen. "Sterile Earth" was calculated by interpolation between Mars and Venus or by letting "Earth" gases react with each other to chemical equilibrium.

Table 2
Atmospheric gases: sources, residence times, and primary sinks.

Gas	Formula	Components of air (ppm) by volume	Sources (atmospheric emissions) (billions of tons/year)			Residence time[f] (years)	Principal sinks[g]
			Abiological Volcanic & tectonic emissions	Biological Microbes, plants, animals	Man-made		
Nitrogen	N_2	780,300	—[a]	1	0	500,000	Utilized by organisms
Oxygen	O_2	209,480	0.001	100	-10	6,000	Utilized by organisms, combusted
Carbon dioxide	CO_2	350	0.01	140	16	2–5	Utilized by organisms
Methane	CH_4	1.7	0	2	0	7–10	Utilized by organisms, atmospheric oxidation
Nitrous oxide	N_2O	0.31	—	1	0	150	Utilized by organisms
Carbon monoxide	CO	0.20 (NH)[b] 0.05 (SH)[c]	0.11	0.1	0.28	0.3	Utilized by organisms
Ammonia	NH_3	0.0001–0.001	0	1.2	0	1 week	Utilized by organisms
Hydrocarbons	$(CH_2)_n$	0.001	0	0.2	0.2	0.01–0.02	Atmospheric oxidation
Oxides of nitrogen	NO_x	$1-3 \times 10^{-5}$[d] $1-2 \times 10^{-4}$[e]	—	—	0.16	1–7 days	Utilized by organisms, atmospheric reactions
Hydrogen sulfide	H_2S	0.0001	—	0.1	0.003	0.005	Atmospheric oxidation
Sulfur dioxide	SO_2	0.00001–0.0001	—	0	0.16	5 days	Atmospheric oxidation
Dimethylsulfide	$(CH_3)_2SCH_3$	0.0001	0	0.2	0	0.01	Atmospheric oxidation

Chlorofluorocarbons						
CFC-11	CFCL₃	0.0003	0	0.0003	75	??
CFC-12	CF₂CL₂	0.0004	0	0.0004	110	??
Sulfur hexafluoride	SF₆	2×10^{-13} ??	0	$+5 \times 10^{-7}$	30	None
Noble gases						
Argon	Ar	9,340				
Helium	He	5.2				
Neon	Ne	18.2	No organism interaction[h]			
Krypton	Kr	1.1				
Xenon	Xe	0.09				

a. Unknown.
b. Northern hemisphere.
c. Southern hemisphere.
d. Remote.
e. Populated.
f. Residence time, which can be thought of as approximately half-life, refers to the amount of time it takes for the values of these gases to fall to $1/e$, or about 37 percent.
g. Fate of the gases as they are removed from the atmosphere.
h. Nongaian gases.

timates; living organisms as new sources of gases are continually discovered. This very large production of ammonia has an important bearing on the maintenance for life of planetary pH. I think biogenic ammonia compensates for the tendency of the planet toward acidity. In regions such as northern Sweden, the northern United States, and Canada, ammonia production is apparently deficient; rain as acid as pH 3 sometimes falls.

Methane is produced in quantities of more than 2 billion tons per annum. I believe the huge production of methane, representing some 8 percent of all of the energy of photosynthesis, is very important for the regulation of the atmosphere. One function of methane is the formation of a very convenient "molecular balloon"; this gas passes the atmosphere to regions where photolysis occurs and hydrogen escapes. Water vapor does not easily enter the upper atmosphere: the tropopause is very cold, and water vapor freezes out to a concentration of 0.5 ppm. Methane, in the same region, has a concentration of 1.5 ppm. Since each methane (CH_4) molecule carries twice as much hydrogen as water, six times as much hydrogen is carried up and outward by methane as by water. In addition, the Earth maintains a net oxidizing state by expelling hydrogen to space. If methane is involved in oxygen regulation, a mature ecosystem is justified in squandering as much as 8 percent of its energy to produce it.

The atmosphere is not a static mixture of gases preserved by Earth's gravitational field. It is a system in dynamic and contemporary balance (table 2). Undoubtedly the immediate origin of the atmosphere is the biota. I am certain that the relative constancy of atmospheric composition over time is actively maintained by sensing and control mechanisms within the biosphere. The human industrial sector, with the possible exception of carbon dioxide emission, contributes relatively little.

Can large-scale atmospheric effects, for example combustion emissions, be used as perturbations to test for Gaia? We first notice air pollution on a large scale by the presence of smoke haze, such as the atmospheric turbidity of a locale such as the British industrial city of Sheffield, a small steel town. By contrast, Bantry Bay in southwestern Ireland is far removed from industry and pollution sources. When the wind blows from the North Atlantic, the air is sparklingly clear.

Visibility at ground level may be more than 40 miles. When the wind blows into Bantry Bay from continental Europe, a source of all sorts of pollution, the picture changes; the visibility range may be reduced to fewer than 1.5 miles. Alan Eggleton and his colleagues at Harwell Laboratory inform us that the rural summertime haze of northern Europe, like that at Sheffield, is a form of photochemical smog frequently associated, like Los Angeles smog, with comparatively high levels of ozone. When the wind blows from continental Europe, a level of about 0.1 part per million of ozone would be expected during the day, to be compared with about one-tenth of that in clear air conditions.

Atmospheric turbidity is a measure of the scattering of incoming sunlight by any particulate matter in the air. Dust particles are blown from the desert by wind or from farm lands under dust bowl conditions. But particulate matter, including fine droplets, may also be produced by reactions among the gases in the atmosphere. Sulfur compounds react with oxidants to produce sulfuric acid droplets or ammonium sulfate aerosols. Trees produce unsaturated hydrocarbons like pinene (a terpenoid; see chapter 14), which polymerizes to form pinene polymer particles, an aerosol that scatters incoming sunlight. Dust particles can be generated *in situ*; they need not have been stirred up. Atmospheric turbidities plotted monthly at Bowerchalke (southern England), Greensborough (North Carolina), and San Bernardino (in the heart of the California smog basin) are indistinguishable. They all show the same high-level seasonal increase. Few people realize that the rural regions of southern England, the Appalachian Mountains, and Los Angeles all share the same density of turbid aerosol in the summertime. Though this turbid aerosol is of photochemical origin at all three sites, the haze at Bowerchalke and Greensborough is quite different from that of Los Angeles. At its worst in southern England or Greensborough, there is little or no odor or eye irritation; the aerosol appears to be principally composed of natural ammonium sulfate or sulfuric acid droplets.

A puzzling feature of smog in rural regions away from industry is that it is most marked with winds from directions which also lack industry. In southern England the densest smogs come with winds from a southeasterly quarter, which traverse many miles of open sea and rural areas before arriving. By contrast, air masses coming from the north over the densely populated industrial regions of the United Kingdom are comparatively free of this sort of haze. Seasonal change in atmospheric turbidity can be measured for air masses from three principal directions at Bowerchalke. Continental air masses have high levels of summertime haze. Air masses coming from a maritime tropical direction off the southern part of the Atlantic, or a maritime polar direction coming from the north, either over the sea or over the industrial regions of the United Kingdom, carry little smog. No significant smog occurs with winds from northerly directions! The densest turbidity in the United States, too, is found not in the densely populated industrial regions, but in the southern Appalachian Mountains, where urbanization is light but trees abound.

A compilation of the areas of turbidity in the northern hemisphere can be made from satellite photographs. The regions of densest turbid aerosol are not the industrial regions of western Europe, the United States, or Japan, but the tropical and desert regions of the world near the equator! The whole of Africa in its middle region lives in a state of permanent haze; this appears to be true also of much of southeast Asia. A sunset on the harbor at Dakar, Senegal, has that same golden look seen in Los Angeles. The Senegal haze, however, is not industrial, for Dakar is quite a small city with little industry; rather, it is the natural haze of Africa. The Canary Islands, photographed from a ship 5 miles offshore, can barely be seen, so dense is the turbidity. Whatever causes this atmospheric turbidity potentially affects the Earth's surface temperature in one way or another. Haze and atmospheric particulates come from the nonhuman biota as well as from industrial and domestic sources.

In the last century the concentration of atmospheric carbon dioxide has increased as a consequence of the ever-increasing burning of fossil fuels. It has risen from 280 parts per million to 350 parts per million, and the increase is beginning to accelerate. This increment corresponds to the retention in the atmosphere of about half of the carbon dioxide from fuel that has been burned. This increase anticipates a warming of the planet by the well-known greenhouse phenomenon: the absorption of infrared radiation by carbon dioxide, which lessens the heat loss of the Earth into space.

These atmospheric changes may be due largely to human activity, or maybe not. Changes in climate might be associated with these

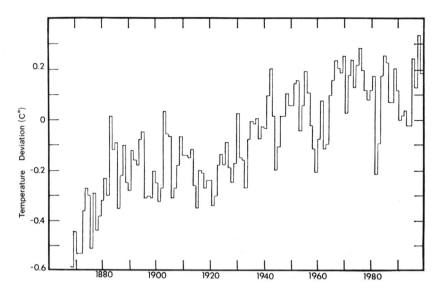

Figure 3
Changes in global mean temperatures since 1860.

measured atmospheric changes. Since about 1925 the climate of the northern hemisphere has changed, and up until the winter of 1970–71 the change had continued in the same direction (figure 3). In the second of the MIT publications I mentioned (*Inadvertent Climate Modification*), a diagram shows the reduction in temperature in the northern hemisphere plotted against latitude for the period 1960–1965 and the period 1965–1971. A clear-cut, quite unequivocal decrease in temperature occurred for all regions higher than about latitude 50° north. A slight warming trend may have occurred near the equator, but it is nowhere near as marked as the apparently continuing decrease in mean temperature in the northern regions. A reverse of the warming trend seems to have occurred. Since this time, however, average global temperatures seem to have been increasing.

Averages, however, are often misleading. A meteorologist friend, Dr. James Lodge of the National Center for Atmospheric Research in Boulder, Colorado, continually reminds himself of this fact with a cartoon on the wall of his office. This cartoon shows a man with his head in an oven and his backside in a refrigerator and a rather dim technician measuring the temperature of his navel. The caption reads

"His average temperature is fine, Doc." So it is with the world. The world's mean surface temperature may not have changed much, but large fluctuations are evident from year to year on a local scale.

Not only is the mean surface temperature in the northern hemisphere changing; other properties are also changing. One is the frequency of westerly wind drift across the North Atlantic. Hubert Lamb, of the British Meteorological Office, has compiled records of westerly wind frequencies going back to as early as records were taken in the past century. The decline of the westerlies in the early 1970s was greater than had ever been observed before. The decline in temperature at this time and the decline in westerly winds would expectedly be associated because the warm winds traversing the Atlantic toward the Arctic Basin are westerlies, and if such winds become infrequent, northern hemispheric temperatures, at least in the regions above the British Isles, become lower over time.

The extent of these climatic changes seems significantly greater than "the climatic noise level." Explanations fall into three categories. The first is "natural/organic." Some authorities suggest that the decline in northern hemispheric temperatures since World War II and through the mid 1970s is largely attributable to increased volcanic activity. Others attribute changes to solar output. Volcanic dust veils had occurred, but fewer were present then than in the nineteenth century. They seem to me insufficient to account for this episode of rapidly declining temperature. The decline was occurring considerably earlier than the most severe of the volcanic dust emissions, e.g., from Mount Agung in Bali (1963–64). The sun's output, which changes little over the sunspot cycle (≈ 11 years), is quite insufficient to account for surface changes on Earth.

Another category of explanations is anthropogenic; it includes factors such as carbon dioxide from fossil-fuel emissions, jet-aircraft contrails (which reflect sunlight back into space), and human dust-raising activities in general, including farming, slash-and-burn agriculture in the tropics, and the production of aerosols as a result of the burning of sulfur compounds. Anthropogenic changes are our own contributions to the environment, and climatic changes may be a response of the global biota to anthropogenic perturbations.

Controversy is intense around the issue of possible effects from industrial, domestic, and agricultural activity. By the early 1970s more than 15 billion tons of carbon dioxide had been injected into the atmosphere, and at least half of this increment still circulates. The rate of increase of carbon dioxide concentration has accelerated so much that it cannot be accounted for merely by emissions.

Meteorologists are in unanimous agreement that CO_2 increase leads to a warmer climate, especially in northern latitudes. Exactly the reverse could happen, however. Both dust and haze reflect sunlight back into space, reducing the heat received from the sun and causing the Earth's surface to cool. Cooling has occurred, but this simplistic explanation does not hold. Hazes in the troposphere absorb more energy than they reflect; a haze in the stratosphere may warm that region also by absorbing energy, but this results, by a strange meteorological sequence, in the cooling of the Earth's surface such as happens when volcanoes inject haze into the stratosphere. Haze near ground level should have a slight warming effect. Almost every man-made effect, from jet contrails to carbon dioxide emissions and haze generation, should cause a rise in mean surface temperature. Obstinately, though, the temperature during this time fell.

The Challenger expedition in the 1950s showed that biological systems readily add methyl radicals to a wide variety of elements, including sulfur. I thought that dimethylsulfide (DMS) might be the major biological sulfur compound emitted into the atmosphere. Challenger had already shown that marine algae and certain land plants emit dimethylsulfide. The production of dimethylsulfide is ubiquitous in the biosphere. Marine algae, soil, and almost all plants emit it. The output of DMS is strongly light-dependent; it may be the missing component of the natural sulfur cycle. It is far more stable than hydrogen sulfide, and so could survive transfer to the stratosphere, where it might oxidize to give sulfate and perhaps a methane sulfonate aerosol. Such an aerosol is well worth seeking; if found, the source will be biological.

Another product of the biota tantalizingly suggestive of important atmospheric change is nitrous oxide (N_2O). N_2O is emitted, mostly by soil microorganisms, at the huge rate of 2.5 billion tons per year. The concentration of N_2O in the troposphere is about 0.5 ppm. In the stratosphere the destruction of N_2O by solar ultraviolet light leads to the production of, among other things, nitric oxide (NO), which modifies ozone production. Nitrous oxide production may affect the

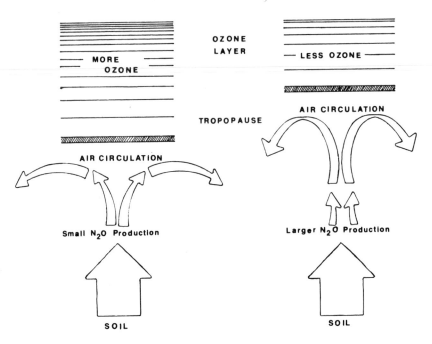

Figure 4
Nitrous oxide (N$_2$O), produced by soil microorganisms, can modify the ozone layer, causing changes in atmospheric circulation patterns.

density of the ozone layer; it may be another biological climate modifier (figure 4).

Regarding recent climatic change and the possible responsibility of man's activities, facts are few and opinions many. But while I think it will be a long time before the complete system that determines the climate is understood, the answers are unlikely to be found if the biota is neglected. The biota has continued to survive and modify its environment for over 3 billion years. Changes which have occurred since the evolution of *Homo sapiens,* and especially more recently since the industrial revolution, seem huge to us; the consequences seem dire and immediate. But devastating environmental change due to rapidly growing populations of young species is a recurring theme of the evolution of life. A strong response of exponentially increasing organisms to their own "pollutants" has happened before. The enforcement of gas-emission standards on internal-combustion engines, the building of "biospheres" by people in Arizona and in the USSR, the announcements both by NASA and by Earthwatch of their plans for "missions to Planet Earth," and the great rise of environmental concerns on the part of industry and educators all begin to exercise a negative feedback on the tendency of our global human population to make its immediate environment unfit for our kind of life. This behavior is typically "gaian"; indeed, the hope I want to leave you with is that Gaia, in fact, truly exists.

Gaia: What's New?

The first presentation on the Gaia hypothesis for our Environmental Evolution course was made in 1973. Now everyone wants to know what's new. What is its current status?

A great deal of new evidence has accumulated. We now have a quite plausible theoretical model of the way Gaia works. A good example of this is the close coupling between carbon dioxide and climate regulation. There is little doubt that increasing carbon dioxide in the atmosphere increases the absorption of outgoing infrared radiation through the greenhouse effect and tends to warm the planet. The evidence for this has strengthened over recent years. Exciting new evidence in the last couple of years has come mostly from analysis of ice cores from Greenland and Antarctica. A geologic record of the carbon dioxide concentration of the atmosphere from the present to tens of thousands of years into the past (well into the last glaciation) can be documented from gas samples from ice taken at different depths. The exciting aspect of this new information is the correlation between CO_2 and temperature. During the last glaciation, the CO_2 concentration fell to somewhat below 200 parts per million; temperature-CO_2 correlation is very close to that of the model predictions made beforehand. Even more exciting: at the end of the last glaciation the carbon dioxide concentration rose close to its present value in a period just short of a hundred years! Geophysical and geochemical processes that presumably control atmospheric CO_2 concentration cannot operate at that speed. In my view, this change in CO_2 concentration was a consequence of the growth and change in population density of the nonhuman biota.

What is the current status of your theoretical work on the Gaia hypothesis?

When the hypothesis was introduced, we felt some biological system must regulate the chemical composition and climate of the planet, but we did not know how. Most of us imagined a very complicated, intricate affair. I thought it might involve something built into the genetic structure of organisms. I am now happily confident that Gaian regulation is a natural and simple consequence of intrinsic properties of life on this planet.

Three fundamental aspects of life determine its tendency to establish a Gaian regulating system. The first is the important fact that life on Earth is strongly constrained by its environment. Life does not flourish when water is frozen, nor when conditions are too hot. More favorable conditions exist between these extremes. Such a constraint applies to all manner of other planetary variables, like acidity; life will not flourish if conditions are either too acid or too alkaline. Life prefers neutrality. Ocean salinity is another constraint. If water is too saline, life cannot grow; if water is so fresh that nutrient salts are lacking, equally life will not continue. Between the extremes lie the best growth conditions. The most important property determining Gaia is the existence of life in the universe of constraints. The second crucial fact is the tendency of all life to grow exponentially whenever or wherever a niche is open, and whenever the environment becomes favorable. The third property relates to diversity. When different organisms emerge, they use opportunities when a new niche opens in different ways, or exploit old niches when other organisms fail to occupy it. So my theoretical approach is based on life's tendency to grow exponentially, limitations to this growth, and organismal diversity. From these assumptions my colleagues and I have been able to produce a simple model of the workings of Gaia. The numerous forms of life interact with their environment in an unbelievably intricate manner in the real world. It is quite impossible, even with the largest computers available, to adequately build a model of the entire world. However, we can investigate the situation by a process of reduction. I have reduced the environment to a single variable—temperature—and the species to a single type—a daisy plant—in order to produce an imaginary world, Daisyworld.

Imagine a planet very like the Earth in many ways, although with less ocean. It is well watered, and plants grow almost anywhere on its surface. It also has a very clear atmosphere, uncomplicated by clouds or greenhouse gases. The surface temperature of the planet is very dependent upon one property only: its albedo, i.e., reflection of sunlight back into space. This imaginary planet, Daisyworld, is at the same orbital distance from its star, identical to our own sun, as the Earth is from the sun. Daisyworld's sun shares a universal property: with age it grows warmer and its output of heat increases. I want to demonstrate how the temperature of Daisyworld varies with and without life as its sun increases its output of heat. The relationship between the growth of daisies and temperature is represented as a parabolic curve. Growth begins at a temperature of about 5°C and increases steadily to a maximum at about 20°C, room temperature. As the temperature rises beyond that, the growth rate declines until all growth ceases at a temperature of 40°C. This choice of growth curve is not arbitrary; it adequately describes growth as a function of temperature for most vegetation.

Growth of daisies has an effect on the environment of Daisyworld. A "species" of daisy that is light-colored and reflects sunlight tends to lower the planetary temperature. When a maximum number of light-colored daisies covers a large proportion of planetary area, the temperature of the planet is at its lowest. Conversely, when very few or no light-colored daisies exist, the planet is darker because of lack of the light reflection tendency, and the planetary temperature is much higher. Small temperature changes take place on Daisyworld depending on the population of daisies. The daisies have the capacity to regulate planetary temperature. We can simulate a lifeless world by holding the daisy population constant, not allowing it to vary. In this case large temperature changes occur with changes in solar output. A lifeless planet does not have the capacity to lessen changes in temperature brought about by increases in solar luminosity. The mean temperature of a lifeless planet can be compared with one inhabited by dark daisies. Assuming that Daisyworld were a lifeless planet covered with just bare rocks, mean planetary temperature would increase as solar luminosity increased. Temperatures would rise from below freezing to about 50–70°C as the solar output steadily rose. Growth of dark daisies would have quite a different effect on temperature as solar luminosity rose. As the planetary temperature reached 5°C, dark daisies would start to grow. Imagine dark daisies that start to grow; because the stand is dark, the daisies will be warmer than their environment. This results in more growth and a little faster spreading. Before long dark daisies will cover a whole area; the temperature of that area will be warmer. This warmth adds to the extra warmth of the daisies. So, with positive feedback, daisy growth rapidly explodes until dark daisies cover a sizable proportion of the planet. The planetary temperature zooms up to close to the most favored value for daisy growth (20°C). It does not continue to rise because daisy growth is discouraged when temperature rises too high, so the planetary temperature remains more or less constant over a wide range of solar luminosity. Dark daisies alone can regulate planetary temperature to a considerable extent.

We now add light daisies and see the effect of competition between two different daisy types. Light daisies prefer to grow at warmer temperatures than dark daisies. When the mean temperature of the planet reaches about 5°C daisy growth commences. The dark daisies grow like mad until the temperature has risen to just above the optimum for growth of dark daisies on the planet. The planet is now warm enough for light daisies to grow, in spite of the fact that their tendency to reflect sunlight makes the environment somewhat cooler. This early stage, favorable for dark daisies, is less favorable for the light ones. As the sun warms up further, the two daisy populations change in number. Dark daisies decrease in numbers as white daisies increase until their growth curves intersect: a point is reached where the light daisies are just as numerous as the dark ones. As the sun warms further, white daisies are more and more favored. Still, they regulate the planetary temperature, and the mean is held very close to the most favorable value for plants. Eventually the sun becomes too hot and the entire system suddenly dies. A sudden rise in planetary temperatures occurs as all life ceases. That is the end of Daisyworld.

Daisyworld is contrived and artificial; it bears little relationship to a real planet. I do believe, however, that in principle the operation of Gaia as illustrated on Daisyworld is a close parallel to what is occurring on our own planet. Indeed, some recent evidence on the possible significance of tropical forest ecosystems and the regulation of planetary and environmental temperature is like that of Daisyworld. In the early days, I wondered why tropical forests were so dark. Their very darkness would make them absorb sunlight, like the dark daisies. Since these are the hottest regions of the Earth, it seemed to me a counterproductive trait to have evolved. Quite recently, what we should have known from the beginning has become obvious. If seen from space, these tropical forest regions of the Earth are not dark at all, but blindingly white. They are covered by white clouds that are the product of evapotranspiration from the tropical forest trees beneath. These clouds stabilize forest temperatures. Moreover, at night, when the sun is not shining, the clouds

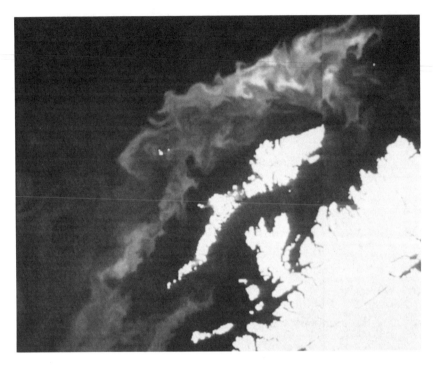

Figure 5
Patrick Holligan's photograph of a coccolithophorid bloom.

tend to disperse, and the very dark color is useful in dissipating the heat that is gathered during the daytime. The tropical forest—dark trees and white clouds—acts toward the regulation of the planet as both dark and white daisies simultaneously. My suggestion is speculative, and I mention it to illustrate how Daisyworld might be extrapolated to Earth. In addition to this tropical forest cloud effect, satellite photographs of oceans show blooms of coccolithophores, appearing to act in the manner of white daisies, that may affect the sea temperature (figure 5). I expect this story to develop more subplots when I come back and repeat it in 10 years.

We should consider more than the effect of albedo in the Daisyworld model. This same sort of environmental and growth feedback model helps explain regulation of concentration of atmospheric carbon dioxide. The growth of the biota continuously pumps carbon dioxide out of the atmosphere into the soil. The concentration of soil CO_2 is 30 times greater than that of the atmosphere. Similar CO_2-

pumping processes occur in the sea. The biota continuously pumps CO_2 and maintains current atmospheric levels, which is probably a major climate-regulating mechanism.

In your books *Ages of Gaia* (1988), and even earlier in *Gaia: A New Look at Life on Earth* (1979), you mention the possibility of a direct connection between the Gaia hypothesis and the phenomenon of plate tectonics. Please explain.

When I prepared this material, I admit the idea was even beyond the category of speculation. Nevertheless, I stuck my neck out and included it. I am glad to report that no less a figure than Don Anderson, Professor of Geology at the California Institute of Technology, in an article in *Science* (Anderson 1984), stated quite specifically that we should consider the possibility that biological influence on the production of eclogite and limestone made plate tectonics possible. We had one closely related notion 10 years ago: that limestone can be a fluxing agent. For movement of the massive tectonic plates, the region of molten material (the magma beneath them) must be fluid and capable of motion. The nature of limestone is such that it lowers the melting point of the rock mixture into which it is drawn. This extra fluidity, present as a result of the subduction of limestone, lubricates the movements of the plates, making the process possible. The limestone—nearly all of which is biological in origin—acts as a fluxing agent, keeping the rocks below the crust molten so that heat is more readily transferred. Convection currents persist. I can't give geological details of the eclogite argument, because it is not my expertise, but I strongly advise reading Anderson's article.

Please explain the relationship between atmospheric CO_2 and limestone.

The amount of CO_2 in the atmosphere depends entirely upon its lithospheric sources and sinks. The ultimate source of CO_2 is outgassing from volcanoes, and the sink for CO_2 is calcium silicate in rocks. In a process called *weathering,* calcium silicate (a very common mineral in igneous and metamorphic rocks) reacts with atmospheric CO_2 in the presence of water and forms calcium bicarbonate and silicic acid, both of which are soluble. These are transported by rivers to the ocean, where the calcium bicarbonate dissociates. The bicarbonate is taken up mostly by organisms in the formation of calcium carbonate shells, skeletons, scales, and other biogenic structures. After death, carbonate sediments form from the rain of dead cocco-lithophores, foraminifera, marine animals, etc. Eventually, under pressure, limestone—primarily $CaCO_3$—forms from the former skeletal material. Later it is subducted to become the fluxing agent I just mentioned. For a better idea of the role of the biota in the formation of minerals I strongly recommend the book by Lowenstam and Wiener (1989). They give us great insight into the mechanisms of Gaia.

What new ideas have you been entertaining?

Perhaps Earth's water has been retained by Gaia. Ocean salinity, water retention, and lateral movement of crustal plates are the ideas concerning us these days. Maybe you can help us work on them!

Readings

Anderson, D. L. 1984. The earth as a planet: Paradigm and paradoxes. *Science* 223: 347–355.

Charlson, R. J., J. E. Lovelock, M. O. Andreae, and S. G. Warren. 1987. Oceanic phytoplankton, atmospheric sulphur, cloud albedo and climate. *Nature* 326: 655–661.

Graedel, T. E., and P. J. Crutzen. 1989. The changing atmosphere. *Scientific American* 261, no. 3: 58–68.

Inadvertent Climate Modification: Report of the Study of Man's Impact on Climate (*SMIC*). MIT Press, 1971.

Lovelock, J. 1979. *Gaia: A New Look at Life on Earth.* Oxford University Press.

Lovelock, J. 1988. *The Ages of Gaia.* Norton.

Lowenstam, H., and S. Wiener. 1989. *On Biomineralization.* Oxford University Press.

Man's Impact on the Global Environment: Assessment and Recommendations for Action. Report of the Study of Critical Environmental Problems (SCEP). MIT Press, 1970.

Sahtouris, E. 1989. *Gaia: The Human Journey from Chaos to Cosmos.* Pocket Books.

Schneider, S. 1989. The changing climate. *Scientific American* 261, no. 3: 70–79.

Schneider, S., and P. Boston, eds. 1991. *Scientists on Gaia.* MIT Press.

Appendix A
Teaching Strategy

Professional geologists, environmental scientists, and biologists can easily teach this material; in many cases they will be learning anew with their students. For the instructor, three books are indispensable supplements to this text: *Traces of Bygone Biospheres,* by Andrey Lapo, *Early Life,* by Lynn Margulis, and *A New Bacteriology,* by Sorin Sonea and Maurice Panisett. Appendix C lists introductory readings from many other fields. Both instructors and students can compensate for any deficiencies in background by consulting them. Plan to adapt our materials to your own needs and to the local ecology.

The course begins and ends at the planetary level. During the first three sessions the instructor leads an exemplary discussion about the geological time scale and the Gaia Hypothesis. Lynn Margulis' videotaped lecture "The Gaia Hypothesis and Early Life" (see below) is comparable to the material in this early portion of the course. The course becomes more participatory as the students grow increasingly familiar with the material, and culminates with students giving their own ten-minute presentations and leading class discussions.

To best appreciate this scientific activity, students should have at least four semesters of any combination of biology, chemistry, astronomy, physics, and geology. Like natural science itself, the program of study evolves and is infinitely expansible. Therefore we have listed in appendix C only the most highly recommended books. In addition to textbooks and secondary sources, it is essential that readings from the primary literature be assigned. Each semester we offer some ten to twenty primary sources as supplementary readings. Those we have used are listed in appendix C.

Students may be evaluated primarily by the quality of their participation and their oral presentations. Over the course of a semester, each student gives three ten-minute presentations and a five-minute presentation on topics of his or her choice, based on the chapters in this volume. Guidelines for preparing these presentations are given below. We ask our students to list the titles of their talks on a large master sign-up calendar. This organizes the topics to be covered in a given class period and allows students to coordinate topics with their classmates. Several short written homework assignments are also required: the time and space assignments, a genetics worksheet, and a geology worksheet. Instructions and samples of these are included in this appendix and should be modified to suit the instructor and the students. In addition, our students create guides for field trips to local sites or institutions of biological interest. Field trips can include visits to museums of science, aquariums, Audubon Society nature centers, university collections, sewage-treatment plants, local conservation areas, and other places of ecological interest, such as salt marshes, bogs, and forests. Plans and questions for two sample field trips are given below. Each student is requested to provide general information about the accessibility of his field site before presenting sample questions and suggested answers. Field trip guides should include explicit directions, hours (where useful), and other information, as in the examples provided below.

Sample Schedule and Minimal Assignments

Week 1	Introductory session
Week 2	Chapter 16
Week 3	Chapter 16
Week 4	Chapters 16 and 1; campus tour*
Week 5	Chapters 2, 3, and 5
Week 6	Chapter 6 or 7, Time Assignment due; agreement on plan for field trip
Week 7	Chapter 8 or 9
Week 8	Chapter 12; Space Assignment due
Week 9	Chapter 10 or 11; Genetics Worksheet due

*Possible visit sites for campus tour: computerized reference library services, map room, rock collection, geology department, petrographic thin section laboratory, meteorological laboratory, herbarium, greenhouse, electron microscope or microprobe laboratory, gas chromatographic–mass spectrometry laboratory, etc. Check your campus for details.

Week 10	Chapter 13
Week 11	Chapter 14 or 15
Week 12	Open discussion; Geology Worksheet and Field Trip Report due
Week 13	Oral final exam

Time Assignment

The purpose of the Time Assignment is to develop an appreciation for the vastness of geological time and for the remoteness of many events that affect us directly today. The assignment is discussed in the class during the fourth or fifth week and should be handed in two weeks later.

Each student is asked to think of and name an event of interest in the history of the cosmos, such as the origin of *Homo sapiens sapiens*, the origin of the Earth-Moon system, evidence of the first life on Earth, the origin of the universe, the orogeny of the Appalachian Mountains, or the end of the last glaciation. Each student must suggest one possibility; if there are sixteen students, the class members, by negotiation, must trim the list by agreeing to ten major events. The assignment is for each student to develop a written time scale (in any form) and place the events on it.

Our criteria for evaluation are the validity of the scale, the use of units (e.g., 1 centimeter = 500 million years), the accuracy of the placement of events on the scale, references, aesthetics, and originality. We present the finest contributions to the entire class and even, when they are extraordinary, post them in the classroom.

To follow up this assignment, we draw attention to Calder's *Timescale: An Atlas of the Fourth Dimension* and to the Elsevier poster of the geological time scale.

Space Assignment

The space assignment requires the students to integrate knowledge crossing various levels of linear dimension, from the molecular (e.g., Ångstroms) to the astronomical (Astronomical Units). Invariably, when asked to arrange the linear dimensions of objects on a scale, they recognize not only the need for a common unit, such as the meter, but also the need for an exponential scale of notation.

As with the Time Assignment, the exercise begins in class, and two weeks are given for completion. Each class member is requested to suggest an object relevant to the course whose linear dimension it would be useful to know. Typical examples are the diameter of the Earth, the distance across a hydrogen atom, the height of the biosphere from the abyss to the top of the troposphere, the diameter of a globular protein, the diameter of a coccoid bacterial cell, and the distance to the edge of the visible universe. After the ten entries of greatest interest to the class are agreed upon, each student pursues the assignment as she or he wishes. After the work has been submitted, we draw attention to Morrison and Morrison's book *Powers of Ten* and show the film of the same name.

Worksheets

Genetics and Mutation

(1) Starting with one cell (at generation 0) which divides at regular intervals, if no cells die, how many cells will there be after

1 generation? ____	2 generations? ____
3 generations? ____	4 generations? ____
5 generations? ____	10 generations? ____
20 generations? ____	N generations? ____

If you start with K cells in the above example, how many cells will there be after N generations?

(2) In March a particular pond has one water lily on it. Every two days the number of lilies doubles. On May 30 the entire pond is covered and looks like a giant lily pad. On what days was the pond one-eighth, one-quarter, one-half covered? Do you think water lilies have such a biotic potential? Define "biotic potential" and explain its significance. What is the point of this exercise for the study of evolution? (Hint: Define "natural selection" for yourself.)

(3) *Penicillium** does not require biotin in its growth medium. *Neurospora*, a similar fungus, does require biotin. Is this observation

---

*Genera, such as *Penicillium* and *Neurospora*, are capitalized and italicized; species are written in lower case and also italicized—for example, *Penicillium crysogenum*. Names of drugs, such as penicillin, are written without capitalization or special fonts.

consistent with the conclusion that biotin plays no role in the cellular biochemistry of *Penicillium*? Explain.

(4) Define and place each of the following on a temporal (functional) diagram that shows how protein synthesis works: DNA, polysomes, mRNA, tRNA, GTP, rRNA, aminoacyl-tRNA synthetase, ribosomes.

(5) Give a real example (that is, specify an organism, a phenotype, and your source of information) for each of the following types of mutations:

point mutation (one or very few base changes)
deletion
chromosomal mutation
aneuploidy.

(6) For each of the following give a one-sentence definition and a referenced example:

replicon
transformation
transduction
transposition
conjugation.

(7) Of the following chromosomal mutations, which kind do you think is the most significant for evolution? Explain your answer.

inversion
duplication
deletion.

(8) Give a referenced example of the mode of action of a chemical mutagen and a measured value for mutation rate.

(9) In 1859 a gentleman farmer in southern Australia imported twelve pairs of rabbits from England to satisfy his passion for hunting. Within a few years, the rabbit became a major agricultural pest on the whole continent. Many ways of eradication were tried without success. In 1959, a virus producing myxomatosis, a disease fatal to rabbits, was deliberately released in the countryside and rapidly spread throughout Australia. It caused such a widespread epidemic that in some areas the rabbit census dropped by a factor of 100 in a matter of weeks. However, year after year, smaller percentages of

the rabbits died. Explain what happened, using the concepts and terms of neo-Darwinism.

(10) Explain how artificial selection may have detrimental effects on organisms used in phenotypic breeding (for example, in breeding for coat color or for egg or milk production). (Hint: Look up artificial selection, phenotype-genotype relations, pleiotrophy, or genetic homeostasis in a comprehensive genetics text.)

(11) What is the "New Synthesis?" (Hint: Look up Julian Huxley or Ernst Mayr.)

(12) A woman with blood type Rh-negative O has four sons and four daughters with a man who has Rh-positive AB blood. Diagram the cross and show the expected blood types of their eight children. How is this example related to "evolution by natural selection"?

Geology

(1) Name and distinguish the three major types of rocks formed on Earth. What are the salient differences among them?

(2) List three localities in the Amherst area (western Massachusetts and the Connecticut River Valley) where you could expect to find a sample of each of the three general rock types. Specify these localities, indicating your references. Bring in (place it, labeled, in a plastic bag with your name, the rock type, and the locality) one identified rock sample from an identified local outcrop.

(3) We are familiar with elemental cycling at the global and local levels, but what is meant by the "rock cycle"? Draw a diagram of the rock cycle to illustrate your answer. (Hint: exogenic, endogenic).

(4) Briefly note the mechanisms behind orogeny (mountain-building), using the ideas of global plate tectonics. Give an example of an orogeny, including the relative movement of plates in the context of a specific geographical location.

(5) Cite two forms of field evidence (be specific about location) that have been used to establish the presence of former glacial activity in the Amherst area. When did the last glaciers recede from New England? (By "field evidence" we mean topographical structures and

patterns, soil deposits, outcrops, and similar features visible in the landscape).

(6) How do meteorites help us to determine the age of the Earth?

(7) What is the fundamental difference between the lithification of detrital sediments (sandstones and shales) and the formation of carbonates?

(8) Define biomineralization. Name two examples of biogenic minerals. What is the evidence that these two minerals are biogenic? (Hint: Look at Lowenstam's book *On Biomineralization*.)

Field Trips

Quabbin Reservation, Central Massachusetts

Times
Visitor Center open Monday–Friday, 7 A.M.–4 P.M.

Directions
Unfortunately, the PVTA will take you only to the intersection of Routes 9 and 202, so a car or a bicycle is necessary (although hitchhiking the remaining 5 miles of Route 9 is probably not out of the question). From campus, make your way to Route 9 East (take a left at Amherst College). About 15 miles down the road, take the left at the sign for Quabbin Reservation/Winsor Dam. The next stop is either the Visitor Center or Winsor Dam.

This self-guided field trip is meant to explore the natural and the "unnatural" aspects of the Quabbin. The trip requires only an hour or two, but you may want to extend it. Though any time is good, early morning is especially pleasant. Binoculars will be useful. The trails may be wet; dress appropriately.

An important aspect of outdoor investigation is the full sensory appreciation of where you are. As you walk the trail, please take time out along the way to listen, smell, touch, and taste. All too often we rely on our eyes and miss a wealth of wonders. Make a conscious effort to stop occasionally to make connections; it is worth it.

The Visitor Center charges no admission. Pamphlets showing the trails in the park area are available free of charge; it is well worth a visit.

Questionnaire

(1) At the Visitor Center, look at the map showing the flow of water from the Quabbin Reservoir to Boston. By what method does the water flow? Draw a diagram to illustrate it.

(2) As you enter the center, there are photographs of bald eagles by Jack Swedberg. How has the existence of the Quabbin become conducive to the reintroduction of mating pairs of eagles to Massachusetts?

(3) Along the back wall of the center are prints of the valley prior to its flooding. Keep these images in mind whenever you walk through the Quabbin Reservation. Why was this valley chosen as the site for the reservoir?

(4) A display case contains a collection of skulls of mammals found within the Quabbin Reservation. What effect, if any, has the establishment of the reservation had on diversity? What do the skulls reveal about the available habitats?

(5) Focusing only on the appearance of the opossum skull, how could you classify the opossum's eating habits (carnivore, . . .)? Of what biogeographical significance is the opossum in New England? What anatomical or physiological features of the opossum are unique to the North American opossum?

(6) What sort of ecosystem is represented by the tank? What is the relationship of the organisms present? What kind of aquatic diversity has the reservoir led to?

The video show on old Quabbin gives a unique glimpse of the past. Take the time to watch it if you can. What was Enfield?

To explore the reservoir, start at the parking area near the Visitor Center.

(7) What observable features of the area are due to glaciation?

Think about the concept of autopoietic systems as you proceed to the Beaver Trail (trail 3), which begins about a mile from the Visitor Center. Look at the Swift River Spillway, just before the turnoff for Winsor Park and Quabbin Hill Tower. This is the first hint of the complex geology of the area. The immediate area of the spillway is a quartz diorite, part of the Belchertown Intrusive.

As you start down the trail, the first impression is one of human presence: the old trails that were a part of the now-dead towns, the strips cleared for powerlines. But even with the clearing, nonhuman life persists.

(8) What kind of community probably occupied this area? How does it compare with the community existing now? Have new habitats been created for wildlife? Explain.

As you make your way along the trail, be aware of how the dominant vegetation has changed. Where the trail forks, head north (to your left). Just as the trail appears to drift into the woods, there is a small pond on the right. Depending on the time of day and the season, everything from algal blooms to mating frogs can be observed—even an occasional deer.

(9) What do you feel is the origin of this pond?

As you walk up the trail, there is a stone wall on your right.

(10) How can we use this human signature of territoriality to understand the needs of others in the community?

Keep your eyes open for a large piece of quartz on the left edge of the trail.

(11) What kind of rock is quartz? What does its presence tell us about the geological forces in the area?

After walking along a low rise, you will find yourself on an outcrop.

(12) What kind of biological weathering has acted on this surface? What sort of evidence is there?

From this point the Beaver Pond becomes visible. View it from a distance first and note any activity.

(13) If "nothing" is visible, how can you determine if beavers are active here?

(14) What other species make use of this created pond? (Look closely into the pond.)

Follow one of the paths up to the far side of the pond to get an idea of the extent of the beaver's domain. There is also an outcrop to the left of the trail where water is running into the pond. Take a close look at the folds and the complex layering.

(15) How does this rock layering differ from that seen in stromatolites?

(16) Draw a diagram of a small section of the folding. What kind of forces do you think could create such folds?

(17) Define autopoiesis. How do the reservoir and the Beaver Pond compare as autopoietic systems?

The major point of this field trip has surfaced with your arrival at Beaver Pond, so retracing your steps at this point is OK. As the trail continues, you will walk through meadow communities, the foundations of houses, and reforested areas. Wild turkeys, bluebirds, a great horned owl, and deer, among other wildlife, have been seen in the meadow.

When you return to the Amherst campus, note in the main entrance of Morrill Science Center the map that diagrams the course of the Quabbin watershed. Can you see where the aqueduct was cut?

Readings

Halpin, D. 1965. The Geometry of Folds and Style of Deformation in the Quabbin Hill Area. Master's thesis in geology, University of Massachusetts, Amherst.

Hollocher, K., and A. Lent. 1987. Comparative petrology of amphibolites in the Monson Gneiss and the Ammonoosuc and Partridge Volcanics, Massachusetts. *Northeastern Geology* 9: 145–152.

Stokes, D. 1976. *Nature in Winter*. Little, Brown.

Blacksha Glass Flower Exhibit, Harvard Botanical Museum, Harvard University

Times
Call the museum for times, prices, and hours.

Directions
At Harvard Square, reached by bus or subway from Park St., go north on Mass. Ave., turn right onto Cambridge St., stay left on Kirkland St., turn left immediately onto Oxford St., and go one block to the university museums. All exhibits with which this questionnaire is concerned are on the third floor of the north wing.

Questionnaire
These questions refer to the glass flowers only. Before entering the turnstyle, look around at the outside exhibit.

Visit all three rooms. Note that the museum cases and the individual exhibits are labeled H-1 through H-9. This questionnaire is concerned primarily with the standing cases in the first room, although several references are made to the wall cases and to other rooms.

(1) Who made these flowers? When were they made? Why are they considered unique? Are they made entirely of glass?

(2) How are the cases arranged? Is this arrangement in evolutionary order? Name any plants represented here that are not angiosperms. What distinguishes cases H-1 through H-3 from cases H-4 through H-9? What does -ae or -aceae mean? (Note that it is on the upper right of each card.)

(3) Case H-1 contains several members of the grass family. What is the technical name of this family? Which species here is of economic importance? Why? After observing the representatives of the family here, specify where on the plant the flowers are generally located.

(4) Are the plants herbacious or woody? Are the flowers single, or are they borne in large numbers? What is the size of the typical single flower? Sketch a typical grass flower and label it. Is it a perfect flower?

(5) What is a common name for the Cyperaceae? Give an example. Why is this family often confused with the grass family? (These plants

can be distinguished from grasses because their leaves are triangular in cross-section.)

(6) Do palms have large or small flowers? (Estimate the size of an individual flower.) Name two palms of economic importance.

(7) Sketch the pineapple flower. Estimate the number of flowers that ultimately make up the edible portion of one pineapple.

(8) Look at *Brodiaca capitate*, *Milla biflora*, and *Ornithagalum umbellatum*. What common food do these resemble? In the plant, is the bulb root or the leaf edible? From the species shown here, estimate the size range and average size of flowers (diameter) in the lily family. What is the most probable number of petals and anthers for lily-family flowers?

(9) What is *Musa paradisiaca*? Sketch the inflorescence and indicate the individual flowers on it. Sketch a cross-section of a typical banana, and indicate where the seeds are and how they are arranged. Estimate the size of the leaf. What evidence indicates to you that bananas are monocots? Where are most orchids from?

(10) Find the heart-leaved willow (Salicaeae, Willow family) in case H-3. How many bumps are there per leaf? What are they? What example of the Betulaceae (Birch family) is displayed here? Sketch the flowers, showing male and female catkins. Is *Corylus* monoecious, or dioecious? Explain.

(11) One of the most common trees on the Boston University campus is *Ulmus americanus*. What is its common name? Sketch the flower, showing its pistil clearly. What happens to the seed? What does the seed look like? Sketch it.

(12) What parts of the *Beta vulgaris* are eaten? What family does it belong to?

(13) The Cruciferae are commonly called the Mustard family. What example is displayed here? Sketch the flower. (The cross shape gives the family its name.)

(14) What product of economic importance comes from plants of the *Papaveraceae* (poppy) family? (Hint: See the Economic Botany exhibit

in the room to the left of the entrance to the Glass Flowers. How many stamens and pistils per flower are there in *Dendromecon*?

(15) *Nepenthes* is the pitcher plant genus. Where does the name come from? (*Nepenthe* means "causes forgetfulness or sorrow" in Greek.) What are the "pitchers"? Are they flowers? What are they for?

(16) What are currants?

(17) Define the following:

angiosperm	monoecious
binomial nomenclature	perfect flower
conifer	plant families
dioecious	plant orders
embryo	seed
fruit	taxon (pl.: taxa)
inflorescence	

Draw a perfect flower and label the following parts: petals, sepals, anthers, stamens, ovary, ovules, receptacles.

Suggestions to Students Preparing Class Presentations

Preparation

Read the assigned chapter and the relevant papers in your packet. Read related chapter(s) in *Early Life*.

Make a list of topics or questions related to the chapter that intrigue you, including some which you think might interest your classmates.

Discuss your ideas with a former student or instructor. After you are sure your instructor or teaching fellow has accepted your topic, record and schedule your title on the master sign-up calendar.

Outline your presentation.

Presentation

Only a single concept can be presented well in a 10-minute talk. Relate each point carefully to that concept. Use acetate diagrams, posters, slides, chalkboard, or whatever else is needed to make each point vivid and memorable. Occasionally repeat the main idea, indicating how the various ancillary points in the presentation are related to the concept. Talk slowly, and stop if you think that the class is not following a line of reasoning.

At the end, summarize the entire talk in a few sentences like those at the beginning, and then invite questions from the class.

To Make Yours an Excellent Presentation

Know your material very well. Do not attempt to teach something you do not understand yourself. Discuss points that may be confusing to you with your classmates and the faculty before the talk.

Discuss your topic with any classmates who have signed up to speak on a similar topic. Coordinate the material to be presented; prevent redundancy by careful planning; divide aspects of the subject matter appropriately.

Discuss your presentation plan well in advance with colleagues (for example, graduate students or professors of zoology, geography, microbiology, or geology). They may be willing to lend you slides, rocks, or other materials. Borrow slides, if possible.

Make your own slides or transparencies. Check local resources for fossils, minerals, or other relevant illustrative materials.

Do not hesitate to consult introductory geology, astronomy, and biology textbooks on matters of background and terminology. Define carefully any new terms. If necessary, review introductory points with the class.

If your topic includes some controversial points, try to create a class discussion by asking provocative but clear questions.

Your presentation need not be formal or stiff. You may encourage class discussion or whatever you wish within your time allotment (usually ten minutes). The main requirements are that your presentation be informative, accurate, and interesting to your fellow students.

Please remember: During your assigned presentation time, you alone are responsible for the quality of the class.

The Interactive Lecture Program

Essential to our way of teaching the Environmental Evolution course are the Interactive Lecture tapes whereby each student, alone in a study carrel, listens to and queries scientists. The Interactive Lecture console, developed at MIT and Polaroid by Stewart Wilson, exemplifies our expectations for advanced science education in the 21st century.

It would, at present, be prohibitively expensive to duplicate the tapes, the electrowriter signals, and other materials. Since the entire program in the original interactive format is available at Boston University and at the University of Massachusetts at Amherst, potential teachers of environmental evolution are invited to visit or enroll in the course.

Our tapes are listed at the end of this appendix. The tape library, because of the importance of the scientists who participated in the recordings, is also an archive for scholars interested in the history of what Gerald Soffen calls "planetary evolutionary biogeochemistry." These taped materials, some of which are in a video format, are invaluable to the way we teach the course.

We use a seminar format based on the tape library, which is always expanding. The lecturers are eminent chemists, geologists, and biologists, most of whom are currently researching the early history of the Earth and the evolution of life. The contributing scientists are chosen not only for their direct involvement in the field of study but also for their ability to communicate clearly.

Each unit consists of the main portion of the lecture (always less than an hour long) and a comprehensive series of questions prepared by students and later answered by the lecturer. Supplementary visual aids (such as color slides, maps, and photographs) and a printed outline of the lecture accompany each tape. Most of the tapes include electrowriter signals that reproduce the lecturer's handwriting on paper.

The lecture format gives the student the opportunity to take part in an "active" learning process through simulated conversation. The student may selectively review the lecture material, obtain supplementary information, and clarify finer points by listening to the question-and-answer tapes. The interactive nature of the format makes it the student's responsibility to learn the material. The quantity of information each student acquires is largely a function of the time he or she puts into listening to, reviewing, and assimilating the material. Because students prepare for class by listening to the assigned audiotaped lecture, class time is free for debate, discussion, student presentation, and further development of the topics. As a result, a large amount of material is presented and understood in the limited class time of a single semester.

The Interactive Lecture console is housed in a comfortable atmosphere conducive to learning. Access to the lecture programs is available by appointment at the student's convenience. With additional course work, usually involving further study of "choice tapes" (also listed below), students may obtain graduate credit under the course title Environmental Evolution.

Tape Library*

"Cosmo-Chemical Evolution"

Cyril Ponnamperuma, Laboratory for Chemical Evolution, University of Maryland

Ponnamperuma discusses the origin of life from interactions of organic chemicals on the prebiotic Earth and gives evidence supporting the chemo-evolutionary theory of the origin of life drawn from the NASA discoveries on meteorites and interstellar dust.

"Polymers Before Monomers?"

Clifford Matthews, University of Illinois, Chicago Circle
15 minutes

Matthews presents the evidence for his controversial hypothesis on the origin of proteins, contrasts his theory with that of Ponnamperuma, and describes its implications for observations of organic matter in meteorites and the outer planets.

"RNA vs DNA" (video)

Antonio Lazcano, Universidad Nacional Autónoma de México
12 minutes

Lazcano reviews various aspects of experimental origin-of-life research and argues that RNA preceded DNA as the genetic material of the earliest organisms.

---

*Tapes are approximately 45 minutes long unless noted otherwise.

"Evidence of Earliest Life"

Paul Strother, Boston University
Strother explains the criteria used for determining whether putative microfossils are actually biogenic, and examines the evidence for life in the early Archean eon based on thin sections of rocks from sites in Greenland, southern Africa, and northwest Australia.

"The Antiquity of Life"

Elso Barghoorn, Harvard University
Barghoorn describes biota from three sites that elucidate the antiquity of life: the Fig Tree Formation in the Swaziland System of southern Africa, the Gunflint Iron Formation of North America, and the Bitter Springs Formation of central Australia.

"Earliest Life: The Rock Record" (video)

Maud Walsh, Louisiana State University
12 minutes
Walsh describes the geological sequence in the Swaziland System, gives evidence that the oldest microfossils are found in what was once a shallow marine environment, and discusses the geological processes involved in the formation of mats and cherts.

"Life in the Proterozoic Eon"

Andrew Knoll, Harvard University
Knoll describes the sedimentary rocks and some of the microfossils preserved in them from 1 billion to 570 million years ago in the Draken Formation of the Arctic Svalbard archipelago.

"Prokaryotic Motility, Eukaryotic Motility, and 'Rubberneckia'"

Sidney Tamm, Boston University
In this set of three lectures, Tamm gives a thorough explanation of our current understanding of the motility systems of prokaryotes and eukaryotes, and of the unique motility system found in the devescovinid protist "Rubberneckia."

"Symbiotic Theory: Cells as Microbial Communities"

Lynn Margulis, University of Massachusetts, Amherst
Margulis presents a current view of the status of endosymbiotic theory. This theory postulates the origin of three classes of organelles of eukaryotic cells (plastids, mitochondria, and undulipodia) from separate lineages of bacteria.

"Spirochetes and the Origin of Undulipodia"

Lynn Margulis, University of Massachusetts, Amherst
Margulis explains her hypothesis for the origin of undulipodia (eukaryotic "flagella" and cilia) within the endosymbiotic theory, and presents the status of experimental evidence supporting the hypothesis.

"Comparison of Planetary Atmospheres: Mars, Venus, and Earth"

Michael McElroy, Harvard University
McElroy hypothesizes that the atmospheres of the inner planets were originally similar. He describes and compares the atmospheres of Mars, Venus, and Earth, and explores the mechanisms of planetary atmospheric evolution that may have occurred on each.

"Gaia"

James Lovelock, F.R.S., Cornwall, United Kingdom
Lovelock suggests that the sum of the organisms on Earth forms a complex system that regulates its environment at the surface of the planet. He presents evidence for the existence of such a system and argues the need to look at the Gaian system as an interacting whole.

"Life's Contribution to the Atmosphere"

James Lovelock and Lynn Margulis
In part I, Lovelock and Margulis contrast the conventional and the Gaian views of the origin and history of Earth's atmosphere. In part II, they discuss evidence for and implications of life's control of atmospheric composition, temperature, acidity, and oxidation state.

"Continental Drift and Plate Tectonics"

Raymond Siever, Harvard University
Siever describes the discoveries that led to the modern version of Wegener's continental-drift theory. He explains the processes of plate tectonics as revealed through studies of fossils, the sea floor and its paleomagnetism, and the distribution of volcanism, earthquakes, faults, and other geological activity.

"Algal Mats of the Persian Gulf"

Stjepko Golubic, Boston University
Golubic describes the different types of coastal microbial (algal) mats that form the sabkha of Abu Dhabi, and the relationship of the living mats to their potential preservation as stromatolites.

"Stromatolites of Shark Bay, Australia"

Stjepko Golubic, Boston University
Golubic describes the formation of different types of stromatolites, and discusses the relationship between the recent stromatolites of Shark Bay and ancient stromatolites of the Proterozoic eon.

"Microbial Activity and Archean Gold Deposits"

Betsey Dyer, Wheaton College
Dyer discusses the role of bacteria in the Archean gold deposits of Witswatersrand, South Africa, and points to the ability of modern bacteria to precipitate gold from solution as evidence for the possibility of that role.

"The Microbial Community at Laguna Figueroa, Mexico"

John Stolz, Duquesne University
Stolz discusses the stratified microbial community involved in the deposition of laminated sediments in Baja California, Mexico, describing the site, the basic structure of a microbial mat, and the organisms that build and inhabit the mat.

"Biomineralization: Production of Minerals by Living Organisms"

Heinz Lowenstam, California Institute of Technology
Lowenstam discusses some of the more than forty minerals produced biogenically inside cells or resulting from the activities of cells. The implications for the fossil record of biomineralization by selected animals (i.e., as teeth and skeletal materials) are detailed.

"Biodestruction and Stabilization of Mineral Surfaces"

Wolfgang Krumbein, University of Oldenburg
Krumbein discusses the relationship of microbes to geological processes, whether destructive (as in the action of lichens on and in rock surfaces) or protective (as in the action of heterotrophs which produce a coating called "rock varnish").

"Plant Chemical Signals and Phanerozoic Evolution"

Tony Swain, Boston University, and Robert Buchsbaum, Massachusetts Audubon Society
Swain introduces the concept of "ecological hormones" (i.e., allelochemicals, semiochemicals) to encompass the interspecific chemical

signals between plants and animals. He presents the chemical structures for several groups of these compounds, and relates them to their pathways and ecological significance.

"The Genetic Mechanisms of Evolution"

Lynn Margulis, University of Massachusetts, Amherst
Margulis discusses the classification of the diverse biota found on Earth and explains some of the basic evolutionary mechanisms that led to this great diversity of life.

"Origins of Life: Historical Development of Recent Theories"

Antonio Lazcano, Universidad Nacional Autónoma de México
Lazcano presents a historical review of the major theories of the origins of life and discusses some of the 20th-century experiments in origins-of-life research.

"Origins of Membranes: Structures and Functions"

David Deamer, University of California, Davis
Deamer discusses the properties of contemporary liposome-forming lipid bilayers and presents his discovery of lipid-like material extracted from the Murchison meteorite. The presence of lipid-like material in meteorites provides a source on the early Earth of molecules that may have formed membranes of the earliest cells.

"The Theory of Plate Tectonics"

Raymond Siever, Harvard University
Siever traces the development of ideas and the sequence of discoveries that led to the synthesis of the theory of plate tectonics, an all-encompassing theory that provides a basis for explaining geological phenomena.

"Mammalian Evolution: Karyotypic Fission Theory"

Neil Todd, Boston University
Todd explains the evidence that chromosomes have fissioned in the evolution of mammals. He explores mechanisms by which these genomic rearrangements may be passed through populations, enabling speciation events. He then uses the controversial theory of karyotypic fission to explain the evolution of family lineages in various groups of tetrapods, such as pigs and dogs.

"Hallucinogenic Plants and Fungi of North America"
Richard Evans Schultes, Harvard University
Schultes describes various ceremonial uses of hallucinogenic plants
and fungi by native peoples of the North American continent.

"Plants, People, and Pollutants"
William Feder, Waltham Field Station, University of Massachusetts
20 minutes
Feder reviews the effects of atmosphere emissions of ozone and
hydrocarbons on the physiology of economically important plants,
and explores the extent to which the atmosphere links people and
their agriculture.

Supplementary Materials

"Five Kingdom Slide Set" (Margulis and Schwartz, 1989 and 1990)
Available from Ward's Natural Science Establishment, Inc., P.O. Box
92912, Rochester, NY 14692-9012.

"Five Kingdoms" (poster, 1991)

"The Gaia Hypothesis and Early Life"
This 1984 lecture given by Lynn Margulis at the NASA Lewis
Research Center is available on video cassettes from NASA Core,
15181 Route 58 South, Oberlin, OH 44074.

"Geological Time Table" (color poster compiled by B. U. Haq and
F. W. B. Van Eysinga; fourth revised, enlarged, and updated edition,
1987)
Elsevier Scientific Publishing Company, Inc., 52 Vanderbilt Avenue,
New York, NY 10017.

"Goddess of the Earth" (videotape, 1985)
This video was produced for the BBC series *Horizons;* it was shown
in the United States as a *Nova* program.

"Powers of Ten" (film, 1978)
This 16-mm color film is available from Pyramid Films, P.O. Box
1048, Santa Monica, CA 90406.

Appendix B
Five-Kingdom
Classification Scheme*

Superkingdom Prokaryota (Chromonemal Organization)

Kingdom Monera (Procaryotae)

Prokaryotic cells, bacteria. Nutrition absorptive (heterotrophic or autotrophic). Anaerobic, aerobic, facultatively anaerobic, microaerophilic or aerotolerant metabolism. Reproduction asexual and chromonemal; sex by conjugation with unidirectional recombination or mediated by small replicons (e.g., viruses, transposons, plasmids, transformation). Nonmotile or motile either by gliding or by bacterial flagella composed of flagellin proteins. Solitary unicellular, filamentous, colonial, or mycelial. Some produce sheaths, spores, or other multicellular resistant structures, sessile or stalked. Cell walls absent (Tenericutes), patchy (Mendosicutes), or composed of peptidoglycans between two lipoprotein membranes (Gracilicutes, Gram-negative) or external to the membrane (Firmicutes, Gram-positive).

SUBKINGDOM ARCHAEOBACTERIA

DIVISION: *Mendosicutes*

Phylum 1.   Methanocreatrices: methane-synthesizing bacteria; anaerobic chemotrophs (*Methanobacterium*)
Phylum 2.   Halophilic and thermoacidophilic bacteria: salt- and heat-tolerant bacteria (*Thermoplasma*)

---

*See L. Margulis and K. V. Schwartz, *Five Kingdoms*, second edition (Freeman, 1988).

SUBKINGDOM EUBACTERIA

DIVISION: *Tenericutes*

Phylum 3.   Aphragmabacteria: mycoplasmas, wall-less bacteria

DIVISION: *Gracilicutes*

Phylum 4.   Spirochaetae: spirochetes (*Spirochaeta, Treponema, Cristispira*)

Phylum 5.   Thiopneutes: anaerobic sulfate- or sulfur-reducing bacteria (*Desulfovibrio*)

Phylum 6.   Anaerobic phototrophic bacteria: purple nonsulfur bacteria (*Rhodospirillum*), green sulfur bacteria (*Chloroflexus*), purple sulfur bacteria (*Chromatium*)

Phylum 7.   Cyanobacteria: blue-green bacteria, blue-green algae (*Pleurocapsa, Nostoc, Oscillatoria*) and Chloroxybacteria: prokaryotic green algae (*Prochloron*)

Phylum 8.   Nitrogen-fixing aerobic bacteria: (*Azotobacter, Rhizobium*)

Phylum 9.   Pseudomonads: Gram-negative, aerobic heterotrophs (*Pseudomonas*)

Phylum 10.   Omnibacteria: Gram-negative aerobic heterotrophic bacteria, enterobacteria, coliforms (*Escherichia, Salmonella*), prosthecate bacteria (*Caulobacteria*), acetic-acid bacteria (*Acetobacter*), Moraxella-Neisseria group (*Neisseria, Moraxella*), predatory bacteria (*Bdellovibrio*), microaerophilic bacteria (*Spirillum*), vibrios (*Photobacterium*), aerobic and facultatively anaerobic rods, chlamydias, and rickettsias

Phylum 11.   Chemoautotrophic bacteria: sulfur-oxidizing bacteria (*Thiobacillus*), ammonia-oxidizing bacteria (*Nitrobacter, Nitrosomonas*), iron-oxidizing bacteria (*Ferrobacillus*)

Phylum 12.   Myxobacteria: heterotrophic aerobic gliding bacteria (*Beggiatoa*), fruiting myxobacteria (*Chrondromyces*)

DIVISION: *Firmicutes*

Phylum 13.   Fermenting bacteria (*Clostridium*)

Phylum 14.   Aeroendospora: aerobic endospore-forming bacteria (*Bacillus*)

Phylum 15.   Micrococci: Gram-positive aerobes (*Paracoccus, Sarcina*)

Phylum 16. Actinobacteria: Gram-positive coryniform and mycelial bacteria (*Actinomyces, Streptomyces*)

Superkingdom Eukaryota (Chromosomal Organization)

Kingdom Protoctista

Eukaryotic cells: membrane-bounded nuclei invariably present, more than a single chromosome per cell. Nutrition heterotrophic, either ingestive or absorptive, or, if photoautotrophic, by measured photosynthetic plastids. All products of evolution of two or more integrated prokaryotic heterogenomic systems. Aquatic microorganisms exclusive of animals, plants, and fungi. Reproduction is asexual, premitotic, or eumitotic sexual. In eumitotic forms, meiosis and fertilization are present, but details of cytology, life cycle, and ploidy level vary from group to group. Organisms are solitary unicellular, syncitial (plasmodial, coenocytic) colonial unicellular, or multicellular. All lack embryos and complex cell junctions (e.g., desmosomes or septate junctions). Most bear undulipodia (eukaryotic flagella or their shorter homologues, the cilia) composed of microtubules in the [9(2) + 2] pattern. Species are aquatic. Primarily unicellular forms are sometimes called protists.

I. Subgroup of phyla in which members lack undulipodia at all stages; complex sexual cycles absent
Phylum 1.   Rhizopoda: amebas, rhizopods
Phylum 2.   Haplosporidia: haplosporidians, parasites
Phylum 3.   Paramyxea: paramyxeans, parasites
Phylum 4.   Myxozoa: myxozoans, fish parasites
Phylum 5.   Microspora: microsporans, fish parasites

II. Subgroup of phyla in which members lack undulipodia; sexual cycles correlated with complex morphology present
Phylum 6.   Acrasea: acrasids, cellular slime molds
Phylum 7.   Dictyostelida: dictyostelids, cellular slime molds that form migrating "slugs" or "hats"
Phylum 8.   Rhodophyta: rhodophytes, red algae, red seaweeds
Phylum 9.   Conjugaphyta: gamophytes, conjugating green algae

III. Subgroup of phyla in which cells of members may reversibly form undulipodia; sexual cycles correlated with complex morphology absent

Phylum 10. Xenophyophora: xenophyophores, deep-sea macroscopic protists

Phylum 11. Cryptophyta: cryptomonads, some "phytoflagellates"

Phylum 12. Glaucocystophyta: glaucocystids, cyanelle-bearing algae

Phylum 13. Karyoblastea: karyoblastean giant amebas

Phylum 14. Zoomastigina: some "flagellates," some "parasites," amebomastigotes, bicoecids, choanomastigotes, diplomonads, pseudociliates, kinetoplastids, opalinids, proteromonads, parabasalians, retortamonads, pyrsonymphids

Phylum 15. Euglenida: euglenids, some "phytoflagellates"

Phylum 16. Chlorarachnida: chlorarachnids, "colored amebas"

Phylum 17. Prymnesiophyta: prymnesiophytes, some "phytoflagellates," algae

Phylum 18. Raphidophyta: raphidophytes, some "phytoflagellates," algae

Phylum 19. Eustigmatophyta: eustigmatophytes, some "phytoflagellates," eye-spot algae

Phylum 20. Actinopoda: acantharians, radiolarians, polycystinids, phaeodarians, heliozoans

Phylum 21. Hyphochytriomycota: some water molds, hyphochytrids

Phylum 22. Labyrinthulomycota: slime nets, thraustochytrids

Phylum 23. Plasmodiophoromycota: plasmodiophorids, some "plant parasites"

IV. Subgroup of phyla in which cells of members may reversibly form undulipodia; meiotic-fertilization sexual cycles correlated with complex morphology present

Phylum 24. Dinomastigota: dinomastigotes, "dinoflagellates," some planktonic algae

Phylum 25. Chrysophyta: chrysophytes, golden-yellow algae

Phylum 26. Chytridiomycota: chytrids, monoblepharids, and other water molds

Phylum 27. Plasmodial slime molds: mycetozoa, "myxomycetes," acellular slime molds

Phylum 28. Ciliophora: ciliates, "infusoria," suctorians
Phylum 29. Granuloreticulosa: foraminifera and shell-less relatives
Phylum 30. Apicomplexa: apicomplexans, "sporozoan parasites"
Phylum 31. Bacillariophyta: diatoms, some algae
Phylum 32. Chlorophyta: green algae, pondweeds, green seaweeds
Phylum 33. Oomycota: oomycetes, some water molds, downy mildews
Phylum 34. Xanthophyta: xanthophytes, yellow-green algae
Phylum 35. Phaeophyta: phaeophytes, kelps, brown algae, brown seaweeds

Incertae Sedis
Phylum 36. Ebridians: some plankton
Phylum 37. Ellobiopsida: parasites

Kingdom Fungi

Haploid or dikaryotic cells; diploids undergo zygotic meiosis to form haploid spores. Organisms are filamentous (mycelial) or secondarily unicellular. They possess chitinous walls and always use absorptive nutrition. Cells always lack [9(2) + 2] undulipodia. The body plan, which may be branched, is composed of hyphae (coenocytic filaments that may be divided by perforate septa). Only single-cell forms are yeasts. Lack pinocytosis and phagocytosis. Extensive cytoplasmic streaming. Propagation by spores.

Phylum 1. Zygomycota: zygomycetes, molds (*Rhizopus, Mucor*)
Phylum 2. Ascomycota: sac fungi or ascomycetes, yeasts (*Saccharomyces*), molds (*Neurospora*)
Phylum 3. Basidiomycota: club fungi, rusts, smuts, mushrooms (*Agaricus, Coprinus*)
Phylum 4. Deuteromycota: fungi imperfecti (*Candida, Penicillium, Aspergillus*)
Phylum 5. Mycophycophyta: lichens, fungal component + cyanobacterial component, or fungal component + green algal component (*Cladonia, Xanthoria*)

Kingdom Animalia

Gametic meiosis; anisogamous fertilization; sperm and egg form a
zygote, which cleaves to form diploid blastula; gastrulation and his-
togenesis generally follow to form multicellular adult with sex organs
in which gametic meiosis occurs. Nutrition heterotrophic; sometimes
ingestive by phagocytosis and pinocytosis, sometimes absorptive.
Extensive cellular and tissue differentiation; desmosomes, septate
junctions, gap junctions, and other differentiated connections
between cells.

Subkingdom Parazoa
Phylum 1.   Placozoa: *Trichoplax*
Phylum 2.   Porifera: calcareous and siliceous sponges

Subkingdom Eumetazoa
Phylum 3.   Cnidaria: coelenterates, hydroids, jellyfish, corals, sea
            anemones
Phylum 4.   Ctenophora: comb jellies
Phylum 5.   Mesozoa: mesozoans
Phylum 6.   Platyhelminthes: flatworms,   planarians,   flukes,
            tapeworms
Phylum 7.   Nemertina: nemertine worms
Phylum 8.   Gnathostomulida: gnathostome worms
Phylum 9.   Gastrotricha: gastrotrichs
Phylum 10. Rotifera: rotifers
Phylum 11. Kinorhyncha: kinorhynchs
Phylum 12. Loricifera: loriciferans
Phylum 13. Acanthocephala: spiny-headed worms
Phylum 14. Entoprocta: entoprocts or kamptozoa
Phylum 15. Nematoda: nematodes,   roundworms   (*Ascaris,*
            Caenorhabditis)
Phylum 16. Nematomorpha: horsehair worms
Phylum 17. Ectoprocta: bryozoa, moss animals
Phylum 18. Phoronida: phoronid worms
Phylum 19. Brachiopoda: brachiopods, lamp shells
Phylum 20. Mollusca: molluscs, monoplacophorans, solenogasters,
            chitons, toothshells, snails, bivalves, squids, octopuses,
            nautiloids

Phylum 21. Priapulida: priapulid worms
Phylum 22. Sipuncula: sipunculid worms, peanut worms
Phylum 23. Echiura: echiuroids, sea cucumbers
Phylum 24. Annelida: segmented worms, oligochete worms, poly-chaete worms, leeches, earthworms
Phylum 25. Tardigrada: tardigrades, water bears
Phylum 26. Pentastoma: pentastomes, tongueworms
Phylum 27. Onychophora: *Peripatus*
Phylum 28. Arthropoda: joint-footed animals, horseshoe crabs, sea spiders, scorpions, ticks, spiders
Phylum 29. Pogonophora: beard worms, tubeworms, vestiminiferans
Phylum 30. Echinodermata: echinoderms, sea lilies, starfish, brittle stars, sea urchins
Phylum 31. Chaetognatha: chaetognaths, arrow worms
Phylum 32. Hemichordata: acorn worms, *Rhabdopleura, Cephaladisas*
Phylum 33. Chordata: notochord-bearing animals, tunicates, sea-squirts, ascidians, lancelets, *Amphioxus,* vertebrates, lampreys, hagfishes, cartilaginous fish, bony fish, amphibians, reptiles, birds, mammals

Kingdom Plantae

Multicellular organisms in which the haploid generation develops from spores, and fertilization produces the diploid embryo that develops into the mature sporophyte, which by meiosis produces spores. Photoautotrophic nutrition: chloroplasts contain chlorophylls *a* and *b*. Organisms exhibit advanced tissue differentiation, many lignified. Production of complex secondary compounds (e.g., polyphenolics, anthocyanins, alkaloids, terpenoids) is common.

DIVISION BRYOPHYTA: *nonvascular embryophytes*
Phylum 1. Bryophyta: hornworts, liverworts, mosses

DIVISION TRACHEOPHYTA: *vascular plants (xylem, phloem tissue)*
Phylum 2. Psilophyta: *Psilotum*
Phylum 3. Lycopodophyta: club mosses and quillworts (*Lycopo-dium, Selaginella, Isoetes*)

Phylum 4.   Sphenophyta: horsetails (*Equisetum*)
Phylum 5.   Filicinophyta: pteridophytes, polypodiophytes, ferns
             (*Polypodium, Osmunda*)
Phylum 6.   Cycadophyta: cycads (*Zamia, Cycas*)
Phylum 7.   Ginkgophyta: *Ginkgo*
Phylum 8.   Coniferophyta: conifers, yews (*Taxus*), pine, spruce, fir
             (*Tsuga, Cedrus*)
Phylum 9.   Gnetophyta: *Gnetum, Ephedra, Welwitschia*
Phylum 10.   Angiospermophyta (Anthophyta, Magnoliophyta):
             flowering plants, monocots (grasses, orchids, lilies,
             palms), dicots (cactuses, roses, daisies)

Appendix C
Background Reading

General

Calder, N. 1983. *Timescale: An Atlas of the Fourth Dimension*. Viking.

Lapo, A. 1987. *Traces of Bygone Biospheres*. Mir, Moscow; Synergetic Press, Oracle, Arizona.

Margulis, L. 1982. *Early Life*. Jones and Bartlett.

Margulis, L., and K. V. Schwartz. *Five Kingdoms*. Second edition. Freeman.

Morrison, P., and P. Morrison. 1982. *Powers of Ten*. Scientific American Books.

Rambler, M. B., R. Fester, and L. Margulis. 1989. *Global Ecology: Towards a Science of the Biosphere*. Academic Press.

Vernadsky, V. 1986. *The Biosphere*. Abridged translation from Russian, based on 1926 French edition. Synergetic Press.

Gaia and Atmospheric Science

Barlow, C. 1991. *From Gaia to Selfish Genes*. MIT Press.

Barlow, C., and T. Volk. 1989. Open systems living in a closed biosphere: Implications for the Gaia debate. *Biosystems* 23: 371–384.

Bunyard, P., and E. Goldsmith, eds. 1988. *Gaia, the Thesis, the Mechanisms and the Implications*. Wadebridge Ecological Centre, Cornwall, UK.

Charlson, R. J., J. E. Lovelock, M. O. Andreae, and S. G. Warren. 1987. Oceanic phytoplankton, atmospheric sulphur, cloud albedo and climate. *Nature* 326: 655–661.

Doolittle, F. 1981. Is nature really motherly? *CoEvolution Quarterly* 29: 58–65.

Dutsch, H. U., ed. 1978. *Influence of the Biosphere on the Atmosphere.* Birkhauser. (Reprinted from *Pure and Applied Geophysics* 116: 213–582.)

Goldsmith, D., and T. Owen. 1980. *The Search for Life in the Universe.* Benjamin Cummings.

Holland, H. D. 1972. The geologic history of seawater—an attempt to solve the problem. *Geochimica Cosmochimica Acta* 36: 637–651.

Joseph, L. 1990. *Gaia: The Growth of an Idea.* St. Martin's Press.

Lovelock, J. 1979. *Gaia: A New Look at Life on Earth.* Oxford University Press.

Lovelock, J. 1986. Geophysiology: A new look at Earth science. *Bulletin of the American Meteorological Society* 67: 392–397.

Lovelock, J. 1988. *Ages of Gaia: Biography of a Planet.* Norton.

Margulis, L., and Lovelock, J. 1989. Gaia and geognosy. In *Global Ecology: Toward a Science of the Biosphere,* ed. M. Rambler, L. Margulis, and R. Fester. Academic Press.

Margulis, L., J. C. G. Walker, and M. Rambler. 1976. Reassessment of roles of oxygen and ultraviolet light in PreCambrian evolution. *Nature* 264: 620–624.

McMenamin, M. A. S., and D. L. S. McMenamin. 1990. *The Emergence of Animals: The Cambrian Breakthrough.* Columbia University Press.

Myers, N. 1984. *Gaia: An Atlas of Planet Management.* Anchor Books.

Sahtouris, E. 1989. *Gaia: The Human Journey from Chaos to Cosmos.* Pocket Books.

Sagan, D. 1988. What Narcissus saw: The oceanic "I/eye". In *The Reality Club,* ed. J. Brockman. Lynx Books.

Sagan, D. 1991. *Biospheres: Metamorphosis of Planet Earth.* Bantam.

Schneider, S. H., and P. Boston, eds. 1991. *Scientists on Gaia.* MIT Press.

Schneider, S. H., and R. Londer. 1984. *The Coevolution of Climate and Life.* Sierra Club Books.

Snyder, T. P. 1985. *The Biosphere Catalogue.* Synergetic Press.

Thompson, W. I., ed. 1987. *Gaia: A Way of Knowing. Political Implications of the New Biology.* Lindesfarne Press.

Trachtman, P. 1984. The search for life's origin. *Smithsonian* 15: 42–51.

Vernadsky, V. I. 1986. *The Biosphere.* Abridged translation. Synergetic Press.

Watson, A., J. Lovelock, and L. Margulis. 1978. Methanogenesis, fires and the regulation of atmospheric oxygen. *BioSystems* 10: 293–298.

Whitfield, M. 1988. Mechanisms or machinations: Is the ocean self-regulating? In *Gaia, the Thesis, the Mechanisms and the Implications,* ed. P. Bunyard and E. Goldsmith, Wadebridge Ecological Centre, Cornwall, UK.

Chemistry (Bio-, Geo-, and Organic) and Bioenergetics

Brownlow, A. 1979. *Geochemistry.* Prentice-Hall.

Delwiche, C. C. 1970. The nitrogen cycle. *Scientific American* 223, no. 3: 136–146.

Fridovitch, I. 1975. Oxygen: Boon and bane. *American Scientist* 63: 54–59.

Harold, F. 1986. *The Vital Force: Introduction to Bioenergetics.* Freeman.

Sagan, D. 1986. Sulfur: Toward a global metabolism. *The Science Teacher* 53: 15–20.

Streitwieser, A., Jr., and C. H. Heathcock. 1981. *Introduction to Organic Chemistry.* Macmillan.

Stryer, L. 1990. *Biochemistry.* Fifth edition. Freeman.

Origin and Early Evolution of Life

Billingham, J. 1981. *Life in the Universe.* MIT Press.

Cloud, P. 1988. *Oasis in Space: Earth History from the Beginning.* Norton.

Cohen, Y., R. W. Castenholz, and H. O. Halvorson. 1984. *Microbial Mats: Stromatolites.* Alan R. Liss.

Day, W. 1984. *Genesis on Planet Earth.* Second edition. Yale University Press.

Ferris, J. P. 1984. The chemistry of life's origin. *Chemical and Engineering News* 62: 22–35.

Guerrero, R., C. Pedros-Alio, I. Esteve, J. Mas, D. Chase, and L. Margulis. 1986. Predatory prokaryotes: Predation and primary consumption evolved in bacteria. *Proceedings of the National Academy of Science* 83: 2138–2142.

Halvorson, H. O., and A. Monroy, eds. 1984. *The Origin and Evolution of Sex.* Alan R. Liss.

Sagan, D., and L. Margulis. 1985. The riddle of sex. *The Science Teacher* 52: 16–22.

Stolz, J. F., and L. Margulis. 1984. The stratified microbial community at Laguna Figueroa, Baja California, Mexico: A possible model for prePhanerozoic laminated microbial communities preserved in cherts. *Origins of Life* 14: 671–679.

Vidal, G. 1984. The oldest eukaryotic cells. *Scientific American* 250, no. 2: 48–57.

Microbiology

Brock, T. D., D. W. Smith, and M. T. Madigan. 1984. *Biology of Microorganisms.* Fourth edition. Prentice-Hall.

Broda, E. 1975. *The Evolution of the Bioenergetic Process.* Pergamon.

Buchanan, E. R., and N. E. Gibbons. 1974. *Bergey's Manual of Determinative Bacteriology.* Eighth edition. Williams and Wilkins.

Schlegel, H. G., and B. Bowien, eds. 1989. *Autotrophic Bacteria.* Science Tech Publishers.

Sonea, S., and M. Panisset. 1983. *A New Bacteriology.* Jones and Bartlett.

Staff, M. P., H. Stolp, H. G. Trueper, A. Balows, and H. G. Schlegel. 1981. *The Prokaryotes.* Two volumes. Springer-Verlag.

Stanier, R. Y., E. A. Adelberg, and J. Ingraham. 1976. *The Microbial World.* Fourth edition. Prentice-Hall.

Microbial Mats and Stromatolites

Cohen, Y., R. W. Castenholtz, and H. O. Halvorson, eds. 1982. *Microbial Mats: Stromatolites.* Alan R. Liss.

Cohen, Y., and E. Rosenberg, eds. 1989. *Microbial Mats. Physiological*

Ecology of Benthic Microbial Communities. American Society for Microbiology.

Walter, M. R. 1976. *Developments in Sedimentology 20: Stromatolites*. Elsevier.

Walter, M. R. 1977. Interpreting stromatolites. *American Scientist* 65: 563–571.

Symbiosis

Gray, M. W. 1983. The bacterial ancestry of plastids and mitochondria. BioScience 33: 693–699.

Margulis, L. 1981. *Symbiosis and Cell Evolution*. Freeman.

Margulis, L., and D. Bermudes. 1985. Symbiosis as a mechanism of evolution: Status of cell symbiosis theory. *Symbiosis* 1: 101–124.

Margulis, L., and R. Fester. 1991. *Symbiosis as a Source of Evolutionary Innovation: Speciation and Morphogenesis*. MIT Press.

Smith, D. C., and A. E. Douglas. 1987. *The Biology of Symbiosis*. Edward Arnold.

Cell Biology

Alberts, B., D. Bray, J. Lewis, M. Raff, K. Roberts, and J. D. Watson. 1983. *Molecular Biology of the Cell*. Garland.

Darnell, J., H. Lodish, and D. Baltimore. 1986. *Molecular Cell Biology*. Scientific American Books.

Freifelder, D. 1983. *Molecular Biology*. Jones and Bartlett.

Wolfe, S. L. 1981. *Biology of the Cell*. Second edition. Wadsworth.

Genetics

Crow, J. F. 1983. *Genetics Notes: An Introduction to Genetics*. Eighth edition. Burgess.

King, R., and W. D. Stansfield. 1990. *Dichotomy of Genetics*. Fourth edition. Oxford University Press.

Suzuki, D. T., A. J. F. Griffiths, and R. C. Lewontin. 1981. *An Introduction to Genetic Analysis*. Second edition. Freeman.

Evolution

Avers, C. 1974. *Evolution.* Harper and Row.

Gould, S. J. 1977. *Ontogeny and Phylogeny.* Belknap Press of Harvard University Press.

Lewin, R. 1982. *Thread of Life.* Smithsonian Books.

Margulis, L., and D. Sagan. 1991. *Microcosmos: Four Billion Years of Evolution from our Microbial Ancestors.* Touchstone.

Margulis, L., and D. Sagan. 1990. *Origins of Sex.* Yale University Press.

Minkoff, E. C. 1983. *Evolutionary Biology.* Addison-Wesley.

Strickberger, M. 1990. Evolution. Jones and Bartlett.

Paleontology

McMenamin, M. A. S., and D. L. S. McMenamin. 1990. *The Emergence of Animals: The Cambrian Breakthrough.* Columbia University Press.

Moore, R. C., ed. 1954. *Treatise on Paleontology.* 45 volumes. University of Kansas Press.

Raup, D. M., and S. M. Stanley. 1971. *Principles of Paleontology.* Freeman.

Simpson, G. G. 1983. *Fossils and the History of Life.* Scientific American Books.

Biomineralization

Lowenstam, H. A., and S. Weiner. 1989. *On Biomineralization.* Oxford University Press.

Westbroek, P., and E. W. De Jong, eds. 1983. *Biomineralization and Biological Metal Accumulation: Biological and Geological Perspectives.* Reidel.

Wilson, J. L. 1975. *Carbonate Facies in Geologic History.* Springer-Verlag.

Environmental Studies

Botkin, D. B., and E. A. Keller. 1982. *Environmental Studies: The Earth as a Living Planet.* Charles E. Merrill.

Strahler, A. N., and A. H. Strahler. 1974. *Introduction to Environmental Science.* Hamilton.

Walker, J. C. G. 1986. *Earth History.* Jones and Bartlett.

Geology and Plate Tectonics

Covey, C. 1984. The Earth's orbit and the ice ages. *Scientific American* 250, no. 2: 58–66.

Gary, M., R. McAfee, Jr., and C. L. Wolf. 1977. *Glossary of Geology.* American Geological Institute.

Greenwood, P. H., and L. R. M. Cocks. 1981. *The Evolving Earth: Chance, Change, and Challenge.* Cambridge University Press.

Jardine, N., and D. McKenzie. 1972. Continental drift and the dispersal and evolution of organisms. *Nature* 235: 20–24.

Raymo, C. 1983. *The Crust of Our Earth.* Prentice-Hall.

Raymo, C. 1984. *Biography of a Planet.* Prentice-Hall.

Scientific American. 1976. *Continents Adrift and Continents Aground: A Scientific American Book.* Freeman.

Scientific American. 1983. *The Dynamic Earth: A Scientific American Book.* Freeman.

Seigel, V. 1980. Earth's shifting surface. In NASA Publication ASA 80-3.

Siever, R., and F. Press. 1983. *The Dynamic Earth.* Freeman.

Appendix D
Geological Time
(not to scale)

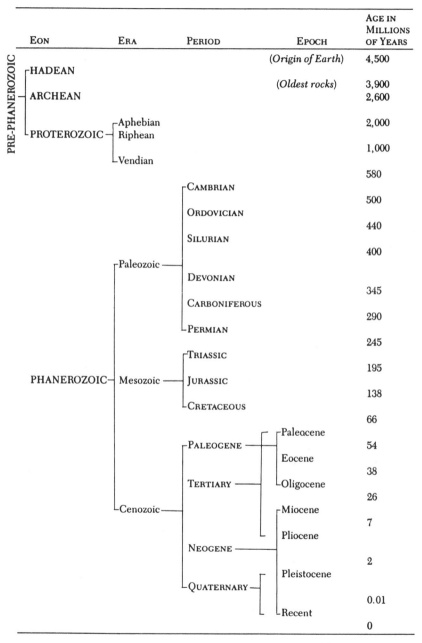

EON	ERA	PERIOD	EPOCH	AGE IN MILLIONS OF YEARS
PRE-PHANEROZOIC			*(Origin of Earth)*	4,500
HADEAN			*(Oldest rocks)*	3,900
ARCHEAN				2,600
PROTEROZOIC	Aphebian			2,000
	Riphean			1,000
	Vendian			580
PHANEROZOIC	Paleozoic	CAMBRIAN		500
		ORDOVICIAN		440
		SILURIAN		400
		DEVONIAN		345
		CARBONIFEROUS		290
		PERMIAN		245
	Mesozoic	TRIASSIC		195
		JURASSIC		138
		CRETACEOUS		66
	Cenozoic	PALEOGENE / TERTIARY	Paleocene	54
			Eocene	38
			Oligocene	26
		NEOGENE	Miocene	7
			Pliocene	2
		QUATERNARY	Pleistocene	0.01
			Recent	0

Source: L. Margulis and D. Sagan, *Origins of Sex* (Yale University Press, 1990).

Appendix E
Modes of Nutrition

The following table lists the sources of energy, electrons, and carbon for metabolism, giving examples of the growth of organisms to which the various prefixes apply.

Energy Sources	Electron sources (or hydrogen donors)	Carbon sources	Organisms and their hydrogen or electron donors

Photo- (light)	Litho- (inorganic and C_1 compounds)	Auto- (CO_2)	Prokaryotes
			  Chlorobiaceae, H_2S, S
			  Chromatiaceae, H_2S, S
			  Rhodospirillaceae, H_2
			  Cyanobacteria, H_2O
			  Chloroxybacteria, H_2O
			
			Protoctista (algae) H_2O
			Plants, H_2O

		Hetero- $(CH_2O)_n$	None
	Organo- (organic compounds)	Auto-	None

		Hetero-	Prokaryotes
			  Chromatiaceae, org. comp.[1]
			  Chloroflexaceae, org. comp.[1]
			
			  Heliobacteriaceae, org. comp.[1]
			  Rhodomicrobium, C_2, C_3

Energy Sources	Electron sources (or hydrogen donors)	Carbon sources	Organisms and their hydrogen or electron donors
Chemo- (chemical compounds)	Litho-	Auto-	Prokaryotes methanogens, H_2 hydrogen oxidizers, H_2 methylotrophs, CH_4, $\quad$ CHOH, etc. ammonia, nitrite oxidizers, $\quad NH_3$, NO_2^-
		Hetero-	Prokaryotes "sulfur bacteria," S manganese oxidizers, Mn^{++} iron bacteria, Fe^{++} sulfide oxidizers, $\quad$ e.g., *Beggiatoa* sulfate reducers $\quad$ e.g., *Desulfovibrio*
	Organo-	Auto-	Prokaryotes clostridia, etc., grown on CO_2 as sole source of carbon (H_2,-CH_2)
		Hetero-	Prokaryotes (most) (including nitrate, sulfate, oxygen and phosphate[2] as terminal electron acceptors) Protoctista[3] (most) Fungi[3] Plants[3] (achlorophyllous) Animals[3]

Table devised in collaboration with R. Guerrero, from *Handbook of Protoctista*, 1990.

1. Organic compounds (e.g., acetate, proprionate, pyruvate).
2. Detection of phosphine: I. Dévai, L. Felföldy, I. Wittner, and S. Plósz. 1988. New aspects of the phosphorus cycle in the hydrosphere. *Nature* 333: 343–345.
3. Oxygen as terminal electron acceptor.

Glossary

actin A class of proteins that are major constituents of the 7-nm-wide microfilaments of eukaryotic cells. Actin microfilaments have molecular weights of approximately 44,000; they are involved in the contraction of muscles and many other intracellular movements.

actinolite A bright green or grayish green silicate mineral of the amphibole group, $Ca_2(Mg,Fe)_5Si_8O_{22}(OH)_2$, which may contain manganese. Actinolite, a type of asbestos, occurs in long, slender, needle-like crystals or in fibrous, radiated, or columnar forms in metamorphic rocks (such as schists) and in altered igneous rocks.

active margin Continental margin characterized by earthquakes, igneous activity, or mountain uplift, i.e., tectonic activity resulting from convergent or transform plate motion.

adaptive radiation The evolution from generalized, primitive species to diverse, specialized species, each adapted to a distinct mode of life. See *cladistic episode, speciation.*

adiabatic (lapse rate) In thermodynamics, this term pertains to the relationship between pressure and volume when a gas or fluid is compressed or expanded without either giving or receiving heat. In an adiabatic process, compression causes a rise in temperature; expansion causes a drop in temperature.

aerobiosis The metabolism of an organism (an *aerobe*) that is active and capable of completing its life cycle only in the presence of gaseous oxygen (O_2). The oxidative breakdown of food molecules and the derivation of energy from them, in which the terminal electron acceptor is O_2, is known as *aerobic respiration*. A zone or environment in which gaseous O_2 is present is known as an *oxic environment or zone*.

aerosol (or atmospheric particulate) A *sol* in which the dispersion medium is a gas (usually air) and the dispersed or colloidal phase consists of solid particles or liquid droplets; e.g., mist, haze, most smokes, and some fogs.

albedo   The relative reflectivity of a body compared with that of a perfectly diffusing surface, measured on a scale from 0 to 1. Black surfaces reflect no incident light and have an albedo of 0. White surfaces reflect all incident light and have an albedo of 1.

algae   A diverse group of eukaryotic, oxygenic, aquatic, photosynthetic protoctists, including single-cell or few-celled forms (protists) and many multicellular descendants (e.g., rhodophytes, phaeophytes, and other seaweeds).

algal laminate   See *stromatolite*.

algal pillar   See *stromatolite*.

allelochemical   See *semiochemical*.

anaerobiosis   The metabolism of an organism capable of completing its life cycle in the absence of gaseous oxygen (O_2). An environment or zone from which gaseous O_2 is absent, either because of physical exclusion or because of the activities of organisms capable of utilizing it, is known as an *anoxic zone or environment*.

anoxic zone or environment   See *anaerobiosis*.

anoxygenic photosynthesis   Photosynthesis in which H_2 or H_2S is the hydrogen donor and no O_2 is produced.

antibody   A protein produced by lymphoid cells (plasma cells) in response to chemicals or microbial substances (antigens) and capable of interacting specifically with its antigen (or a chemically similar substance), leading to the amelioration, removal, or alteration of that antigen from the animal.

antigen   A substance that, upon introduction into the body of vertebrates and some marine animals, stimulates the production of specific antibodies. An antigenic protein molecule may carry several distinct sites, epitopes, or antigenic determinants.

archaeobacteria (Archaea)   A distinct group of prokaryotes, as determined by their ribosomal RNA, lipids, and other properties, which includes the methanogenic, the extreme halophilic, and certain acidophilic, thermophilic sulfur bacteria.

asthenosphere   Upper portion of the mantle; the layer of the Earth just below the *lithosphere*, composed of rocks more plastic than the surface, in which isostatic adjustments take place, magmas may be generated, and *seismic waves* are strongly attenuated. It is equivalent to the upper *mantle* of the Earth.

atmosphere The mixture of gases that surround a planet. On Earth it is chiefly oxygen (20%) and nitrogen (79%), with some argon (1%) and carbon dioxide (0.03%) and smaller quantities of hydrogen, helium, methane, krypton, neon, nitrogen oxides, xenon, and other gases.

autopoiesis Organismal self-maintenance; metabolically active, self-bounded, and self-generating system (e.g., a cell). A prerequisite to reproduction and thought to have preceded reproduction in evolution; also spelled *autopoesy* or *autopoiesy*. From the Greek for "self-making."

banded iron formation A distinct type of sedimentary rock consisting of alternating layers of more and less oxidized iron oxides embedded in a chert matrix. Most of the economically important concentrations of iron in the world are found in Proterozoic (2.5 billion to 570 million years ago) banded iron formations.

basalt Dark-colored, fine-grained igneous rocks (iron, calcium, magnesium silicates), whether intrusive or extrusive.

biocoenosis See *community*.

biogenesis The production of a living cell, a mineral (e.g., a $CaCO_3$ shell), a gas (atmospheric oxygen), or a structure (stromatolite) from a parent organism or a living community of organisms. The doctrine that all life has been derived from previously living organisms.

biomineralization The formation of minerals by living organisms. Two kinds are known: *biologically controlled* or *matrix-mediated* biomineralization, i.e., intracellular precipitation of a given mineral type under genetic control of the cell (magnetite in magnetotactic bacteria, calcite by *Coleps* or coccolithophorids) and *biologically induced* biomineralization, i.e., production of acid, which changes local pH, or other environmental alterations that in turn cause potentially mineralizable material to precipitate (e.g., extracellular precipitation of iron and manganese oxides by *Leptothrix, Bacillus,* or other bacteria; precipitation of amorphous calcium in lakes due to algal activity).

biosphere The place where all the living things on Earth (the biota) reside. Extending from the top of the troposphere to below the abyss, it is the environment of the system of life at the surface of the Earth.

biota The sum of the living matter (all organisms) on Earth (the flora, fauna, and microbiota taken together).

biotic potential The number of organisms that can be produced in a single generation, or unit of time, which is characteristic of the species, measured in maximum number of offspring per generation, maximum number of spores produced per year, or equivalent terms. It illustrates the tendencies of organisms to increase exponentially when their conditions for material growth are satisfied.

bioturbation The disruption, churning, stirring, or other movement and local disturbance of sand, mud, or other sediments by live organisms.

calcification The hardening of tissue in live material or the replacement of organic material by calcium salts (especially $CaCO_3$) in fossilization.

calcium carbonate The common rock-forming mineral $CaCO_3$ (limestone).

carbonaceous chondrite A type of *meteorite*.

chasmolith An ecological term referring to microorganisms living in rock crevices produced by erosion or by endolithic organisms. See *endolith* and *epilith*.

chert A hard, extremely dense or compact, dull to semi-glassy, cryptocrystalline sedimentary rock, consisting dominantly of cryptocrystalline silica with lesser amounts of micro- or cryptocrystalline quartz and amorphous silica (opal); it sometimes contains impurities such as calcite, iron oxide, and the remains of siliceous and other organisms.

cladistic episode An adaptive radiation in evolution, i.e., the splitting of a lineage of descent into two species or higher taxa.

clast An individual constituent, grain, or fragment of a sediment or rock produced by the mechanical weathering (disintegration) of a larger rock mass from the supporting, protective structures of animals, plants, or microbes, whether whole or fragmentary.

coacervate An aggregation of colloidal droplets that form when a solution of polypeptides, nucleic acids, and polysaccharides is shaken. Interpreted by A. I. Oparin to be a type of "protobiont."

coenocyte Plasmodium; syncitium. A multinucleate structure (thallus) lacking septa or cell walls; thallus with siphonous, syncitial, or plasmodial organization.

community A unit in nature composed of populations of organisms of different species living in the same place at the same time. *Microbial communities* are those lacking significant populations of animals and plants. A group of species living together as a community is also known as a *biocoenosis*.

crust See *lithosphere*.

cybernetic system An engineered, regulatory, multi-component control complex with sensory, amplification, and positive and negative feedback properties.

Daisyworld A first attempt by Lovelock to apply cybernetic-style modeling to the Gaia hypothesis to demonstrate how the surface temperatures of terrestrial planets might be modulated by biota. The Daisyworld biota consists of light and dark daisies whose differential growth rates in varying temperature regimes determine changes in planetary albedo.

diagenesis (mineral)   Recombination or rearrangement of a mineral that results in a new mineral.

diagenesis (sedimentary)   All the chemical, physical, and biological changes, modifications, or transformations undergone by a sediment after its initial deposition (i.e., after it has reached its final resting place in the current cycle of erosion, transportation, and deposition) and during and after its lithification, exclusive of any surficial alteration (weathering) and metamorphism. *Early diagenesis* refers to diagenesis occurring immediately after deposition or burial. *Late diagenesis* refers to deep-seated diagenesis which occurs a long time after deposition, when sediment is more or less compacted into a rock, but still in the realm of pressure-temperature conditions similar to those of deposition.

dolomite   Calcium-magnesium carbonate, a common rock-forming rhombohedral mineral, $CaMg(CO_3)_2$, found in extensive beds as a compact limestone or dolomite rock; it is also precipitated directly from seawater, possibly under warm, shallow conditions. See *limestone*.

eclogite   High-temperature-and-pressure equivalent of basalt from Earth's interior. This bimineralic mantle rock forms the matrix for diamonds explosively exuded from kimberlite pipes. It is composed of garnite and clinopyroxene (an iron-poor calcium, magnesium silicate) and occasional traces of diamond, graphite, corundum, rutile (titanium dioxide), or coesite (high-temperature-and-pressure form of quartz).

ecological hormones   See *Semiochemicals*.

ecosystem   A unit in nature composed of communities or organisms in which the biologically important elements (carbon, sulfur, nitrogen, phosphorus, oxygen, etc.) entirely cycle within the unit. The biologically essential chemical elements tend to cycle more rapidly within ecosystems than between them.

elongation factor TU (EFTU)   A protein that complexes with ribosomes to promote elongation of polypeptide chains; it dissociates from the ribosome when translation is terminated. Elongation factor TU is responsible for alignment of the AA-tRNA complex in the "A" site of the ribosome in protein synthesis.

endolith   An ecological term describing microorganisms living in tiny openings in rocks or rock crevices that have been produced by the metabolic activities of the endolithic organisms themselves. See *epilith, chasmolith*.

epilith   An ecological term referring to the biota living on the surface of rocks and/or stony material. See *chasmolith, endolith*.

ESA European Space Agency (France, Germany, Netherlands, Italy).

eubacteria All bacteria other than the Archaeobacteria (or Archaea) (i.e., mycoplasms, omnibacteria or Gram-negative rods, myxobacteria, cyanobacteria, actinobacteria, etc.). They differ from the archaeobacteria in that their cell walls contain neuraminic acid, and they have distinctive lipids, tRNAs, rRNAs, and RNA polymerases.

eukaryote A nucleated organism (protoctist, fungus, animal, or plant).

eukaryotic "flagella" See *Undulipodium*.

evaporite A nonclastic sedimentary rock composed primarily of minerals produced from a saline solution that became concentrated by the evaporation of the solvent; especially, a deposit of salt precipitated from a restricted or enclosed body of seawater or from the water of a salt lake. An example is gypsum, a widely distributed mineral consisting of hydrous calcium sulfate: $CaSO_4 \cdot 2H_2O$. Gypsum is the most common sulfate mineral and is frequently associated with *halite* and anhydrite in evaporites or in thick, extensive beds interstratified with limestones, shales, and clays (especially in rocks of Permian and Triassic age).

facies Layer of rocks; the unit of study in stratigraphy. The sum of all primary lithologic and paleontologic characteristics exhibited by a sedimentary rock and from which its origin and environment of formation may be inferred; the general aspect, nature, or appearance of a sedimentary rock produced under or affected by similar conditions; a distinctive group of characteristics that differs from other groups within a stratigraphic unit.

Faint Young Sun Paradox Since the Archean eon, solar luminosity has increased as determined by all models of stellar evolution based on modern cosmogeny, and therefore the surface temperature of the Earth should have been below freezing in the past or boiling now; yet fossil evidence suggests that the Earth's surface temperature has remained constant during that time (from 3.4 billion years ago to the present), or that it has decreased.

fermentation Any process in which energy derived from metabolism (catabolism) of organic substrates is used in the generation of ATP via substrate-level phosphorylation. In all fermentations, the degradation of organic compounds in the absence of gaseous oxygen yields energy, while other organic compounds act as the terminal electron acceptors. Bacteria capable of obtaining energy via fermentation are known as fermenting bacteria.

flagellum An extracellular structure of some bacteria composed of homogeneous protein polymers, members of a class of proteins called flagellins; moves by rotation at the base; relatively rigid rod driven by a rotary motor embedded in the cell membrane that is intrinsically nonmotile and sometimes sheathed. See *undulipodium*.

formation   A geomorphological unit of study in field geology; a geographically distinguishable naturally formed topograhic feature, commonly differing conspicuously from adjacent objects or material, or being noteworthy for some other reason; especially a striking erosional form on the land surface.

fossil   Any remains, trace, or imprint of a plant, animal, or microbe, or communities formed by them, that has been preserved, by natural processes, in the Earth's crust since some past geologic time; any evidence of past life. It is termed a *microfossil* if it is too small to study without the aid of a microscope, whether it is the remains of a microscopic organism or part of a larger organism. A sedimentary structure which consists of a fossilized track, trail, burrow, tube, boring, or tunnel resulting from the life activities (other than growth) of an organism, made on or in soft sediment at the time of its accumulation, is termed a *trace fossil.*

Gaia hypothesis   The idea that the biota regulates specific aspects of the biosphere, that life on Earth forms a single metabolic physiological system in which over 30 million types of organisms metabolize, grow, and die, each producing and removing gas. Each interacts with the elements C, H, O, N, P, and S. Their interactions lead to modulation of the Earth's temperature, acidity, and atmospheric composition. The idea was first stated in the late 1960s by the atmospheric chemist James E. Lovelock.

Galileo   NASA space mission (1990–2000) to orbit Jupiter and send a probe to contact and analyze the Jovian atmosphere.

gene   The unit of study in analysis of heredity of all organisms. From mating organisms and study of the distribution of traits in their offspring it can be inferred that hereditary units (genes) occupy specific positions (loci) within the nuclear genome, or chromosome in eukaryotes. Composed of DNA, these units of function can show one or more specific effects on the phenotype of the organism; they can mutate to one or more allelic forms or recombine with other such units. Three classes of genes are recognized: (1) *structural genes,* which are transcribed into mRNA and then translated into polypeptide chains, (2) *structural genes,* which are transcribed into rRNA and tRNA molecules which are used directly, and (3) *regulatory genes,* which are transcribed but serve as recognition sites for enzymes and other proteins involved in DNA replication and transcription. See *genome, replicon.*

genome   All the genes carried by an individual or cell, i.e., a single gamete (or haploid organism); the bacterial genophore (nucleoid) and its plasmids or, in diploid eukaryotes, the set of chromosome pairs. The minimal sum of the genetic material required to determine an organism or set of genes inside an organelle. See *gene, replicon.*

geochemical process   Chemical changes occurring in rocks (i.e., organic compound transformation during diagenesis in the formation of shale or coal from mud, or chemical transformation of one mineral to another under the pressure and temperature changes in metamorphism.)

geochronology The study of time in relation to the history of the Earth, especially by the absolute-age and relative dating systems developed for the purpose. See *radioactive decay*.

Glossopteris **flora** The Gondwanaland plant community dominated by this genus of cycadofilicalean (seed fern) trees, indicating the southern-hemisphere distribution of Paleozoic forests. ·

gypsum An evaporite mineral consisting of hydrous calcium sulfate ($CaSO_4 \cdot 2H_2O$). See *evaporite*.

halite The evaporite mineral NaCl. It is native salt, occurring in massive, granular, compact, or cubic-crystalline forms and having a distinctive salty taste.

hematite The common iron mineral alpha-Fe_2O_3. It is found in igneous, sedimentary, and metamorphic rocks, both as a primary constituent and as an alteration product. See *banded iron formation*.

hydrolysis The splitting of a molecule into two or more smaller molecules with the addition of the elements of H_2O. See *polymer*.

isotope One of two or more species of the same chemical element having the same number of protons in the nucleus but different atomic weights, (i.e., different numbers of neutrons).

isotopic fractionation The relative enrichment of one isotope over another in a system, due mainly to the differential effects of temperature but also to kinetic effects, activity coefficients, etc. on the slight mass differences of the isotopes.

karst A type of topography formed over limestone, dolomite, or gypsum by dissolving or solution, that is characterized by closed depressions or sinkholes, caves, and underground drainage.

limestone A sedimentary rock consisting chiefly (more than 50% by weight or by areal percentages under the microscope) of calcium carbonate, primarily in the form of the mineral calcite, and with or without magnesium carbonate; specifically, a carbonate sedimentary rock containing more than 95% calcite and less than 5% dolomite.

lithification The conversion of newly deposited, unconsolidated sediment into a coherent and solid rock, involving processes such as cementation, compaction, desiccation, crystallization, recrystallization, and compression. It may occur concurrent with, or shortly or long after, deposition.

lithosphere   The solid portion of the Earth at its surface, above the mantle, as compared with the *atmosphere* and the hydrosphere; the *crust* of the Earth. See *asthenosphere*.

Magellan   NASA space mission (1990–1992) to analyze from orbit the surface geomorphology of Venus, using radar.

magnesium calcite   A variety of calcite: $(Ca,Mg)CO_3$. It consists of randomly substituted magnesium carbonate in a lattice of calcite. See *limestone*.

magnetite   A black, isometric, strongly magnetic, opaque mineral of the spinel group: $(Fe,Mg)Fe_2O_4$. It constitutes an important ore of iron. See *banded iron formation*.

mantle   See *asthenosphere*.

Mariner   U.S. flyby missions (1964–1971) to Mars and other inner planets.

metabolism   The sum of enzyme-mediated biochemical reactions that continually occur in cells and organisms and provide the material basis for autopoiesis.

meteorite   Any meteoroid that has fallen to the Earth's surface in one piece or in fragments without being completely vaporized by intense frictional heating during its passage through the atmosphere. Most meteorites are believed to be fragments of asteroids and to consist of primitive solid matter similar to that from which the Earth was originally formed. There are three classes of meteorites: *Stony meteorites* consist largely or entirely of silicate minerals and comprise more than 90% of all meteorites seen to fall. *Iron meteorites* consist generally of nickeliferous iron (solid solution of iron with 4% to 30% or more of nickel). *Carbonaceous chondrites* are friable, dull black, chondritic stony meteorites containing hydrated, clay-type silicate minerals (usually fine-grained serpentine or chlorite) and considerable amounts and a great variety of organic compounds (hydrocarbons, fatty and aromatic acids, porphyrins).

microbe   Microorganism. Prokaryote, fungus, or protoctist requiring a microscope for visualization.

microbial community   A community made up of microorganisms.

microbial mat   A benthic structure composed of a community of microorganisms, usually dominated by phototrophic bacteria, such as the cyanobacterium *Microcoleus*, that bind and trap sediment (and sometimes actively precipitate minerals). Microbial mats are living precursors of stromatolites.

microfossil   See *fossil*.

microtubule   A slender, hollow structure made primarily of tubulin proteins (alpha-tubulin and beta-tubulin), each with a molecular weight of about

50,000, arranged in a heterodimer. Microtubules are of varying lengths but usually invariant in diameter at 24–25 nm. They form the substructures of axopods, mitotic spindles, kinetosomes, undulipodia, haptonemata, nerve-cell processes, and many other intracellular structures. See *mitotic spindle, undulipodia.*

mitotic spindles   Composed of microtubules, kinetochores, and often centrioles or centrosomes. Transient proteinaceous structures associated with mitotic cell division limited to eukaryotic organisms.

monomer   Subunit of a polymer.

monophyly   The condition of a trait or a group of organisms that evolved directly from a common ancestor. Sister taxa are monophyletic. See *taxon.*

NASA   The National Aeronautics and Space Administration of the United States.

negative feedback mechanism   A property of a system in which production or amplification of a material or a product leads to inhibition of that same production. For example, in feedback inhibition of metabolic control, the end product of a metabolic pathway acts as an inhibitor of an enzyme, or step, within that pathway.

oolite   A sedimentary rock, usually a limestone, made up chiefly of ooliths cemented together. An *oolith* is one of the small, round, accretionary bodies in a sedimentry rock resembling the roe of fish and having diameters of 0.25–2 mm (commonly 0.5–1 mm).

organelle   "Little organ"; a visibly distinct structure inside any type of cell, composed of a complex of macromolecules and small molecules. Examples include those lacking genomes (i.e., carboxysomes, ribosomes) or containing their own genomes (mitochondria, plastids, and nuclei).

organic geochemistry   A science within geology or chemistry that studies naturally occurring carbonaceous and biologically derived substances of geological interest.

organo-sedimentary structures   Biogenic rocks such as stromatolites.

oxic environment or zone   See *aerobiosis.*

oxidation   The combination of a molecule with gaseous or atom oxygen or the removal of hydrogen from a molecule. Since electrons are transferred to the oxidizing reagent, which becomes reduced, oxidation and reduction (q.v.) are always coupled in what are called oxidation-reduction reactions. Reduction is classically defined as the addition of hydrogen or electrons. Natural forms of oxidized and reduced sulfur are shown in the accompanying diagram.

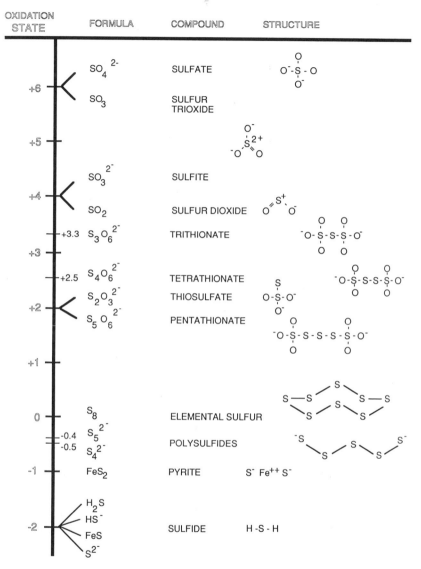

Sulfur oxidation states in nature.

oxidation state The propensity of a compound to accept electrons (or their equivalent, H atoms). Oxidation states vary from fully oxidized (oxygen itself, great tendency to violently accept electrons) to hydrogen gas (nonoxidized, fully reduced, no tendency to accept more electrons). The change of oxidation state of elements such as sulfur or nitrogen (from fully oxidized sulfate through fully reduced nonoxidized sulfide). Intermediates such as thiosulfate or elemental sulfur are crucial for chemical transformations in nature. Life is based on incessant changes in oxidation state of carbon, sulfur, hydrogen, and nitrogen.

oxidizing atmosphere An atmosphere that contains oxidized gases such as CO_2, H_2O, and N_2, and detectable (greater than trace) amounts of gaseous, free oxygen (O_2).

oxygen The eighth element of the periodic table. It has an atomic number of 8, a valence of -2, and a molecular weight of 16 grams per mole. See *oxidation state.*

ozone O_3, triatomic oxygen. A highly reactive gas with both tropospheric and stratospheric sources.

paleomagnetism The study of natural remanent magnetism in order to determine the intensity and direction of the Earth's magnetic field in the geologic past.

passive margin Leading border or subducting margin of tectonic plate, i.e., in the East Pacific, to be compared with trailing margin (i.e., mid-Atlantic rift), at which new igneous materials are forming. Continental margin characterized by thick, relatively undeformed sediments with only limited tectonism related to divergent plate motion

petrographic thin section Polished slices of rock thin enough to allow light to pass through them; used to detect microfossils in a cryptocrystalline matrix. See *chert.*

pheromone An example of a semiochemical.

photo-oxidation The production of singlet-state oxygen ($^1O_2$), a very powerful oxidant and rapidly lethal upon formation in the cell, by the reaction of certain photosensitive pigments with light in the presence of O_2 (molecular oxygen).

photosynthesis A mode of nutrition that permits cell growth with light captured by chlorophyll as energy source, usually accompanied by the production or organic matter from carbon dioxide and a hydrogen donor (such as hydrogen gas, H_2; water, H_2O; hydrogen sulfide, H_2S). In *oxygenic photosynthesis,* H_2O is the hydrogen donor and O_2 is produced. An organism capable of growth and metabolism using only light energy and inorganic carbon reduction (from CO_2 to all needed organic constituents of its cells) is a *photoautotroph*. See *anoxygenic photosynthesis*.

phototroph An organism that fills its energy requirements from light. See *photosynthesis*.

phylogeny Family tree. Diagram or other representation of hypothesized sequences of ancestor/descendant relationships of groups of organisms reconstructed from hypotheses of their evolutionary history.

Pioneer NASA missions to Venus, Jupiter, and Saturn. Goals include reconnaissance, elucidation of structure, dynamics, and chemical composition of the atmosphere and ionosphere, and study of magnetic fields and solar-wind interaction. (Early 1970s through mid 1980s.)

plasmodium See *coenocyte*.

plasmogenesis Concept of the origins of protoplasm from inorganic or prebiotic colloidal materials. This term refers mainly to an early-20th-century movement dedicated to the experimental study of the origins of life, dominated by Alfonso Herrera.

plate tectonics Global tectonics based on an Earth model characterized by a small number (10–25) of large, broad, thick plates (blocks composed of both continental and oceanic crust, and mantle). Continents are the raised portions of the plates. Each plate "floats" on some viscous underlayer in the mantle and moves more or less independently of the others and grinds against them (like ice floes in a river), with much of the dynamic activity concentrated along the periphery of the plates. Plates are propelled from the rear by *sea-floor spreading*; oceanic crust is increased by convective upwelling of magma along the mid-oceanic ridges. The older crust moves away from the new material at a rate of 1–10 cm per year. This is thought to provide the power source for plate tectonics. Linear margins of plates are locations of volcanic, earthquake, and other tectonic activity.

polar wandering curve The apparent movement during geologic time of the Earth's rotation and magnetic poles, suggested by shifts in the climatic zones and by paleomagnetic determinations. Possibly all indications of polar wandering can be accounted for by continental displacement. See *plate tectonics*.

polymer A macromolecule composed of a covalently bonded collection of repeating subunits or monomers linked together during a repetitive series of similar chemical reactions. Each strand of DNA is a linear polymer of nucleotide monomers. Characteristic structure of proteins (amino acid monomers), nucleic acids (nucleotide monomers), and many other substances.

population A local (geographically defined) group of nonspecific organisms sharing a common gene pool; also called a *deme*. A group of organisms belonging to the same species and living in the same place at the same time.

prebiotic chemistry Laboratory experiments or theoretical calculations of chemical interactions thought to have occurred on the Hadean or Archean Earth prior to the appearance of life but relevant to it.

primary metabolism The metabolism involved in the production and utilization of primary metabolites, those components required for cells, i.e., minimal autopoietic units.

primary metabolite An organic compound that is produced metabolically and is essential for completion of the life cycle of the organism that produces it (e.g., any of the 20 protein amino acids or nucleotides in RNA and DNA). Chemical component required for autopoiesis.

prokaryote Bacterium.

protein synthesis The process of protein formation by cells. The formation of a protein directed by a specific messenger RNA (mRNA) molecule is known as *translation*. The formation of an RNA molecule (including mRNA) from a DNA template by complementary base pairing is called *transcription*. This process is mediated by an enzyme known as *RNA polymerase*. Translation occurs in a *ribosome* (q.v.). (Ribosomes consist of two unequal subunits bound together by magnesium ions. These subunits consist of roughly equal parts of ribosomal RNAs (rRNA) and protein.) As the 5′ end of the mRNA moves through the ribosome, a lengthening polypeptide chain is produced. *Transfer RNAs* (tRNA) are molecules that function here to transfer amino acid residues to the growing polypeptide chain. The newly formed protein is released once the 3′ end of the mRNA has moved through the ribosome.

proteinoid microsphere Spheres visible with the light microscope, 0.1–10 μm in diameter, which are products of thermal copolymerization of amino acids.

protoctists Algae, amebas, ciliates, slime molds, foraminiferans, seaweeds, water molds, and other eukaryotes; all multigenomic aquatic eukaryotes except plants, animals, or fungi. *Protists* are the few- or single-celled members of the kingdom.

pseudomorph A mineral whose outward crystal form is that of another mineral species; it has developed by alteration, substitution, incrustation, or paramorphism.

punctuated equilibria A term describing a pattern seen in the fossil record of relatively brief episodes of speciation followed by long periods of species stability. See *speciation*.

radioactive decay The spontaneous radioactive transformation of one nuclide to another, or of the energy state of the same nuclide (a species of atom characterized by the number of neutrons and protons in its nucleus).

Essential to geochronology, this process is quantified in radiometric dating methods used to determine the age, in years, of rocks.

redox potential   A quantifiable measure of the relative susceptibility of a substance to oxidation and reduction. See *oxidation, oxidation state.*

reduction   See *oxidation.*

regolith   A general term for the entire layer of fragmental, loose, incoherent or unconsolidated rock material, of whatever origin (residual or transported) and of very varied character, that nearly everywhere forms the surface of the land and overlies or covers the more coherent bedrock. Found on the surfaces of the moon, Mars, and Earth, it includes rock debris (weathered in place) of all kinds: volcanic ash, glacial drift, alluvium, loess and eolian deposits. On Earth, detritus, plant remains, and soil are included.

regression   The retreat or contraction of the sea from land areas, and the consequent evidence of such withdrawal. The opposite of *transgression.*

replication   A duplicating process requiring copying from a template; i.e., the copying of genetic material.

replicon   A genetic element that behaves as an autonomous unit during DNA replication. In bacteria, the genophore (visible in electron microscopy as the nucleoid) functions as a single large replicon, whereas eukaryotic chromosomes contain hundreds of replicons in series. Small replicons include plasmids, viral nucleic acids, transposons, or other DNA capable of autonomous replication. See *gene, genome.*

reproduction   Any process that augments the number of cells or organisms; not to be confused with sex or replication. See *sex, replication.*

respiration   The oxidative breakdown of food molecules and release of energy from them; the terminal electron acceptor is inorganic and may be O_2 or, in anaerobic organisms, nitrate, sulfate, or nitrite. See *oxidation.*

reverse transcription   DNA synthesis from an RNA template, mediated by reverse transcriptase. See *protein synthesis.*

ribosome   See *protein synthesis.*

RNA polymerase   See *protein synthesis.*

rRNA   See *protein synthesis.*

sabkha   A salt flat or low salt-encrusted plain restricted to a coastal area, as on the Arabian peninsula along the Persian Gulf. See *microbial mat.*

scytonemine   Brownish, light-protective sheath pigment of unknown chemical composition found in cyanobacteria such as members of the genus *Scytonema.*

secondary metabolism   The metabolic pathways that produce and utilize secondary metabolites. See *secondary metabolite, primary metabolite.*

secondary metabolite   A metabolically produced organic compound that is not essential for completion of the life cycle of the organism that produces it (e.g., alkaloids, flavonoids, and tannins). They seem to play primarily ecological roles, and may serve as pheromones or stress-response compounds (phytoalexins). See *secondary metabolism, semiochemicals.*

secondary plant metabolites   See *semiochemicals.*

sedimentary rock   A rock resulting from the consolidation of loose sediment that has accumulated in layers; e.g., a *clastic rock* consisting of mechanically formed fragments of older rock transported from its source and deposited in water, air, or ice, or a chemical rock (such as rock salt or *gypsum*) formed by precipitation from solution, or a biogenic rock (such as certain *limestones*) consisting of the remains or secretions of plants, animals, and microbes.

sedimentary sequence (stratigraphic sequence)   A set of deposited beds that describes the geologic history of a region.

seismic wave   A general term for all elastic waves produced by earthquakes or generated artificially by explosions.

semiochemicals   Chemical signals released in the environment that mediate interactions between different species. Examples are *allelochemicals* (chemicals secreted by an organism that influence behavior in a member of another species), which are the chemicals introduced into the environment by one species to suppress the growth or reproduction of another. Some allelochemicals are *secondary plant metabolites.* A chemical exchanged between members of the same species that affects behavior is termed a *pheromone.* Examples of such pheromones are the sex attractants, alarm substances, aggregation-promotion substances, territorial markers, and trail substances of insects. Generally these signals may be termed *ecological hormones.*

serial endosymbiosis theory   The theory that undulipodia, mitochondria, and plastids originated respectively as motile, respiring, and photosynthetic free-living bacteria that established symbioses with other bacterial hosts, such as the extant *Thermoplasma*—i.e., that these organelles began as xenosomes. The theory that eukaryotic cells evolved from bacterial ancestors by a series of symbiotic associations that occurred in a specific temporal sequence.

sex   Any process that recombines genes (DNA) in an individual cell or organism from more than a single parental source. Sex may occur at the nucleic acid, nuclear, cytoplasmic, and other levels.

silica   The chemically resistant dioxide of silicon: SiO_2. It occurs naturally in five crystalline polymorphs: in cryptocrystalline form, in amorphous and hydrated forms, in less pure forms (i.e., sand and chert), and combined in silicates as an essential constituent of many minerals.

siliceous rock   A rock containing abundant silica, especially free silica rather than silicates.

silicification   A process of fossilization whereby the original organic components of an organism are replaced by silica, as either quartz, chalcedony, or opal.

sinter   A chemical sedimentary rock deposited as a hard incrustation on rocks or on the ground by precipitation from hot or cold mineral waters of springs, lakes, or streams; specifically, siliceous sinter (an opaline variety of *silica* deposited as an incrustation by precipitation from the hot mineral waters of a hot springs or geyser) and calcareous sinter.

soil   Organic-rich *regolith* of planet Earth.

solar luminosity   The total amount of radiant energy at all wavelengths emitted into space per unit time by the entire solar surface. See *Faint Young Sun Paradox.*

speciation   1. The evolutionary process leading to the division of an ancestral species into offspring species that coexist in time; horizontal evolution or speciation; cladogenesis. 2. The gradual transformation of one species into another without an increase in species number at any time within the lineage; vertical evolution or speciation; phyletic evolution or speciation. See *sympatric speciation, phylogeny.*

stratigraphy   Representation, in geology of rocks, in which layers or strata are arranged as to geographic position and chronological order of sequence.

stratosphere   An upper portion of a planetary atmosphere, above the troposphere and below the mesosphere, characterized by relative uniform temperatures and horizontal winds. On Earth, its lower limit varies from about 8 to 20 km; its upper limit is around 45 km. The temperature in this region is around −75°C.

stromatolite   Laminated carbonate or silicate rocks, organo-sedimentary structures produced by growth, metabolism, trapping, binding, and/or precipitating of sediment by communities of microorganisms, principally cyanobacteria. Produced by benthic bacterial communities, they are still called *algal pillars* and *algal laminates.*

subtidal zone   See *tidal zone.*

supratidal zone   See *tidal zone.*

symbiogenesis   Evolutionary innovation by establishment of permanent symbioses. As originally coined by K. S. Merezhkovsky in 1920, the term is defined as the origin of organisms (species) through combination and unification of two or many organisms entering into symbiosis.

symbiont See *symbiosis*.

symbiosis The prolonged physical association of two or more organisms belonging to different species. The levels of partner integration in a symbiosis may be behavioral, metabolic, gene product, or genic. A *symbiont* is a member of a symbiosis; an organism that lives with another of a distinct species or kind for most of the life cycle of both. The permanent symbiosis is referred to as the *holobiont* (e.g., the lichen); the partners (algae, fungi) are the *bionts*.

sympatric speciation An uncommon process by which populations inhabiting (at least in part) the same geographic range become reproductively isolated until they form new species. See *speciation*.

syncitium See *coenocyte*.

tannin (tannic acids) Secondary metabolites from the bark and fruit of many plants which are derivatives of flavonoids (condensed tannins) or triesters of glucose or other sugars (hydrolyzable tannins) with one or more trihydroxybenzene carboxylic acid. Several types of polyphenolic organic compounds.

taxon (plural: taxa) The general term for a taxonomic unit, whatever its rank. Examples range from most inclusive (kingdom, phylum, class) to least inclusive (genus, species, variety).

taxonomic unit A named group of organisms, that are placed in the taxon on the basis of features they have in common, or on the basis of their ancestry, or both.

terrestrial planet A planet similar to Earth in terms of size and mean density and possession of derived oxidizing atmospheres. Usually the inner planets, Mercury, Venus, Earth, and Mars, but sometimes Pluto is included.

tidal zone (also littoral zone) Pertaining to the benthic ocean environment or depth zone between high water and low water; also, pertaining to the organisms of that environment. *Subtidal zone* refers to that part of the littoral zone that is between low tide and about 100 meters. *Supratidal zone* pertains to the shore area marginal to the littoral zone, just above high-tide level.

transcription See *protein synthesis*.

transform fault A strike-slip fault characteristic of midoceanic ridges and along which the ridges are offset. Analysis of transform faults is based on the concept of *sea-floor spreading*. See *plate tectonics*.

transgression The spread or extension of the sea over land areas, and the consequent evidence of that advance (such as strata deposited unconformably on older rocks, especially where new marine deposits are spread far and wide over the former land surface). Also, any change (such as rise of sea level or subsidence of land) that brings offshore, typically deep-water environments to areas formerly occupied by nearshore, typically shallow-water conditions, or that shifts the boundary between marine and nonmarine deposition, or between deposition and erosion outward from a marine basin. The opposite of *regression*.

translation See *protein synthesis*.

transposon One kind of transposable element in both prokaryotes and eukaryotes that is immediately flanked by inverted repeat sequences, which in turn are immediately flanked by direct repeat sequences. Transposons usually possess genes in addition to those needed for their insertion (e.g., genes for resistance to antibiotics, sugar fermentation, etc.).

tRNA See *protein synthesis*.

tropopause See *troposphere*.

troposphere The lowest level of a planetary atmosphere, in which the temperature decreases steadily with increased altitude. On Earth extending from the surface of its upper boundary, the *tropopause* (q.v.), at a height of about 8 to 20 km, depending on the latitude and the time of year. Turbulence is greatest in this region, and most of the visible phenomena associated with the weather occurs here (for example, cloud formation). See *stratosphere*.

tubulin Major protein of undulipodia and mitotic spindles. See *microtubule*.

unconsolidated sediment In geology, clastic, unlithified material (precursor to conglomerate) in which consolidation resulting from deposition was too rapid to give time for complete settling. See *sedimentary rock*.

undulipodium A cell-membrane-covered motility organelle usually show-ing feeding or sensory functions and composed of at least 200 proteins. Microtubular axoneme with [9(2) + 2] substructure is covered by plasma membrane and limited to eukaryotic cells. Includes cilia and eukaryotic "flagella." Each undulipodium invariably develops from its kinetosome. The principal protein component of microtubules, and thus a major structural protein of the undulipodia, is *tubulin*. Tubulin is a dimer composed of alpha and beta subunits, each of molecular weight 55 kd. See *flagellum* and *microtubule*.

uniformitarianism The fundamental principle or doctrine that geologic processes and natural laws now operating to modify the Earth's crust have acted in the same regular manner and with similar intensity throughout geologic time, and that past geologic events can be explained by phenomena and forces observable today; the concept that the present is the key to the past.

vaterite A rare hexagonal mineral: $CaCO_3$. It is trimorphous with calcite and aragonite, and consists of a relatively unstable form of calcium carbonate. See *limestone*.

Venera A series of Soviet space missions to Venus (1975 to present) emphasizing surface science from survivable "soft landers" (as opposed to the atmospheric science emphasized on the NASA Mariner and Pioneer missions).

Viking NASA exploratory mission to Mars (1975–76) involving two orbiters, astronomical measurements, and two landers replete with scientific instruments. Viking sought life on Mars.

virus An ultramicroscopic, obligate, intracellular, small genome incapable of autonomous replication. Viruses are not autopoietic entities; they reproduce only by entering a host cell and using its protein synthetic system.

Voyager Comprehensive reconnaissance missions, launched in the late 1970s, to Jupiter, Saturn, Uranus, and their satellites; forerunner to Galileo.

xenosome An organelle of documented external origin (i.e., kappa particles or *Chlorella* of *Paramecium*).

Sources Used in Compiling Glossary

Brock, T. D., and M. T. Madigan. 1988. *Biology of Microorganisms*. Fifth edition. Prentice-Hall.

Campbell, N. A. 1990. *Biology*. Second edition. Benjamin/Cummings.

Gary, M., et al. 1974. *Glossary of Geology*. American Geological Institute.

King, R. C., and W. D. Stansfield. 1990. *A Dictionary of Genetics*. Fourth edition. Oxford University Press.

Margulis, L. 1982. *Early Life*. Science Books International.

Margulis, L., and D. Sagan. 1986. *Origins of Sex*. Yale University Press.

Margulis, L., J. O. Corliss, M. Melkonian, and D. J. Chapman, eds. 1990. *Handbook of Protoctista*. Jones and Bartlett.

Press, F., and R. Siever. 1986. *Earth*. Fourth edition. Freeman.

Rambler, M. B., L. Margulis, and R. Fester, eds. 1989. *Global Ecology*. Academic Press.

Sagan, D., and L. Margulis. 1988. *Garden of Microbial Delights*. Harcourt Brace Jovanovich.

Stanier, R. Y., et al. 1986. *The Microbial World*. Fifth edition. Prentice-Hall.

Wyatt, S., and J. Kaler, 1974. *Principles of Astronomy*. Allyn and Bacon.

Credits

Chapter 1
Figures 1, 2, 3, 4:
NASA.

Figure 6:
Jeremy Sagan (Presentation Express).

Chapter 6
Figure 1:
Drawing by J. S. Alexander.

Figures 2, 3:
From S. Golubic, "Microbial mats and modern stromatolites in Shark Bay, Western Australia," in *Planetary Ecology,* ed. D. E. Caldwell, J. A. Brierley, and C. L. Brierley (Van Nostrand Reinhold, 1985). Copyright 1985 Van Nostrand Reinhold. Reprinted with permission.

Chapter 7
Figure 3:
Elso S. Barghoorn.

Figure 6:
Maud Walsh.

Chapter 8
Photo of author:
Boston University Photo Services.

Figure 1:
From "Algal belt and coastal sabkha evolution, Trucial Coast, Persian Gulf," in *Stromatolites* (Developments in Sedimentology, volume 20), ed. M. R. Walter (Elsevier, 1976). Copyright 1976 Elsevier Scientific Publishing Company. Reprinted with permission.

Figure 2:
From S. Golubic, "Organisms that build stromatolites," in *Stromatolites* (Developments in Sedimentology, volume 20), ed. M. R. Walter (Elsevier, 1976). Copyright 1976 Elsevier Scientific Publishing Company. Reprinted with permission.

Figure 3:
From S. Golubic and J. W. Focke, *"Phormidium hendersonii* Howe: Identity and significance of a modern stromatolite-building microorganism," *Journal of Sedimentary Petrology* 48: 751–764. Copyright 1978 Society for Sedimentary Geology. Reprinted with permission.

Figures 8, 9, 12:
Dr. Robert K. Park.

Figures 10, 11, 13:
From S. Golubic, "The relationship between blue-green algae and carbonate deposits," in *The Biology of Blue-Green Algae* (Botanical Monograph 9), ed. N. Carr and B. A. Whitton (Blackwell, 1973). Copyright 1973 Blackwell Scientific Publications. Reprinted with permission.

Chapter 9
Figure 1:
From P. E. Playford and A. E. Cockbain, "Modern algal stromatolites at Hamelin Pool, a hypersaline barred basin in Shark Bay, Western Australia," in *Stromatolites* (Developments in Sedimentology, volume 20), ed. M. R. Walter (Elsevier, 1976). Copyright 1976 Elsevier Scientific Publishing Company. Reprinted with permission.

Figure 2:
From S. Golubic, "Stromatolites, fossil and recent: A case history," in *Biomineralization and Biological Metal Accumulation*, ed. P. Westbroek and E. W. Jong (Reidel, 1983). Copyright 1983 D. Reidel Publishing Company. Reprinted with permission of Kluwer Academic Publishers.

Figure 4:
From S. Golubic and H. J. Hofmann, "Comparison of modern and mid-Precambrian Entophysalidaceae (Cyanophyta) in stromatolitic algal mats: Cell division and degradation," *Journal of Paleontology* 50: 1074–1082. Copyright 1976 Society of Economic Paleontologists and Mineralogists. Reprinted with permission.

Figure 7:
Hans J. Hofmann, Department of Geology, University of Montreal.

Chapter 10
Figure 4:
David G. Chase.

Figures 3, 5, 7:
Drawings by Christie Lyons.

Figure 8:
Drawing by Laszlo Meszoly.

Figure 12:
Drawing by Laszlo Meszoly.

Chapter 11
Figure 1:
David G. Chase.

Figure 3:
Drawing by Laszlo Meszoly.

Figures 2, 9, 10, 14:
Drawings by Christie Lyons.

Figures 4, 5, 11:
Drawings by Kathy Delisle.

Figure 16:
Robert Obar.

Chapter 13
Figure 1:
Drawing by Sheila Manion-Artz.

Figure 3:
From *The Floor of the Oceans,* based on bathymetric studies by B. C. Heezen and M. Tharp. Copyright 1977 Marie Tharp. Reprinted with permission.

Figures 4–13:
From F. Press and R. Siever, *Earth,* fourth edition (Freeman, 1986). Copyright 1986 W. H. Freeman and Company. Reprinted with permission.

Figure 14:
Paleomap Project, Christopher R. Scotese, University of Texas, Arlington.

Figure 15:
From R. L. Larson and W. C. Pitman, *The Bedrock Geology of the World* (Freeman, 1985). Copyright 1985 R. L. Larson and W. C. Pitman. Reprinted with permission.

Chapter 14
Figures 1, 2, 4, 5, 6, 7, 8, 9, 10:
Drawings by Sheila Manion-Artz.

Figure 3:
William Ormerod.

Photo of author:
Boston University Photo Services.

Figure, page 379:
Drawing by Sheila Manion-Artz.

Addresses of Contributors

Robert Buchsbaum
Massachusetts Audubon: North Shore
Endicott Regional Center
346 Grapevine Rd.
Wenham, MA 01984

David W. Deamer
Dept. of Zoology
University of California
Davis, CA 95616

Stjepko Golubic
Boston University
5 Cummington Street
Boston, MA 02215

Andrew H. Knoll
Botanical Museum
Harvard University
26 Oxford Street
Cambridge, MA 02138

Antonio Lazcano
Faculty of Sciences
Dept. of Biology
Universidad Autónoma de México
04511 Mexico D.F.

James E. Lovelock
Coombe Mill
St. Giles on the Heath
Launceston
Cornwall PL15 9RY
United Kingdom

Lynn Margulis
Dept. of Botany
University of Massachusetts
Amherst, MA 01003

Clifford Matthews
Dept. of Chemistry
University of Illinois
Chicago Circle
Mail Code 111
Box 4348
Chicago, IL 60680

Michael McElroy
Pierce Hall
Harvard University
Cambridge, MA 02138

Cyril Ponnamperuma
Laboratory for Chemical Evolution
University of Maryland
College Park, MD 20742

Raymond Siever
Dept. of Geology
Harvard University
Cambridge, MA 02138

Paul Strother
Dept. of Geology
Boston University
Boston, MA 02215

Neil Todd
Carnivore Genetic Newsletter
26 Walnut Place
Newtonville, MA 02160

Index

Italic page number indicates presence of illustration.